Modernizing .NET Web Applications

Everything You Need to Know About Migrating ASP.NET Web Applications to the Latest Version of .NET

Tomáš Herceg

Apress®

Modernizing .NET Web Applications: Everything You Need to Know About Migrating ASP.NET Web Applications to the Latest Version of .NET

Tomáš Herceg
Praha, Czech Republic

ISBN-13 (pbk): 979-8-8688-0616-2   ISBN-13 (electronic): 979-8-8688-0617-9
https://doi.org/10.1007/979-8-8688-0617-9

Managing Director, Apress Media LLC: Welmoed Spahr
Acquisitions Editor: Ryan Byrnes
Development Editor: Laura Berendson
Editorial Project Manager: Gryffin Winkler

Cover designed by eStudioCalamar

Cover Photo by Sandro Katalina on Unsplash (unsplash.com)

Distributed to the book trade worldwide by Springer Science+Business Media New York, 1 New York Plaza, Suite 4600, New York, NY 10004-1562, USA. Phone 1-800-SPRINGER, fax (201) 348-4505, e-mail orders-ny@springer-sbm.com, or visit www.springeronline.com. Apress Media, LLC is a California LLC and the sole member (owner) is Springer Science + Business Media Finance Inc (SSBM Finance Inc). SSBM Finance Inc is a **Delaware** corporation.

For information on translations, please e-mail booktranslations@springernature.com; for reprint, paperback, or audio rights, please e-mail bookpermissions@springernature.com.

Apress titles may be purchased in bulk for academic, corporate, or promotional use. eBook versions and licenses are also available for most titles. For more information, reference our Print and eBook Bulk Sales web page at http://www.apress.com/bulk-sales.

Any source code or other supplementary material referenced by the author in this book is available to readers on GitHub. For more detailed information, please visit https://www.apress.com/gp/services/source-code.

If disposing of this product, please recycle the paper

Table of Contents

About the Author

 **Tomáš Herceg** lives in the Czech Republic, and has been a Microsoft MVP since 2009. He runs a software consulting company called RIGANTI, and he has founded DotVVM, an open-source framework for building web apps using a popular MVVM design pattern. He often speaks at conferences and user groups, and he is the founder of Update Conference, the largest .NET developer event in the Czech Republic.

Tomáš spent a large part of his career helping his customers with technical decisions, such as cloud migration, microservices architecture, Domain-Driven Design, and modernization of large legacy applications. He wrote many technical articles about .NET development and conducted numerous courses and hands-on labs. Writing this book seemed like the next step forward.

About the Technical Reviewer

 **Joel Lopes** is a Staff Software Engineer at Cruise LLC, where he specializes in creating cloud services for autonomous vehicle maps and routing with a strong emphasis on scalability, reliability, and availability. He is a senior member of IEEE, a Fellow of BCS, and a Fellow of IETE and has been honored with several awards for his significant contributions to the industry. Before joining Cruise, Joel accrued over a decade of experience architecting robust and secure software at major cloud providers like Microsoft and Google. He conceptualized YAML configuration as code for Azure Engineering Systems on top of Azure DevOps release and led release systems instrumental in developing private clouds such as Azure Government Cloud, Azure Germany, Azure China, Azure Secret Cloud, and Azure Top Secret Cloud. He also played a crucial role in developing hybrid cloud solutions for Azure's core build system. Joel holds a master's degree in Computer Science from the University of Missouri, Kansas City, and a bachelor's degree from the University of Mumbai.

Acknowledgments

On this place, I would like to express my gratitude to several people without whom this book would not exist.

To Mehdi, my dear husband, who supported me when I came up with the crazy idea of writing a book and every single day of this eight-month-long adventure.

To my family, who encouraged and helped me with whatever I chose to do and who always respected my decisions even when they had different opinions. Nothing is more valuable to me than accepting someone for who they are, and they succeeded in doing so for my entire life.

To Wolfgang Amadeus Mozart, whose Magic Flute, Don Giovanni, and other phenomenal operas were playing in my headphones most of the time while I was writing, researching, and thinking.

To Michal Altair Valášek, who helped me with the security parts of the book and gave me a lot of useful advice on getting the ASP.NET Identity examples right. Also, he was the person who taught me ASP.NET Web Forms at the beginning of my career. I remember every one of the sessions he presented in the Aquarius meeting room of the former Microsoft building in Prague. I was still in high school, and every month, with my fresh driver's license, I drove almost 200 kilometers to attend his session at 6 PM and another 200 kilometers to get back home before midnight to be ready for school I had to attend the next day.

To Štěpán Bechynský and Dalibor Kačmář, two amazing people from Microsoft Czech Republic, who convinced me to apply to study at Charles University even when I thought I was not going to finish it. Although I quite quickly confirmed my expectations that most of the knowledge taught in the lectures would not be directly useful or applicable to what I wanted to do, I did not see the importance of the foundations and principles on which computer science stands, and this is the most valuable thing the university taught me. The frameworks and libraries change, but the principles remain.

To Roman Jašek, who reviewed parts of the text while we were traveling to attend the MVP Summit in Seattle and provided valuable feedback.

To Stanislav Lukeš, the most active contributor to the DotVVM project, without whom the project would never be more than a simple conference demo. In 2014, I published an initial prototype on GitHub and briefly mentioned it during one of my sessions at the MS Fest community conference. The same day, someone with a nickname exyi submitted a pull request to the repository and continued doing that ever since. Thank you for this amazing journey.

To people at Apress, who reached out to me with the idea of writing a book and helped me throughout the entire process. To my technical reviewer, who pointed out numerous suggestions on how to make the book text and examples better.

And finally, to all the people at RIGANTI, my day-to-day inspiration, who passionately work on our projects and deal with all the technical challenges we encounter. You help me learn new things and keep my mind open to trying new ways and concepts. You are the most amazing group of people to work with.

CHAPTER 1

Introduction

Every keynote of the annual Microsoft Build conference has a slide about how many developers are missing in the IT industry. Even with the rise of artificial intelligence and the introduction of tools like GitHub Copilot or ChatGPT, there are not enough developers to build and maintain applications. Even though these tools are improving every day and can help with the lack of workforce in our industry, I think the situation will not change anytime soon. Faster than ever, the requirements for new applications, digital transformation, and automation of manual processes create new demand for new software.

Try to look at any state administration; most of their activities still involve moving hand-filled forms or manual transfer of information from one system to another. Making this digital and automated requires a tremendous amount of work for solution architects, system integrators, and developers.

More and more lines of code are written by the developers or generated by AI-powered tools, and all this code needs to be maintained, often for years. Many companies and developer teams struggle to keep their projects updated to the new versions of libraries and frameworks, even when the versions being used contain security vulnerabilities. The worldwide deficit in the number of developers forces businesses and organizations to prioritize delivering new features rather than keeping the codebase in perfect condition.

© Tomáš Herceg 2024
T. Herceg, *Modernizing .NET Web Applications*,
https://doi.org/10.1007/979-8-8688-0617-9_1

The significance of this problem rises dramatically when the new version of the developer platform brings significant breaking changes. This is how technological debt emerges and grows.

The New Generation of .NET

A significant step in accumulating technological debt was created when Microsoft introduced .NET Core 1.0 in 2016. It was not just another update of .NET; a more precise term would be the *new generation*. The .NET Core and its subsequent versions, which are called just .NET, contain plenty of improvements in terms of performance, application architecture, and maintainability. However, they come with a great deal of challenges when you want to migrate to them from any previous version.

Table 1-1 shows the releases of .NET Framework and .NET Core, later renamed to .NET. You can see that .NET 5 was the successor of .NET Core 3.1. In the rest of this book, for any statement about .NET Core without a specific version, you can safely assume it is also valid for .NET 5, 6, 7, and subsequent releases from the .NET Core branch. I am going to refer to it also as "the new .NET".

You can notice that .NET Framework occasionally gets new versions, too. Since .NET Framework is an essential component of Windows, its release cycle and support are bound to the Windows life cycle.[1] However, Microsoft officially states that this branch of .NET will only be getting security fixes in the future, and all the new development will be done to the .NET Core branch. .NET Framework is undoubtedly not going away in the upcoming years; many Microsoft products (including Visual Studio and various components of Windows) are built using the .NET Framework.

---

[1] See https://dotnet.microsoft.com/en-us/platform/support/policy/ dotnet-framework

Table 1-1. *Versions and release dates of .NET Framework and .NET Core*

.NET Framework Branch	Release Date	.NET Core Branch	Release Date
.NET Framework 4.6.2	August 2016	.NET Core 1.0	June 2016
		.NET Core 1.1	November 2016
.NET Framework 4.7	April 2017	.NET Core 2.0	August 2017
.NET Framework 4.7.1	October 2017	.NET Core 2.1	May 2018
.NET Framework 4.7.2	April 2018	.NET Core 2.2	December 2018
.NET Framework 4.8	April 2019	.NET Core 3.0	September 2019
		.NET Core 3.1	December 2019
		.NET 5	November 2020
		.NET 6	November 2021
.NET Framework 4.8.1	August 2022	.NET 7	November 2022
		.NET 8	November 2023

Bridging the Gap with .NET Standard

.NET is not just a runtime for running C#, VB.NET, and F# code. It is also a rich set of libraries, API, and, most importantly, complete frameworks for creating web, desktop, or mobile applications.

Because the API surface of these two branches differed and Microsoft wanted to allow easier code sharing between them, .NET Standard was introduced. While both .NET Framework and .NET Core are runtimes accompanied by a collection of libraries, .NET Standard is entirely different. You can think of it only as a list of APIs, something like a contract to be implemented by some runtime. Instead of using Portable Class

Libraries,[2] you can create a standard Class Library project that targets a specific version of .NET Standard. Thanks to this, the library is guaranteed to interact only with the APIs present in the .NET Standard, and thus the same DLL can be used with .NET Framework and .NET Core versions that implement this standard. If you try to call an API that is not part of .NET Standard, the compiler will produce an error.

.NET Standard ceased to fully serve its purpose since its version 2.1 was not implemented by any version of .NET Framework. Thus, the latest version of .NET Standard that is useful for modernization techniques described in this book is .NET Standard 2.0, which is implemented by .NET Framework 4.6.2+[3] and .NET Core 2.0+. Table 1-2 shows the platforms' compliance with various versions of .NET Standard.

Table 1-2. *.NET Framework and .NET Core compliance with*
.NET Standard[4]

.NET Standard Version	Compatible .NET Framework Version	Compatible .NET Core Version
.NET Standard 1.6	.NET Framework 4.6.2+	.NET Core 1.0+
.NET Standard 2.0	.NET Framework 4.6.2+	.NET Core 2.0+
.NET Standard 2.1	-	.NET Core 3.0+

---

[2] Portable Class Library was an older concept that allowed compiling the same code to target multiple platforms. See https://learn.microsoft.com/en-us/ xamarin/cross-platform/app-fundamentals/pcl for more information.

[3] Technically, .NET Framework 4.6.1 claims to implement .NET Standard 2.0, but there are several compatibility issues in various NuGet packages. It is recommended to upgrade to a newer version.

[4] See https://learn.microsoft.com/en-us/dotnet/standard/net-standard for a complete listing of supported runtimes with all versions of .NET Standard.

What Has Changed

There were numerous changes in the Base Class Library[5] itself, but these don't create significant issues when migrating the code from .NET Framework to .NET Core.

In most cases, the edits in the code are only cosmetic; for example, sometimes you must use a different overload of some method or another constructor. For instance, in .NET Framework 4.7.2, the ToHashSet extension method gets an argument of type IEqualityComparer, but this overload is missing in the .NET Standard 2.0. If you migrate the code directly to .NET Core 2.0 or higher, you will not even notice this, as the same overload is present in .NET Core. However, a small code change will be necessary when the code is moved into a class library targeting .NET Standard, as shown in Listing 1-1.

Listing 1-1. An example of overload supported in .NET Framework and .NET Core but missing from .NET Standard 2.0

```
IEnumerable<string> names = new[] { "ABC", "abc" };

// does not work in .NET Standard 2.0
var uniqueNames = names.ToHashSet(
    StringComparer.CurrentCultureIgnoreCase);

// works in .NET Standard 2.0
var uniqueNames = new HashSet<string>(names,
    StringComparer.CurrentCultureIgnoreCase);
```

---

[5] The Base Class Library is the basic set of APIs included in .NET. It contains the built-in data types to represent strings, numbers, and dates; it contains collections, APIs to work with input and output, globalization and culture-based formatting of values, representing text in various encodings like UTF-8, and more. https://en.wikipedia.org/wiki/Standard_Libraries_(CLI)#Base_Class_Library

Some APIs in .NET Core have slightly different behavior, often because of added support for Linux and Mac OS. This is the case of UseShellExecute in the ProcessStartInfo class.[6] Since some .NET areas are just a thin wrapper over the Windows API, you can find methods that throw PlatformNotSupportedException on non-Windows platforms because it is not possible to implement such APIs.

Furthermore, some APIs like Code Access Security or Remoting were removed completely; luckily, they were not used often.

The situation is dramatically different when it comes to application frameworks like ASP.NET MVC, Entity Framework, WPF, and almost all others that are part of .NET. Some of these frameworks were available even in the first version of the .NET Core, albeit with a handful of breaking changes. This is the case with the previously mentioned ASP.NET MVC and ASP.NET Web API.

Others, such as Windows Forms and WPF, were added later, namely, in .NET Core 3.0. They also introduced numerous incompatibilities, especially in the design-time experience in Visual Studio, but they are officially supported.

Several libraries, for example, the Entity Framework and ASP.NET Identity, were completely reimplemented, heavily changed, and renamed to Entity Framework Core and ASP.NET Core Identity.

Finally, some frameworks have no alternative in the new .NET Core world. This is the case of WCF (Windows Communication Foundation) which is available for the new platform only as an open source community–maintained project called *CoreWCF*. An even bitter story is the story of ASP.NET Web Forms, which was so challenging to reimplement

---

[6] The differences in the shell execute behavior are described in the documentation page at https://learn.microsoft.com/en-us/dotnet/core/compatibility/fx-core#change-in-default-value-of-useshellexecute

for .NET Core without introducing significant breaking changes that it was decided not to support this technology on the new platform at all. There is no similar framework available on the .NET Core. Thus, migrating a Web Forms application necessarily means rewriting all pages and UI components to use a different presentation technology.

Even though the programming language remained the same on the old and the new versions, all the frameworks have been modified or rethought to work in the new era of cloud and distributed applications. There is clearly more focus on performance, removing unnecessary robustness, and making things more lightweight (as you can see, for instance, in the Minimal API approach introduced in .NET 6). Much work has also been done to get rid of tight coupling with operating system components like IIS (Internet Information Services). The old ASP.NET depended heavily on the infrastructure brought by IIS, while the new ASP.NET Core is completely decoupled from the web server.

Another excellent example of this drift is Entity Framework. The querying mechanism in Entity Framework 6 was very robust and designed for databases with hundreds or even thousands of tables. The startup time and the time to the first query were not the most critical metric because most workloads were server applications running for days or weeks, and the cadence of releases was significantly lower in the days before the rise of DevOps. Restarts of such applications were infrequent and did occur several times a month at most. Business-critical applications were typically running in clusters of several physical or virtual machines. In contrast, when you look at the Entity Framework Core, its first versions supported only basic queries, and the focus of the team was split between excellent query performance and providing a pleasant experience when working with smaller database models that suit the modern microservices approach. This approach is more fruitful in cloud environments where the application running in containers can be stopped and started many times a day, either because of frequent releases or various auto-scaling configurations where the underlying infrastructure moves the application

7

instances between servers. You can also notice a shift in the EF team's attention to a more expressive API for defining the database model in the code, clearly inspired by favorite approaches like Domain-Driven Design. Even the most recent versions of Entity Framework Core do not beat the power of the query translator in the old Entity Framework 6. However, as a developer, you have more convenient ways to express how your database model will look and how it will be mapped to the database schema.

The new .NET Core was definitely a great step forward, and practically all application frameworks that are part of today's .NET ecosystem were significantly improved to better suit today's requirements for modern applications. However, in most cases, it is extremely difficult to take the codebase of a project targeting .NET Framework and run it on the new .NET. The upgrade process, often referred to as *modernization*, usually requires weeks or months of planning, code editing, and testing.

Ten Thousand Feet View of the Book

Each chapter of this book looks at different aspects and stages of this modernization challenge, explains the differences between the old and new, and offers advice or examples of the decision that needs to be made and steps that need to be taken.

In this chapter, I will try to give an overview of the changes that happened in various application frameworks between .NET Framework and .NET Core and lay out the high-level migration steps to be taken.

Chapter 2 will discuss the most common reasons for modernization, including the nontechnical ones such as explaining the benefits to company management and other stakeholders. I will also compare the complete rewrite approach with the incremental modernization and discuss their pros and cons.

In Chapter 3, I will discuss the steps to take before you start the modernization journey. I will talk about side-by-side migration using YARP (Yet Another Reverse Proxy) and compare it with an in-place approach that can be done using an open source framework called DotVVM. Dealing with change requests and bug fixes during the modernization will also be one of the crucial topics discussed in the chapter.

Chapter 4 will focus on the communication frameworks: WCF, ASP. NET SignalR, and old ASP.NET Web Services. I will show their equivalents available in the .NET Core world: ASP.NET Core SignalR, CoreWCF, and SoapCore open source projects. I will also show how to use an HttpContext adapter package to prepare the codebase for migration to the new .NET.

In Chapter 5, I will explain how to migrate data access code. Starting with the classic ADO.NET approach, where not many things have changed, I'll spend most of the time describing the migration journey for Entity Framework 6, which is the most favorite ORM in the .NET world. I will briefly mention other technologies, namely, LINQ to SQL, and show what code changes you can expect.

Chapter 6 will talk about migrating from legacy identity providers. I will begin with the old ASP.NET Membership and Role providers and describe how to migrate from ASP.NET Identity to its new version called ASP.NET Core Identity. Since the new library uses a different format of hashed passwords stored in the database, I will also show two strategies on how to migrate them safely: one will require all users to reset their passwords, and the other will store passwords in the old format in a safe way and migrate them to the new format on the first successful sign-in.

In Chapter 7, I will show a minimum-effort migration method of an ASP.NET Web Forms application using an open source MVVM framework called DotVVM. The reason for using DotVVM is that it is the only .NET-based web framework that supports both the old .NET Framework and the new .NET Core worlds, and so it can be used as a bridge

9

between these two worlds. I will also show how much easier it is to migrate applications where the business logic is well separated from the presentation code and how many things will have to be changed in applications where the business logic is spawned anywhere from the database to code-behind or even markup files.

Chapters 8 and 9 will focus on the most universal method of modernization of web applications – the side-by-side approach based on the YARP. In these chapters, I will explain how to create a new project for the migrated pages, how to configure the proxy to redirect the traffic to the legacy application for pages that have not been rewritten yet, and, most importantly, how to deal with all complications arising from the fact you are running two separate applications: creating the single sign-on experience for the two applications, synchronizing the session data, invalidating the cache on changes made in the other application, and more.

The last chapter will close the modernization topic with some examples and tips on separating business logic and keeping it independent of the presentation technology. This allows you to save a lot of effort if you face a similar "platform restart" as it happened with the arrival of .NET Core. In general, the web frameworks have a shorter life span than the back-end code; thus, it makes sense to be prepared for the future replacement of the presentation technology.

Get Ready

Naturally, no single path would suit all applications and teams. In each case, you will have to consider not only technical but also business and real-world aspects, which sometimes prove to be more challenging than changing the code itself. There are even cases when modernization does not make sense from the business perspective, especially when the project is not business-critical, and its long-term maintenance costs are negligible.

What makes this task even more challenging is that, most commonly, the developer team cannot dedicate all its capacity to the migration itself. Still, it must deliver new features and fix issues in the meantime. That is why modernization typically needs to be done in small incremental steps. An approach similar to A/B testing[7] can be involved to prevent a complete unavailability of essential functions or to be able to quickly retreat and return to the previous implementation in case of issues. You could see this approach in recent years in many consumer applications; there is a button to try the new experience, but you can always fall back to the old one. In combination with good telemetry, the developer team is able to deliver new functionality quickly and make sure it works seamlessly without risking that the users will not be able to do the things they want.

About the Author

It is always good to know something about the person whose text you are reading. Each of us has different backgrounds, worked for different companies, participated in projects of various sizes, talked to different customers and stakeholders, and hunted different bugs. Even though I have seen many software projects in various circumstances, indeed, I have not seen everything, and my worldview is thus incomplete. Feel free to confront the ideas you read in this book with your own experience and environment.

---

[7] A/B testing is an approach where the same functionality is implemented twice. Some percentage of users are forwarded to first implementation, while the rest use the second implementation. In combination with telemetry, you can evaluate which one performs better. In the case of modernization, you can do A/B testing by preserving the old implementation of a feature while rolling out its new version gradually.

I started programming in QBASIC when I was seven years old. I spent almost all my teenage life in front of the computer screen where you would most of the time see Turbo Pascal, Visual Basic 3 to 6, followed by Visual Studio .NET and all its subsequent versions: 2003, 2005, and so on.

I liked building games; the most complex was a 3D multiplayer strategy from the Antic Greece world, including even the AI player and a simple scripting language with an interpreter for implementing campaign missions. I also built numerous websites in PHP and ASP.NET Web Forms. For many of them, I got paid, which helped me study in Prague, the capital of the Czech Republic. With one of my friends, I created the largest website dedicated to programming in .NET in Czechia and published hundreds of articles and blog posts there. In 2009, I got my first Microsoft MVP award.

I got a bachelor's degree at Charles University in Prague. At first, I wasn't amazed by the school much. Although they gave me a solid theoretical background in computer science and algorithmic thinking, I wanted to learn more practical skills and get experience from real-world projects. That is why I quit the master's program, and in my incredible naivety, I founded a software consulting company called RIGANTI. I loved programming but didn't realize that as the CEO, I would hardly have time to write code. On the other hand, it allowed me to be part of hundreds of software projects and get the big picture of the day-to-day challenges of the developers without the need to spend thousands of hours on each one. I had the chance to see the struggles and complications of mobile development in Xamarin; I saw how much time it took to make a great web UI before jQuery, as well as in the modern JavaScript framework era. I got insights into the challenges of optimizing SQL indexes, hunting memory leaks caused by invalid registrations in a dependency injection container, and much more. I got invited to dig into the code many times, especially when my colleagues were dealing with some mysterious issue.

For most of the years, my job was not the day-to-day developer's work. However, I was present whenever important technological decisions were made. I helped design Azure-based solutions for global companies,

I got the opportunity to see the birth of innovative products in several startups, and even saw low-level programming of hardware devices in manufacturing companies.

Seeing these projects from the management level allowed me to better understand the business incentives and motivations of the stakeholders. I learned, often the hard way, how important it is to communicate with the developers and customers. Every single time, the technical issues we ran into could be solved in a matter of hours or days. Still, it was always the lack of communication that caused problems and broken relationships that were so difficult to restore.

One important category of projects coming to RIGANTI was legacy applications developed by someone else, and our task was to maintain these applications. In this kind of work, the developers always appreciate good architecture, especially the separation of the codebase into layers. Additionally, we found that it is good when the codebase is somehow predictable. No matter what architectural patterns or conventions are used, it is helpful when your intuition helps you navigate the code and find what you are looking for. With many projects, we didn't have this luxury; business logic was literally everywhere. In combination with non-existing or at least incomplete documentation, we clearly saw that even the tiniest changes in the application can be expensive to fix.

The company participated in several modernization projects and helped our customers fight their technological debt; this is how this book was born. It summarizes several years of my observations and experience. I sincerely hope that you find these insights helpful.

Application Framework Equivalents in the .NET Core World

The old .NET Framework introduced several application frameworks which are widely used in thousands of web applications. This section briefly introduces the modernization of applications using each of these frameworks.

One category of frameworks includes *ASP.NET Web Forms*, *ASP.NET MVC*, and *ASP.NET Web Pages*. All these technologies can be used to create web user interfaces, and at the end of the day, their main job is processing HTTP requests and rendering the corresponding HTML output.

The second category includes *ASP.NET XML Web Services*, *WCF (Windows Communication Foundation)*, *ASP.NET Web API*, and *ASP.NET SignalR*. These libraries were widely used to implement communication interfaces between multiple applications and often allowed .NET to interact with other platforms, such as Java and PHP.

A special category belongs to *LINQ to SQL* and *Entity Framework*, Object-Relational Mapper libraries widely used to retrieve and store information in SQL databases.

And finally, there is *ASP.NET Identity*, a universal library to implement identity, role management, and persistence of user accounts. This technology was often combined with *Entity Framework* as many developers prefer storing user information and application data in the same database.

Frameworks for Web UI

Let's start with the first category of presentation frameworks. The oldest of them is *ASP.NET Web Forms*, which tried to offer a similar level of simplicity in building user interfaces as we know from the world of desktop applications. A few years after its release, *ASP.NET MVC* was introduced to provide an alternative approach to building web applications. Finally, *ASP.NET Web Pages* allowed to strip off a part of MVC boilerplate code.

ASP.NET Web Forms

In ASP.NET Web Forms, the individual pages of the application were defined in `.aspx` markup files accompanied by code-behind files. The markup file contained an HTML code enhanced with the concept of server controls, page directives, and data-binding expressions. Whenever the server received an HTTP request, the hierarchy of server controls defined in the page was instantiated; the sequence of `Init`, `Load`, and `PreRender` life cycle events was called; and finally, the server controls rendered HTML, which could be interpreted by the browser. The entire page had to be one big `<form>` element, and any time the user clicked any button, the form was submitted to the server. This action was called the *postback*. The server extracted the values from the request body, which included a special hidden field called *View State*, which enabled Web Forms to restore the hierarchy of server controls to the exact state as it was at the end of the previous request. This concept helped to create a *stateful experience* on top of the stateless HTTP communication. The application logic was invoked, and a newly rendered HTML was sent back to the browser.

This process did not lead to the best user experience. When the users interacted with the page and caused the postback, they had to wait until the server produced a completely new HTML. It wasn't unusual that the page flickered or was unresponsive for a while, and the postback itself could take a significant amount of time because of the size of the state-persisting hidden field. This was the primary reason why many .NET developers did not like this technology at all. In numerous cases, it was extremely difficult to keep the view state field reasonably small, especially on pages containing many controls or multiple sections.

Later, this concept was enhanced by ASP.NET AJAX, an extension to Web Forms, which used JavaScript to replace the full postback with an asynchronous AJAX call, which allowed the server to render just the part of the page that was expected to change. It was done by the `UpdatePanel` control. The user experience became significantly better, but the view state field remained the biggest problem.

After the first versions of .NET Core arrived, Microsoft announced that ASP.NET Web Forms was not going to be supported on .NET Core because it would be extremely difficult to avoid making significant breaking changes. Given the amount of existing Web Forms applications with hundreds or thousands of pages, the effort required to perform complete functional testing would probably discourage many people from even trying the upgrade. Additionally, ASP.NET Web Forms were tightly integrated with the IIS, so tightly that it was almost impossible to run ASP.NET Web Forms applications reliably in a different web server environment.

The Web Forms included several smaller frameworks, for example, the Membership, Role, and Profile providers. These technologies were predecessors of ASP.NET Identity and provided a useful abstraction over storing the user account information. Although the .NET Framework is still supported by Microsoft, the algorithms the Membership providers use to store passwords in the database are not considered secure by today's standards.

Another problem with this technology is that it tried to make things simple, and in some cases, it went a bit too far. Using components like `SqlDataSource` provided a quick way of implementing CRUD interfaces with a minimum amount of code, but it did not push the developers to separate business logic from the presentation concerns. It is no wonder that this approach was preferred by many. It was the fastest way to achieve the goal, it was also presented in most of code samples, and Visual Studio offered a nice tooling to auto-generate the SQL queries. All other methods required more effort. Additionally, .NET Framework did not offer a more sophisticated API or framework for database querying than ADO.NET at that time. The same SQL queries that appeared in `SqlDataSource` would just move somewhere else, without giving you any other benefits such as a more powerful querying API.

The `aspx` markup also allowed the developers to place any code blocks, such as conditions or loops anywhere in the hierarchy of server controls. This greatly increased the chance that important business logic would be spawned in random places in the HTML markup. These two aspects complicate the modernization process and make it error-prone.

Because there is no equivalent or similar technology present in the world of .NET Core, all pages and user controls have to be rewritten into some other presentation technology. Chapter 7 shows the in-place way of modernization where the pages can be rewritten using an open source DotVVM framework to be later migrated to .NET Core. Chapters 8 and 9 show another way of porting such applications. The effort greatly depends on the code quality, especially in the `aspx` markup and code-behind files.

ASP.NET MVC

The second technology that contributed a huge part to the old .NET Framework web world was ASP.NET MVC. It addressed the loudest criticism of Web Forms thanks to removing the view state, and it allowed the developers to have precise control over the rendered HTML output. The first versions of ASP.NET MVC used the same `aspx` extension for markup files, although using server controls was not allowed.

In the later versions of MVC, the Razor language was introduced and was the distinctive feature that brought a lot of popularity to this framework. Listing 1-2 shows the difference between the old and the new syntax.

Listing 1-2. Examples of ASPX and Razor view syntax

```
<!-- ASPX-based syntax -->
<%@ Page Language="C#" Inherits="System.Web.Mvc.ViewPage" %>
<section>
<% using (Html.BeginForm())
   { %>
    <label for="UserName">User Name:</label>
    <%= Html.TextBox("UserName") %>

    <label for="Password">Password:</label>
    <%= Html.Password("Password") %>

    <input type="submit" value="Log in" />
<% } %>
</section>

<!-- Razor syntax -->
@model LoginViewModel
<section>
    @using (Html.BeginForm())
    {
        @Html.AntiForgeryToken()

        @Html.LabelFor(m => m.UserName)
        @Html.TextBoxFor(m => m.UserName)

        @Html.LabelFor(m => m.Password)
        @Html.PasswordFor(m => m.Password)
```

```
    <input type="submit" value="Log in" />
  }
</section>
```

In MVC, the code that defines the user interface is clearly separated from the code that loads the data, handles the user actions, and guides the navigation throughout the application. When the server gets an HTTP request, the routing engine finds the corresponding controller and method (called *action* in the MVC terminology) and invokes it with the arguments bound from the query string or request body. The result is then passed to the view, which produces the output for the browser. Thanks to this separation, the view has no way to interact with the controller before the action is finished.

This separation greatly enhances the testability of such applications. It is not difficult to write unit or integration tests for the controllers; you can just create an instance of the controller, call methods, and verify that they return the correct results. ASP.NET MVC also introduced an abstraction over the `HttpContext` object, which allowed the creation of mocks for the tests.

The successor of ASP.NET MVC in the .NET Core world is named ASP.NET Core MVC. Although there are many similarities between these two frameworks, there are some changes that need to be made when migrating to the new version. Most of them come from the different architecture of ASP.NET Core which is multiplatform and where the request pipeline is composed in the Startup class. This concept was present in .NET Framework only after the introduction of OWIN.

ASP.NET Core also incorporates dependency injection as one of the fundamental platform concepts. If the .NET Framework application leveraged any dependency injection library, you need to either replace it with the built-in `IServiceProvider` in ASP.NET Core or integrate the solution within.

The complexity of migration depends on whether you use the old `aspx` views that are not supported on the .NET Core or whether Razor views are used. If you use the older view engine, you need to rewrite all pages to the Razor syntax. In case you are already using the Razor syntax, there may be numerous small code changes, but, overall, the ASP.NET Core MVC is similar.

ASP.NET Web Pages

ASP.NET MVC was very popular, especially for implementing public-facing websites. However, in simple applications which consisted of mostly static pages, the layer of controllers felt unnecessary. In fact, most of the controllers were empty or contained just one action. That is why a third presentation technology was introduced on the .NET Framework; it was called ASP.NET Web Pages and allowed to use plain Razor views to implement fully functional pages.

One great benefit of this approach was the option to add a controller to the page later. While the page remained simple and contained just a few moving parts, a plain Razor view was enough. When the page started growing, you could add the controller to implement more advanced logic.

The successor of ASP.NET Web Pages on .NET Core is ASP.NET Razor Pages. This framework is conceptually similar, but it offers more advanced features, and it is useful even for more interactive web applications. The view can define a section with a code and use an MVVM-inspired approach to work with the state of the page.

Upgrading Web Pages to Razor Pages is relatively smooth, but it is often thanks to the fact that websites using this technology are very simple. You can expect namespace changes and numerous smaller code edits.

Communication Frameworks

The preferred way of communication between applications changed quite frequently over the years. The beginning of the 21st century was dominated by SOAP (Simple Object Access Protocol). In the .NET world, it was provided by the *ASP.NET XML Web Services* framework.

Later, Microsoft introduced *Windows Communication Foundation* (WCF), which attempted to provide robust and extensible abstraction over the information exchange between multiple applications. The feature set of this framework was quite impressive; it supported various protocols, including bidirectional messaging. Even from an architectural standpoint, the technology looked well designed. However, the complexity of its configuration model and inferior performance discouraged many developers from using it.

When it was clear that REST was becoming the most popular technology, Microsoft added *ASP.NET Web API* to address the demand. It was possible to make REST endpoints using WCF; however, ASP.NET Web API proved to be the ideal choice. Inspired by the MVC approach, each request is handled to corresponding controller action based on the routing rules, and URL or request body parameters are parsed and bound as arguments of the invoked method. The method can then return a result representing an abstraction over an HTTP status code and the content of the response.

A completely different type of communication is provided by *ASP.NET SignalR*. While the aforementioned technologies work on the request–response basis, the purpose of this library is to provide real-time bidirectional communication. The client establishes a persistent connection with the server, and while the connection is active, any of the parties can send messages to the other. The connection is made preferably using the WebSockets technology, but when it is not possible, the library uses HTTP long polling[8] or Server-Sent Events[9] to emulate the persistence. From the developer's perspective, this logic is abstracted away, and the library offers either sending string messages or using an RPC interface provided by *SignalR hubs*. There are client libraries for JavaScript and other platforms.

ASP.NET XML Web Services

Each XML Web Service is represented by a file with `.asmx` extension and a class with methods the clients can call. The requests and responses are XML-serialized SOAP messages. Each service also provides a WSDL[10] definition, which can be used to generate client proxies in various languages.

---

[8] HTTP long polling is a special use of the classic HTTP request–response scheme. The client sends a request to the server, but the connection is kept open, and the response is not produced until there is a notification the server needs to deliver to the client. If there are no notifications for some time (usually 30 seconds), an empty response is generated, and the client issues a new HTTP request immediately. This approach works well even in environments with various restrictions on request or connection time limits imposed, for example, by a proxy server which is on the way between the server and client. More details can be found at `https://datatracker.ietf.org/doc/html/rfc6202#section-2.1`

[9] Server-Sent Events are also based on classic HTTP request–response scheme, but the server responds using the MIME type `text/event-stream` and occasionally sends notifications separated by a pair of newlines. The response stream is open until the connection is terminated; usually, there are no timeouts for the duration of a single request applied. More information can be found at `https://developer.mozilla.org/en-US/docs/Web/API/Server-sent_events`

[10] WSDL (Web Services Description Language) is a standard describing the interface of services and their operations. More information can be found at `www.w3.org/TR/wsdl/`

This technology became obsolete in the .NET Framework times already, and it was advised to switch to WCF, but I have seen it still in use in many projects. In the .NET Core world, no built-in package would implement the SOAP client or server. However, there are several open source solutions available. Based on the number of downloads on NuGet, the most popular alternatives are CoreWCF[11] and SoapCore.[12]

The migration in terms of required code changes is not difficult. You need to change the service classes to inherit the base classes from the SoapCore or CoreWCF packages and update the method definitions and Data-Transfer Object classes to use appropriate attributes guiding the serialization. In addition to that, you need to register and configure the library in the application startup class, including the authentication. If you use any Web Service extensions, they also need to be migrated.

A trickier part would be to ensure that all transferred objects are serialized and deserialized correctly as there may be subtle changes because of using another implementation of the SOAP serialization.

Windows Communication Foundation

WCF is still heavily used today, although even during the era of .NET Framework its popularity started to decline in favor of ASP.NET Web API. This technology was introduced as part of .NET Framework 3.0 and came with a highly ambitious plan to enable building service-oriented applications. Each service provided a contract in the form of an interface, and it was consumed either using proxies that could be generated in the runtime or using IDE or a command-line tool. The concrete details of communication (which protocol is used, how the communication is secured, and so on) were specified in the configuration file. Under some

---

[11] CoreWCF repository URL: https://github.com/CoreWCF/CoreWCF
[12] SoapCore repository URL: https://github.com/DigDes/SoapCore

circumstances, it was even possible to change the way of communication without recompiling and redeploying the application just by changing the configuration.

Later versions of WCF allowed to specify configuration in the code which proved to be safer; having the entire configuration of the communication layer defined in a configuration file could be a source of runtime errors as many configuration changes would not be possible without appropriate code changes. However, the overall complexity of the configuration remained; it was just moved to another place.

Migrating WCF services to .NET Core requires using the *CoreWCF* project. It is an open source WCF port maintained by the community and supported by the .NET Foundation. It does not support all features, such as support for distributed transactions, and advanced security concepts. Version 1.0 did not include the named pipes and message queue transports, but these were added in version 1.4. Additionally, new features have been added, such as support for the ASP.NET Core authentication model, making it easier to use JWT[13] bearer tokens.

The migration requires you to install the NuGet package of CoreWCF, change namespaces, and register all services in the startup class. The XML-based configuration files are supported, as well as specifying the configuration in code.

If your services are not consumed by a third party (all clients are under your control, and you can modify them), replacing WCF with gRPC[14] can be a viable alternative. gRPC provides a feature set close to WCF, is

---

[13] JSON Web Token is a format for transferring security tokens with support of encryption and digital signatures, designed so the tokens could be used in URLs or other environments with restricted set of usable characters. More information can be found at `https://datatracker.ietf.org/doc/html/rfc7519`

[14] gRPC is a communication technology which uses Protocol Buffers, a binary format of messages, and provides a request-response-based Remote Procedure Call mechanism. More information can be found at `https://grpc.io/docs/`

supported in all commonly used programming languages, and offers superior performance over WCF thanks to utilizing HTTP/2 and using space-efficient binary format.

ASP.NET Web API

ASP.NET Web API was Microsoft's response to the rising popularity of REST. While it was possible to implement RESTful services using Windows Communication Foundation's `WebHttpBinding`, the lightweight solution of Web API seemed to fit the new world of diverse REST endpoints.

In ASP.NET Web API, the collections of operations exposed to web clients are organized in controllers, similar to ASP.NET MVC. The main concepts from MVC, such as routing, parameter binding, or filters, are also available in Web API. Although ASP.NET Web API supported XML as a message format, JSON was used in a vast majority of cases. The framework did not introduce much abstraction; the developers had direct access to request headers and could work with the response stream, which was helpful, especially when working with larger binary payloads or custom data formats.

In contrast to the previous two technologies that could not exist without endpoints to provide the WSDL metadata of services and their operations, this feature was always considered optional in the world of ASP.NET Web API. Consuming the REST API can be done with pure *HttpClient*; it is unnecessary to generate proxy classes. However, browsing the API description and generating clients proved useful when working with larger API surfaces. OpenAPI and Swagger[15] became popular and were made available through several implementations, with *NSwag* and *Swashbuckle* having the most downloads on NuGet.

---

[15] OpenAPI is a language-agnostic standard that describes REST API endpoints in a JSON format. Swagger is a set of tools to design endpoints, generate client proxies and servers, and more.

The migration to ASP.NET Core requires switching the namespaces of controllers, registering them in the startup class, and adding attributes that explicitly state HTTP methods (in ASP.NET Web API, they could be inferred from the method names). Since some default behaviors of parameter binding also changed, rigorous testing is necessary to prevent introducing breaking changes.

If you use *Swashbuckle* or *NSwag* to generate OpenAPI JSON contracts, additional changes will be needed as these tools use different conventions to auto-generate operation names on .NET Framework and the new .NET. You can use a diff tool to compare the old and new OpenAPI specifications to make sure there are no breaking changes. Even if the format of HTTP requests and responses is the same, when the developers generate proxy classes, you want to avoid renaming the generated methods.

ASP.NET SignalR

ASP.NET SignalR works in a completely different way than the other frameworks. Unlike previous cases where communication is always initiated by the client, SignalR provides an easy way to communicate in both ways and at any time. As it was mentioned earlier, WebSockets are used, if possible, but SignalR can fall back to other kinds of emulating the "persistent connection," which uses normal HTTP requests, for example, when running on an older web server that doesn't have support for WebSockets.

On the server, the SignalR developers can use two core concepts: persistent connections and hubs. The persistent connection is a low-level mechanism that provides only OnConnected and OnDisconnected methods and a way to send and receive string messages. Typically, JSON-serialized payloads are used, but you are free to use any format of your convenience. Hubs provide an RPC-like interface where you can define methods that can be invoked from the client. The hub connection on the client can also define methods that can be invoked from the server. When you invoke a method on one side, its name with serialized arguments is sent to the other side, a corresponding method is called, and the result, if any, is serialized and sent back to the caller.

On the client side, the SignalR developer initiates a connection to the server and subscribes to its events, for example, receiving a message, invocation of a method defined on the client, disconnecting, and so on.

When both server and client are .NET, SignalR provides an option to use strongly typed hubs. This allows the creation of a shared library with an interface defining the contract for the hub methods and having a type-safe way of calling the hub. In other cases, you need to make sure that the invoked method name and passed arguments match the method signature on the other side.

The migration from ASP.NET SignalR to ASP.NET Core SignalR starts with changing the NuGet packages, making some namespace changes, changing the client-side libraries, and rewriting the initialization of SignalR connection in all client applications. The implementation of both server and client sides of the framework is completely different, albeit the principles are unchanged.

ASP.NET Core SignalR doesn't support the persistent connection approach, so all persistent connections must be migrated to hubs. For simple cases, it can be done just by defining a `SendMessage` method with one string argument on both sides, but if there are various kinds of messages involved, I would strongly recommend creating specific methods for each kind of message. Instead of your own serialization of messages, you can replace this approach with passing objects or multiple arguments to hub methods.

ASP.NET SignalR could auto-generate JavaScript client proxies; this was done by including a script pointing to a magic URL specified in the configuration (`/signalr/hubs` by default). In ASP.NET Core SignalR, you need to call the hub methods using the `invoke` method on the connection, as the auto-generated hub proxies are not supported.

The JavaScript version of ASP.NET Core SignalR does not require jQuery, and it is important to mention that it does not support Internet Explorer. Though already unsupported by Microsoft, it is still used in some organizations.

The .NET API for establishing and configuration of connections and implementing hubs has been slightly changed, yet the code changes are not substantial, and there are probably not many applications with hundreds of hubs. More error-prone situations are going to be on the JavaScript side where there is no way to emit compile-time errors, and rigorous testing will thus be required. The new ASP.NET Core SignalR is written in TypeScript, and it is worth using it as it makes sure the API is used correctly.

Data Access Libraries

After we dealt with the web UI frameworks and libraries for communication, we should look at the data access side, which is present in most applications, especially in the world of .NET, so popular in enterprises.

The foundation of data access, the ADO.NET framework, has not been significantly changed, and most of the code working with DbConnection and DbCommand (or their database-specific variants like SqlConnection and SqlCommand) will work without any code changes. The worst thing you can meet is the need to replace some assembly references or NuGet packages.

The first ORM[16] introduced with .NET Framework 3.5 was LINQ to SQL. It was soon superseded by Entity Framework introduced in .NET Framework 4.0, but for some time it was a choice of many developers.

---

[16] Object-Relational Mapper allows working with SQL databases through an abstraction where the records stored in relational tables are represented as objects (in the sense of object-oriented programming). The mapper can load data from the database and use it to materialize objects and later synchronize the changes made to the objects back to the database.

Entity Framework was at first a built-in component of .NET Framework, but soon it became clear that being tied to the long release cycle of .NET would prevent it from adding new features quickly enough. This is why it was decoupled and distributed as a NuGet package.

The first versions of Entity Framework used the Database First and Model-First approach where the database was represented by a layered EDM[17] model. Visual Studio includes a designer for these models, and it was possible either to generate the model from the database or build it from scratch with the designer. This approach had many problems. The designer was slow when working with large models. The feature that could update the model based on changes made to the database schema often dropped manual changes the developer made to the model. The underlying XML file describing the model could get easily corrupt and had to be repaired manually. The latter issue happened often when working in the team in a version-controlled environment; anytime when two developers updated the file, there was a conflict that was difficult to resolve.

In Entity Framework 4.1, the Code First approach was announced, and it rapidly became the preferred way for most developers. The successor of Entity Framework, Entity Framework Core, dropped support for the designer experience and EDM models, and the only possible representation of the model is the approach introduced with Code First.

---

[17] The Entity Data Model is an XML-based description of the Conceptual Model Layer (the model with which you work in your application code), the Storage Layer (the schema of the underlying database), and a Mapping Layer (how the Tables from the Storage Layers are mapped to Entity Sets in the Conceptual Model Layer, and so on).

LINQ to SQL

LINQ to SQL does not have any alternative in the new .NET, and migration to Entity Framework Core (or another ORM technology) is needed.

Even though the model is represented in an XML file (.dbml) and could be theoretically used to generate another model representation, a more reasonable approach is to generate the Entity Framework Core model from the database. You will need to update the namespaces, change SubmitChanges to SaveChanges (or to SaveChangesAsync but that will require making the entire call chain asynchronous), InsertOnSubmit to Add, and DeleteOnSubmit to Remove. Most of the changes will be related to the fact that the Entity Framework Core scaffolder will generate different names for navigation properties between the tables.

In general, the Entity Framework Core query translator is way more robust than the LINQ to SQL, so there is a good chance you will not run into any query that LINQ to SQL is able to translate and Entity Framework Core is not.

However, there is at least one feature that is unique to LINQ to SQL: the delay-loaded properties. It is a setting on a property in some model class that was commonly used on varbinary(max) columns. When the entity was loaded, this value of such delay-loaded property was not retrieved until the property was actually accessed. This feature was often used for entities that contained pictures or other files. In Entity Framework Core, the solution is to map the same database table to two entities: one with all columns and the other with just the small-sized columns. You can then use the heavy entity only when you need to access the file data and use the light entity in all other cases.

Everything will need to be tested because there may be slight differences in how LINQ to SQL translated the queries.

Entity Framework

Entity Framework Core is a perfect example of Phil Karlton's famous "naming is hard" principle. There were a lot of good reasons to name this technology just by adding the "Core" suffix. After all, it was added to the new branch of .NET either (and removed several versions later). When you look at a code querying data or working with entities, you will probably not be able to tell whether it is Entity Framework or Entity Framework Core.

However, the inner implementation of EF Core is completely different and makes one of the greatest challenges when doing the migration to the new .NET. Using almost the same name suggests that it will be similar, and it is to some extent. But there are thousands of tiny differences and edge cases that require thorough testing.

On the other hand, the old Entity Framework is a rare example of a component originating in the .NET Framework era which is supported on the new .NET. Its versions 6.3 and 6.4 target both .NET Framework and. NET Standard 2.1.

This gives you an option to postpone the migration to Entity Framework Core to a later time, after the application gets migrated to the new .NET. Alternatively, it may be a completely reasonable and viable decision to stay with Entity Framework and not migrate to Entity Framework Core; the benefits might not be so interesting in comparison with other improvements.

If you decide to do the migration, there will be several stages.

First, if the model is defined in the EDM file, it needs to be ported to the Code First representation. In the newer versions of Entity Framework, the model classes are generated from the EDM file using T4 templates, but it is not sufficient to just use them as the Code First model. They do not contain all the metadata from the EDM model, for example, whether the value is required, the maximum length of a string column, or precisions of numeric values. You would need to go through all entities and manually decorate their properties using attributes. If you decide to generate the Code First model from the database instead, you will run into a separate set of issues caused by different conventions to infer the names of navigation properties. This gets especially problematic if the EDM model is customized manually; in such case, it holds information that is not available in the database, so it cannot be reflected by the scaffolder.

Second, the API to configure the model has evolved a lot, and the OnModelCreating method will need many code changes. Also, the constructor in the DbContext class will probably change, as the way of configuring the database connection and concrete storage provider is also different.

Third, the Entity Framework Migrations were also completely changed and reimplemented. The good news is that the old migrations may not be needed to upgrade; you can remove them and consider the current schema of the database as the initial state for the Entity Framework Core Migrations. By doing this, you will lose the ability to revert the schema to previous versions, but in many cases, it is not a significant issue.

Finally, the greatest challenge will be going through all the queries and making sure that Entity Framework Core will be able to translate them. The query translator in the old Entity Framework was very robust, and albeit it often generated long and suboptimal SQL code, the complexity of LINQ queries that you were able to pass to it was sometimes astounding. Even queries with advanced use of multiple GroupBy aggregations were translated without larger problems. In Entity Framework Core, you need to be much more cautious; sometimes, even relatively simple constructs cannot be translated.

After reading the previous paragraphs, you might have got the impression that Entity Framework Core is a step back. What is the point of migration if it means plenty of work and then it cannot even translate all the queries?

There are actually many good reasons to migrate to it. The major one is the performance. The library, including its query translator, was completely rewritten, and one of the reasons was to change the architecture so it would work better in smaller applications which is the new trend after the era of large enterprise monolithic applications for which the old Entity Framework was designed for. You will see this effect immediately in terms of the startup time of the application. The initialization and time to first query are way faster with Entity Framework Core.

The second reason is a larger feature set, especially in the area of model customization. Although it was possible to configure mapping in Entity Framework, the model could not diverge from the database schema substantially. Entity Framework Core supports a plethora of new concepts, such as owned entities, property value conversions, and constructors with parameters. Features like global filters allow you to automatically inject Where clauses to all places in which you work with access to a particular entity, making many things easier. Support for table-valued functions greatly extends the interoperability of the ORM with native means of the underlying database. And finally, Entity Framework Core supports even non-relational data stores such as Azure Cosmos DB, a cloud-native document database.

The decision whether to migrate or not, and whether to do it together with the rest of the application or as a second step, is not an easy one. I will discuss it in more detail in the next chapter.

Membership and Identity

One of the most important requirements in web development is authentication (verification of the user identity based on provided credentials) and authorization (enforcing access permissions of a particular user, usually based on their role membership). Throughout history, .NET presented several solutions for this area.

Membership Providers

With .NET Framework 2.0, ASP.NET introduced the Membership, Role, and Profile providers. These providers took care of the preceding requirements. For example, the MembershipProvider offered a set of methods for creating users, verifying their passwords, handling the access lockout, or resetting the password. The role provider allowed the developers to manage roles, and their member users, while the profile provider could store custom information about any user.

You can provide your own implementations for these providers by specifying them in the web.config file, but most developers used the defaults which persisted all data in a Microsoft SQL Server database.

In some cases, I have seen applications where the developers decided to implement this functionality on their own. A common complaint was that the database schema created by the default providers was heavy and difficult to use with the remaining database tables. However, there are often numerous security vulnerabilities in custom implementations of this functionality. Implementing secure storage for hashed passwords is not an easy task at all, and it is almost impossible to do right without a deep understanding of cryptography and its practical application. Furthermore, with the increasing computing power, it is necessary to regularly update the hashing algorithms to keep the credentials safe in case of a data breach.

The complexity of the database schema was reduced with ASP.NET Universal Providers package, but the rising popularity of external identity providers (often based on OAuth/OpenID Connect protocols) required an even more advanced solution as the membership model worked with assumptions that were no longer met; for example, the users suddenly did not need a password.

If your application uses membership, role, or profile providers, the best option is to migrate to ASP.NET Core Identity. Since it uses a different database schema, you will need to migrate the current users, roles, and profiles. A problem that arises during this migration is that ASP.NET Core Identity uses a different algorithm to calculate the password hashes. You do not have the clear-text form of the password at the time of migration to compute its hash using the new algorithm. There are two ways to handle this issue; either you will not migrate the passwords at all and require the users to set new passwords, or you can implement a mechanism that will rehash the password in the new format on the next user successful sign-in as it is the only moment when we have the password in the clear-text form. The details of the rehashing will be covered in Chapter 6.

Additionally, if you call static methods on `Membership`, `Roles`, or `ProfileManager` in your code, you will need to migrate to the equivalent APIs of ASP.NET Core Identity. The signatures of the equivalent methods are different; on the other hand, there are only a few pages that need to call this API in most applications.

ASP.NET Identity

ASP.NET Identity provides a superset of features of the old providers, and along with the concept of roles, it also allows us to store claims and external login information for each user. For example, if you want to allow the users to sign in using a social network, there will be no password for that user in the database, but the application will need to remember the ID of the user used by the social network. If the site supports more external identity providers, a single user may need to store multiple external logins. The claims can store any other security-related information about the user; a common use case is storing the ID of a tenant in multi-tenant applications.[18]

---

[18] In a multi-tenant application, a single instance of the application serves multiple customers, or *tenants*, whose data and configuration are isolated from the others. The tenant is not the same thing as the user; in most cases, tenants represent organizations, and each organization can be accessed by multiple users. In addition to the user identity, the application often needs to know the tenant the user interacts with, as there are users who can access multiple tenants.

The ASP.NET Identity works with the concept of identity stores. Like the providers, you can use one of the built-in stores, for example, the Entity Framework Core store, but you are free to provide your own implementation.

The migration path is similar to the migration from the membership providers. You will need to migrate the data from the ASP.NET Identity tables to the ASP.NET Core Identity tables, which have a different schema. The same complication will be with the passwords: they cannot be migrated immediately as the hashing algorithm is different.

There is an extra challenge that you can run into when using Entity Framework 6. There is no official implementation of the ASP.NET Core Identity store for Entity Framework 6; there is the Entity Framework Core store available. This can be solved by one of the three methods:

1. Implement your own EF6 store, possibly covering only the subset of functionality you need. This can mean a significant effort, and if you plan to migrate to Entity Framework Core later, this effort would be invested only in a temporary solution.

2. Migrate Entity Framework 6 to Entity Framework Core at the same time. As mentioned in the previous section, this is the most effortful option. On the other hand, there are plenty of benefits coming from moving to EF Core.

3. Use Entity Framework Core to access the users and roles through ASP.NET Core Identity API and Entity Framework 6 to access the remaining database tables. This is probably the option with the least effort; however, it can be the source of subsequent issues as the user entity will be represented by two

different classes, it would be not possible to make transactions across two DbContexts without the cumbersomeness of distributed transactions, and others. However, it can be a temporary solution until the migration from Entity Framework 6 to Entity Framework Core is done.

Other Unsupported Technologies and APIs

To investigate whether the project uses other APIs which are not supported on the new .NET, there is a tool called .NET Upgrade Assistant. It is available either as a Visual Studio extension or as a command-line tool.

One of the functions of this tool is to analyze a project or a solution and identify the tasks that need to be done. It can also help with performing some of the tasks (like upgrading NuGet packages, performing some code changes, and so on).

To install the command-line version of the tool, you will need to run the command in Listing 1-3 in a command line.

Listing 1-3. Command to install .NET Upgrade Assistant

```
dotnet tool install upgrade-assistant --global
```

After the tool is installed, you can run it on the `.csproj` or `.sln` file to generate an HTML report using the command-line command in Listing 1-4.

Listing 1-4. Command to analyze a project or solution. Replace YourProject.csproj with a path to your project or solution file

```
upgrade-assistant analyze --format HTML YourProject.csproj
```

When the analysis is finished, an HTML file will be generated on the disk. Figure 1-1 shows an excerpt from the document showing the recommendations the tool will produce. For example, you can see that it noticed that the application is using ASP.NET Identity UserManager and SignInManager classes, and it suggests replacing them with ASP.NET Core Identity equivalents. Also, it instructs us to change the namespaces of the ActionFilterAttribute and replace the ApiController from the old ASP.NET MVC with the ControllerBase from the ASP.NET Core. Additionally, it detected that the application calls HttpContext.Current which is not available on the ASP.NET Core and recommends using the new HttpContextAccessor API.

Path	Details ↑	Baseline
⌄ UA0013_G: Replace usage of Microsoft.AspNet.Identity, Microsoft.AspNet.Identity.UserManager`2, Microsoft.AspNet.Identity.Owin.SignInManager`2 34		
ⓘ file:///D:/Work/DotvvmWeb/src/Dotv... /LicensesController.cs	ASP.NET identity should be replaced with ASP.NET Core identity. For more details, see https://docs.microsoft.com/aspnet/core/migration/identity	New
ⓘ file:///D:/Work/DotvvmWeb/src/Do... /CurrentUserProvider.cs	ASP.NET identity should be replaced with ASP.NET Core identity. For more details, see https://docs.microsoft.com/aspnet/core/migration/identity	New
ⓘ file:///D:/Work/DotvvmWeb/src/DotvvmWeb/Do.../Startup.cs	ASP.NET identity should be replaced with ASP.NET Core identity. For more details, see https://docs.microsoft.com/aspnet/core/migration/identity	New
Show All		
⌄ UA0002: Types should be upgraded 21		
ⓘ file:///D:/Work/Dotvvm... /SetJsonLdContentTypeAttribute.cs	Type 'ActionFilterAttribute' should be replaced with 'Microsoft.AspNetCore.Mvc.Filters.ActionFilterAttribute'	New
ⓘ file:///D:/Work/DotvvmWeb/src/Dotv... /LicensesController.cs	Type 'ApiController' should be replaced with 'Microsoft.AspNetCore.Mvc.ControllerBase'	New
ⓘ file:///D:/Work/DotvvmWeb/src/Dotv... /ActivityController.cs	Type 'ApiController' should be replaced with 'Microsoft.AspNetCore.Mvc.ControllerBase'	New
Show All		
> UA0010: Attributes should be upgraded 20		
⌄ UA0005: Do not use HttpContext.Current 16		
ⓘ file:///D:/Work/DotvvmWeb/src/Dotv... /LoggingController.cs	HttpContext does not have a Current property; get the context from a controller or use HttpContextAccessor instead	New

Figure 1-1. *An excerpt from the report generated by the .NET Upgrade Assistant*

It is probable that most recommendations will be related to switching the application frameworks mentioned earlier in this chapter. However, there are some APIs that are not supported on the new .NET, such as AppDomain and Code Access Security or .NET Remoting. There are also some APIs that should be avoided as they will start throwing exceptions in the future, for example, binary serialization. The tool should identify all these problems and give you an idea of how complicated they will be to replace.

Summary

In this chapter, I have briefly described the changes introduced by the new generation of .NET, starting with .NET Core 1.0 and continuing to the new, yearly released .NET 7 and 8. I have mentioned all major application frameworks for building web user interfaces, building API interfaces, and providing data access and highlighted the path of their migration. After reading this chapter, you should have a high-level overview of the changes that your projects will require, which is a great starting point for Chapter 2, where I will discuss how to plan the modernization process and make sure all its stages are covered.

Table 1-3 provides a summarization of the application frameworks and the steps to be taken during the modernization.

Table 1-3. *Application frameworks on .NET Framework, their equivalents on the new .NET, and steps necessary to migrate*

.NET Framework	New .NET	Effort of Migration	Steps
ASP.NET Web Forms	–	High	Rewrite all pages and user controls and related business logic to a different presentation technology
ASP.NET MVC	ASP.NET Core MVC	Low	Change namespaces, resolve compile errors
ASP.NET Web Pages	ASP.NET Razor Pages	Low	Change namespaces, resolve compile errors

(*continued*)

Table 1-3. (*continued*)

.NET Framework	New .NET	Effort of Migration	Steps
ASP.NET XML Web Services	SoapCore	Medium	Refactor the services to the SoapCore representation, migrate the authentication and SOAP extensions
WCF	CoreWCF	Low	Change namespaces, resolve compile errors, replace missing features with another approach
ASP.NET Web API	ASP.NET Core MVC	Low	Change namespaces, resolve compile errors, compare OpenAPI definitions, and provide additional metadata to reach identical API surface
ASP.NET SignalR	ASP.NET Core SignalR	Low	Change namespaces, resolve compile errors, migrate persistent connections to hubs
LINQ to SQL	Entity Framework Core	Medium	Scaffold EF Core model from the database, change namespaces, resolve compile errors, replace missing features with another approach

(*continued*)

CHAPTER 1   INTRODUCTION

Table 1-3. (*continued*)

.NET Framework	New .NET	Effort of Migration	Steps
Entity Framework	Entity Framework Core	High	Change namespaces, resolve compile errors, replace missing features with another approach, edit model configuration to achieve an identical database schema, test all queries, and make sure EF Core can translate them
Membership providers	ASP.NET Core Identity	Medium	Change namespaces, resolve compile errors, migrate the data to the tables generated by ASP.NET Core Identity, resolve the migration of passwords by manual reset or re-hashing on the user sign-in
ASP.NET Identity	ASP.NET Core Identity	Medium	Change namespaces, resolve compile errors, migrate the data to the tables generated by ASP.NET Core Identity, resolve the migration of passwords by manual reset or rehashing on the user sign-in

CHAPTER 2

Justifying the Modernization

After reading the previous chapter and reviewing your project's codebase, you should have an overview of the steps necessary to migrate the application to the newest version of .NET. In this chapter, I would like to discuss the benefits of migration, both technical and nontechnical. As a matter of fact, the nontechnical reasons are often overlooked, even though they may be actually more important than the technical challenges.

At the end of the day, it is the business people who make the final decision whether the project should be modernized or not. Being able to explain the situation to the company management and give them strong arguments for the shareholders or investors may make the difference between having an easy-to-maintain project with a happy developer team and a big pile of legacy code no one wants to touch. Various studies show[1] that the technical state of key software projects positively influences the company's business results.

---

[1] Forsgren, Nicole, Jez Humble, and Gene Kim. Accelerate: The science of lean software and DevOps: Building and scaling high performing technology organizations. IT Revolution, 2018.

The book explains how the performance of software delivery teams, low technological debt, and adoption of DevOps practices positively affect the company's business results. Although the modernization to the newest version of .NET is only one of the entry conditions measured in the research, I believe it is an important one: it also affects the team motivation, better suits today's preference for cloud environments, and last but not least, makes hiring new developers significantly easier.

To Modernize or Not to Modernize

The fact that something is possible does not necessarily mean it is a good idea. Technically, migration of any .NET Framework project to the newest .NET is always possible, but the required effort may greatly vary. Thus, evaluating whether such an effort corresponds to the business value and aligns with the company's future strategy is always necessary.

Let me offer several examples of projects I have seen at RIGANTI in recent years and some reasoning on whether the modernization makes sense.

Example 1: Application in Maintenance Mode with a Negligible Number of New Requirements

This project started in 2012, and it is a large ASP.NET Web Forms application with approximately 150 web pages, dialog windows, or components. It is accompanied by a Windows Service to process operations in the background. It communicates with Microsoft Dynamics NAV web services using the Windows Communication Foundation. The WCF is also used in the background service to accept requests from the web application. The web interface uses third-party components Progress Telerik UI for ASP.NET AJAX. The data access layer is built with Entity Framework using the EDMX model (not the Code First approach).

The application was completed in 2014, and since then, maintenance and support have been provided. There have been new requirements, but the total number of developer hours spent on them between 2015 and 2023 is only about 2000, which corresponds to around 250 hours of work per year. Most of the requirements were quite trivial tasks: adding several form fields to existing pages, adding change tracking and auditing to more important entities, or fixing issues after upgrades to the newer version of Microsoft SQL Server.

The customer will likely require a facelift of the user interface in the upcoming years; the current UI does not follow today's design trends, and the users have been reporting various responsivity issues on mobile devices. However, since the application is tailor-made to the customer's internal processes, the business logic will probably remain without changes.

Since ASP.NET Web Forms does not have an equivalent on the new .NET, all 150 web pages or components would need to be rewritten to some other presentation technology. Most of them are quite complex. Thus, it is reasonable to expect that the migration of solely the Web Forms part would take hundreds of hours. Adding the other pieces of the puzzle (WCF, Entity Framework, and others), we can easily see that there is not much business value in migrating the project. Even if the time to implement new requirements would drop by 50% after the migration, the return on investment would be unreasonably high.

Eventually, the business conditions might change, and the benefits of modernization would have to be reconsidered. However, there is also a good chance that the application would be replaced by some third-party SaaS solution that would be customizable enough to meet the company's requirements.

Example 2: Complex and Actively Developed Admin Portal

The second project is also an ASP.NET Web Forms application, which is used by just a few employees; however, it is a key component of the customer's business. Its purpose is managing the company's products and services, supervising the partner activity, calculating commissions, and financial reporting.

The application is actively developed and extended with new features because of changing market conditions and regular announcements of new types of products with different parameters. The application cannot be replaced easily; it was developed for more than 15 years, and many of the business processes are not well documented; they lay in the code of stored procedures or somewhere deep in the code-behind files of .aspx pages. A small internal team of two developers maintains and develops the application. Their capacity is limited as this project is not their only responsibility. One of the developers is close to retirement age, and the company is looking for a replacement; however, it is not easy to find developers willing to work with ASP.NET Web Forms projects today.

Most of the other projects in the company have been started later, and they are already using .NET Core 3.1 or .NET 6. This particular application is one of the last reasons for running Windows Server machines; all other applications are being migrated to Docker containers with a vision to run in Microsoft Azure cloud. Getting rid of the last Windows Servers would reduce the company's IT infrastructure expenses, especially the costs of an external vendor who manages the Windows machines.

In this case, the company decided to modernize the ASP.NET application using the in-place migration using the DotVVM framework described in Chapter 7. The side-by-side method described in Chapters 8 and 9 would require extracting the business logic in a class library, and since this logic is spawned in various places in the project and there are some parts of the application where no one remembers how they should work, the in-place method was believed to be easier and less risky.

Because the team did not have the capacity to perform the migration themselves, RIGANTI was asked to provide the missing developer resources. The customer's team could focus on implementing the new requirements (the new pages and parts of the application were implemented directly in DotVVM – the new presentation technology).

The goal was to first modernize the application with minimal changes to the UI and business logic, followed by refactoring and cleanup of unused modules.

After the migration was completed, the project was deployed as a Docker container to a Kubernetes cluster in Microsoft Azure.

Example 3: Ecommerce Solution Transformed into Multiple Applications

RIGANTI acquired the task of maintaining this project in 2011. We have participated in its development for a couple of years and later handed it over to our partner company that maintains the solution until today. Even at the time this project came to us, it was quite dated already; it started at the time of ASP.NET Web Forms 1.0. The application was a complex ecommerce site accompanied by an admin portal, both implemented in one large ASP.NET Web Site project.[2]

The quality of the codebase was poor when the project came to us, and we had to deal with numerous bugs at the beginning. Most were related to a data access layer generated from the database schema by some unknown and obscure tool. It did not use transactions, and what was more, SQL connections did not get disposed properly. Most errors were caused by exhausting the connection pool; if multiple SQL commands were run in a sequence (each of them opening a new connection), there was a good chance that some of them would fail, leaving the database in an inconsistent state.

The codebase at the beginning was already enormously large, and thousands of new features were added over the years. In fact, more and more applications started to emerge around this one core website.

---

[2] ASP.NET Web Site project is a special kind of Visual Studio project without a project file. All files in the website directory are considered as a part of the project; there is no file that would bind them together.

There were various reporting tools, portals for partners, several APIs for third-party integrations, numerous integrations to partner systems, and more. Most of the new applications did not use ASP.NET Web Forms; some started to use ASP.NET MVC and ASP.NET Web Pages, and some used the combination of ASP.NET Web API and a client-side JavaScript framework. In fact, it appears that the developer team tried almost everything they could: Angular, React, and Vue.js.

The rapidly changing business always required to focus on delivering new features and improvements rather than refactoring and modernizing the code, but luckily, some effort was put into improving the code quality. The original website was redesigned many times, and some part of the old and unreliable business logic was replaced with each redesign. When the API for third parties was implemented, some areas of the application were ported to use this API internally. There were never intentional plans to change the single monolithic application into a microservices solution, but it was naturally going in that direction, and it would not be off the line to call some new components true microservices.

The project is still actively developed; there are several teams working on it, and it is a crucial piece of the customer's business. Several of the applications are business-critical, and any outage would have a significant financial impact.

Since the project consists of multiple loosely coupled applications, and their importance varies, it is necessary to create a strategy for the modernization of such a large solution. This strategy should provide clear answers on which parts of the project should be migrated and in what order.

Numerous criteria can be included in the decision process. Here is a list of some of them:

- *Frequency of deployments and code changes*: Less frequently changed projects are not that important to modernize.

- *Age of the codebase and technology stack*: Older technologies have higher risks of becoming unsupported and lacking developers familiar with these technologies.

- *Performance and throughput*: New versions of .NET include numerous performance optimizations and low-allocation APIs, which can bring significant performance improvements and lower operation costs.

- *Quality of the codebase and separation of business logic from other concerns*: Projects with low code quality can benefit more from a full rewrite than from modernization.

- *Business importance of the component*: When the budget for modernization is limited, you should spend it on the parts that are important to the business.

In the case of this project, the modernization is still ongoing. The first part which was chosen for a full rewrite was the old ASP.NET Web Forms application. Since it is a public-facing site that must be optimized for search engines, ASP.NET Core MVC was used as it offers the highest level of control over rendered HTML. It was the oldest part of the codebase and the most important. Because of removing almost all business logic and replacing it with the newer implementation in the API, which already existed, the reliability of this application greatly improved; finally, we got rid of the old, generated data access layer full of fundamental design issues.

Incremental modernization of this part was not necessary, as the entire rewrite could be done within six months, which was acceptable for the customer. In case of a longer time frame, modernization could be a better approach as the end users would be able to use the new parts of the application sooner, which also means that we would get the feedback earlier.

For other parts that were written in ASP.NET MVC, a migration to ASP.NET Core MVC was done. There was another ASP.NET Web Forms application for partners, which is being rewritten into React, and since it is also a large website with hundreds of pages, an incremental side-by-side modernization is used here. A new application is being developed aside from the old one, and parts of the old application are being incrementally shut down and replaced by the new implementation. All this is done using YARP, which forwards the traffic from the new implementation to the old one in case the requested page has not yet been migrated.

There are dozens of other smaller applications that are not critical; some of them are just tools that are run manually, and since most of them do not change frequently, they are still using the .NET Framework, and it is probable that they will not have to be migrated at all. Eventually, their functionality will be reimplemented in some other component to better fit the new use cases. In some cases, it is already happening. The functionality of some of the single-purpose tools has become a standard functionality of another application, and the tool is not needed anymore.

Takeaways

As you can see from the preceding examples, only technical aspects are insufficient to make decisions. All stories mentioned at least the importance of the project to the customer's business, the size of the team, the speed of development, and the information we know about the budget.

This information may not be available to developers, especially in larger enterprises. In order to make a good decision, you need to ask about the entire business situation of the project. Is the project making money for the company? How important is it? What is the vision of its future development? Is the business being disrupted and is there a larger change on the horizon?

Often, you need to find the right people to ask in your organization. In smaller or medium-sized companies, you may be able to reach the CTO or a person in an equivalent position directly; they should be able to give you the right context or help with the decision. In larger enterprises, there is typically someone responsible for solution architecture, that is, deciding what applications will be used, how they will be integrated, and so forth.

Even when you know the answers, it may still not be enough to be certain whether the benefits coming from modernization are going to justify the costs. But gathering as much information as possible is never a bad idea.

Benefits of the New .NET

The important question that will be asked eventually is what do we get if we modernize this application? From the management perspective, there may be nothing wrong with it. The application just works, and the team is able to resolve most issues in a timely manner. Especially if the application only serves as an internal tool, invisible to the customers, the motivation to make any changes is often very low.

The management people will probably not be very enthusiastic about the technical benefits of upgrading to the new .NET. However, they will understand different aspects, for example, how difficult it is to hire new developers willing to work with legacy technologies, such as ASP.NET Web Forms. This section mentions both technical and nontechnical arguments for what the company can gain from the migration.

Technical Arguments

From .NET Core 1.0, the new branch of .NET was developed with three main things in mind: performance, scalability, and cross-platform needs. Also, the entire codebase was open sourced, and we can watch how the new version is being developed, what discussions the .NET team has about the new features, or what changes actually made it to each release.

Performance Improvements

A nice demonstration of the importance of performance for the .NET team is to look at the number of pull requests from the performance area that were merged to the main branch in the .NET repository.[3] Figure 2-1 shows that the number of performance-related pull requests rises with every version of .NET. Naturally, many of these changes touch only particular small areas of .NET, often improving the performance of just a single method. However, every release also brings several large-scale improvements from which practically all .NET applications benefit.

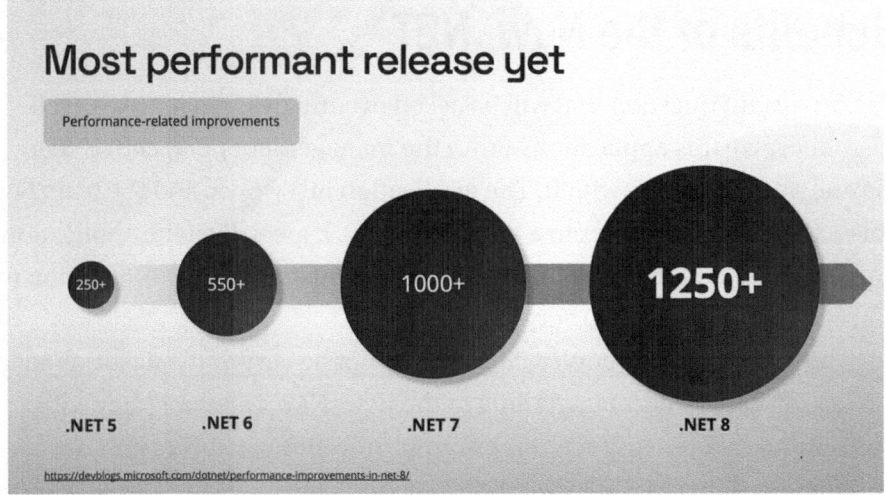

Figure 2-1. *Slide from .NET Conf 2023 showing the number of performance-related improvements in the recent versions of .NET*

---

[3] I have not been successful in finding how exactly the .NET team calculated the number of performance-related improvements. In the GitHub repository of ASP. NET Core, some PRs are marked with the Perf label, but the Runtime repository does not use such label and probably has a different strategy. The numbers were announced in a .NET Conf 2023 Keynote session: www.youtube.com/watch?v=mna5fg7QGz8&t=116s

There are detailed blog posts[4] written by Stephen Toub for every major release describing many of the improvements in very great detail, including code samples and relevant benchmarks.

I think it is important to have at least a 10,000-foot view of the improvements across these versions of .NET and understand the principles on which they stand. That is why the rest of this section will go through all major areas, sometimes digging into a detailed example for the purpose of illustrating what is under the hood.

Just-In-Time Compiler

The most impressive magic starts inside JIT. It is the layer responsible for taking the IL instructions emitted by the C# compiler (or other .NET language compiler) and translating them to the machine code based on the concrete processor architecture and capabilities. The overall performance of the application is influenced by both speed of the JIT itself (how long it takes to compile the IL code) and the performance of the machine code produced by it (how many optimizations the JIT can do).

From .NET Core 2.0 up to .NET 8, there were several big improvements to the JIT, each of them having a significant impact. The good thing about it is that the enhancements in this layer are speeding up all .NET applications, not just those that start using some specific feature of the new .NET.

---

[4] https://devblogs.microsoft.com/dotnet/performance-improvements-in-net-8/
https://devblogs.microsoft.com/dotnet/performance_improvements_in_net_7/
https://devblogs.microsoft.com/dotnet/performance-improvements-in-net-6/
https://devblogs.microsoft.com/dotnet/performance-improvements-in-net-5/
https://devblogs.microsoft.com/dotnet/performance-improvements-in-net-core-3-0/
https://devblogs.microsoft.com/dotnet/performance-improvements-in-net-core-2-1/
https://devblogs.microsoft.com/dotnet/performance-improvements-in-net-core/

Tiered Compilation

When a .NET application is started, JIT does not compile the entire assembly and all its references; that would be terribly slow. Instead, each method is compiled as late as possible – once it is first invoked. There is a good chance that many methods are not going to be compiled at all as they are never invoked.

The more optimizations the JIT does to the method in order to produce the best-performing machine code, the longer the compilation takes. If the method is running for a long time or if it is going to be invoked repeatedly, it is worth spending more time to generate optimal machine code. Unfortunately, most methods are called just once, and, thus, doing advanced optimizations often does not pay off.

The tiered compilation introduced in .NET Core 3.0 allows the JIT to emit the machine core for a method quickly with almost no optimizations on the first execution ("Tier-0"), and when the method is called multiple times, recompile it with the full set of optimizations ("Tier-1"). The recompilation happens on a background thread, and after it is done, all call sites to the method are patched to point to the new address of the better-optimized version. This provides a good trade-off: the JIT does not spend much time on methods where optimizations are important and invests more time only into methods that seem to be called often.

In the subsequent versions of .NET, this mechanism was improved by two other concepts: OSR (On-Stack Replacement) and PGO (Profile-Guided Optimization).

The problem of the plain tiered compilation is methods that run once, but they take a long time to finish – typically when there are loops. It is beneficial to optimize such methods even on the first execution, but the JIT is not able to tell how long the method is going to run. As a simple-enough heuristic, the JIT looks at whether the method contains loops (backward-going jumps, to be precise). If it does, the tiered compilation is not used, and the method is compiled the slow way – with all the optimizations. Unfortunately, such an optimization may do more harm than good if the loop performs only a few or even zero iterations.

The On-Stack Replacement was added in .NET 5 as an opt-in feature and has been enabled by default in .NET 7. Basically, it allows the method code to be replaced not only between its invocations but even while it is running. The Tier-0 compilation adds some instrumentation code to track the number of actual iterations, and when it surpasses a certain limit, the Tier-1 compilation is triggered. The On-Stack Replacement then transfers the state (local variables, registers) and jumps to the corresponding location in the newly compiled version of the method.

The second principle – Profile-Guided Optimization – uses instrumentation to collect data about the execution patterns of the application and then feeds it to the compiler to further optimize the output. Because the "static" flow of PGO requires significant developer effort to set up (compile the application with instrumentation, run it and "simulate" the typical execution patterns, and then recompile it again fed with the gathered data), .NET uses a "dynamic" approach in which the execution patterns are collected automatically during the Tier-0 compilation. Consequently, they are utilized in the Tier-1 compilation, requiring no interaction of the developer. The Dynamic PGO was introduced in .NET 6 as a preview feature and is turned on by default in .NET 8.

Because the instrumentation also consumes some time, an additional tier was inserted between Tier-0 and Tier-1. First, the code is compiled unoptimized and uninstrumented; after a few invocations, the instrumentation is added, and after another set of invocations, the Tier-1 compilation based on the results of instrumentation is triggered.

Implementing this feature into the .NET runtime involved a tremendous amount of work. One of the tiny pieces needed to even get started is counting the number of invocations of a method. Originally, the .NET team implemented the counter without any locking or using the Interlocked class. In general, this is a dangerous approach. Lost updates may happen[5] as the methods can be called from multiple threads. In this particular case, it was believed to be good enough – there is no need to know the exact number; an approximate number would do well. However, the team later found out that the inaccuracy was not acceptable in some cases, so they implemented their own thread-safe approximate counter.[6]

Inlining

One of the frequent optimization done by JIT is inlining of methods. When a method is inlined, its body is copied to the place from which the method is called. The actual method call is avoided – it would require manipulation with the stack and jump to another area of the memory that may not be CPU-cached. The copied method body can also be further optimized, for example, by substituting constants passed as arguments or eliminating unused branches, as shown in Listing 2-1.

Listing 2-1. When the FormatNumber is inlined, only the branch for the "f" format is pulled up to the Main method

```
// BEFORE INLINING
public void Main()
{
    var number = FormatNumber(42, "f");
    Console.WriteLine(number);
```

---

[5] Incrementing a variable is not an atomic operation. When the scheduler switches the thread during the incrementation, the changes to the variable may get lost. You can easily simulate this by creating two threads and incrementing the same variable in a for loop one million times. After both threads finish, you would expect the variable to be 2,000,000; however, the actual number will be much lower as some incrementations got lost. See https://learn.microsoft.com/en-us/dotnet/api/system.threading.interlocked?view=net-8.0#remarks for more details.

[6] https://github.com/dotnet/runtime/blob/main/docs/design/features/ScalableApproximateCounting.md

```
}

public string FormatNumber(int value, string format)
{
    switch (format)
    {
        case "f":
            return DoSomethingWithValue(value);
        case "d":
            return DoSomethingElseWithValue(value);
        default:
            return DoFallback(value);
    }
}

// AFTER INLINING
public void Main()
{
    var number = DoSomethingWithValue(42);
    Console.WriteLine(number);
}
```

This mechanism, of course, comes with a trade-off. Imagine an inlined method that is used from 100 places in the application. Its body would be copied many times, making the assembly larger. This can cause plenty of other drawbacks – apart from slower assembly loading and higher memory consumption of the application, it can also lead to many CPU cache misses. When the inlined method is called frequently and from different places, its instructions will exist in memory in many instances (for each callee) and will not fit in the CPU cache. Without the inlining, these instructions would be present in memory only once and would be likely reused.

One of the key roles of JIT is to decide when it makes sense to inline a method. Also, the larger the method is, the more complicated the inlining is, so there is also a limit on the method size to be considered for inlining.

Inlining was present even in the old .NET Framework, albeit with pretty strict limits (it automatically disqualified methods larger than 32 bytes of IL code, methods with a complex flow control such as `try/catch` block, virtual methods, and so on). Each version of the new .NET extends the capabilities of inlining. .NET 7, for example, enhanced support for cross-assembly inlining. Due to some special treatment of string literals in JIT, cross-assembly inlining of methods using string literals was not supported before. Now it is.

The inlining is further enhanced with devirtualization and constant folding. Devirtualization is a technique allowing to speed up virtual method calls. When a virtual method is called, the runtime must look at the actual instance type and find the correct method in the virtual method table. In many situations, the method can be determined at the compile time, for example, when the method is called on a sealed type. In .NET Core 2.1, the JIT learned how to devirtualize `EqualityComparer<T>.Default.Equals` used in `Dictionary` and other collections. For `Int32`, it can devirtualize and inline the call to a plain `int` comparison (no type can inherit from `int` and thus override its `Equals` method), speeding up the operation more than twice.

Constant folding allows the compiler to evaluate expressions with constants at compile time. The basic example is replacing `num` `*` `3` with 6 in case `num` is a constant with a value of 2. It can be powerful in combination with inlining. If you look closely at Listing 2-1, when the `FormatNumber` method is inlined, the `format` argument becomes a constant – the compiler knows its value. It can then propagate the constant to the `switch` statement and eliminate all the branches except for the `"f"` one.

Thanks to this mechanism, the JIT is able to propagate constants into various functions, including Math operations or even a DateTime constructor. Thanks to this, the new DateTime(2023, 9, 1) can be simplified to new DateTime(0x8DBAA7E629B4000), where the ugly constant is the internal representation of the DateTime type – the number of ticks (100ns intervals since the midnight of January 1, 0001). The complicated calculation needed to obtain this internal representation from the numbers 2023, 9, and 1 does not even happen at the runtime.

Other JIT Improvements

Over the years, the JIT introduced various other improvements, for instance, bounds checking removal or elimination of branching.

.NET was designed as a memory-safe environment; thus, each access to an array requires to be sure that the index is within the bounds of the array. In some cases, the JIT is able to prove that the index cannot be outside the range, and therefore it can omit the check, improving the performance. The palette of patterns recognized by JIT expands with every version of .NET.

For example, .NET 8 supports removing the bounds check when accessing the array using _array[(uint)_index % _array.Length]. This pattern is often used in collections using the hash table, such as Dictionary. By applying the % operation, the _index can never exceed the maximum index of the _array.

JIT also tries to remove branching where possible. Each if statement, ternary operator, or loop slows down the execution of the program by introducing a possible jump to a different location. CPUs like to pipeline the operations – while the current instruction is executed, the next instruction is already being prepared. Each jump introduces uncertainty on which instruction will be the next one. That is why CPUs have branch predictors – a heuristic that predicts the result of the condition and performs the next instructions in advance. This is great when the predictor is correct, but when it makes a mistake, some work has to be undone. Eliminating the branch can significantly speed up the program.

There are a couple of examples of removing branches. One of them is a ternary operator, which results in either 0 or 1 – the condition and jump may be replaced by a bit manipulation. The code i >= 0 && j >= 0 on uint may be simplified to (i | j) >= 0, which eliminates a branch introduced by the && operator.[7] A lot of performance gains were also achieved on higher levels in the application code by removing duplicate or unnecessary checks. This is true for many improvements in the performance of collections that will be mentioned later.

Vectorization

Another technique used to gain better performance is vectorization. Modern CPUs support SIMD[8] instructions that work with vectors – sequences of several numeric values. These instructions take vectors on the input and perform some operation on each element, producing another vector.

In .NET, these operations are exposed through the Vector types. There are methods for arithmetic, bitwise operations, comparisons, and more. If the CPU does not support vectorized instructions, the code falls back to non-vectorized, loop-based implementation.

---

[7] The && operator (conditional logical AND) introduces a branch – if the expression on the left is false, the expression on the right is not evaluated at all. Converting to | (logical OR) removes the branch. See more details in the issue: https://github.com/dotnet/runtime/issues/61940

[8] SIMD – Single instruction, multiple data.

JIT uses vectorization to zero longer blocks of memory – instead of zeroing by 4- or 8-byte blocks, it can work with significantly larger vectors, such as 32 bytes. Based on which vector sizes are supported, the JIT can emit a sequence of vector instructions to zero a block of memory of any size required.

Garbage Collector

One level above the JIT sits the GC responsible for removing objects that are not needed anymore. The GC itself is a monumental piece of engineering, and I encourage every .NET developer to read the excellent *Pro .NET Memory Management* book by Konrad Kokosa[9] – it provides a great insight into how .NET works with memory.

Before .NET 7, the garbage collector worked with segments, large blocks of memory with size of gigabytes in the server mode or hundreds of megabytes in the workstation mode. The strategy was changed to work with smaller regions of 4 megabytes which is more flexible when the memory needs to be repurposed from one generation to another. For example, when generation 0 has enough free space, it may be used by generation 2 instead of reserving a new large segment. This helps to reduce the memory requirements of .NET applications, especially when some segments cannot be released because of pinned objects.

.NET 8 can also work with dynamic heap count. In the server mode, the number of heaps was based on the number of logical cores. Now, it can be dynamically increased or decreased to balance throughput and memory footprint. This approach is described in more detail in a blog post[10] by Maoni Stephens.

---

[9] Kokosa, Konrad, Christophe Nasarre, and Kevin Gosse. Pro .NET Memory Management: For Better Code, Performance, and Scalability. Apress, 2024.
[10] Dynamically Adapting To Application Sizes: https://maoni0.medium.com/dynamically-adapting-to-application-sizes-2d72fcb6f1ea

A great deal of improvements in the GC performance derives from a side effect of rewriting native parts of the .NET runtime into managed code – significant parts of the .NET runtime, such as ThreadPool, were rewritten from C++ to C#. When the garbage collection is in progress, the threads may need to be suspended, so the GC can move blocks of memory and fix all the object references the threads are working with. When the thread is in the unmanaged C++ part, the GC must wait until it gets to the managed world to be able to safely suspend it. This increases the pause the GC may need, with a direct negative impact on the application performance. Therefore, less time spent in the unmanaged code leads to faster garbage collection.

New Performance-Related Types

The Base Class Library (BCL) contains the base types used in any .NET application and a myriad of standard functions and APIs. In the .NET Core branch, it got several interesting new enhancements. Span<T> or ValueTask<T> are not just new types in the BCL. Their introduction in the framework required changes in the runtime and also new language features.

Even if your application code does not use these new concepts directly, you can be sure that they are used internally in many BCL functions you work with, not mentioning the number of things that take place even before your Main method gets invoked.

Span and Memory

The Span<T> and Memory<T> types are an example of an API that most developers do not interact with directly, but even though, they get tremendous benefits from it.

One group of functions where the performance greatly affects the throughput works with large arrays or long strings. This group includes various parsers, formatters, serializers and deserializers, queue processors, and so on. Imagine you have a large array or a long string, and you must pass it to a function that only needs its part. Making a substring or copying the particular segment of the larger array to a new small array would be terribly slow. One way to go is to do it like the Write method on System. IO.Stream: it takes the array, offset, and count arguments. However, this approach is problematic from various viewpoints:

- The API of your functions is poisoned with the same groups of arguments that always come together. There will probably also be overloads without the offset and count arguments to make the cases when you work with the entire array more convenient.

- The code inside the method must calculate which array indices it will work with. It often performs its own bounds checking, in addition to the checks .NET must do anyway.

- Such a method cannot work with an array coming from the unmanaged world, for example, in the form of a pointer and a number of items. Before working with such an array, you would need to copy the memory into a standard .NET array, bringing a significant performance penalty.

- In performance-critical scenarios, you may want to have the array on the stack. Unfortunately, the classic arrays or strings cannot do that without the unsafe option, which comes with another drawback: possible access violations, the necessity to pin objects to prevent them from being moved by GC, and so on.

Span<T> is a solution to this problem. It allows access to a continuous region of memory (on a managed heap, on the stack, or provided by the unmanaged world) in a memory-safe way and with very low overhead.

Basically, the Span contains a pointer to the beginning of the memory region, and a number of items in the region, with the T generic argument defining the size of the item. As shown in Listing 2-2, you can create a Span from an array on the heap, the stack, or an arbitrary pointer obtained from an unmanaged function.

Listing 2-2. Examples of creating Span<T>

```
using System;
using System.Runtime.InteropServices;

// Example 1: Span created from an array
Span<byte> bytes = new byte[10];

// Example 2: Read-only span created from a string
ReadOnlySpan<char> chars = "Hello world";

// Example 3: Span created from a stack-allocated array
Span<byte> stackBytes = stackalloc byte[10];

// Example 4: Span created from an unmanaged memory
unsafe
{
    // allocate 10 bytes
    IntPtr ptr = Marshal.AllocHGlobal(10);
    try
    {
        Span<byte> unmanagedBytes = new Span<byte>(
            (byte*)ptr, 10);
    }
    finally
    {
        // free the memory
        Marshal.FreeHGlobal(ptr);
    }
}
```

You can see that the Span<T> also has the read-only version ReadOnlySpan<T>, which is used for the string. Since strings in .NET are immutable, creating Span<char> from them is impossible. But the read-only version is fine.

Once you have the Span or ReadOnlySpan, you can access the individual elements using the indexer. In order to provide memory safety, .NET will do bounds checking. If you try to access a negative index or go past the number of elements in the Span, you will get IndexOutOfRangeException.

Spans are typically used with value type parameters, and the indexer on the Span is declared as ref return, a feature introduced in C# 7. Thanks to this, you can modify the underlying memory directly – the getter will return a reference to the particular block of memory without making a copy of it, as a normal getter would do. You can see how the indexer is declared in Listing 2-3.

Notice the ref keyword at the declaration of the indexer and at the return clause. Also, see the readonly keyword at the ReadOnlySpan<T> indexer: the struct cannot be modified via the returned reference. Because the indexer returns the reference to the struct, there is no need to declare the setter in Span<T>.

Listing 2-3. Ref return indexer on Span<T> and ReadOnlySpan<T>

```
// Span<T>
public ref T this[int index]
{
    get
    {
        if ((uint)index >= (uint)_length)
            ThrowHelper.ThrowIndexOutOfRangeException();
        return ref Unsafe.Add(ref _reference,
            (nint)(uint)index);
```

```
    }
}

// ReadOnlySpan<T>
public ref readonly T this[int index]
{
    get
    {
        if ((uint)index >= (uint)_length)
            ThrowHelper.ThrowIndexOutOfRangeException();
        return ref Unsafe.Add(ref _reference,
            (nint)(uint)index);
    }
}
```

An incredibly useful feature of Spans is slicing. The Slice method creates another Span for a subsegment of the original Span, without copying memory as string.Substring would do. If you ever implemented your own tokenizer or parser, you probably recall that it is all the time about reading a long string or array and juggling with indices. Since you want to avoid making memory copies, you keep the input string as is and just remember the current position. Each function of the parser will have to do arithmetic on the indexes. With Span, you could abstract this away by passing just the slice representing the text that has not been consumed yet.

Spans have some limitations – for instance, they cannot be stored on the heap, as it would be difficult for the GC to fix the pointers when moving the underlying managed array (the pointer is different than an object reference; it may point anywhere inside the array). Spans cannot thus be boxed; they must always remain on the stack. They cannot be captured for lambdas or used in async methods as they would become fields of the compiler-generated async state machine class.

The Memory<T> and ReadOnlyMemory<T> types are the rescues for this problem. Internally, they contain a classic object reference and then the index and length representing the "span" in the data area of the object. Since the object references are tracked normally by GC, the instances of these types can appear on the heap normally and do not have the previously mentioned restrictions. When needed, you can obtain Span from Memory and ReadOnlySpan from ReadOnlyMemory.

As you will see shortly, introducing the spans unleashed a great amount of performance improvements in many other .NET areas.

Allocation-Free Parsing

In the previous section, I mentioned writing parsers. Imagine that one of the tokens that appears in the custom format you need to parse is a number. At some point, you need to call Int32.TryParse (or Double. TryParse) to verify the number format and obtain the actual value of the token. However, these functions required a string argument. You may have carefully written your parser to work just with the long string and use index arithmetic, but for parsing numbers, you had to create a substring eventually.

With the introduction of spans in .NET Core 2.1, the new overloads that accept them appeared in various places. For example, Int32. TryParse(ReadOnlySpan<Char>, out Int32) allows us to pass a read-only span instead of a string.

Listing 2-4 shows a trivial parser which can read a long input of decimal numbers separated by any number of white characters. Notice that its TryAcceptNumber method is implemented without spans. It tries to read the characters from the current position in the input string and detects whether the sequence continues with a valid decimal number. If so, it returns true and sets the parsed value and moves the "cursor" to the new position. If the input does not continue with a number, it returns false.

The input string can be long – that is why the function does not use Substring on it and uses the currentPosition variable to track which portion of it has already been consumed. However, to call double.TryParse, it needs to cut out the relevant portion of the input string by calling Substring, which introduces the string allocation.

Listing 2-4. A simple parser example without spans

```
// the parser state variables
string inputString = "...";
int currentPosition = 0;

while (currentPosition < inputString.Length)
{
    if (TryAcceptNumber(out var number))
    {
        // process the read number
        ...
    }
    else if (char.IsWhiteSpace(inputString[currentPosition]))
    {
        currentPosition++;
    }
    else
    {
        throw new Exception(
            $"Unsupported char at {currentPosition}!");
    }
}

bool TryAcceptNumber(out double number)
{
    // read until there is a digit or dot, or until the end
```

```
var tokenLength = 0;
while (
    currentPosition + tokenLength < inputString.Length &&
    (char.IsDigit(
        inputString[currentPosition + tokenLength])
        || inputString[currentPosition + tokenLength]
            == '.')
) {
    tokenLength++;
}

if (tokenLength == 0)
{
    // does not continue with digit characters
    number = 0;
    return false;
}

// test whether the read token is a valid number
if (double.TryParse(
    inputString.Substring(currentPosition, tokenLength),
    CultureInfo.InvariantCulture,
    out number))
{
    currentPosition += tokenLength;
    return true;
}
    return false;
}
```

Imagine the input string is long and potentially contains thousands of such numbers – the allocation overhead can be significant. The `string` instances not only get created but need to be tracked by the GC and eventually removed from the memory.

Also, notice the while loop used to detect whether the string continues with a digit or the dot char or whether we have reached the end of the string; there are not many better ways how to achieve that. Additionally, we need to add the currentPosition to indexes everywhere to read the correct portion of the input.

When you look at Listing 2-5, there are a couple of changes. First, we will create a span for the part of the string we work with – starting with currentPosition. This means that we will no longer need to add it everywhere to the index. Searching for the next non-digit or non-dot character can be done using the IndexOfAnyExcept method. Such a method does not exist on string, but it does exactly what we need here. If the end of the span is reached, the return value will be a negative number. Technically, the method accepts ReadOnlySpan<char> as an argument, but there is an implicit conversion from char[] to this type. Remember that you cannot declare the numberTokenAllowedChars field as a ReadOnlySpan as it cannot end on the heap. You have to make the span inside the method where you need to use it. However, this is quite efficient and does not involve any allocation.

The most important thing here is the Slice call, which replaces the Substring. This is how we pass a subsegment of the underlying memory without the need for copying – the main performance benefit of this example.

Listing 2-5. A simple parser example using spans

```
// parser constants
char[] numberTokenAllowedChars = new[] {
    '0', '1', '2', '3', '4', '5', '6', '7', '8', '9', '.' };

...

bool TryAcceptNumberWithSpan(out double number)
{
```

```
ReadOnlySpan<char> span =
    inputString.AsSpan(currentPosition);

// read until there is a digit or dot, or until the end
var tokenLength =
    span.IndexOfAnyExcept(numberTokenAllowedChars);

if (tokenLength <= 0)
{
    // does not continue with digit characters
    number = 0;
    return false;
}

// test whether the read token is a valid number
if (double.TryParse(
    span.Slice(0, tokenLength),
    CultureInfo.InvariantCulture,
    out number))
{
    currentPosition += tokenLength;
    return true;
}
    return false;
}
```

Although this might look like a boring academic exercise, the impact is dramatic. Thanks to spans, you can write allocation-free parsers. The .NET Core 3.0 introduced the new, really fast JSON parser – System.Text.Json. Thanks to spans, it can be that fast.

You can find span-based overloads in various data types – numbers, dates, Guid, Enum, StringBuilder, encodings, and more.

ValueTask

You may have noticed that the Stream got the new ReadAsync and WriteAsync overloads which accept Memory<byte> or ReadOnlyMemory<byte>. Thanks to that, they can get rid of the offset and count arguments, as the memory types can represent a subsegment of an actual array. In many cases, using Memory can save you from instantiating a new array just for the purpose of passing it to the Stream read and write methods.

Another significant benefit of these new methods is a different return type – ValueTask<T>, in this case, ValueTask<int> (the methods return the number of bytes read or written). Value tasks have been introduced in .NET Core 2.0 to help with methods that are by nature asynchronous but return the result synchronously in most cases. This applies to many streams; they typically have their own internal buffers to be more efficient.

When you try to read 100 bytes from a network stream, there is a good chance that the data have already been received and stored in some internal buffer of the stream, so the ReadAsync method may return immediately. If the data is not yet available and the method must wait (asynchronously), it will likely receive more bytes from the wire at once. The method will then return 100 bytes, but the remaining data will be stored in the buffers, allowing the subsequent read to be synchronous again.

For long streams, the read or write methods are called frequently. Since Task is a reference type, each call to these methods would allocate a new object. The result tasks can be cached for some data types – for example, .NET pre-allocates Task<bool> for true and false results. But ReadAsync and WriteAsync return a number of bytes, which may be different for every call.

ValueTask is a value type that contains the result of the operation for successful synchronous tasks and allocates a complete Task instance only for asynchronous or unsuccessful operations, storing the exception thrown inside.

Imagine you need to download 100 MB of data and use 64 kB chunks. It would mean 1600 calls to the ReadAsync method and thus possibly hundreds of Task objects that would be allocated although they were not needed (assuming that some calls would actually require them as the operation will not be synchronous).

It is surprisingly difficult to get the accurate size of a managed object, but if you look in the Task[11] class source code, you can get at least some idea of how heavy the tasks are. If you omit all static fields of the Task, you will see two integer fields, one enum field (which is also backed by an integer), and six fields of a reference type. The integers and enums are 12 bytes in total. On 64-bit platforms, each object reference is 8 bytes, which is 48 bytes for all six fields. The total size is 60 bytes, and if you add the .NET object header and method table pointer, which is 16 bytes on a 64-bit platform, you get to a total of 76 bytes. If the task has a result, add the size of the result value (either the size of the reference for reference types or calculate the size of the value type). Normally, the objects are aligned to multiples of 8, which will round it to 80 bytes. The real numbers can differ, but they are certainly not going to drop to 0, which is the allocation of the ValueTask.

I have created a simple benchmark comparing the memory allocation of the overload returning Task and ValueTask when downloading a 100 MB file. I used plain insecure HTTP to filter out an additional overhead caused by encrypted communication. As shown in Listings 2-6 and 2-7, the memory savings depend on the speed of download vs. the speed of processing the received data. If the data arrive faster than they get processed, more calls to ReadAsync end as synchronous, decreasing the total allocation.

---

[11] See https://github.com/dotnet/runtime/blob/v8.0.0/src/libraries/
System.Private.CoreLib/src/System/Threading/Tasks/Task.cs

Listing 2-6. Benchmark – download of 100 MB file – slower processing than download

Method	Mean	Error	StdDev	Allocated
ClassicTasks	10.32 s	0.039 s	0.036 s	116016 B
ValueTasks	10.34 s	0.045 s	0.042 s	744 B

Listing 2-7. Benchmark – download of 100 MB file – faster processing than download

Method	Mean	Error	StdDev	Allocated
ClassicTasks	52.71 ms	2.173 ms	6.374 ms	135.48 KB
ValueTasks	51.53 ms	2.460 ms	7.253 ms	29.53 KB

Even if you do not plan to download large files, imagine a web application that processes thousands of small requests. Saving a few bytes on each read or write is a significant metric that helps ASP.NET Core to be one of the fastest web platforms by TechEmpower benchmarks.[12]

Similar overloads for reading and writing that utilize `ValueTask` were also added to `Socket`, `WebSocket`, `TextReader`, and other places. This lowers the need for memory allocation for network and filesystem communication.

Source Generators

Source generators are a feature that quickly found its use in various .NET areas. They can be used for many different purposes, but the typical use case in the performance area is to avoid calling Reflection or emitting IL code at runtime and generate this code at the compile time instead.

---

[12] See `www.techempower.com/benchmarks/`

The source generator is a program that is invoked after the compiler parses the application's source code. Its goal is to analyze the application source code provided by the compiler and generate additional source files (if needed). After the generator finishes, the augmented output is passed to the next stage of the compiler, which transforms it into the IL representation.

There are a lot of libraries that use Reflection heavily at the application startup. For example, the Entity Framework looks at your `DbContext` class and emits the model from there. ASP.NET browses the assembly looking for API or MVC controller classes. A popular mapping framework, AutoMapper, looks for type maps defining which property in the source object will be mapped to which property in the destination. Scrutor scans assemblies for service interfaces and their implementation, allowing convention-based service registrations. Not all these activities can be done at the compile time,[13] but some of them can. Source generators can help in these cases.

New JSON Parser

For a long time, .NET was lacking an official and good implementation of JSON.[14] Instead, the open source library `Newtonsoft.Json` created by James Newton-King dominated the .NET world and was referenced even by the official Microsoft packages for years.

---

[13] Many of these libraries use C# code to configure themselves. This is a problem for the source generator – it is invoked at the compile time. It has no way to run the code which configures the library itself. This is the case of AutoMapper or Scrutor – the configuration of maps or service scans is done by a code that needs to be invoked.

However, there are other mapping libraries that are configured using attributes. These can be easily read by the source generator.

[14] Actually, there were `DataContractJsonSerializer` and `JavaScriptSerializer`, but they never got popular and widely used, partly because of numerous limitations. See `www.newtonsoft.com/json/help/html/JsonNetVsDotNetSerializers.htm` for more info.

System.Text.Json is a namespace introduced in .NET Core 3.0 which contains an implementation of fast, allocation-free parser and serializer/deserializer. It is built with using Span types and can work directly with UTF-8, which brings additional performance boots (the parts of the JSON received over the wire as UTF-8 bytes do not need to be transcoded to .NET strings of two bytes per character and can be parsed directly).

In every .NET release since then, the new JSON parser was improved to be even faster.[15] For example, beginning with .NET 6, it got a great speed-up thanks to the source generators. Normally, when the JSON parser reads the input and materializes the object, it needs to use Reflection to create object instances and set their properties. By using the source generator (see Listing 2-8), the Reflection can be avoided by generating code that builds objects and sets their properties directly.

Listing 2-8. Declaring the source-generated JSON serializer context

```
using System.Text.Json.Serialization;

[JsonSerializable(typeof(Customer))]
[JsonSerializable(typeof(Category))]
partial class GeneratedJsonContext : JsonSerializerContext
{
}
```

The JSON source generator emits the implementation of the CustomerJsonContext class. As you can see in Figure 2-2, it creates several files. If you look at them, you will find methods that serialize objects just by invoking WriteStartObject, WriteString, and other methods on

---

[15] An exhaustive set of benchmarks for real-world scenarios can be found in a .NET blog article at https://devblogs.microsoft.com/dotnet/the-convenience-of-system-text-json/. Look for JsonSerializer (corresponds to the new System.Text. Json) and NewtonsoftJsonSerializer entries.

the Utf8JsonWriter instance. Similarly, there are methods that prepare metadata and delegates for construction and writing properties of the concrete types used in the serialization.

This eliminates the need for the serializer to use the Reflection at runtime, further reducing the number of allocations. The Reflection objects contain many fields, making them quite heavy, and the Reflection calls are order of magnitude slower than normal property access.

Figure 2-2. *Files generated using the JSON source generator*

Optimizations in Base Types and Collections

The new concepts described in previous sections unleashed thousands of small but important performance optimizations in foundation types that practically every application needs. Let's briefly look at what has improved in the .NET branch over the years.

Parsing and Formatting

It is pretty surprising that even in basic things like parsing decimal point numbers, there is apparently still some room for improvement, and there is even ongoing research.[16] Thanks to it, the parsing `float` and `double` values became about twice as fast in .NET 7.

Similar improvements were made to `DateTime` and other date/time-related types. An interesting take is using a relatively new algorithm based on Euclidean affine functions[17] to speed up calculations of individual date parts (`Day`, `Month`, `Year`, and so on) from the `DateTime`'s internal representation.

Parsing and formatting of `Guid` also get some improvements in .NET 6. In all these scenarios, `Span`s are used to prevent unwanted memory allocations.

Vectorization for Strings

A myriad of use cases involves working with long texts. The `String` class implements several algorithms which can benefit from vectorization. The .NET Core 2.1 started using vectorization on the `IndexOf` and `LastIndexOf` methods, and more methods were reimplemented to utilize the same concept in the subsequent versions.

---

[16] See https://nigeltao.github.io/blog/2020/eisel-lemire.html
[17] See https://arxiv.org/abs/2102.06959

To give an idea of how this works, imagine first a naïve implementation of the IndexOf function (let's ignore for a while the culture-specific or case-insensitive comparisons, and for the sake of simplicity, let's assume that we search for a single char and not for a substring). As you can see in Listing 2-9, it will probably have a for loop iterating each char in the string and comparing it with the char you are looking for.

The vectorized version will check whether the hardware supports vector instructions. If so, it can process multiple chars at the same time. Depending on the concrete machine, the vector size may be different (e.g., my CPU can work with Vector<byte> with a size of 32 bytes). Basically, the searched buffer is segmented into blocks of the same size as the vector, and the algorithm asks whether any of the vector components is equal to the character being searched. For this to work, you need to make a vector for the character being searched – just repeat the character the same number of times as the vector size. Then, there is a vector operation Vector.EqualsAny you can use to perform a byte-per-byte comparison of the two vectors. Note that the array size may not be aligned with the vector size; in such cases, the rest of the array needs to be processed sequentially, which is also the case when the vectorization is not supported by the hardware at all.

Listing 2-9. Naïve sequential and naïve vectorized version of IndexOf. For simplicity, it works with bytes instead of strings and chars

```
int NaiveIndexOf(byte[] text, byte searchedChar)
{
    for (var i = 0; i < text.Length; i++)
    {
        if (text[i] == searchedChar)
        {
            return i;
```

```
        }
    }
    return -1;
}

int NaiveVectorizedIndexOf(byte[] text, byte searchedChar)
{
    var textSpan = text.AsSpan();
    var start = 0;

    if (Vector.IsHardwareAccelerated)
    {
        // make a vector of the searched char
        // (repeat the same char to fill the entire vector)
        var searchedVector = new Vector<byte>(searchedChar);

        // search in blocks of a supported vector size
        while (start + Vector<byte>.Count <= textSpan.Length)
        {
            var textVector =
                new Vector<byte>(textSpan.Slice(start));
            if (Vector.EqualsAny(textVector, searchedVector))
            {
                // we have found a block with a match;
                // do not move and search sequentially
                break;
            }
            // no match, let's continue with the next block
            start += Vector<byte>.Count;
        }
    }
```

```
    // process the rest of the array sequentially
    for (var i = start; i < textSpan.Length; i++)
    {
        if (textSpan[i] == searchedChar)
        {
            return i;
        }
    }
    return -1;
}
```

Please note that the real implementation is far more complex than what I have shown here to demonstrate the principles of using vectorization. If the code needs to work with non-ASCII encodings, perform culture-specific comparisons, or deal with case insensitivity, the comparison is not a trivial byte equality check. Various tricks are involved when the searched string is not just a single, such as searching for its first and last chars with appropriate distance between them – this can be vectorized and eliminates most of the matches, requiring scanning the string sequentially in fewer cases.

Similar improvements were also made to the Trim, Split, Replace, and Reverse methods. New methods such as IndexOfAnyExcept were added on Span which help to implement various parsers and are utilized by other methods used by the String type.

String encodings also heavily rely on vectorization. Many operations on the Latin1 encoding used for parsing HTTP protocol messages became vectorized in .NET 5.

C# 11 added support for UTF-8 string literals, which can also help in applications working with long chunks of text that are intended to be sent or received over the wire. This allows you to avoid conversions from classic UTF-16 representation of the String class and have these instances already prepared in UTF-8. Most parsing and formatting methods already support ReadOnlySpan<byte>, which also helps avoid unnecessary conversions, mainly in serialization and deserialization scenarios.

Collections

All collections present in .NET also got special attention to work faster. My favorite pull request from the earlier days of the .NET Core is #9539 Faster List Add[18] which optimizes the performance of the List<T>.Add method. It is hard to imagine an application that would not use it at least once; thus, almost every application benefits from this change.

The original implementation is shown in Listing 2-10; the new one is much more complicated.

Listing 2-10. Original implementation of the List<T>.Add method

```
// Adds the given object to the end of this list.
// The size of the list is increased by one.
// If required, the capacity of the list is doubled
// before adding the new element.
public void Add(T item) {
    if (_size == _items.Length) EnsureCapacity(_size + 1);
    _items[_size++] = item;
    _version++;
}
```

The List class uses the _items array to store the items, and the _size field contains the actual number of items. The internal array's default capacity is 4, and when the newly added item does not fit into the array, a new array with a doubled capacity is created. As you can see, the original implementation called the EnsureCapacity method in such cases. By the

---

[18] See https://github.com/dotnet/coreclr/pull/9539

way, the EnsureCapacity method contained an additional check of the array size, which was unnecessary.

Listing 2-11. Improved implementation of the List<T>.Add method

```
[MethodImpl(MethodImplOptions.AggressiveInlining)]
public void Add(T item)
{
    var array = _items;
    var size = _size;
    _version++;
    if ((uint)size < (uint)array.Length)
    {
        _size = size + 1;
        array[size] = item;
    }
    else
    {
        AddWithResize(item);
    }
}

// Non-inline from List.Add to improve its code quality
// as uncommon path
[MethodImpl(MethodImplOptions.NoInlining)]
private void AddWithResize(T item)
{
    var size = _size;
    EnsureCapacity(size + 1);
    _size = size + 1;
    _items[size] = item;
}
```

As you can see in Listing 2-11, the new implementation adds several changes. Instead of accessing the class fields, their instances were captured in local variables. The comparison of array size is done in uint, now a common idiom in most of the .NET codebase. While the Add method is instructed to perform aggressive inlining,[19] the AddWithResize method is not inlined as it is not the hot execution path.

This change to List.Add (and other similar changes to other List methods) decreased the time to make 100 million adds and removes on a list by approximately 25%.

The implementation of adding items into List has been later changed in several subsequent pull requests to avoid an unnecessary second check of the array size.

Given some other collections in .NET use the List internally, they also benefit from this improvement. Just in .NET Core 2.0, Queue, ConcurrentQueue, SortedSet, and ConcurrentBag got similar optimizations.

Particular attention was given to speeding up Dictionary, the second most popular collection of .NET. A significant performance improvement was gained by replacing the modulus (%) operation with multiplications and bit shifts. This operation is used to calculate to which bucket the value belongs based on its hash code, and this optimization has a significant impact.

The concurrent collections were updated to require slow locking in fewer cases. There were various improvements to immutable collections as well.

.NET 8 introduced **frozen collections** – a third group of collections optimized for fast reading. The reason for introducing this new group was that the immutable collections were optimized for a different

---

[19] Be cautious when using the attribute in your code – unnecessary use can have the opposite effect of damaging the performance. See https://learn. microsoft.com/en-us/dotnet/api/system.runtime.compilerservices. methodimploptions?view=net-8.0

criterion – fast creation. They are immutable, but quite ironically, they expose `Add`, `Delete`, and other "mutation" methods. These methods do not change the collection itself but return a new collection – the result of the mutation. Also, the internal implementation of the immutable collection is designed to "share" the data with their parents. For example, the `ImmutableDictionary` does not use a hash table internally; instead, it is represented as a self-balancing tree. To clone such a collection and add an entry is very fast, but the algorithmic complexity of read operations is thus $O(\log n)$ instead of $O(1)$ for a hash table, which means the reads are much slower. The frozen collections solve this problem – they are also immutable but optimized for reading, not for quick allocation and quick mutation into new instances.

You should use immutable collections when you need to be able to quickly create "mutated" collections. The frozen collections are great for places where you create them once and then use them for a long time without the intent to modify them.

Summary

I believe I mentioned the most important highlights of what you can expect from the new .NET in the performance area. There is much more. As mentioned at the beginning of this subsection, each release of .NET gets hundreds of pull requests whose intent is to improve performance. The effects of each optimization in the runtime and the BCL are multiplied any time when such API is used on some higher layer – in libraries, frameworks, and even on hosting infrastructure. Many components of Azure are also written in .NET.

One interesting side effect of the improvement in .NET was the introduction of YARP – a fast reverse proxy based on ASP.NET Core. It benefits from all the improvements made to the .NET, as its main purpose is to enable high throughput with as few allocations as possible.

It was adopted by the Azure App Service team[20] in order to lower the infrastructure costs. The experienced improvement in throughput was almost 80%. Pretty impressive!

Developer Productivity

The new .NET offers numerous improvements in the efficiency of the developer's inner loop. More than a hundred times a day, you make a code change, compile the application, and run it to see whether the new works or not. You interact with the version source control system to track changes made to the source files. Most projects today depend on external libraries and packages. Each of these areas received significant enhancements in recent years.

Better Developer Tools

The previous section already mentioned various performance optimizations; thanks to them, every run of the application will be faster. But not only that, the C# compiler and MSBuild, the build system for .NET applications, are also written in .NET. You can benefit from faster compile times and faster restoration of NuGet packages, and thanks to the new project system[21] in Visual Studio, which is used for the new SDK-based projects, many IDE operations are also significantly faster.

Visual Studio, still the most popular IDE in the .NET world, gets feature and performance updates every few months. Instead of waiting two or three years for the new major version, significant updates are

---

[20] See https://devblogs.microsoft.com/dotnet/bringing-kestrel-and-yarp-to-azure-app-services/

[21] A project system is a mechanism responsible for loading the project file (e.g., .csproj), identifying all project items, creating a hierarchical representation, and allowing the IDE (Visual Studio) to interact with the items. What you see in the Solution Explorer window is how the project system sees your project; it is a bit different view than what you would see directly in the filesystem.

delivered more frequently.[22] For example, an update 17.5 for Visual Studio 2022 from March 2023 brought a significant performance improvement, reducing build times for the new .NET projects by up to 80%. The update 17.8 improved the speed of running a project when pressing F5 by about 20%. Although some of these improvements help speed up work with .NET Framework projects as well, many are related to the new project system and SDK-style projects (see the "Version Control" section). The old projects still use the old, COM-based project system.

Enabling to run .NET workloads on Linux and Mac opened a huge space for other IDEs. Some developers prefer a lighter tool over heavy full-featured products, choosing Visual Studio Code. It is worth mentioning that there are two levels of support of C# in VS Code. There is a free open source C# extension that uses the OmniSharp engine,[23] and there is also a licensed extension called C# Dev Kit which provides a feature set similar to the Visual Studio. Individuals, academic employees, and open source developers can use it for free with the same terms that apply to Visual Studio Community. For organizations, the C# Dev Kit is included with the Visual Studio subscriptions.[24]

Many developers moved to a competitive product offering – JetBrains Rider.[25] Offering the same features as the popular ReSharper extension for Visual Studio, this IDE works on all platforms and quickly became the first choice for a part of the community.

---

[22] See `https://devblogs.microsoft.com/visualstudio/visual-studio-performance-highlights-delivered-in-2023/` for more info about recent improvements in build and solution acceleration.

[23] See `www.omnisharp.net/`

[24] The full license terms can be found at `https://marketplace.visualstudio.com/items/ms-dotnettools.csdevkit/license`

[25] See `www.jetbrains.com/rider/`

Hot Reload

At the beginning of this section, I mentioned the developer's inner loop. Hot Reload is an incredibly useful feature that can save vast amounts of time.

For years, we have been used to the scheme when even a trivial change to the source code required rebuilding and restarting the entire application. With some exceptions, like Web Site projects at the times of ASP.NET Web Forms, once you touched the C# code or anything that was translated to the C# code (e.g., editing the forms using the designer interface in WinForms or WPF projects), there was no reasonable way in .NET how to reflect these changes in the running process.

The first step of the journey was Edit and Continue, a feature of the debugger introduced in 2005 that supported applying simple changes in the code. However, it did not work in many project types, and for years, it supported only 32-bit applications. This restriction was lifted in 2013, but even after that, there were no visible improvements to this mechanism until 2021, when .NET Hot Reload was introduced.

The Hot Reload allows the developers to modify code while the application is running and apply these changes without restarting the process. Not all kinds of changes are supported, but the list of supported modifications[26] grows with every .NET release.

For example, you can add methods, fields, constructors, and other members to existing types (except for enums and interfaces). Adding members to existing objects or types is quite safe because the original code had no way of interacting with these members (they did not exist yet). When new fields are added to objects, they must be stored somewhere else, as it is impossible to go through the entire stack and heap and move

---

[26] See https://learn.microsoft.com/en-us/visualstudio/debugger/supported-code-changes-csharp?view=vs-2022

and extend the object bodies. But again, the original code did not interact with them, and the new code will be emitted in a way to obtain these fields from the alternative location (you can imagine some dictionary that holds the additional members for each object; the only requirement is that it should cooperate with the GC and remove the additional members when the object gets removed from the memory; this is exactly what the ConditionalWeakTable collection does).

The Hot Reload can also quite safely modify method bodies; the new IL will be injected into the process to be JIT-compiled the next time the method is invoked.

There are some limitations when adding or editing lambda expressions; it may require capturing new variables which is not supported. It is possible to modify async methods, but you cannot change regular methods returning Task to async ones.

Starting with .NET 8, it is possible to make changes to code that works with generic types. Renaming members other than fields, including parameter types, is supported in most cases. In many cases, changing the return types of methods works too (naturally, you need to also update all places from which the method is called).

The Hot Reload is well integrated with the IDEs – when you pause the project and edit the code, you can easily apply it to the running application. When it is not possible, the IDE will perform a full rebuild and restart. The ASP.NET Core was also augmented with a mechanism that detects code changes or process restarts and tries to update or recover from it automatically, for example, by updating the UI or reloading the web page in the browser.

Hot Reload also offers an API to libraries and frameworks to listen for an event that the process was patched. Many libraries cache information about types obtained through Reflection. These caches need to be updated after the code changes are applied because the underlying types might have changed.[27]

For many developers, Hot Reload completely changed the way they used to work. Previously, they were making code changes and occasionally ran the project (with the debugger) to see whether the application behaved correctly. With Hot Reload, the first thing they do is run the project (often without the debugger because it disables some functionalities in the IDE), and then they modify the code and watch the real-time changes in the application. Some edits are applied via Hot Reload; for some of them, the process must be restarted. The ASP.NET Core browser refresh middleware will automatically handle everything and refresh the page in the web browser as needed. Combined with the faster startup of the new .NET applications, the typical developer inner loop became way more efficient and productive.

Version Control

Over the years, Git has become practically an industry standard for source code versioning. Around it, a huge ecosystem of products and services evolved, democratizing things that were extremely difficult to set up before. The concepts of Continuous Integration or Continuous Delivery are not anything new, but with easy-to-get tools like GitHub Actions, even individuals or small organizations can adopt them easily, with minimum costs and effort. Tools like Dependabot[28] which scan repositories and

---

[27] For example, the open source framework DotVVM clears pre-compiled pages and serialization maps when code changes are applied. See `https://github.com/riganti/dotvvm/blob/main/src/Framework/Framework/Runtime/HotReloadMetadataUpdateHandler.cs`

Notice the `MetadataUpdateHandlerAttribute` at the top which decorates the class responsible for handling this event.

[28] See `https://docs.github.com/en/code-security/dependabot`

identify vulnerabilities in project dependencies help to make software projects more secure.

Many companies migrated away from Microsoft's TFVC,[29] the source control system used in Microsoft Team Foundation Server (later renamed to Azure DevOps Server), mostly in favor of Git.

The new .NET is much better prepared for team environments where frequent conflicts occur when multiple developers modify the same files. The greatest example in .NET Framework projects is the .csproj file. This file contains a complete list of files included in the project. Also, each NuGet package reference is specified in both packages.config and the .csproj file. Listings 2-12 and 2-13 show relevant excerpts from these files.

Listing 2-12. An excerpt from the packages.config file showing references to ASP.NET Web API packages

```
<packages>
  ...
  <package id="Microsoft.AspNet.WebApi"
          version="5.3.0" targetFramework="net472" />
  <package id="Microsoft.AspNet.WebApi.Core"
          version="5.3.0" targetFramework="net472" />
  <package id="Microsoft.AspNet.WebApi.Owin"
          version="5.3.0" targetFramework="net472" />
  <package id="Microsoft.AspNet.WebApi.WebHost"
          version="5.3.0" targetFramework="net472" />
  ...
</packages>
```

---

[29] Team Foundation Version Control is a centralized source control version system present in Visual Studio Team Foundation Server, later renamed to Visual Studio Team Services and even later to Azure DevOps. To prevent conflicts, it worked with the concept of "checking-in" files, disallowing to edit them by other team members.

Listing 2-13. An excerpt from the project file showing references to corresponding libraries

```
<Project ...>
  ...
  <ItemGroup>
    <Reference Include="System.Web.Http, Version=5.3.0.0,↵
Culture=neutral, PublicKeyToken=31bf3856ad364e35,↵
processorArchitecture=MSIL">
      <HintPath>..\packages\Microsoft.AspNet.WebApi.Core.5.3.0↵
\lib\8net45\System.Web.Http.dll</HintPath>
    </Reference>
    <Reference Include="System.Web.Http.Owin, Version=5.3.0.0,↵
Culture=neutral, PublicKeyToken=31bf3856ad364e35,↵
processorArchitecture=MSIL">
      <HintPath>..\packages\Microsoft.AspNet.WebApi.Owin.5.3.0↵
\lib\net45\System.Web.Http.Owin.dll</HintPath>
    </Reference>
    <Reference Include="System.Web.Http.WebHost,↵
Version=5.3.0.0, Culture=neutral,↵
PublicKeyToken=31bf3856ad364e35,↵
processorArchitecture=MSIL">
      <HintPath>..\packages\↵
Microsoft.AspNet.WebApi.WebHost.5.3.0\lib\net45\↵
System.Web.Http.WebHost.dll</HintPath>
    </Reference>
  </ItemGroup>
  ...
</Project>
```

Not only that this duplicity creates occasional issues when these files get out of sync (the NuGet tooling thinks that it references some version of a NuGet package, but the reference in the project file points to another DLL location). Another issue arises from the need to specify even transitive dependencies – the packages that are not referenced by your project directly but are required by some of the dependent packages. The excerpts show several references even though a single reference would be sufficient; the other packages could be added automatically because the main package depends on them. This complicates things when you upgrade or remove package dependencies; there is no easy way to tell whether the package is required by the project or whether it was added just as a dependency of some other package that may have already been removed from the project. Keeping the list of dependencies clean and up to date is thus quite difficult in the old .NET Framework projects.

Package References

The solution for this problem (which is, by the way, available even for the old .NET Framework projects, although with some restrictions) is called PackageReference. It is a new element supported by MSBuild that replaces the traditional Reference elements generated from the entries in packages.config.

Instead of the relative path to DLLs in the packages folder, it contains the name and version of the NuGet package. The transitive dependencies are handled automatically, which allows you to define only the packages your project uses directly. This is much easier to keep clean and concise, as shown in Listing 2-14. The packages.config file is no longer needed.

Listing 2-14. An example of the PackageReference element

```
<Project ...>
  ...
  <ItemGroup>
    <PackageReference Include="Microsoft.AspNet.WebApi.WebHost"
      Version="5.3.0" />
  </ItemGroup>
  ...
</Project>
```

Another great advantage of the new .NET is that the NuGet packages are downloaded in a machine-level cache, not in the `packages` directory created in every solution folder. This helps to save a significant amount of disk space, as multiple projects will probably use a large subset of the same packages, which are now stored only once in the user profile folder (e.g., `C:\Users\`*YourUserName*`\.nuget` at Windows). Thanks to this, the package restore can be faster as some packages may have already been in the cache if you used them in some other project.

One of the caveats is that the new NuGet package references solve various issues caused by incompatible assembly versions of dependent packages. For example, if you reference libraries A and B, which both have a dependency on library C but in different versions, in the .NET Framework, you need to tell the assembly loader to redirect the load attempt from the older version to the newer version of that assembly. This was done typically in the `.config` file of the application, as shown in Listing 2-15. Multiple packages may need `Newtonsoft.Json` in various versions, but the config entry will redirect all these dependencies to the latest version.

Listing 2-15. An example of assembly binding redirect configuration

```
<runtime>
    <assemblyBinding xmlns="urn:schemas-microsoft-com:asm.v1">
        <dependentAssembly>
            <assemblyIdentity name="Newtonsoft.Json"
                              culture="neutral"
                              publicKeyToken="30ad4fe6b2a6aeed" />
            <bindingRedirect oldVersion="0.0.0.0-13.0.0.0"
                             newVersion="13.0.0.0" />
        </dependentAssembly>
    </assemblyBinding>
    ...
</runtime>
```

You can probably remember the cases when this section got out of sync with the actual NuGet package versions (typically on version downgrades). The application crashed with an exception because the version of the assembly on the disk was different than expected.

All this disappears with the new .NET. If libraries A and B depend on C in different versions, the higher version of C is selected automatically. If you directly reference package C in a lower version than any of the other packages need (direct dependencies win over transient ones), you will get a compiler warning that a package downgrade was detected. You can fix it easily by requesting a newer version, and you will notice this problem at the compile time, not in the runtime.

SDK-Style Projects

The format of `.csproj` files on the new .NET has also changed. The goal was to make these files briefer, take advantage of reasonable defaults, and prefer a convention-based approach, which greatly reduces the number of times you need to change these files. And in the remaining cases, the format of these project files allows easy manual editing, without forcing you to use the Project Properties editor experience in Visual Studio.

This helps with merging conflicting changes. The version control systems often mark the conflicts in the project file, which makes their XML content syntactically invalid. The IDE then refuses to load such files, and being able to resolve the conflict just with a text editor is a great benefit. Not to mention the fact that the conflicts are not that rare.

Whenever the developer added a file to a project in the old projects, it resulted in a change in the `.csproj` file. Because of that, the file's version history was polluted with plenty of trivial changes, which made it much harder to find the important ones. Also, even when a source code file was present in the filesystem, it was not considered to be a part of the project unless it was explicitly included in the `.csproj` file. It was sometimes confusing to see the compiler complaining about a missing class, but the file was there when you looked in the filesystem. Listing 2-16 shows how the C# files were registered in the old file format.

Listing 2-16. An excerpt from the old format of the project file listing all source code files

```
<Project ...>
  ...
  <ItemGroup>
    <Compile Include="Controllers\AuthenticationController.cs" />
    <Compile Include="Controllers\InsiderController.cs" />
    <Compile Include="Controllers\ScriptingController.cs" />
    <Compile Include="Controllers\ExportController.cs" />
    ...
  </ItemGroup>
  ...
</Project>
```

Looking at this old format, you can easily imagine a myriad of possible conflicts that can occur whenever two developers add a controller at the end of this section, not speaking about the changes caused by moving files between folders or performing larger structural changes in the project. What is the added value of an explicit list of all source code files in the first place?

The new SDK-style project files, as they are called, can specify the Sdk attribute on the root Project element, which can link to a specific SDK. This SDK contains a set of MSBuild targets and tasks responsible for compiling, packing, and publishing code. They also specify many defaults, enabling the project files to specify much fewer things. Listing 2-17 shows a complete project file for a console application. The simplicity is astounding if you compare it with the old format. Most things, such as the root namespace, assembly name, and other defaults, are just inferred from the project filename or the specified target framework version.

Listing 2-17. A simple SDK-style project file for a console application

```
<Project Sdk="Microsoft.NET.Sdk">
  <PropertyGroup>
    <OutputType>Exe</OutputType>
    <TargetFramework>net8.0</TargetFramework>
  </PropertyGroup>
</Project>
```

It is also much easier to publish your own Class Library projects as NuGet packages. You do not need to hand-craft the .nuspec files to define the package metadata; instead, most information is inferred from the .csproj file you already have. You can also specify additional metadata using MSBuild properties,[30] such as PackageId, Version, PackageTags, Authors, Company, and more.

---

[30] See https://learn.microsoft.com/en-us/nuget/create-packages/creating-a-package-msbuild#set-properties

Entity Framework Migrations

You can save a lot of time when dealing with conflicts in Entity Framework Migrations. In order to detect changes made to the Entity Framework model and emit the corresponding migration code when calling Add-Migration, the migration engine in both EF (Entity Framework) and EF Core compares the current model with the last-known model snapshot.

However, in the old Entity Framework, the model snapshot is stored as a Base64 blob in a .resx file. When multiple developers add migrations and then commit the changes, the model snapshot does not contain all the migrations, and because it is Base64 encoded, it is impossible to merge. In such cases, the recommended way was to unroll the migrations and create them again. However, due to the way this mechanism was designed, even detecting that there was a conflict was not easy – the error messages often pointed to something else, and the hard part was even realizing what happened.

The migrations were redesigned in Entity Framework Core. The model snapshot is stored as a standard C# file, and it is generated in a deterministic way. Thanks to that, most conflicts in this file can be resolved automatically or with a simple manual edit, and there is no need to regenerate migrations.

Support for Linux and Containers

Since .NET Core 1.0, .NET is officially supported on Linux and Mac OS, and the introduction of .NET 6 and .NET MAUI, a multiplatform technology to build desktop and mobile applications, also added Android and iOS as supported platforms.

Many companies started deploying their workloads using containers and running them in various cloud environments, with Kubernetes as the most popular orchestrator. The great advantage of containers is that the developers have much better control of the OS and its installed dependencies. The `Dockerfile`, from which the container image is built, typically starts with the base image, which contains a tested combination of an OS and version of the application runtime such as .NET.

Upgrading the application to the newer version of .NET does not require any change on the server; it is only about running a new container which is built from a base image with the new version of the operating system and the .NET runtime. There is no need to install or configure anything on the server. Of course, this comes with a new responsibility. Now, it is the developer or DevOps specialist who oversees that the application is using the newest security updates of the .NET version being used. It will not get updated automatically without rebuilding the Docker image.

For example, if you look at the Docker Hub page[31] for the .NET runtime containers, you will see a bunch of versions that guarantee to have a particular version of the underlying operating system, a particular version of .NET, and all the dependencies it needs. Your job is only to copy the application files into the container and specify the entry point – the command that will be executed when the container is started.

Listing 2-18 shows how a `Dockerfile` for a .NET application can look like. As you can see, the first stage defines the container used for running the application (`dotnet/aspnet:8.0`) and indicates on which ports the application will be listening. The second stage uses the SDK container (it is much larger than the first container because it contains the complete .NET SDK – compilers and other tools). It copies the `.csproj` file into the container and performs the package restore operation. Subsequently, it copies the remaining files and builds the project.[32] The third stage takes the results of

---

[31] See `https://hub.docker.com/_/microsoft-dotnet`

[32] The reason why these operations are split into two is caching. When Docker finds out that the project file has not changed since the last run, it skips the `dotnet restore` command and continues with copying the remaining source code files. This can save significant amount of time.

the second one and publishes the result files for deployment. These files are picked by the final stage (running again in the ASP.NET runtime container specified in the first stage) and copied to the final destination. Finally, the entry point is specified. This entire workflow may look too complicated; however, it is designed to be extensible and efficient when executed multiple times.

Listing 2-18. An example Dockerfile for an ASP.NET Core application

```
# First stage - define the target container
FROM mcr.microsoft.com/dotnet/aspnet:8.0 AS base
USER app
WORKDIR /app
EXPOSE 8080
EXPOSE 8081

# Second stage - restore and build
FROM mcr.microsoft.com/dotnet/sdk:8.0 AS build
ARG BUILD_CONFIGURATION=Release
WORKDIR /src
COPY ["SampleApp/SampleApp.csproj", "SampleApp/"]
RUN dotnet restore "./SampleApp/./SampleApp.csproj"
COPY . .
WORKDIR "/src/SampleApp"
RUN dotnet build "./SampleApp.csproj" \
    -c $BUILD_CONFIGURATION \
    -o /app/build

# Third stage - publish the files
FROM build AS publish
ARG BUILD_CONFIGURATION=Release
RUN dotnet publish "./SampleApp.csproj" \
    -c $BUILD_CONFIGURATION \
    -o /app/publish /p:UseAppHost=false
```

```
# Fourth stage - finalize the container
FROM base AS final
WORKDIR /app
COPY --from=publish /app/publish .
ENTRYPOINT ["dotnet", "SampleApp.dll"]
```

Although Windows containers can be used to run even .NET Framework applications, their heaviness and limited support in non-Microsoft cloud environments makes them much less useful. That is why Linux containers are the preferred way of deployment in many organizations.

Being able to run on Linux also opens new opportunities to decrease the costs of hosting larger .NET applications. Looking at the virtual machine prices in most used cloud platforms, each of them offers Linux virtual machines or Linux-backed SaaS offerings for hosting .NET workloads for lower prices than their Windows alternatives, mainly because of license costs and higher hardware requirements. The smallest .NET workloads can be run on tiny Linux devices such as Raspberry Pi.

When considering migration of any large application from the .NET Framework to the new .NET, the savings on hosting infrastructure can be one of the greatest long-term benefits.

Architectural Improvements

The new versions of .NET offer several new concepts in the platform architecture. A collection of NuGet packages starting with `Microsoft. Extensions` provides abstractions and implementations of various high-level concepts, such as configuration, logging, caching, dependency injection, resiliency, telemetry, and more.

When working in the .NET Framework, I often found areas that seemed overengineered to me (such as the XML-based configuration model that was extensible using the `ConfigurationElement` API), as well as areas that were completely missing. For example, the .NET Framework did not contain any universal dependency injection container. A lot of libraries emerged to solve the problem, but each was defined in a different way. Although the interface `IServiceProvider` was present, most libraries do not use it and provide their own way of interacting with the DI (Dependency Injection) container. The same story was with logging, caching, and other aspects.

Additionally, a lot of things were (and some still are) provided by static methods, which hurt the testability of the code. The code that uses `DateTime.UtcNow` or `ConfigurationManager.AppSettings` static members is hard to cover by tests, and you are often required to create your own interfaces around these static concepts.

The .NET 8 finally introduced the `TimeProvider`, an abstraction over the system time you can use to easily simulate various dates in tests and make sure the code behaves correctly. The new `Microsoft.Extensions.Configuration` library no longer relies on static members and thus can be used in the tests easily, possibly testing multiple configurations in various tests without the need to use mocks.

Configuration

In the .NET Framework, the configuration was defined in XML files. In web applications, the configuration file was typically named `Web.config`; in other kinds of applications, the config file used the same name as the executable file with added `.config` extension.

The configuration file format supported inheritance – the default machine-wide configuration could be specified in `Machine.config` to be applied to all .NET applications running on the machine. The application could come with its own hierarchy of configuration files, which was commonly used in web applications hosted in IIS.

The individual configuration sections could be locked to prevent overriding on the higher levels of the hierarchy. The format also supported encryption of selected sections for secure storage of passwords and other secrets, and everything was extensible so the developers could register their own configuration sections and enforce their own validation rules to make the configuration consistent.

While this feature set looks quite impressive, the reality was that most features were not in use in most .NET applications. Seeing hundreds of deployed ASP.NET applications, I rarely met one where the connection strings would be actually stored in encrypted form. It was quite difficult to configure it, and it complicated the diagnostics of such applications. The extensibility offered by defining custom configuration sections was so cumbersome that many developers just resigned and put everything in the appSettings section (a generic key-value storage that was easy to use). As I already mentioned in the previous section, the configuration was typically accessed by calling static members on the ConfigurationManager, which caused problems in tests where you needed to test various configurations.

The new .NET comes with the Microsoft.Extensions.Configuration package with a brand-new concept of configuration. It does not have all the bells and whistles, such as encrypted sections, but it is easily extensible and offers features that were not available in the old model, for example, overriding the configuration using environment variables, an approach popular especially in the world of containers.

The first important thing is that the configuration has no predefined sections or structure. Its schema is completely up to you. Some conventions (e.g., the ConnectionStrings section) are worth following, but no one forces you to do so.

The configuration is basically a key-value storage where the keys can be hierarchical (separated by a colon or double underscore sequence). Arrays can be mapped too; the key is the zero-based index of the array element.

Listing 2-19 shows a sample JSON configuration file. If you try to load this file, you will see configuration keys ConnectionStrings:MainDB, SampleValue, SampleArray:0, and SampleArray:1.

Listing 2-19. A sample JSON configuration file

```json
{
  "ConnectionStrings": {
    "MainDB": "FileName=database.db"
  },
  "SampleValue": "value",
  "SampleArray": [
    "item1",
    "item2"
  ]
}
```

Apart from JSON, there are more configuration providers. I have already mentioned environment variables, but there are more – Azure Key Vault, INI or XML files, key-per-file provider (used in Kubernetes environments – the key is the filename, the value is the content of the file), or command-line arguments.

One provider that deserves special attention is the User Secrets provider. Its purpose is to prevent the developers from placing secrets in the standard configuration file that is committed to the version control. Instead, the User Secrets will create a dedicated JSON file in a special location in the user profile folder that is not part of the repository (e.g., C:\Users*MyUserName*\AppData\Roaming\Microsoft\ UserSecrets*SomeId*, where *SomeId* is specified in the .csproj file as the UserSecretsId MSBuild property).

The configuration can have multiple layers; each subsequent layer can override the values from the previous layers. When you create a default ASP.NET Core application, there are several layers:

1. The first layer comes from the `appsettings.json` file in the application directory.

2. The second layer is another JSON file called `appsettings.Environment.json` in the application directory, where *Environment* is `Development`, `Production`, or any other name you define using the `ASPNETCORE_ENVIRONMENT` environment variable. When you run the application in your dev environment (e.g., from Visual Studio or by running `dotnet run` in the command line), the environment will be `Development`. When you deploy the application, the environment will be `Production` by default.

3. The third layer is User Secrets. This layer is added only when the Environment is `Development`. User Secrets should not be used in production.

4. The fourth layer is environment variables.

This means that you can use environment variables to override anything in User Secrets. Furthermore, User Secrets can override anything in the `appsettings.Development.json`, which can override `appsettings.json`.

In ASP.NET Core applications, the configuration object will be prepared automatically – you can just request `IConfiguration` using the dependency injection mechanism. If you want to load your own configuration, you can use the `ConfigurationBuilder` to build your own chain of providers, as shown in Listing 2-20.

Listing 2-20. Building your own chain of configuration providers

```
var configuration = new ConfigurationBuilder()
    .AddJsonFile("appsettings.json")
    .AddJsonFile(customConfigPath, optional: true)
    .AddEnvironmentVariables()
    .Build();
```

The final important feature is the support for binding configuration to objects. The IConfiguration interface provides various methods to access values, sections, or children. Listing 2-21 shows how to read various entries from the configuration mentioned in Listing 2-19.

Listing 2-21. Reading and binding the configuration entries

```
// returns plain string value
config["SampleValue"];

// goes in the ConnectionString section and obtains MainDB value
config.GetConnectionString("MainDB");

// gets all child entries from the ConnectionStrings collection
config.GetSection("ConnectionStrings").GetChildren();

// binds the section SampleArray into an array of strings
config.GetSection("SampleArray").Get<string[]>();
```

Because the configuration does not use static members, it is very easy to mock the IConfiguration instance and provide custom configuration for tests. There is even an in-memory provider to specify configuration in code, without the need for external files or artifacts.

Dependency Injection

The dependency injection design pattern became a fundamental part of most frameworks in the new .NET. In any nontrivial project, business logic lives in many different classes. There are popular design principles in use like DRY (Don't Repeat Yourself) or SRP (Single Responsibility Principle), which guide you toward reusing common parts of the code as well as separating logic with multiple responsibilities. Both these principles lead to many different classes, some of which will necessarily depend on others.

For example, when an MVC controller `CustomersController` needs an instance of Entity Framework `DbContext` (let's call it `EcommerceDbContext` for now) to perform some operation with a database, we can say that `CustomersController` depends on `EcommerceDbContext`. At some point, the controller will need an instance of the context, and the question is how it shall obtain this instance.

The natural answer would be, "Let's call `new()`." However, the context may need some other dependencies, such as a configuration (its connection string and other settings). Sometimes, it is also wise to reuse instances. If the `CustomersController` also needs `ILogger`, there is no added value in creating new instances every time – the loggers are typically written in a thread-safe way, and in case they employ some internal buffering or caching, having multiple instances of them may cause more harm than good. However, deciding how exactly the dependent instances shall be created is not the responsibility of `CustomersController`. Its purpose is something completely different – handling API requests concerning the customers.

The Inversion of Control principle thus tells us that the class should not require concrete dependencies but just their interfaces. This simplifies replacing the real implementation with its mock when writing tests and opens a space for multiple implementations of the same component or involving various decorators or interceptors. There is also an Explicit

Dependency Principle which says that all dependencies of a class should be explicit. Just by looking at the class declaration (not implementation), you should get a clear idea of what the class needs to do its job.

Listing 2-22 shows our CustomersController. As you can see, the class declares its dependencies as constructor arguments. If you look at the constructor, you can see that the class interacts with the database and needs logging. If the Explicit Dependency Principle is followed, you can be almost certain that when you supply correct dependencies, the class will work, and there shall be no hidden surprises like runtime crashes because of missing configuration.

Listing 2-22. Declaration of a class having its dependencies supplied in constructor

```
public class CustomersController : ControllerBase
{
    private readonly IEcommerceDbContext dbContext;
    private readonly ILogger<CustomersController> logger;

    public CustomersController(
        IEcommerceDbContext dbContext,
        ILogger<CustomersController> logger)
    {
        this.dbContext = dbContext;
        this.logger = logger;
    }
    ...
}
```

The last missing piece of this puzzle is how the instance of CustomersController is created. Provided everything is configured correctly, the ASP.NET Core MVC will be responsible for creating the controller instance any time an HTTP request arrives and points to a route handled by this class. In order to supply the correct arguments to the controller's constructor, it needs to know how its dependencies shall be created. What object shall it pass to the `IEcommerceDbContext` parameter?

This is where a dependency injection container comes into its place. At the application startup, the container needs to be configured to know the rules and conventions to resolve each dependency. It needs to be informed that if someone needs `IEcommerceDbContext`, they shall obtain an instance of the `EcommerceDbContext` class, and a new instance shall be created for each use (this is called *Transient lifetime*). When someone needs `ILogger<T>`, an instance of `ConsoleLogger<T>` shall be provided (substitution of the concrete type for `T` is another feature of DI containers called *open generics*), and the same instance may be shared for all consumers (referred to as *Singleton* lifetime).

In the old .NET Framework world, there were many popular DI containers – Unity Container,[33] Castle Windsor, Autofac, Ninject, SimpleInjector, and many others. They had way more features than I described in the previous paragraphs, but the common core was the same for all of them.

The .NET Core branch came with a built-in solution packaged as `Microsoft.Extensions.DependencyInjection`. There are two important interfaces – `IServiceCollection` and `IServiceProvider`. The `IServiceCollection` allows registering services (interfaces and their implementations) while specifying their lifetimes (*Transient*, *Singleton*, and *Scoped*, which means that the instance will be shared by all consumers within the same scope; in ASP.NET Core, it is the scope of a single HTTP request). Once the service collection is configured, the `IServiceProvider` can be created to provide instances of registered services to anyone who will need them. In most scenarios, you do not need to interact with the `IServiceProvider` directly – the framework you use will use it somewhere under the covers.

---

[33] Unity Container (`http://unitycontainer.org/`) is a different project than Unity (cross-platform gaming engine).

When HTTP requests come, and their routes resolve to actions in the `CustomersController` class, ASP.NET Core MVC will call `GetService<CustomersController>` on the `IServiceProvider`. The provider will look at the class constructor, create all the dependencies first (by recursively calling `GetService<IEcommerceDbContext>` and so on), and then invoke the constructor with the correct arguments.

It will respect the lifetime settings of the individual services; if they are configured as *Singleton*, it will return the same instance to all consumers. If the service is registered as *Scoped*, it will return the same instances to all consumers within the same scope – the async call context assigned to the particular HTTP request. The framework (in this case, ASP.NET Core MVC) needs to tell the provider when the scope begins and ends. This is done by calling the `CreateScope` method, which returns a new `IServiceProvider` just for the scope. When the entire container is disposed, all instances created by the container which are `IDisposable` are disposed too. The same behavior applies to the scopes – when a scope ends, all disposable instances bound to the scope are disposed.

Listing 2-23 shows how the services can be registered. Most frameworks provide their own extension methods on the `IServiceCollection`.

Listing 2-23. Examples of registering services in the IServiceCollection

```
public void ConfigureServices(IServiceCollection services)
{
    // singleton service - defined by concrete type
    services.AddSingleton<ILogger, ConsoleLogger>();

    // scoped service - defined by a custom factory method
    services.AddScoped<IEcommerceDbContext>(
        serviceProvider => new EcommerceDbContext(...)
    );
```

```
// transient service - just the concrete type without
// interface
services.AddTransient<PortalConfiguration>();

// registration of framework via extension method
services.AddMvc(options => { ... });
}
```

The idea of having a built-in dependency injection container is great for framework authors as they have universal interfaces that they can rely on. There is still room for community-authored DI containers, which offer more features; on the other hand, many users are happy with the built-in container.

The built-in container has some limitations; for example, it does not support open generics. This problem can be solved by a nice library called *Scrutor*.[34] It keeps the built-in `IServiceProvider`, but it enhances the configuration API of `IServiceCollection` with convention-based registrations, for example, to automatically register all classes that implement a particular interface. It also supports the missing open generic parameters in service registrations.

Logging

The old .NET Framework came with the `Trace` and `Debug` classes, which allowed applications to emit text-based messages and configure trace listeners, which could store them in text files, Windows Event Log, or other destinations. The logging mechanism could be configured in code or using the old `.config` files.

Although this API worked well and was frequently used by various libraries and frameworks, it had some unpleasant limitations. The most important one was that the traces did not have any predefined structure – each log entry was just a plain text value. For example, when the code

---

[34] See `https://github.com/khellang/Scrutor`

reported an exception, ToString() was called on it. The error message, the stack trace, and other data you need to include in the trace (date and time, IP address or identity of the user, and so on) were stored just as text that would need to be parsed later, possibly incurring inaccuracies or errors.

There were several libraries that filled this gap, such as *log4net*, *Serilog*, and *NLog*. They had to bring their own interfaces and services for logging as it was hard to hook to the built-in Trace API based on static methods.

The new .NET comes with Microsoft.Extensions.Logging package, which contains a new, structured log system that is extensible and quite flexible. Everything starts with the LoggerFactory class, which allows configuring the logging pipeline and then creating ILogger instances for different parts of the application (so-called categories – typically, the fully qualified name of the class producing the log entries is used as the category).

When the pipeline is configured, you can specify the exporters – they tell where the log entries will be sent, for example, on a console output, to a file, or to some external service such as Azure Application Insights. It is also possible to specify filters for each destination – for example, all messages from a category starting Microsoft.EntityFrameworkCore.* with severity *Information* or lower will be filtered out. Thanks to the filters, your logs will not be poisoned by thousands of uninteresting messages and will contain only the information that matters. This is important, especially for modern diagnostics services like Azure Application Insights, where the costs depend on how much data is ingested. You only want to collect useful diagnostics data to avoid unnecessary costs.

In many applications, you will not interact with the LoggerFactory directly. As you will see in the next section, the logging destinations and filters are configured as part of the host builder API. When you need to emit log messages, you can just request an argument of type ILogger<CustomersController> where CustomersController will be transformed into the fully qualified name and serve as the logging category. As shown in Listing 2-24, you can emit messages of various levels and attach additional metadata with them.

Listing 2-24. Example of using ILogger

```
public class ApplicationEventIds
{
    public static readonly EventId CustomerLoaded
        = new EventId(100, "CustomerLoaded");
}

// specify EventId to easily match the same event
logger.LogDebug(ApplicationEventIds.CustomerLoaded,
    "The customer entity was loaded.");

// specify message template and arguments
logger.LogInformation(
    "The order {OrderId} was created at {Date:s}.",
    orderId, DateTime.UtcNow);

// specify exception
logger.LogError(exception, "Order cannot be processed.");
```

The new logging model quickly became popular as it is extremely easy to use – just request ILogger<T> in the constructor and start emitting log entries. There is still space to integrate it with popular libraries to augment its capabilities. Now, these libraries have a common API surface built into the platform they can attach to.

Also, most libraries and frameworks started to use the logging system extensively. If you use Entity Framework Core, you will see all SQL queries sent to the database, and you can easily suppress them using filtering if you are not interested in those. ASP.NET Core logs all requests and exceptions to the console, and again, it can be easily adjusted using the filters based on the hierarchical category names.

Hosting

A great deal of changes arose also in the area of hosting .NET applications. In the world of the old .NET, there were several different application models. Console and desktop (Windows Forms or WPF) applications had the typical entry point in the form of the Main method. In desktop applications, the Visual Studio IDE tried to hide it from the developers (at least the less experienced ones) to prevent them from making unintended changes that could break the designer and other parts of the tooling.

Web applications, however, did not have this typical entry point. The applications were intended to load into the IIS worker process. Instead of the entry point, the Global.asax file which declared a class inheriting from System.Web.HttpApplication was searched for. From there, the ASP.NET application was configured and prepared for running. Later, the support for another entry point in the form of OWIN Startup Class was added to allow more flexible building of the HTTP request pipeline. In fact, this was the predecessor of ASP.NET Core, and a lot of patterns we now have in the new .NET originate from the OWIN era.

In the new .NET, all applications have the same entry point – the Main method, albeit it can be hidden when you turn on the top-level statement feature. This allows you to write the entry-point code directly into the file without the namespace, class, and method declaration. The compiler will wrap it into the Main method automatically. The important change here is that even web applications are normal .NET console applications that can be launched as normal processes. Removing the mysterious way of loading the application assemblies in the worker process and requiring the tight integration with COM ISAPI interfaces allowed running ASP.NET Core applications with almost any web server or even in a stand-alone mode where the built-in Kestrel web server is used.

Another change is that the various types of applications were unified within the Host Builder pattern. Each nontrivial application, no matter if it is just a console application, a background service, or a web application,

114

requires some basic infrastructure to operate – configuration, logging, dependency injection, and integration with the outside environment (web applications interact with the web server within which they run, background services need to listen for various signals from the operating system that guides their startup and shutdown, and so on).

Listing 2-25 shows the entry point of an ASP.NET Core application. The code uses the top-level statement approach. It is not enclosed in any method; you can imagine the Main method around it.

Listing 2-25. An example of a host builder for a web application

```
var builder = WebApplication.CreateBuilder(args);

// Add services to the container
builder.Services.AddMvc();

var app = builder.Build();

// Configure the HTTP request pipeline.
app.UseRouting();
app.UseAuthorization();
app.MapControllers();

app.Run();
```

As you can see, the code calls WebApplication.CreateBuilder, which prepares the host builder with defaults for web applications. You can configure the IServiceCollection via builder.Services, and you can extend the configuration or logging options through the builder variable. Once everything is ready, you can build the application instance by calling Build.

The application then configures the HTTP request pipeline and plugs in the desired middlewares and frameworks. Finally, it calls Run, which will start waiting for the requests. The entire process takes just a few lines and offers good flexibility to configure the main aspects of the application, such as where it loads configuration, how the logging will look, and so on.

Listing 2-26 shows how to create a background service which can be hosted as Windows Service or a Systemd daemon on Linux.

Listing 2-26. An example of a host builder for worker service

```
var builder = Host.CreateApplicationBuilder(args);

// Add services to the container
builder.Services.AddSystemd();
builder.Services.AddWindowsService();

// Register the worker service to be run
builder.Services.AddHostedService<Worker>();

// Run the worker
var host = builder.Build();
host.Run();
```

As you can see, the way of preparing the infrastructure for different kinds of applications has been unified and is very similar. There are integrations to both Windows- and Linux-based operating systems to interact with their platform-specific mechanisms like receiving the shutdown signals.

The hosted services have a universal interface IHostedService with StartAsync and StopAsync methods and can also be used in web applications. This allows you to reuse some code between various types of applications, having the same way of accessing the configuration, logging, and other important mechanisms.

All .NET applications can be launched as normal processes; they do not require any external logic baked into separate products like IIS. This makes them much more agnostic about the environment in which they will run. With the rise of cloud platforms, this has become more important than ever.

Other Packages

There are multiple packages starting with `Microsoft.Extensions.*` to help with common tasks or patterns. Most of them also have a separate package ending with `*.Abstractions` – such packages are great to be referenced by libraries and frameworks. They contain only the interfaces, not the actual implementation.

I have already covered the `Configuration`, `DependencyInjection`, `Hosting`, and `Logging` ones.

The `Microsoft.Extensions.Caching` package provides a great mechanism for caching, in both local and distributed versions. The built-in `MemoryCache` provides an in-process cache with support for absolute or sliding expiration[35] and an option to specify priorities for the cached items.

By default, the cache does not care if the process is running out of memory; in fact, there is no reasonable way to measure the size of objects stored in the cache. However, you can set a size limit on the cache and specify the sizes of each stored item explicitly; in such cases, the cache will evict items based on priorities and sizes to fit within the limit. There is also an option to explicitly call the `Compact` method.

If you need to use the distributed cache, you can find several production-ready implementations of the `IDistributedCache` interface defined in the abstraction package, for example, `Microsoft.Extensions.Caching.StackExchangeRedis` for Redis or `Microsoft.Extensions.Caching.SqlServer` for Microsoft SQL Server. In contrast to the memory cache, the methods on this cache are asynchronous as they expect the retrieval and storage operations to take longer.

---

[35] Absolute expiration means that the cache item will be evicted at an explicitly specified date and time. Sliding expiration is defined by an interval; if the cache item is not accessed for longer than the specified interval, it is evicted.

Another interesting package that was added in .NET 8 is `Microsoft.Extensions.Resilience`. With the rise of microservices architecture, many applications started talking with other components. Such applications are often hosted in cloud or container orchestrator environments like Kubernetes, where the infrastructure may occasionally decide to restart or move the individual workloads to another server instance, which may cause short-term downtimes. One failed dependency can then lead to cascading failures. For example, if service A calls service B and service B calls service C, which is down, the failure propagates to service A.

The resilience package allows the implementation of the retry logic, timeouts, or a circuit breaker – a mechanism that temporarily stops calling the failed service in case it experiences a higher number of errors in the recent time interval than a configured threshold.

Listing 2-27 shows how the package can be used to configure the resiliency pipeline on an `HttpClient`. If a request fails due to a network issue, HTTP status 500 or above, or specific HTTP codes like 429 (Too many requests) or 408 (Request timeout), the call will be retried three times, with a one-second wait after the first failure, and exponentially growing wait times on subsequent failures. The listing uses the `Microsoft.Extensions.Http.Resilience` package, which provides the extension methods and handlers for the `HttpClient` that implements this logic.

Listing 2-27. Configuring the resiliency pipeline on an HttpClient

```
services.AddHttpClient()
    .AddResilienceHandler("retry", builder =>
    {
        builder.AddRetry(new HttpRetryStrategyOptions
        {
            MaxRetryAttempts = 3,
            Delay = TimeSpan.FromSeconds(1),
```

```
        BackoffType = DelayBackoffType.Exponential
    });
});
```

The package allows you to use standard resilience pipelines with reasonable defaults for usual cases or implement them on your own. They are not limited to `HttpClient` only – you can use them in a generic way to wrap any code.

Conclusion

As you can see, the new .NET brings a large number of new concepts, runtime improvements, and new libraries, which makes the development much more convenient. Although the list is not by any means exhaustive, I believe I tried to describe the most fruitful parts where I see the greatest benefits.

Nontechnical Arguments

If you look at any of the previous pages in this chapter, I believe they provide quite convincing reasons for technical people – developers, software architects, technical leads, CTOs, and others. However, none of the arguments presented is probably going to work when talking with the business people – project and product managers, board members, or business owners.

The modernization of any nontrivial application requires significant effort, and thus all stakeholders should have a good understanding of the situation. Is such a challenging crusade really necessary? What will be the benefits for the business and the customers? What will happen if we stay with the old version? What would be the best time to start? For how long will we need to maintain the old solution? How much is it going to cost?

The answers to most of these questions are not easy. In fact, some of them may be impossible to find out with acceptable accuracy. In the rest of this chapter, I will try to present nontechnical benefits and gains. Chapter 3 will dig into more details about planning the modernization and estimating the required effort and timings.

The text in this section still uses technical terms and will not be easily understandable to persons without a technical background. However, as a technical person, you can filter out the parts that are irrelevant to your specific scenario and highlight the things that apply while translating the general terms into concrete improvements. For example, with the knowledge of the project, the generic statement about flexible deployments thanks to the support of containers can be translated to "we will be able to deploy a new version in a matter of hours instead of days, and we will not have to install new versions of libraries on the server with every other deployment."

Hiring and Motivation of Developers

The first version of .NET Framework was introduced in 2001, and its version 2.0, released in 2005, was the first successful and widely adopted version which got a lot of traction. The older generation of .NET developers comes from these days. Their knowledge and experience with the new branch of .NET depends on the projects they have been involved in.

.NET was never strong in attracting young developers and startup communities. It was always perceived as too enterprise technology created by Microsoft. This started changing only in recent years; one of the reasons is the huge effort of several people in Microsoft working on developer relations. They produce a lot of learning content, do regular live coding on Twitch, and more. These activities help to attract students and young people to the .NET community. Most of these new community members started using .NET quite late and completely skipped the old era. Therefore, their knowledge of the old .NET technologies is going to be rather limited.

An important component of software development is learning. Every five to ten years, we use quite different approaches to design and build applications. Most developers are used to learning new things regularly and trying new concepts in their projects.

When it comes to working on a legacy project built on technologies and frameworks from 2008 or 2014 (the last significant feature updates of the .NET Framework), it is becoming increasingly difficult to find developers who have experience with these technologies and who are willing to work with them.

The younger .NET developers, whose careers started just several years ago, might never have seen the old .NET Framework. The new versions are not completely different; the C# language is still being used, but they will still be unfamiliar with many concepts.

The developers with experience with the old era may have the knowledge to work on such projects, but if they have ever tried the new .NET versions already, they may have a difficult time going back. The libraries, frameworks, tools, and performance of the old world are significantly less comfortable to work with, not to speak about the lack of the learning component. Most developers prefer to stay in motion and have a chance to use the latest versions. Without that, their value in the job market will decrease over time. If they decide to leave for another company eventually, not knowing the latest versions of .NET would be a visible handicap to them.

For sure, there is still a large group of developers who would happily use the old versions or even learn them, provided that the project offers another kind of delight. The project may be from an industry that matches the developer's personal interests. For example, I have one friend who always dreamed about working as a developer in the space industry. For him, the need to work with legacy technologies was not a big issue; he finally got a chance to work in his dream company.

It can be a project with a significant positive impact on society, such as an application for dispatching ambulance teams to the places of reported incidents accompanied by a mobile application you could use in low-coverage areas to call for help. We have participated in such a project at RIGANTI, and most developers liked the project for what it was doing, not caring much about the concrete and sometimes obscure technologies that had to be used because of integrations with various third parties. Sometimes, the application involves an interesting architectural pattern (like Domain-Driven Design), and the technological debt is thus not a problem – the code is still quite nicely maintainable and easy to work with. Or maybe the project involves nontrivial algorithms that attract people looking for a bit of intellectually challenging work.

Of course, some developers prefer working with the technologies they already know to learning something new. This does not have to be bad – such people tend to stay on the projects for years, often having incredibly profound know-how about the context, user scenarios, and business logic. There are plenty of projects where such a strategy is greatly appreciated – there is not much business value in modernizing them or introducing new concepts, but the long-term stability of the project is important.

All in all, it is significantly more difficult to hire developers to work on legacy .NET projects. Many developers either do not have experience with the old frameworks and libraries because they started with .NET in recent years, or they prefer to work with the new versions to keep their knowledge up to date. The number of developers willing to work with legacy technologies will decrease over time, and motivating them will be more difficult or costly.

Higher Operating and Maintenance Costs

The first part of this chapter mentioned many performance-related improvements that Microsoft and the community worked on in the recent versions of the .NET. Every such improvement helps to speed up applications, which may translate to lower operating and infrastructure costs, especially for larger deployments. The support of Linux also offers savings on Windows Server licenses.

One good, albeit hard-to-reproduce, example of the savings achieved by migration to the new .NET comes from the Microsoft team, which takes care of the Bing search engine. There are not many projects of the scale of Bing; however, it is realistic to believe that similar savings can be achieved on smaller projects as well. The Bing team published a blog post[36] where they described a 34% improvement when they switched from .NET Framework 4.7.2 to .NET Core 2.1. They also mention a great improvement in the reduction of deployment time thanks to the ReadyToRun images – it is also an important metric to consider in large deployments.

Later, when the Bing Ads Campaign Platform was migrated to .NET 6 and moved to Azure Kubernetes Service, the team experienced a drop in memory consumption by 40–50%.[37] In larger solutions, such savings allow you to significantly reduce the number of servers in on-premises deployments, and they directly translate to lower bills in cloud environments where you can use auto-scale features.

Another example is the experience of the team running Stack Exchange, a popular network whose Stack Overflow website is known to every developer on the planet. Interestingly, the primary motivation was not the performance. Instead, they saw huge benefits in increased efficiency of development and maintenance of the codebase, new opportunities and scenarios for testing, as well as a more flexible deployment model (they have many private deployments for their enterprise customers in various environments). Their reasoning for the migration is nicely summarized in an X (formerly Twitter) thread:[38]

---

[36] See https://devblogs.microsoft.com/dotnet/bing-com-runs-on-net-core-2-1/

[37] See https://devblogs.microsoft.com/dotnet/bing-ads-campaign-platform-journey-to-dotnet-6/

[38] See https://twitter.com/Nick_Craver/status/1031858480888639488

*We're migrating Stack Overflow to .NET Core. **It's not because of performance.** There are enough major wins without even factoring performance for us to move. Any performance gains are 100% in the bonus category. We'd migrate with a 0% perf improvement.*

...

What if we had one way to deploy testing, on-prem, and hosted for Enterprise? Or at least very few ways of assembling the same LEGO pieces. That's what .NET Core is. It's very modular and enables a litany of wins for us.

—Nick Craver, Architect Lead for Stack Overflow

You can find plenty of examples of successful modernizations, mostly presenting nice charts of lowered CPU or memory consumption right after the deployment. There are not many deeper analyses of the long-term savings enabled by better maintainability of the code and increased developer comfort. Additionally, it is hard to quantify the value or lower risks coming from using more secure libraries. However, they can be reasonably expected, thanks to the effort Microsoft and the community put into making every version of .NET better. Because Microsoft itself uses .NET in most of its products, it also gets a large share of benefits and savings from migrating to its new versions.

To illustrate the possible licensing savings, let's consider an example of an Azure-hosted application. Let's say that the application runs on a Windows Server virtual machine with 8 GB of RAM and 2 virtual CPUs. The average CPU utilization is lower than 20%, so we can safely assume this will not worsen after migrating to the new .NET.

Table 2-1 shows the costs of the Windows- and Linux-based virtual machines and Windows- and Linux-based Azure App Service plans (platform-as-a-service offering for hosting web applications) hosted in the same data center (West Europe). You can see that the savings are significant – the license cost is almost 50% of the price.

Table 2-1. *Comparison of prices of Windows and Linux virtual machines in Azure (pay-as-you-go pricing, no discount, West Europe data center)*

Offering	Operating System	Monthly Price
Azure Virtual Machine D2v3 – 2 CPUs, 8 GB RAM 50 GB temporary storage	Windows	$154.76
	Linux (Ubuntu)	$87.60
Azure App Service P1V3 – 2 Cores, 8 GB RAM 250 GB storage	Windows	$246.74
	Linux	$129.94

An additional gain of the migration to Linux is the lower overhead of Linux-based systems compared to Windows Server. The same hardware configuration with Linux will most likely allow the application to utilize more RAM than on Windows Server, even if you uninstall all unnecessary components. The minimalist nature of Linux allows it to run on tiny devices like Raspberry Pi, often used in various IoT scenarios. Windows can also run on IoT devices, but the hardware requirements and the license costs for production deployments are both higher.

Security Considerations

The .NET Framework is tied to the support life cycle of Windows.[39] Until the application runs on a supported version of Windows Server, Microsoft provides security fixes to the .NET Framework runtime in the same way as for any other component of Windows. It is highly recommended to upgrade all applications running on .NET Framework to its latest version to not fall out of support.

---

[39] See https://dotnet.microsoft.com/en-us/platform/support/policy/dotnet-framework

The support policy of the new .NET is not tied to the life cycle of Windows. Instead, you can choose between LTS (long-term support) and STS (standard-term support) releases.[40] For example, .NET 8 is an LTS release with a three-year support period (the release date is November 14, 2023, and the support ends on November 10, 2026). During this time window, Microsoft will release security updates and announce them on the .NET blog[41] as well as in the .NET Announcements GitHub repository.[42]

On Windows, the security patches are distributed via Microsoft Update. If your application uses self-contained deployments (the framework libraries are distributed together with the application) or is based on container images, you must publish a new version of the application with the patched framework libraries or based on the patched container image.

The new .NET brings many security improvements in terms of better architecture and design of its features and libraries. Some aspects, such as algorithms for hashing user passwords in ASP.NET Core Identity packages, are more secure because of using modern versions of algorithms and up-to-date recommendations. The new .NET also allows Microsoft to update such mechanisms in the next major version without the fear that it may break the current applications.

One important feature of the new .NET is getting rid of the reliance on the *Machine Key*. This key was used for several purposes, for example, the protection of authentication tokens. The application could override the auto-generated key with its own one, which was often used in cluster deployments. However, the framework was designed to work with just one key at a time, which complicated its rotation. If you decide to rotate the key (which should be done regularly), it will invalidate all authentication tickets

---

[40] See `https://dotnet.microsoft.com/en-us/platform/support/policy/dotnet-core`

[41] See `https://devblogs.microsoft.com/dotnet/`

[42] See `https://github.com/dotnet/announcements/issues`

and all information protected by the key. In modern frameworks (including the new .NET), multiple keys can be used, and there is an overlap time window during which both keys work. This allows the information protected by the old key to be reissued using the new key to avoid interruption.

Also, the process of key rotation is not automated and thus depends on manual effort. There were more problems with the machine key design described on the .NET blog.[43] That is why the machine key approach can be replaced[44] by the Data Protection framework, the same mechanism ASP.NET Core uses, and it works even in quite old versions of the .NET Framework. The solution in the new .NET can store the keys in multiple destinations like Azure Key Vault and performs automatic key rotations.

Many .NET applications need to store the passwords of the users in the database. Since doing that in a secure way is very difficult and requires advanced knowledge of cryptography, even the old versions of .NET Framework provided an API that could be used by developers. The new versions of .NET offer the ASP.NET Core Identity library, whose hashing algorithm is the most current, and its parameters are updated between the major .NET releases to meet up-to-date standards.

If the application still uses the .NET Framework, there is a chance that it still uses the Membership Provider API (introduced in ASP.NET 2.0 in 2005), the ASP.NET Universal Providers (introduced in 2011), or the old ASP.NET Identity library (its version 2.2 released in 2015, last patch in 2023). In general, the older the library is, the weaker algorithms with a lower number of iterations it is going to use. The strength of the algorithm and the number of iterations directly affect the complexity of retrieving the original passwords in the event of a database breach.

---

[43] See https://devblogs.microsoft.com/dotnet/cryptographic-improvements-in-asp-net-4-5-pt-1/ and https://devblogs.microsoft.com/dotnet/cryptographic-improvements-in-asp-net-4-5-pt-2/

[44] See https://learn.microsoft.com/en-us/aspnet/core/security/data-protection/compatibility/replacing-machinekey?view=aspnetcore-8.0

The old Membership Providers allowed the developers to store the passwords in a plaintext or encrypted form, both of which are not considered secure by today's standards. If the application is not going to be migrated to the new .NET, the password security should be migrated to at least the latest version of ASP.NET Identity, where the hashing algorithm is extensible and can be eventually updated to use the recommended approach. Finally, implementing the two-factor authentication is advisable.

The last significant effort in terms of improving security was making it simple to avoid having secrets baked into the codebase. The old .NET Framework did not motivate the developers to store connection strings separately from the application code. The concept of Web Config Transformations[45] assumes that the production keys will be in the `Web. Release.config`, a file that was a standard part of the project. It was much easier for the developers to have the secrets in the code, and it required a significant effort to use the correct and secure approach.

Another feature of a similar kind was the one-click publish functionality. It was convenient for the developers to be able to publish a project in the production directly from Visual Studio. However, it relied on XML files, which were also part of the codebase. They contained database connection strings and sometimes even the passwords of the server user account used for the deployment.

The new .NET configuration model is designed to easily separate the secrets from other configuration values, and there are many concepts that simplify the process for the developers, such as the User Secrets technology. All tutorials and code samples in the official documentation show the correct way of handling the secrets and emphasize the importance of following these guidelines. Additionally, there are automatic analyzers that detect the presence of secrets in the code and warn the developer about that or even prevent them from committing the code change.

---

[45] See `https://learn.microsoft.com/en-us/previous-versions/aspnet/ dd465326(v=vs.110)`

There is still a lot of effort in making sure that the application is secure which are not related by any means to the .NET platform. Most security issues are caused by mistakes in the application code made by developers that were not discovered by testing and quality assurance. However, achieving the same level of security requires more effort on the .NET Framework than on the new .NET, as some aspects of the platform are better designed and architected out of the box. The newer implementation of security mechanisms, such as password hashing, is based on more up-to-date standards and recommendations.

Summary

I believe I demonstrated the powers of the new branch of .NET in all important areas. In some sections, I went quite deep into the details, but I believe that it helps to understand the principles and the way in which .NET performance and architecture improvements are guided. It helps to get an intuition of what you can expect from the future.

The next chapter will focus on planning the modernization and provide several tips on how you can try it on some small part to get an idea of the complexity of this journey.

CHAPTER 3

Before You Start

After reading the previous chapter, you are familiar with the benefits of moving the application to the latest version of .NET. In this chapter, I will discuss the details of how to get there and how to best prepare for this journey.

Choosing the Right Strategy

I have used the word "modernization" in the book, but what exactly does it mean? Is it just upgrading the packages and code changes that happen only in the application folder? Does moving parts of the functionality outside of the original application still fall into the scope of the word "modernization"? What about a complete rewrite, where we focus on creating an entirely new application but with the potential reuse of at least some functions?

If you search for definitions of modernization, they typically mention a process of updating existing legacy software solutions to new platforms, versions, or best practices. Sometimes, they even mention changing the application architecture, for example, from a monolithic approach to microservices. Since this area is remarkably interesting for cloud platform providers, you will commonly find mention of the cloud in the sentence following the definition. Additionally, most definitions do not use the term *application*. They typically use a more generic term *system* or *software*, which may stand for a solution composed of multiple applications.

© Tomáš Herceg 2024
T. Herceg, *Modernizing .NET Web Applications*,
https://doi.org/10.1007/979-8-8688-0617-9_3

Modernization is the act of updating organizational processes, systems, and tools to the most current versions or best practices. In the context of cloud computing, modernization is the process of transitioning an organization's applications, processes, and data management to a cloud-first approach. The goal is to improve organizational and technological performance, enhance the quality of customer and employee experiences, and accelerate time to market for new offerings and updates.

—Microsoft Azure, Cloud Computing Dictionary[1]

Application modernization is the practice of updating older software for newer computing approaches, including newer languages, frameworks, and infrastructure platforms. This practice is also sometimes called legacy modernization or legacy application modernization. It is the software development equivalent of renovating an older home to take advantage of improvements to efficiency, safety, structural integrity, and so forth. Rather than retiring an existing system or replacing it wholesale, legacy modernization extends the lifespan of an organization's applications while also taking advantage of technical innovations.

—VMware Glossary, Application Modernization[2]

---

[1] See https://azure.microsoft.com/en-us/resources/cloud-computing-dictionary/what-is-application-modernization

[2] See www.vmware.com/topics/glossary/content/application-modernization.html

As we can see, modernization does not require all changes to happen in the original application. We can split one application into multiple pieces, or if the system consists of multiple applications, we can merge them into one or even replace some of them with an existing SaaS solution. Modernization does not even have to touch all application components; some parts may remain completely unchanged.

All the definitions also emphasize the goals and benefits – extending the lifespan of the solution, improving efficiency (lowering the costs of running the software and increasing developer productivity) and performance (not only technological but also organizational), and so forth. If we focus on these goals, we can perceive any technical improvement to the software that aims to achieve these goals as modernization.

Example: Modernizing a Large E-learning Website

One side project we did at RIGANTI was a training center called DotNetCollege. It offered a large variety of courses for developers, mostly about .NET, web development, and software architecture. For this purpose, we created a website that covered and automated all processes of this company. The public-facing part presented the visitors with all the scheduled courses. The visitors could browse the entire library of the topics, sign up for any course, and pay with a credit card. The system automatically issued invoices and tax receipts. Based on complex rules configured in the admin part, it also calculated the compensation for the trainer.

The admin part had ten modules, including a CRM to track ongoing conversations with larger customers, a module for creating and sending newsletters and generating posts to social media, and more. There was a separate section for trainers where they could interact with the course attendees (share files or other course materials with them) and track their earnings.

The solution also contained a background service that was responsible for sending scheduled emails (e.g., "the course you have registered for starts next Monday," and so on) and also spinning up the virtual machines with preinstalled software for the attendees.

Figure 3-1. Structure of the example application

Figure 3-1 shows the structure of the application. It was developed in 2014 in quite a short time using the most current technologies of that time: .NET Framework, ASP.NET MVC, Entity Framework 6, and ASP.NET Identity.

From the first moment, the application was hosted in Microsoft Azure. It was a monolithic app – everything except the background service was a single deployable unit. The background service was a separate console application hosted as Azure Web Job, but it was just a tiny layer that called the same business logic as the web application. Figure 3-2 shows the projects in the solution. The arrows illustrate the project dependencies (BL stands for *business layer*, and DAL stands for *data access layer*; both are class libraries).

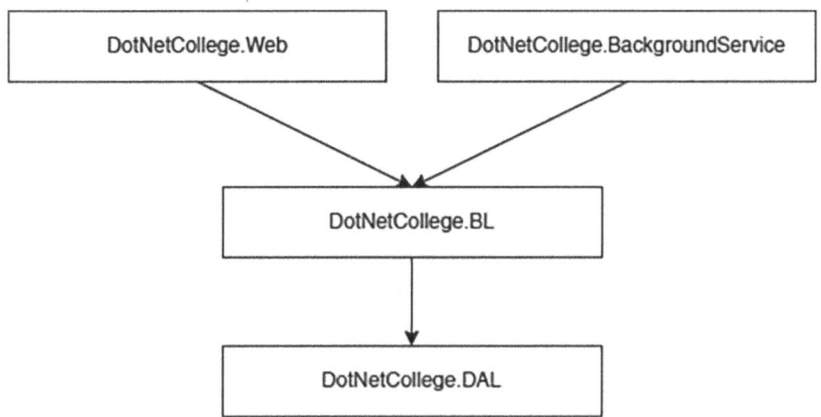

Figure 3-2. *Monolothic architecture of the example application*

The decision to modernize this application was taken in 2023. Even though the application was monolithic and could be modernized as it was, we did not pick the most straightforward way.

- The CRM module provided the basic functionality we needed, but there are a lot of SaaS solutions that offer more features, such as integration with email marketing tools, social media analytics, or advertising platforms. We decided to remove this module from the application and migrate the data outside. The integrations were easy to do because our selected CRM platform offered a nice REST API.

- The same decision was made for the marketing module. Today, there are many solutions for email marketing that provide nice API integration and have so many features that it does not often make sense to build them yourself.

- The background service was a separate application running as Azure Web Job, but ASP.NET Core has the concept of hosted services that allow running background tasks. That is why we decided to merge these applications into one and created two `IHostedService` implementations for the periodic operations the background service did. In advanced scenarios, it is recommended to use libraries like Quartz.NET[3] or Hangfire,[4] which can correctly handle extreme cases like missed ticks,[5] but this was not important for us.

---

[3] See www.quartz-scheduler.net/

[4] See www.hangfire.io/

[5] It is not trivial to implement a reliable periodic timer. For example, if you want to run a task every top of the hour, the naïve implementation would probably check whether the `DateTime.UtcNow.Minute` is zero. If you do the check once per minute, you should not miss any tick. However, the application may be down at that minute, and the tick will be missed, or it may restart during the zero minute, and the tick may occur twice. Also, there is no guarantee that the timer will tick exactly every minute – it can be slightly later based on the process and thread scheduling done by the OS. In an extreme case, the timer can tick, for example, at 1:59:59.988 and then at 2:01:00.012. The advanced libraries use persistent storage to track whether the task was executed and guarantee *at least once* semantic.

- We were also considering splitting the application into multiple parts (separate the public-facing part from the admin, trainer, and course attendee dashboards), but we found out that the added value did not justify the effort.

As you can see from these points, we tried to minimize the scope before taking any further steps. The SaaS solutions we selected offered us more features and made modernization faster and less risky. There are monthly costs for using these external services, but even if we account for ten years, they are lower than the development effort of migration, testing, and further maintenance and development of these modules.[6]

The major decision – whether to choose incremental changes or do a full rewrite of the application – awaited us. Before I share which option we chose, let's look at these two alternatives in more detail.

Incremental Changes

The method I refer to as "incremental changes" tries to split the process of modernization into small units, which can be deployed to production during the process.

There is no exact specification of how big these deployment units shall be. However, with today's popularity of DevOps, even several deployments per day are not unusual. If the team uses an agile approach, the frequency of deployments can be aligned with sprints. There may be periods of time when a substantial area is reworked, and the application can be

---

[6] Even if you are happy with the functionality and do not expect any changes, there may be external factors such as new regulations (one example for all was GDPR), company acquisitions or mergers, and stricter requirements of web browsers (HTTPS everywhere) that may require considerable effort. SaaS providers are commonly able to implement these requirements more efficiently as the costs are shared by all their customers.

in an uncompilable state for a while. However, when speaking about incremental changes, such periods should not be long – a few days at most. Naturally, such things should never happen in the main branch. I will talk in the following sections about using version control and workflows you can set up.

Frequent deployments allow you to get feedback from the users quickly, which helps to lower the risks of introducing bugs. The earlier a bug is discovered, the easier it is to fix and the less material damage it can cause. If you get a bug report for a feature you worked on yesterday or last week, you can still remember the context and will be able to identify the cause more quickly. In case of critical bugs that cause data loss or inconsistencies, it is crucial to discover and remove them quickly. The longer they are present in the system, the more damage and costs they can introduce.

A/B testing and gradual feature rollouts can help you to make sure a possible problem in the modernized functionality will not prevent the users from doing their jobs. You can keep the old version of the modernized area along with the new implementation and enable the new version only for a limited number of users. Based on metrics such as the number of exceptions, you can decide whether the feature is mature enough to be rolled out for everyone or whether additional work is needed. Alternatively, you can let the users opt in for the new experience while preserving the option to revert to the old UI. There is also a mechanism of feature flags which can enable or disable a particular functionality based on configuration. When introducing a new feature, you can have an easy way of turning it off when it starts causing unexpected issues after the deployment.

Of course, this brings additional complexity, and you can expect an extra effort to have both versions of the same feature in the system. It is always a trade-off between lower risk and a more effortful approach. You do not have to apply this approach dogmatically – use it for critical features or when it makes sense.

In-Place Modernization

In some cases, it is possible to modernize the application in place. It means that all changes will happen in the application directory. The application will be deployed the same way it used to be. No additional server configuration is necessary (except for installing the new version of .NET).

Naturally, this approach has many restrictions. Since there will be parts that depend on .NET Framework libraries, to modernize them, you will have to stick to technologies that support .NET Standard. You will make incremental changes to the application to remove everything that is not compatible with .NET Standard, and once you get to the point that your code fully compiles for the .NET Standard API surface, you will be able to perform the final switch of the target framework to the new .NET.

This method will be applicable to many class library projects. For example, in the DotNetCollege solution, this was the case of DotNetCollege.DAL and DotNetCollege.BL projects.

The data access layer project contained the Entity Framework 6 model (DbContext, entity classes, enums, migrations, and so on). Since the EntityFramework package supports both .NET Framework 4.5 and .NET Standard 2.1 targets, we can continue using it even with the newest .NET. You can start by upgrading this project to the new SDK-style project.

Because .NET Framework cannot use .NET Standard 2.1 (it only supports .NET Standard 2.0), you have to make the project multi-targeted, as shown in Listing 3-1. Instead of the TargetFramework element, you specify TargetFrameworks (notice the added s at the end) with a semicolon-separated list of target framework monikers.[7] These multi-targeted projects will produce multiple output assemblies. If you

---

[7] Target framework moniker identifies a particular version of .NET. See https://learn.microsoft.com/en-us/dotnet/standard/frameworks#supported-target-frameworks

look in the bin/Debug folder, you will see subfolders net8.0[8] and net472 with the compilation outputs.

You can use MSBuild conditions to specify dependencies or project items only for a specific target framework. For example, the ASP.NET Identity package does not exist for .NET 8, so I had to use the Condition attribute in Listing 3-1 to apply it only for .NET Framework 4.7.2 target. We will have to replace this package with something else later.

Listing 3-1. An example of a multi-targeted SDK-style project

```
<Project Sdk="Microsoft.NET.Sdk">
  <PropertyGroup>
    <TargetFrameworks>net8.0;net472</TargetFrameworks>
    <OutputType>Library</OutputType>
  </PropertyGroup>
  <ItemGroup>
    <PackageReference Include="EntityFramework"
            Version="6.4.4" />
  </ItemGroup>
  <ItemGroup Condition=" '$(TargetFramework)' == 'net472' ">
    <PackageReference
        Include="Microsoft.AspNet.Identity.EntityFramework"
        Version="2.2.4" />
  </ItemGroup>
</Project>
```

---

[8] We could use netstandard2.1 instead of net8.0, but since the class library is used only by one application that will run on .NET 8, there is no added value in targeting .NET Standard 2.1. If it was a universal library, .NET Standard 2.1 would be a better choice. When writing universal libraries, you aim to keep the dependencies as loose as possible.

When you use the new SDK-style project file, you can use preprocessor symbols in the C# code to use different implementations for each framework. For example, the NETFRAMEWORK symbol will apply only for .NET Framework target. Similarly, there is NETSTANDARD2_0 that will apply only for frameworks compatible with .NET Standard 2.0. There is also a group of symbols for version ranges, such as NET6_0_OR_GREATER, defined for .NET 6 and all higher versions. You can refer to a complete list of preprocessor symbols.[9] The usage of these symbols is shown in Listing 3-2.

Listing 3-2. Using the preprocessor symbols for different framework targets

```
using System.Data.Entity;
using DotNetCollege.DAL.Entities;

#if NETFRAMEWORK
using DotNetCollege.DAL.Migrations;
using Microsoft.AspNet.Identity.EntityFramework;
#endif

namespace DotNetCollege.DAL
{
#if NETFRAMEWORK
    public class AppDbContext
        : IdentityDbContext<AppUser, AppRole, int,
            AppUserLogin, AppUserRole, AppUserClaim>
    {
        static AppDbContext()
        {
```

---

[9] See https://learn.microsoft.com/en-us/dotnet/standard/frameworks# preprocessor-symbols

```
        Database.SetInitializer(
            new MigrateDatabaseToLatestVersion<
                AppDbContext, Configuration>());
    }

    public AppDbContext() : base("DB")
    {
    }
#else
    public class AppDbContext : DbContext
    {
        // TODO: integrate with ASP.NET Core Identity later
#endif
```

The details of replacing ASP.NET Identity will be covered in detail in Chapter 6. During the migration of DotNetCollege, we also migrated from Entity Framework 6 to Entity Framework Core. However, this step can be postponed as Entity Framework 6 also works with the new .NET. I will be discussing this migration in Chapter 5.

Before looking at another method, let us briefly look at what was inside the DotNetCollege.BL project. Figure 3-3 shows the project folders in the Solution Explorer view.

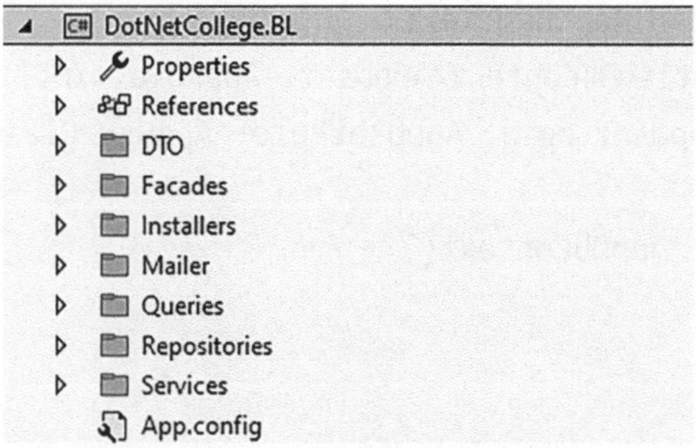

Figure 3-3. *Folders present in the business layer project*

This project contains the entire business logic of the application. The DTO folder contains Data-Transfer Objects,[10] plain C# classes with properties that are the input and output of Services and Facades. Both folders actually contain services – classes that encapsulate business logic. The distinction between these two is whether they are used directly from the UI (we decided to call them Facades) or whether they are for internal use (used by Facades or other Services). Technically, all classes in the Services folder could be internal.[11]

The Repositories and Queries folders contain code that works with the means of the data access layer – the Entity Framework. Every database query that returns a collection of DTOs is wrapped as a class in the Queries folder. For example, a class named OrderListQuery can return a list of orders with support for various filtering capabilities (the filters for the query are represented by another class, OrderListFilterDTO, that can be easily passed to the UI). All query objects are inherited from a base class that contains common functionalities like sorting and paging.

The layer of Repositories is often perceived as an antipattern. However, in the case of this application, it was just a thin layer that helped us to clarify dependencies between classes. If a service declares a dependency on DbContext in its constructor, the only thing you can tell is that it interacts with the database. It gives you a more precise picture if it declares a dependency on IRepository<CustomerEntity>. As a matter of fact, this can be very helpful in the incremental change approach as you can use a different implementation of the repository for each entity. This allows you to migrate the data access layer incrementally, for example, by aggregates.[12]

---

[10] See https://martinfowler.com/eaaCatalog/dataTransferObject.html

[11] At the time of implementing the first version of the DotNetCollege application, we used this convention in many RIGANTI projects. In the recent years, we moved away from it – mostly because of shifting to a Domain-Driven Design or other types of architecture.

[12] Aggregate is a group of entities tightly coupled by relationships that only make sense to be worked with together. See https://martinfowler.com/bliki/DDD_Aggregate.html

The `Mailer` folder contained T4 templates[13] that were responsible for composing HTML bodies of emails generated by the application. The `Installers` folder contained rules for Castle Windsor, a dependency injection container used in the application.

Thanks to the abstraction we had, we did not have to make many changes:

- The `Mailer` folder with email templates was removed as the SaaS solution replaced it. One of the benefits was that the marketing team could manage the templates itself in a WYSIWYG (What You See Is What You Get) editor instead of passing every change on to the development team, which had to update the templates and redeploy the entire application.

- The `Installers` folder was replaced with an extension method that registered the services in the `IServiceCollection`. The Castle dependency injection container is not used anymore.

- The base generic class of the `Repository<T>` was only slightly updated to support Entity Framework Core. The concrete implementations for each entity did not have to be changed at all; most of them just inherited the base class and added no extra functionality.

- The same applies to the base class of `Query` objects. Because of the changes in the query translation engine, all query classes (there were about 40 of them) had to be manually reviewed and sometimes rewritten to work with Entity Framework Core. However, we had to

---

[13] See `https://learn.microsoft.com/en-us/visualstudio/modeling/code-generation-and-t4-text-templates`

change only about 20% of them. One query provided a very complicated reporting functionality with multiple nested aggregations and generation of time periods. It had to be reimplemented as a SQL Table-Valued Function and then invoked using the `FromSql` method[14] of the new Entity Framework Core.

- The `Services`, `Facades`, and `DTOs` did not have any dependencies on Entity Framework – they worked with it through the abstractions of repositories and queries. Therefore, they did not need any changes in order to compile. During testing, we found only several places that stopped working because of lazy loading, which is disabled by default in Entity Framework Core. In such places, we added the missing `Include` calls or created a special query object for the case. This, in fact, helped with the performance of the application – lazy loading can cause significant penalties, especially in the SELECT N+1 problem.[15]

---

[14] `FromSql` allows you to pass a parameterized SQL query to the database and treat it as `IQueryable`. Because of this, you can wrap the query with additional filtering, sorting, and any other transform. You have to be careful – if used incorrectly, it can lead to a SQL injection attack; this is probably the reason why Entity Framework 6 never introduced such a functionality. See `https://learn.microsoft.com/en-us/ef/core/querying/sql-queries`

[15] The SELECT N+1 problem in ORMs typically occurs when you make one query to load a collection of database entities (the N represents their count) and then trigger lazy loading when processing each item. The code performs poorly as it needs 1+N (sequential) database queries. See `www.thinktecture.com/en/entity-framework-core/entity-framework-core7-n1-queries-problem/` for more information.

Unfortunately, the project had only a few automated tests. Most areas were not covered at all. That is why the migration required rigorous manual testing of all application features. Having enough reliable tests would make modernization much easier.

The in-place modernization is often used for Class Library projects. It can be used for web applications as well, but the limitation is to use a presentation framework that supports .NET Standard. One such framework is DotVVM, an open source project that lets you build web applications using the Model-View-ViewModel[16] pattern. Because of the support of both .NET Framework and the new .NET, you can install DotVVM NuGet packages in the .NET Framework project and incrementally "reimplement" every web page using DotVVM. After all pages are ported to DotVVM, the target framework can be changed to the new .NET, and the application will continue working. I will discuss this migration path in detail in Chapter 7.

Side-by-Side Modernization

For many projects, the side-by-side modernization will be the only way. Because of significant differences in the technologies and frameworks, it is not possible to use both old and new libraries in the same project.

Instead, the modernization process starts with creating a new application based on the new .NET and using the up-to-date packages and frameworks. After that, you can incrementally move functionality from the original application to the new one while providing a user-friendly way to transition between these applications. You can make it so smooth that

---

[16] MVVM (Model-View-ViewModel) is a design pattern used for the application presentation layer. The View defines the contents and look of the graphics interface. The Model represents the data and business logic of the application, for example, in a form of domain objects and services. The ViewModel represents the current state of the UI and handles the commands coming from the user (e.g., button clicks). See `https://learn.microsoft.com/en-us/dotnet/architecture/maui/mvvm`

the users will not be able to recognize that they interact with two different websites. If both applications run on the same domain, use the same CSS styles and layout, and have a single sign-on functionality, the experience for the user can be completely seamless.

On the other hand, sometimes you want to show the users that the application is being upgraded, and the redesign is often a part of the modernization process. A common example of this is adding support for mobile devices and tablets by implementing a responsive layout. It is more of a business decision whether the modernization should involve changes in the user interface or not. Doing these two tasks together may require less effort than doing them separately. However, modernization is already a complex process – including other activities increases the risks and makes this process even longer.

A common approach to side-by-side migration is utilizing a reverse proxy to forward the traffic from one application to the other. If an HTTP request can be handled by the first application, it is done so. Otherwise, it is forwarded to the second application to be processed. This is a typical use of the Chain of Responsibility[17] design pattern. Figure 3-4 shows the flow of the request – if the request URL does not match any route in the first application, it is passed to the second one. The requests for routes / orders or /order/{id} are handled by the new application – these routes have already been migrated. All others are passed to the old application by the proxy.

---

[17] See https://refactoring.guru/design-patterns/chain-of-responsibility

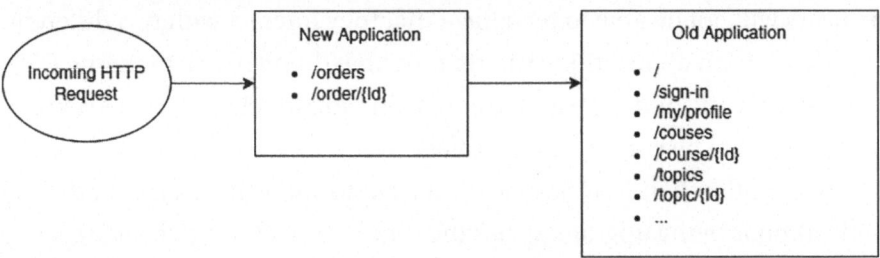

Figure 3-4. *Chain of Responsibility pattern created by the reverse proxy*

The Chain of Responsibility pattern is not only used between the two applications. When you register middlewares into the ASP.NET Core request pipeline, the same semantics are involved. Based on the order of registration, the first middleware receives all incoming HTTP requests. It either handles them itself or passes them to the next middleware. If none of the middlewares can process the request, the HTTP 404 (Not Found) response is generated.

The reverse proxy is, therefore, plugged as the last middleware in the new application. Any request not processed by the new application is sent to the old one. This is exactly what happens when you right-click any old ASP.NET project in Visual Studio and use the .NET Upgrade Assistant extension[18] to start a side-by-side migration. Visual Studio creates a new ASP.NET Core project using the newest .NET version and installs YARP[19] as the last middleware in the pipeline. Your responsibility is to configure it to point to the URL of the old application. Listing 3-3 shows how the generated ASP.NET Core project looks like.

---

[18] See https://dotnet.microsoft.com/en-us/platform/upgrade-assistant
[19] See https://microsoft.github.io/reverse-proxy/

Listing 3-3. New ASP.NET Core project using YARP to forward
unhandled requests to the old application

```
var builder = WebApplication.CreateBuilder(args);
builder.Services.AddSystemWebAdapters();
builder.Services.AddHttpForwarder();
builder.Services.AddControllersWithViews();

var app = builder.Build();

if (!app.Environment.IsDevelopment())
{
    app.UseHsts();
}
app.UseHttpsRedirection();
app.UseStaticFiles();

app.UseRouting();
app.UseAuthorization();
app.UseSystemWebAdapters();

app.MapControllers();
app.MapForwarder("/{**catch-all}",
    app.Configuration["ProxyTo"])
    .Add(static builder => {
        ((RouteEndpointBuilder)builder).Order = int.MaxValue;
    });

app.Run();
```

The AddHttpForwarder registers YARP into the service collection,
and MapForwarder registers it in the request pipeline. The AddSystemWeb
Adapters and UseSystemWebAdapters register the Microsoft.AspNetCore.
SystemWebAdapters package that simplifies the migration of code

depending on `System.Web`, especially static members like `HttpContext.Current`. It is expected that you will share code between the two applications, and providing the adapters for the old API means you will need to make much fewer changes in this shared code.

Among the other middlewares, you can see that `MapControllers` is called before the `MapForwarder`. This is important – the MVC controllers, which will eventually handle all requests, should have priority over sending the requests to the old application.

Naturally, you can play with this default template to adapt it to your needs. I have already mentioned the A/B testing, which assumes that both old and new versions of the page will be present in the solution. Based on some URL parameter or a setting in cookies, you can decide whether the request will be handled immediately or forwarded to the other application.

There are three important caveats. First, introducing a second application requires a configuration change on the server and a change in the deployment process. Until now, there was just one application hosted on the server. You will need to update the web server configuration, so the application moves to another domain or port (in fact, it should be an internal address that is better not accessible from the Internet, for example, `localhost:8080`). Additionally, you will need to deploy the new application on the server and configure it to run on the original domain (in our case, `www.dotnetcollege.cz`). The proxy needs to be pointed to the old application (`localhost:8080`).

The second caveat is that sometimes the old application looks at the request URL to detect which domain it is running on and uses this information for various purposes, for example, to generate links. Some multi-tenant applications pick their configuration based on the domain on which they are accessed.

Most proxies provide the original request URL in `X-Forwarded-Proto`, `X-Forwarded-Host`, and `X-Forwarded-For` HTTP headers. The application may require some code changes to read the actual request URL from these headers; after moving it to another domain, it would see `localhost:8080` as a request URL. Additionally, some applications perform automatic HTTP to HTTPS redirects. If you use a reverse proxy, you typically configure HTTPS only on the first application in the chain and use HTTP for the rest. If this is the case, you will need to disable the automatic HTTP to HTTPS redirection in the old application. Otherwise, you will get into a redirect loop.

The third problem is that suddenly you have two applications instead of one, which has numerous implications. Many applications do not care much about concurrency and were not written with scalability in mind. They can cache some things in memory, use the session storage to persist temporary information between multiple requests, store some data in the filesystem, use in-memory locks or other in-process synchronization primitives, and so on. This may cause various glitches when some requests come to the new application, and others come to the old application. The cache in one application may still hold data the other application has already modified. One application might have saved something in the filesystem. However, it is not visible to the other application unless you configure both of them to look in the same directory (and deal with potential file-locking problems). The session can be configured to store the data in a shared database, but this has performance implications (get and store operations on the session can become orders of magnitude slower) and requires the data to be serializable. The in-memory locks synchronize access to resources only in the scope of a single process, which may create race conditions when the same critical section is entered in both processes at the same time.

Another common problem is the single sign-on experience. ASP.NET uses a different format of authentication cookies than ASP.NET Core, and you will need to invest some effort in making sure that the user identity will be accessible by both applications. To implement it in a secure way is not trivial.

All these issues will be discussed in more detail in Chapter 8.

Full Rewrite

The previous method of modernization is suitable for scenarios in which the "new" application is similar to the old one. Its user interface may be redesigned or facelifted; the individual pages or parts may contain many small, local changes; the navigation and menus may be restructured; and so forth. But it is still the same application when looking at it from a distance.

I would like to highlight the option of using modernization as an opportunity to make greater changes. Most old applications are not outdated only from the technological point of view but also from other perspectives. The business may have changed in recent years, the trends and priorities may have shifted, and the application may be good at solving problems that are not important anymore or be far behind the expectations of the users.

A great example is the transformation that happened in retail banking in recent years. I will describe my experience living in the Czech Republic, but I believe most aspects have been very similar in other parts of the world.

Until a few years ago, opening a bank account required visiting one of their subsidiaries, proving your identity by showing your ID or passport, signing several paper forms, and depositing some funds in cash. When I got my first account in 2004 (I was 15 or 16 years old), the bank told me about a brand-new feature – a web application from which I can control my bank account. I still remember that ugly interface. From viewing the HTML of the pages, I recognized it was written in Java. The application was slow; every operation took about ten seconds. It worked only in Internet Explorer 6. If you tried to access it from another browser, it refused to load. The feature set of this application was very small – in fact, you could only see the account's transaction history and make a wire transfer.

Around 2015, the bank web application was still the same. It received several new features over the years. They somehow solved the support for other web browsers, but the UI was not meeting the requirements of the time. When you tried to access the application on a mobile device, the experience was horrific. Even the first step of navigating the menu was very hard to do without zooming down the page and having to chase those small buttons.

The application was "account-centric." In case you had multiple accounts, you had to switch between them. Other bank products were covered by the application in quite a weird way. For example, there was a special "account" called "Insurance products" in the list of accounts in the menu, which opened a completely different interface for managing insurance contracts. It was probably the easiest way for the developers to implement it, but the new requirements clearly went against the structure of the entire application as it was originally designed.

Currently, the bank has a new web and mobile application. It was rewritten from scratch, and, more importantly, its entire concept was completely changed. The center of everything is the customer, which is a good decision as many customers have more than one product. The other products are first-class citizens in the application and have the same importance as the bank accounts in the UI. The application interface is mobile-first, and the mobile app shares the same graphics design with the web interface.

I have not investigated it further, but the mobile applications do not seem to be "hybrid apps" – native applications that use the platform's web browser component to render a web page. This means the bank had to implement multiple applications – one for the Web and one for each mobile platform (unless they used some multiplatform framework like Xamarin, Flutter, or React Native; in such case, it would be just one mobile application for all mobile platforms).

Introducing the new applications certainly required a deep change in the bank processes. The applications offer a self-service experience to acquire new products without the need to visit the bank subsidiary. Today, you can even open a bank account just from the mobile application – without even visiting the bank. The application can verify the identity of new customers through a government identity portal which the Czech citizens can use to access various e-government services. On this identity portal, there are various means of authentication, for example, reading the chip of your identity card (if you have a Smart Card reader) or signing in to another bank's application (if the bank has already verified your physical identity). Therefore, if you have any bank account in the Czech Republic, you already have a valid e-government identity, which allows you to open an account in any other bank without going there physically.

An important feature of the new applications is the two-factor verification of outgoing payments and other operations. If you make a wire transfer to an account that is not yours, the banks commonly require you to authorize the transaction in a mobile application or by some other method, such as a text message. Today, most banks also allow you to use this method to sign contracts and approve other operations like changing the limits of your cards.

As you can see, the banks could not only use the in-place or side-by-side incremental modernization of their software. Instead, they had to make a significant shift based on evolving users' expectations ("I will not have to go to the bank or post office") while rethinking many of their internal processes. One customer web application was replaced by not one but two or more applications. We cannot see how many such shifts the banks needed to make in their internal systems, but even your most conservative estimate would probably constitute significant effort. The authentication model was integrated with the government identity provider, and there were surely many significant architectural changes behind the scenes to make this migration possible.

This is not only the modernization of a single web application – this is a complete digital transformation of the bank's business. Maybe your company is going through a similar process, and thus a similar "big bang" will be a better choice than an isolated modernization of a single legacy application.

As I mentioned in Chapter 2, it is necessary to look at this problem not only from the technical point of view but also from the perspectives of all stakeholders. The chance of successful delivery will rise when the technical decisions are aligned with the company strategy and other changes in the industry that may be already in progress.

A full rewrite does not mean that all new code must be written from scratch. Naturally, even huge parts of code and functionality can be shared if the technology allows. Often, the business logic from the old application is exposed as an API to be consumed by the new applications. A transition period when both new and old applications can run simultaneously is also quite common, and it is not unusual for such periods to take years.

However, the full rewrite option allows you to change the underlying technology completely. New applications can be written using different languages or tools. The database technology may be completely modified, involving a complex process of data migration. There are often tendencies to replace relational databases with document databases, change architecture from a CRUD-based approach to Domain-Driven Design, etc. Such changes are so significant that it is necessary to make a new implementation. This approach typically requires more effort than the "safe" way of incremental changes, but greater changes may lead to greater benefits.

Back to the Example

Earlier in this chapter, I promised to share our way of modernizing the e-learning website. Feel free to return to Figure 3-1 to recall the situation.

Two applications (website and background service) were merged into one ASP.NET Core application. We used the in-place way of migration, followed by a graphics refresh. We rewrote all ASP.NET MVC pages and controllers to DotVVM while changing the design pattern from MVC to MVVM. The refactoring of controllers to viewmodels proved to be quite easy, and since we had the business logic well separated in the business layer and the models coming to the MVC views could remain unchanged, the migration was smooth. The MVVM pattern was useful in the admin area, which contained many complex forms. The user experience was greatly improved because full postbacks in MVC were replaced with AJAX calls which DotVVM does out of the box.

The full rewrite approach was used only for the parts that were replaced with SaaS solutions. Instead of migrating the CRM and newsletter modules, we implemented an integration to the REST API of these external services. Some calls were triggered from the e-learning application (e.g., when the user created an account and subscribed to the newsletter, we called the REST API to add them to the subscriber list). We used webhooks to handle events from the external services. When an opportunity in the CRM was moved to the Contract Signed stage, the CRM called the e-learning portal REST API to prepare a new private course order for the customer.

After all the MVC pages were reimplemented in DotVVM (the Git history showed us that this process touched only about 7% of files in the entire codebase), the project was changed to target the latest version of .NET. There were a couple of remaining dependencies on the `System.Web`, but most of them were one-line changes. The largest problem was a migration from Entity Framework to Entity Framework Core and moving from ASP.NET Identity to ASP.NET Core Identity. It required reviewing all query objects, reimplementing some of them, fixing various lazy loading problems, and migrating user account tables to the new structure.

This was the longest step during which the project could not be compiled; it took about a week. In the previous phases, the application could still work as it targeted the old .NET Framework, and the time to rewrite an MVC page to DotVVM one was between 1 hour and 1.5 days. We used branches in Git, which allowed us to work on these changes in parallel and fix issues in the current code at the same time.

The final application was deployed to Azure App Service. We used the same Azure resource that we were using for years to host the old version – we just replaced the old application binaries and files with the new ones. This was probably not the best choice – the application suffered from runtime issues occurring randomly every few days. We never found the exact cause of the issue, but the problem disappeared when we created a new Azure App Service resource and deployed the application again (copying the exact same files). Some issues with the old resource probably arose when the target framework was changed; maybe there were some remaining files or artifacts from the old version somewhere in the filesystem, which interfered with the new binaries targeting the new runtime.

Estimating the Effort

The two most popular questions of the management are "How much is it going to cost?" and "How quickly can we deliver it?" If you know the answers for each considered option, making the business decision is then simple. It is as simple as implementing a nontrivial feature when you have a detailed specification, including a profound analysis of all edge cases and potential conflicts with the software's existing functionality. Please let me know what was the last time you had this luxury.

In any project larger than what can fit in one's mind, you always live in a world of uncertainty. This gets worse on team projects where you don't know the details of what other team members do. Every management position suffers from the same problem; you almost never have enough information and accurate data to make a qualified decision.

A common trick to escape this trap is to make decisions that are reversible. Let us try this option, and if it proves wrong, retreat to an alternative path and learn. It is crucial to first agree on the definition of wrong – how do you find out it is going wrong? Otherwise, people may tend to "hide" the problem or keep trying even when it should already be clear the way is not feasible.

In the case of modernization projects, applying this trick would mean, for example, trying to migrate several pages and evaluating the required effort. If it is above expectations, a change of strategy or approach will be necessary. But how do you know the threshold?

Divide and Conquer

There is a great book, *Software Estimation: Demystifying the Black Art*, by Steve McConnell,[20] which describes all the challenges and practices of estimating the effort.

An important technique mentioned in the book is using past data. If the modernization project is not the first in the company, try to get insights from previous projects. The data tells you something even if the situation or technologies were different. Similarly, if the modernization project you are participating in is known not to be the last one, make sure you collect the effort required for individual areas, so this data is not lost.

In most cases, you will not be able to find a similar project to compare with. Another method, especially counting and classification, can be of great help. You find a repeating element (e.g., web page, component, feature, or database table) and count the number of instances that fall into Very Small, Small, Medium, Large, and Very Large buckets. You can estimate (or better measure) an effort required for one instance in each bucket, and based on that, you can extrapolate the total effort.

---

[20] See www.microsoftpressstore.com/store/software-estimation-demystifying-the-black-art-9780735605350

It is recommended to have a difference of at least a factor of 2 between the buckets. You may adjust the number of buckets to less or more – I often ended up using just Small, Medium, and Large buckets.

Example: Estimating the Effort

Let us return to the example of the e-learning website. The process of modernization can be split into the following high-level tasks:

1. Replace the CRM and Newsletters module with an API integration to external SaaS services.

2. Replace the MVC pages and controllers with DotVVM pages and viewmodels.

3. Migrate Entity Framework 6 to Entity Framework Core – review and fix all query objects and repository methods.

4. Migrate ASP.NET Identity to ASP.NET Core Identity, including migration of user accounts.

5. Resolve the remaining issues (access to unsupported .NET Framework APIs) when switching to the target framework.

6. Merge the background service into the web application.

7. Update the application deployment process.

I will not dig into point 1 as it would require a detailed user story and feature breakdown. Since it is a "full rewrite" case, the way of estimating its effort is similar to any other greenfield implementation.

Point 2 is more interesting – it involves rewriting MVC views into DotVVM views (different syntax), refactoring MVC controllers into DotVVM viewmodels, and testing to make sure the new implementation works the same way.

As mentioned earlier, we have split the pages into buckets based on their complexity:

- *Small*: Mostly static pages, just a few controller methods

- *Medium*: Medium-sized pages without complicated logic, such as JavaScript blocks or large third-party components

- *Large*: Complex pages (more than 200 lines of code) with complex logic or special behaviors

We have found subcategories of pages that were very similar to each other, and they could be put all into the same bucket without detailed classification. This was the case in the admin area, where almost half of the pages contained only a data-grid component with standard features like filtering, sorting, and paging. We placed all of them in the Medium category.

The other half of the pages in the admin area contained a form to insert or edit a single entity. This group of pages was split into all three buckets. Some entities were really trivial (various code tables with only ID and description). The vast majority of entities contained quite a lot of properties to be edited, but there was no sophisticated logic or processes behind them; these fell into the Medium category. A few entities, such as Order or a Course, involved a complex workflow and various state changes, and thus they went to the Large bucket.

We tried to estimate the effort first, but after that, we selected three pages from each bucket we believed to represent the category best. Table 3-1 shows the comparison of original estimates and the actual effort.

Table 3-1. Original and measured estimates for pages in each bucket

Page Complexity	Estimated Effort	Measured Effort (First 3 Pages)
Small	1.5 hours/page	1.9 hours/page
Medium	5 hours/page	6.4 hours/page
Large	20 hours/page	12.7 hours/page

As you can see, we tend to underestimate the simple pages and overestimate the difficult ones. However, there are two important things to note.

First, choosing only three pages from each bucket is by far not a good enough sample. In our case, the application was not extremely large; if we chose ten pages from each category, we would have already migrated a substantial portion of it.

Second, the migration of the first few pages may be more difficult than the average. Some initial steps must be taken at the beginning, for example, preparing some helper functions or infrastructure. Additionally, the team may not have any previous experience with this activity, and thus their productivity may improve over time. On the other hand, there is a good chance that you will not choose the pages where you expect the worst complications in the sample, even unintentionally. All in all, it is better to have at least some empirical evidence than guesses.

I strongly recommend keeping track of the team's effort on each page and periodically reviewing how the actual values are evolving. At the beginning of the project, the numbers may oscillate, but with more pages being migrated, the value will become stable eventually.

Table 3-2 shows how the estimate evolved after each sprint. The initial guess led to a total effort of 508 hours. The actual effort was about 15% higher. After the evaluation phase, the estimate was closer to the actual effort. You can see that during Sprint 1, the team dealt with some complications as the estimated effort rose up to 623.5 hours. The team immediately reached out to inform me that we may need an extra sprint to complete the migration of the pages. Figure 3-5 shows how the effort per page evolved over time.

161

Table 3-2. *Evolution of estimated effort hours based on actual progress*

	Initial Guess	Evaluation	Sprint 1	Sprint 2	Sprint 3
Simple	24	30.4	33.7	31.7	31.7
Medium	156	249.6	274.8	267.2	268.3
Large	324	274.2	315.0	292.4	283.6
TOTAL	**504**	**554.2**	**623.5**	**591.3**	**583.6**

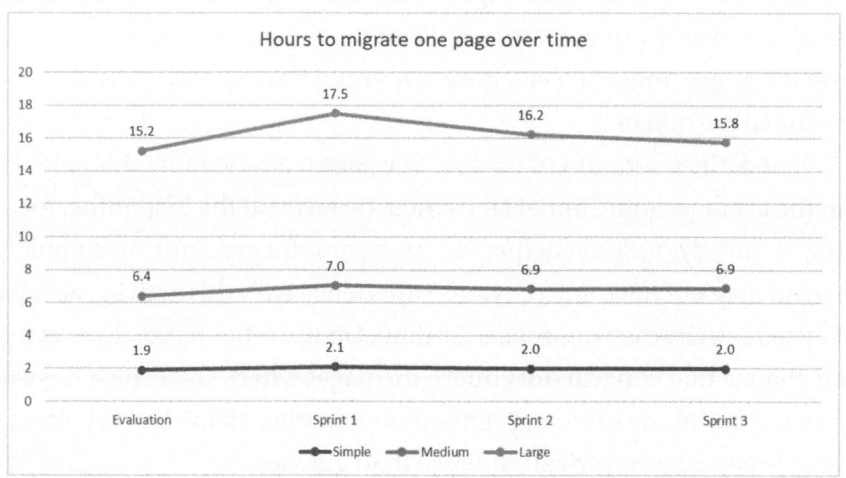

Figure 3-5. *Evolution of the "hours per page" metric over time*

Please note that the numbers may be very different in your project. There are multiple factors that can greatly affect the migration complexity – the experience and size of the team, how well is the business layer separated, whether you do or not do a graphics redesign during the process, whether the testing of migrated pages is included in the effort or tracked separately, and so on. In our case, the migration was done by two experienced developers (one working full-time, the other working part-time) and one tester (part-time). There were additional hours for project management; however, they were tracked separately and not divided between the migrated pages.

You can use a similar approach in other high-level migration steps listed at the beginning of this section. If you switch from Entity Framework to Entity Framework Core, you will need to review all queries that use the DbContext to make sure the new query translator will be able to generate appropriate SQL. If you do not have all queries wrapped in separate classes (which makes identification and classification of the queries much easier), you can search for all usages of the Entity Framework context and start from there.

Adding, updating, and removing entities did not change much, so you can ignore these occurrences. However, any LINQ calls on this context object should be investigated, especially when they contain GroupBy or similar complex functions. Simple Where and OrderBy clauses will probably work without differences. In the case you use mapping libraries like AutoMapper to generate projections on IQueryable, you should review and classify all defined mappings.

A similar situation happens with lazy loading. You can review all entities and their navigation properties and count the number of occurrences where lazy loading may appear. Based on that, you can estimate how much time you spend on resolving each instance.

This approach can give you a better insight into the complexity of modernization activities. I recommend reevaluating the initial guesses by using the actual effort regularly. There are plenty of tools to track time, for example, Toggl.[21] It requires some effort until the team learns to track the work to the required level of detail, but when used correctly, the data are very helpful. In our case, the developers were a bit reluctant to do such detailed time tracking at the beginning, but when they saw the usefulness

---

[21] See https://toggl.com/

of the data for planning, the complaints quickly disappeared. In fact, after the project, the developers reported that they liked the stress-free nature of the technically complicated project, thanks to the ability to foresee the future.

The tracked time can be linked to issues, tasks, or tickets in work planning tools such as Azure DevOps or JIRA, which offer rich interfaces to create various kinds of reports.

Preparing the Environment

Even in the 2020s, I occasionally encountered legacy projects developed without proper tooling, such as source control. The reasons are different – one of them is that the application was created by people who were not software developers, and they made the application as a side effect of their regular work to simplify some repeating tasks. A lot of people who are not primarily developers can use VBA in Excel or Access, and it is not that far from eventually writing a VB.NET application.

I don't try to blame anyone here. On the contrary, I am quite impressed when I see such applications – their authors often invested their free time and fought many obstacles to achieve something that seemed impossible.

With the rise of AI and low-code or no-code platforms, we can expect more applications created by hobbyists or people who are not developers. Sometimes, these applications evolve into crucial tools used by a substantial part of the company, and eventually they may outgrow their creators and require a real developer team to take care of them.

Prior to starting modernization, it is a good idea to resolve all these "sins of the past." If the application does not use a version control tool, take the opportunity to configure it (and include this activity in the effort estimate, including the time the team will need to learn and adopt these practices). If there is no proper logging or monitoring, invest some time to add it to the project. If the codebase contains hard-coded secrets, allocate some time to move it to a secure place.

Cleanup

Unused features and code tend to accumulate in every project: methods or classes that are not called, pages that are not necessary anymore, long blocks of commented-out code, configuration entries that no one uses, and NuGet packages that are not necessary. You probably know the temptation to remove some code that Visual Studio reports to have zero references, followed by a quick retreat for fear of breaking something.

All these items may increase the effort during modernization. You may spend hours upgrading some old package and resolving dependency conflicts only to find out that it was not used anywhere. All this effort could be used for something else.

Some projects contain huge parts of code needed at some time in the past, but they are not called anymore. This code may cause compile errors when updating the target framework. If it is not used, there is no point in fixing errors in it.

Commented-out code blocks are another thing to be dealt with. I once heard someone say, "Any commented-out line of code that is not uncommented on the same day is useless. No one will ever return to it tomorrow or any time in the future." Unfortunately, I do not remember where I heard that, so I am unable to give appropriate credit to the author of this quote, but it has a point. The longer the blocks are present in the code, the lower the chance they will ever be used. Do not fear deleting them – you can always find them in the version history if needed. Such blocks make the code harder to read, and what is worse, they can confuse the diff tools when resolving merge conflicts.

There is a concept called YAGNI (You Aren't Gonna Need It). It is usually applied in the opposite direction (do not introduce new things because you just foresee you will need them), but it is useful to think about it from the other side. You probably already have some unnecessary things in the project. What are the chances you will need them again? The developers who designed and implemented them may not even work at the company, or they just do not remember how these things worked and why they were written like that. Since these parts of the application were not used recently, they may not even be functional, and they are probably not covered by tests. Bringing them to life may require even more work than implementing them again.

To identify NuGet packages that are not needed, you can use tools like ReSharper,[22] which can identify and remove unused packages. Visual Studio 2019 and 2022 offer similar functionality, but, unfortunately, it is available only for the new SDK-style projects.

You should test the application after applying this tool, as some packages will not be referenced directly but loaded via Reflection. These tools will not be able to detect that and may remove something the application needs.

The rule of thumb is to get rid of everything the application does not need in order to reduce the surface you will need to work with during modernization.

Review Project Dependencies

Thanks to .NET Standard, most .NET libraries distributed as NuGet packages support both branches of .NET. However, the introduction of built-in mechanisms like dependency injection or a new logging model in the new .NET led the library authors to adapt these libraries to accommodate these patterns.

I have seen several blog posts advising the developers to start with an upgrade of all packages to their latest possible versions supported on .NET Framework. The idea is to get as close to the final state as possible before starting the large chunk of work you must do as quickly as possible. In general, it sounds reasonable, but I have met several cases when this approach added some extra work instead of removing it.

---

[22] The feature is called Optimize NuGet references: `https://blog.jetbrains.com/dotnet/2016/02/22/resharper-ultimate-10-1-eap-3/`

One example is *AutoMapper* which removed the static API in its
version 9.0.[23] Listing 3-4 shows how the library was used before and after
the change. When upgrading, applications using the static API require
code changes in many places. The changes are trivial – instead of using the
static `Mapper` class, you use an `IMapper` instance, and wherever you call
an extension method (such as `ProjectTo`), you need to pass the mapping
configuration to it. The problem occurs when your project does not use
dependency injection – you have no easy way to get the `IMapper` instance
in all these places (other than making a static class yourself which you
would want to get rid of eventually). In this case, it is easier to postpone
the upgrade of AutoMapper until you run on the new .NET and have the
dependency injection available out of the box.

Listing 3-4. Differences in AutoMapper usage

```
// AutoMapper 8.0
// static API - configuring maps
Mapper.CreateMap<NewsletterEntity, NewsletterDetailModel>();

// static API - using maps for a single object or IQueryable
var model = Mapper.Map<NewsletterDetailModel>(
    newsletterEntity);
var models = dbContext.Newsletters
    .ProjectTo<NewsletterDetailModel>();

// AutoMapper 9.0+
// new API - configuring maps
var config = new MapperConfiguration(cfg => {
    cfg.CreateMap<NewsletterEntity, NewsletterDetailModel>();
});
var mapper = config.CreateMapper();
```

---

[23] See www.jimmybogard.com/automapper-9-0-released/

```
// new API - using maps for a single object or IQueryable
var model = mapper.Map<NewsletterDetailModel>(
    newsletterEntity);
var models = dbContext.Newsletters
    .ProjectTo<NewsletterDetailModel>(
        mapper.ConfigurationProvider);
```

Some libraries depended on platform-specific APIs, which changed between ASP.NET and ASP.NET Core. Therefore, instead of publishing a new version, they introduced another package. For example, this is the case of *Swashbuckle*, a popular library for generating OpenAPI (Swagger) definitions for Web APIs. The package for .NET Framework is called Swashbuckle, but ASP.NET Core projects use Swashbuckle.AspNetCore instead.

You cannot reference the new packages until the project targets the new .NET. In many cases, although the name of the package has the same prefix, the API inside may be very different (changed namespaces, different API for initialization and configuration, and so on). Upgrading the old packages to the latest version may not make much sense, as the new package will be different anyway.

All in all, I would not apply the advice mentioned earlier dogmatically. If the latest version of a package supports both .NET branches and is not expected to depend on platform-specific features like ASP.NET Core closely, it should be safe to upgrade it as a separate step before modernization. However, if the currently used version of the package works with the new .NET already, you can delay the upgrade to a later time.

In general, the only intent of this package review is to move as much work away from the main phase of modernization as possible. This phase is already complicated enough to burden it with work that can be done separately – before or after.

Monitoring and Diagnostics

Another frequent issue of legacy applications is the lack of logging, monitoring, and collection of diagnostic data. At times when these applications were created, we did not have the luxury of today's services like Azure Application Insights, which can collect exceptions, logs, and metrics and provide dashboards with advanced analytics.

Collecting all exceptions with a complete stack trace is a must-have, but any other logged information is very useful when hunting issues possibly caused by changes in the application.

If you do not want to use cloud offerings such as Application Insights, there are libraries to collect and store the diagnostic data locally. On many servers, IIS was configured to write all unhandled exceptions into Windows Event Log.

Another popular choice for old ASP.NET was Elmah.[24] It can hook onto ASP.NET runtime and collect all unhandled exceptions. It supports storing the diagnostic data in the SQL database and offers a simple web interface to browse the collected data. It also offers a cloud-based solution which may be helpful – storing exceptions in the database may not be the ideal long-term solution.

The default destination for many .NET developers is Azure Application Insights. Microsoft invested a lot of effort to make the configuration easy, and thus installing it in a .NET Framework project is just a matter of a few clicks in Visual Studio.[25] It will add a couple of NuGet packages to the project, and a configuration file called `ApplicationInsights.config` will be created. In this file, you can fine-tune which data you want to collect, and you need to specify the connection string (it contains the URL of the

---

[24] See `https://blog.elmah.io/elmah-tutorial/`
[25] See `https://learn.microsoft.com/en-us/azure/azure-monitor/app/asp-net#add-application-insights-automatically`

ingestion server and the instrumentation key of your Application Insights account). The default configuration is quite reasonable – I recommend starting without any changes and looking at the results in a couple of days.

The service is paid based on the amount of ingested data, so eliminating unnecessary information can lower the costs. You can configure sampling[26] that reduces the amount of data while preserving the statistical correctness – for example, the service will store only 10% of data, but the algorithm will try to pick unique events and drop events that repeat often, remembering only the counts. The results reflect the number of occurrences of each event when viewing the data.

While knowing about every exception is crucial, an optional but useful area of interest is the metrics. Using just a few lines of code, you can instrument your code to track that some event happened and how many times. For example, if you have an ecommerce site, you may report a metric that users placed an item in the cart, submitted an order, proceeded with the payment, signed in to their accounts, and so forth. If you have a worker to process some items in the background, the time required to process an item can also be interesting information to collect.

You can use these metrics to make sure the application is healthy and the critical processes run smoothly. Services like Application Insights allow you to set up alerts based on metrics using a time-window query. For example, if the number of events "user added item in cart" in the last hour is zero, it indicates a significant problem in the application we should focus on. Similarly, if processing an item in the worker normally takes ten seconds, we can set up a rule to watch the average item processing time and inspect it every few minutes. If the average time is more than 30 seconds, there is probably some performance issue. The alerts can send emails and SMS, trigger a REST API, or deliver a push notification to the Microsoft Azure application on the phone.

---

[26] See https://learn.microsoft.com/en-us/azure/azure-monitor/app/sampling-classic-api

The added value of good application monitoring and diagnostics is tremendous. In my experience, it can reduce the time for investigation of issues by an order of magnitude. Given that the configuration of such tools takes almost no time, the return on investment is very quick. The alerts can tell you about a problem even before the customers notice – this is priceless.

In the case of side-by-side migration or full rewrite, you may store the logs and metrics in the same place. In such cases, make sure the telemetry contains an identification from which application it originates and uses the same format. Otherwise, you would not be able to easily compare the data.

Version Control

Modernization, in general, involves numerous changes in the codebase. It is crucial to have the ability to track why any change was made and in what context it was. This is almost impossible without a proper source code versioning tool.

There are still applications developed and maintained without versioning tools like Git. Even if you work on the project as a single developer, the versioning tool can be of a huge help. If you hesitated to configure it because of lack of time or just waited for the right moment, you should do it now before starting to make significant changes in the code.

Some teams still use TFVC,[27] the mechanism of version control implemented by Microsoft Team Foundation Server, which was later renamed to Azure DevOps Server. Although Microsoft still supports this technology and is used in numerous enterprises, many organizations have started migrating to Git, today's de facto industry standard. Git is much more flexible than the centralized TFVC, does not require developers to be connected to the server to check out files or access the version history, and

---

[27] See https://learn.microsoft.com/en-us/azure/devops/repos/tfvc/what-is-tfvc

integrates with other developer tools and services that provide features like pull requests, forking repositories, etc. Also, Git has a different concept of branches – only one branch is checked out at a time in the repository instead of having all branches lying on the disk in folders next to each other. This allows you to have many more branches – they come with almost no overhead in contrast to TFVC.

If your application is still on the TFVC and you plan to migrate to Git eventually, I strongly recommend doing it before the modernization. During the migration,[28] Microsoft recommends not preserving the history (because of the different ways of branches), which means that you would potentially lose the largest benefit of the version control – being able to look back and track reasons for any change in the code.

Git Workflows

Many teams already use Git but do not get the most benefits from its features. I saw projects where everyone committed and pushed changes into the main branch without any tests or gates, which often broke the build and wasted the time of multiple people dealing with compile errors. This unsystematic approach can cause various problems during modernization.

During modernization, there will be situations when you need to do trivial edits to code in hundreds of files, for example, changing namespaces, using different method overloads, migrating from static API (HttpContext. Current) to dependency-injected instances, and so on. If you do not use branches, you will either have to push one very large commit with all the changes involved or use smaller commits that will leave the code in an uncompilable state. The larger the commit is, the higher the chance of getting merge conflicts and the harder it is to resolve them.

---

[28] See https://learn.microsoft.com/en-us/azure/devops/repos/git/
import-from-tfvc#migrate-from-tfvc-to-git

There are several popular workflows for using Git in larger teams and projects.

GitHub Flow

One of the popular workflows is GitHub flow.[29] In this flow, the `main` branch does not allow direct commits – it is locked. Instead, to start working on a feature or a bug fix, you create a new branch from `main`. Using descriptive names is recommended; some teams agreed on using prefixes such as `feature/new-customer-dashboard` or `fix/order-details-performance`.

After the branch is created, you can commit your changes to it. Each commit should contain an isolated, complete change and should be described properly in the commit message. You can push as many commits as needed, including revert commits. When the change is ready, you create a pull request and let others review it. They may suggest changes, which are resolved by additional commits.

Most platforms today support CI/CD pipelines which are triggered when the PR (pull request) is created – they will build the code, run automated tests, and optionally prevent the PR from merging if there is an error. When the pull request is approved, it can be merged into the `main` branch. This branch should always be ready to deploy – it shall not contain any unfinished features.

There can be many branches worked on in parallel. It is good to streamline the process not to have PRs waiting to be reviewed for a long time as it increases the chance for merge conflicts.

---

[29] See `https://docs.github.com/en/get-started/using-github/github-flow`

Gitflow

Gitflow[30] is a more complex workflow that originated in the early days of Git. Although its popularity is declining, mostly because of its unnecessary complexity for smaller teams and projects, I believe it is important to understand it, as you may come up with a simplified or modified version of it that will work for you.

The idea is to have two branches – main[31] and develop. The first branch contains the version that is deployed in production and uses tags to indicate the release number. The second branch is the branch where all the development happens. To implement a feature or a fix (meaning a fix for an issue that happened in the development branch but did not get into the production yet), you create a new branch from develop.

When the new version (e.g., 0.3) is getting ready, and all features intended for this version are finished and merged into develop, a release branch named release-0.3 is created. From this moment, the develop becomes the branch for 0.4 features.

The release branch can be deployed to test or staging environments and allows you to commit and push the last fixes. Once it is ready to release, it is merged into both main and develop (so the bug fixes made to this branch would not get lost).

If you need to fix an issue in production, you should create a hotfix branch (e.g., hotfix-order-summary-perf-issue) from main. After the issue is resolved in this branch, it is merged into main. It is usually also merged into develop, except for the cases when the issue is resolved in the development version by another means.

---

[30] See www.atlassian.com/git/tutorials/comparing-workflows/gitflow-workflow

[31] The original definition of Gitflow used the name master (conforming to the default branch name in Git), but most tools and services switched to the name main recently. I prefer the name main as well. See https://sfconservancy.org/news/2020/jun/23/gitbranchname/

Trunk-Based Development

Trunk-Based Development[32] started getting traction in recent years as a reaction to the weakness of Gitflow's lengthy feature branches. If you work on a feature that is not going to the current release but is planned for the future, with Gitflow, the feature branch will not be merged until the develop branch switches to the new version.

The Trunk-Based Development flow heavily relies on continuous integration – every change pushed to main needs to be verified by automated build and tests.

In this flow, you should focus on making small commits and merge them into the main branch often, ideally every day, after running the tests. The main branch should always pass the tests and be ready to deploy.

It is possible to use feature branches (a variant called Scaled Trunk-Based Development), but even these should be merged regularly and should not live longer than a few days. Unfinished features or features being prepared for a future release need to use feature flags to disable the code path conditionally.

The code review is done either before merging feature branches or by sequentially reviewing the commits pushed into main.

Conclusion

There are more workflows than the two I mentioned; however, these three should be enough to give you an idea.

In general, the GitHub flow and Trunk-Based Development may work better for projects where most or even the entire team capacity will focus on modernization or in cases when modernization is not going to leave the codebase in an uncompilable state for longer than a few days. In such cases, you will be able to work in small batches and possibly deploy in

---

[32] See https://trunkbaseddevelopment.com/

production often to get immediate feedback from the customers. If you expect one or a few complex features which could prevent the project from being compiled without errors for some time, I believe it is not a big deal to break the short-lived branch policy in these rare cases, meaning that you can have a feature branch that lives longer than a few days even if you follow Trunk-Based Development. Especially when switching the target framework and replacing or upgrading some libraries, you can expect hundreds of compile errors, and resolving all of them is rarely a matter of just a few hours.

Gitflow or a similar approach with two branches may be better when modernization is only one of the team activities, and you expect more changes in the current version running in the production. These changes will be happening in the `main` branch through the hotfix branches (feel free to create your own naming conventions – you do not have to call standard requirements hotfixes), while modernization will take place in the `develop` branch. There is a risk of conflicts, especially when larger refactoring is going to happen in the `develop` branch. In some cases, you will have to reimplement the hotfixes manually as cherry-picking them may not be possible due to file moves or heavy changes in namespaces. If you can avoid refactoring until the later stages of modernization, I recommend doing so. Any unnecessary deviation of the two branches will increase the chance of merge conflicts.

Feel free to build your own workflow if none of these three fits your project. However, make sure that every team member understands the chosen flow and follows it.

Summary

In this chapter, I compared the way of making incremental changes with the full rewrite approach. Both methods have their benefits and can be combined in larger solutions consisting of multiple applications.

I showed several methods of getting rough estimates of the effort required for various parts of modernization. By dividing countable elements into buckets and estimating the effort for one item, you can get an overall estimate of required effort, and by tracking and reevaluating these numbers after every sprint, you can get a better insight into the progress and remaining amount of work.

Finally, I discussed various activities you should do before you start modernizing your application. This includes removing unnecessary code and dependencies, upgrading some NuGet packages, implementation of logging and monitoring, and preparing the source control tools.

Chapter 4 will talk about migration of API-based applications using ASP.NET Web Services, WCF, ASP.NET Web API, or ASP.NET SignalR.

CHAPTER 4

Migrating APIs and Web Services

This chapter will focus on replacing communication frameworks present in .NET Framework with their ASP.NET Core equivalents. Because none of the technologies is supported in the new .NET as it is (with the same NuGet packages and namespaces), you will need to either use the full rewrite approach or the side-by-side incremental migration.

The full rewrite option is basically copy-pasting the whole project and updating it to the new API as one big step. You can deploy the new version to production after it is finished, which is also the moment when you can abandon the old version entirely.

The side-by-side modernization allows migrating the API incrementally and potentially using various A/B testing techniques. For example, you can establish a custom HTTP header that can be used to opt in for the new API, and so on. You can also get early feedback from the users, and because most API apps do not use session or cookie-based authentication, a lot of the complexity of the side-by-side approach mentioned in previous chapters disappears.

© Tomáš Herceg 2024
T. Herceg, *Modernizing .NET Web Applications*,
https://doi.org/10.1007/979-8-8688-0617-9_4

Before You Start

Before digging into the details, it is useful to think about the risk of introducing breaking changes. If your API is used by third parties or if there are many client applications that are outside of your control, achieving an equal API surface and the same behavior will be the primary goal. It is important to mention that a breaking change may occur even when the API itself does not change. Any team running a heavily used API service can probably recall some scenarios when even a small performance-related change of a single endpoint broke the clients. Clients often do not call the API in the most efficient way; there are frequent cases of calling the same endpoints with the same parameters repeatedly instead of having these calls cached. Therefore, even if you introduce a small slowdown of the API, the overall experience may be worse by a multiple because a single action in the application may require many API calls.

However, retaining the same API may not always be the top priority. Many APIs have only a few clients, and your team may also own their codebase. Allowing changes on both ends of the communication channel offers some additional benefits.

For example, when migrating ASP.NET Web API controllers to ASP.NET Core MVC, the System.Text.Json library is used instead of Newtonsoft. Json. This can lead to subtle differences in the serialization of transferred objects. For instance, System.Text.Json treats polymorphic types differently – it requires an explicit listing of possible inherited types that can be used in a property of a base type. Listing 4-1 shows how the two serializers produce a different output unless you add the JsonDerivedType attribute on the base class.

Listing 4-1. Serialization of polymorphic types using Newtonsoft.
Json and System.Text.Json

```
public class Zoo
{
    public Animal[] Animals { get; set; }
}

// Without adding these attributes, System.Text.Json will
// only serialize the Name property from the base class
//[System.Text.Json.Serialization.JsonDerivedType(typeof(Dog))]
//[System.Text.Json.Serialization.JsonDerivedType(typeof(Cat))]
public abstract class Animal
{
    public string Name { get; set; }
}

public class Dog : Animal
{
    public string Breed { get; set; }
}

public class Cat : Animal
{
    public int FluffinessLevel { get; set; }
}

Console.WriteLine(
    System.Text.Json.JsonSerializer.Serialize(zoo));
Console.WriteLine(
    Newtonsoft.Json.JsonConvert.SerializeObject(zoo));
```

```
// Output from System.Text.Json
// {
//    "Animals": [
//       {
//          "Name": "Fido"
//       },
//       {
//          "Name": "Whiskers"
//       }
//    ]
// }
//
// Output from Newtonsoft.Json
// {
//    "Animals": [
//       {
//          "Breed": "Golden Retriever",
//          "Name": "Fido"
//       },
//       {
//          "FluffinessLevel": 10,
//          "Name": "Whiskers"
//       }
//    ]
// }
```

System.Text.Json uses a different setting model that is not 1:1 to Newtonsoft.Json. Any customization to JsonSerializerSettings needs to be transformed to the new API. You will also need to reimplement all custom converters, as the API and its semantics are different. If you can use the same JSON serialization library in the client applications as well, you can save some headaches.

In the case of ASP.NET SignalR, modifications to the client applications are necessary. The new SignalR Core uses a different internal protocol; thus, all clients must be updated to support that. This can be especially painful when your SignalR API is used by third parties; they will need to update their client code.

Another area of consideration is the API versioning. Some developer teams struggle with complaints about breaking the clients by deploying changes in their APIs, and the introduction of API versioning can be the solution to this problem. Modernization might be the right moment to introduce this mechanism if it was not present before. Please note that the versioning of the APIs comes with additional complexity and some overhead in the maintainability of the code (e.g., keeping track of which versions are unused and can be safely removed), so I do not advocate for it in all cases. But if you expect it to bring immediate benefits or feel that it should have been added to the application a long while ago, modernization is a great opportunity to involve it.

Refactoring on the Way

I have seen plenty of applications where the business logic was written directly in the controllers, web service implementations, or code-behind files of `.aspx` pages. This can make the situation much more complicated, especially when you choose the side-by-side approach I described in previous chapters. Having two applications requires being able to share code containing all the logic, and this sharing is not possible if the code depends on the old ASP.NET libraries, which are not part of the .NET Standard. Some situations can be solved by using the `Microsoft.AspNetCore.SystemWebAdapters` package that adds some of the old `System.Web` API and adapts it to the new infrastructure, but it does not cover everything.

Ideally, the code in API controllers and service implementations should be trivial; it can deal with matters specific to the web environment, such as translation of exceptions to SOAP or JSON responses and handling HTTP status codes and REST semantics, but it should avoid implementing the core application logic (e.g., enforcing business rule validation, accessing the database, and so on). This should be implemented in lower layers of the application, and the controllers or web services shall only invoke this business logic. Having the business layer represented as a separate class library project makes it much easier to introduce multi-targeting or port it to use .NET Standard or the new .NET.

In the case of in-place migration, refactoring business logic away from controllers or services may not seem as urgent as in the side-by-side scenario, but it is a good idea anyway. If the application survives another decade, it might need to be modernized again, and the same problem will reappear, only with much more business logic accumulated over the years.

Refactoring can have other beneficial effects, for example, discovering parts of code that are not used or identifying repeated code that can be exposed as a shared method or service. I have found many trivial mistakes and issues in several projects thanks to refactoring, such as missing permission checks or incomplete validations. I managed to improve the application's security and reliability because the refactoring forced me to look at the code more closely and understand what it does.

CODE SAMPLES FOR THIS CHAPTER

The migration of API applications is demonstrated in the GitHub repository available via the book's product page at `https://github.com/Apress/Modernizing-.NET-Web-Applications`. You can find the entire solution in the `chapter04` folder.

For each technology mentioned in this chapter, there is a collection of projects named using the following convention (for `Soap`, `Wcf`, `WebApi`, and `SignalR`):

- ModernizationDemo.*Soap*: The original implementation in .NET Framework

- ModernizationDemo.*Soap*Core: The modernized version running on ASP.NET Core

- ModernizationDemo.*Soap*Tests: Tests running against both versions to ensure the behavior of the API has not changed

The Soap section also contains an example of using gRPC to demonstrate the rewrite of ASP.NET Web Services to this technology. Feel free to consult the examples in the repository and experiment with them.

If you want to run the projects, follow the instructions in the Readme file in the chapter04 folder.

ASP.NET XML Web Services

XML Web Services is the oldest technology to implement RPC-like interfaces based on the SOAP protocol. It was present even in the earliest versions of .NET Framework, and despite all its problems, using it was incredibly simple. You just had to place the .asmx file in the project and implement the service, decorating its methods with the WebMethod attribute. On the other end, you added a service reference in the project and entered the URL of the service. Visual Studio did all the hard work for you – it downloaded the WSDL schema and generated the client code. Listing 4-2 shows the implementation of the web service and client code calling the service.

Listing 4-2. XML Web Service server-side and client-side code

```
// server-side
[WebService(Namespace = "http://tempuri.org/")]
[WebServiceBinding(ConformsTo = WsiProfiles.BasicProfile1_1)]
[System.ComponentModel.ToolboxItem(false)]
public class Products : System.Web.Services.WebService
{
    [WebMethod]
    public List<ProductModel> GetProducts()
    {
        ...
    }

    [WebMethod]
    public ProductModel GetProduct(int id)
    {
        ...
    }
    ...
}

// client-side
var productsClient = new ProductsClient.Products();
productsClient.Url = "http://your-server/Products.asmx";

var products = productsClient.GetProducts();
```

The code generator in Visual Studio also generated async versions of the methods (GetProductsAsync) in the client proxy class. However, since it was introduced before .NET 4.0, the methods do not use the Task-based approach and thus are not awaitable. To use it in an asynchronous way, you need to register a handler to the GetProductsCompleted event and then call GetProductsAsync. When the response is received, the event will be triggered. Because this approach is not very comfortable to use,[1] many developers preferred the synchronous API. This may be one of the moments when you may want to modernize the client applications as well. You will be able to take advantage of the modern asynchronous API.

Migrating to SoapCore

The least-effort method is to use the *SoapCore*[2] library which implements the SOAP protocol on the server. Porting the individual services is just a matter of changing the attributes on methods and adding the right startup configuration.

First, change the System.Web.Services.WebMethod attributes to System.ServiceModel.OperationContract on every method exposed from the service. Then, decorate the service class with the System.ServiceModel.ServiceContract attribute. You may have already seen these attributes before – they were used in WCF.

As mentioned in the previous section, I recommend reviewing all the methods to see if they contain any business logic. If they do, extract it into a separate class in the business layer. One important advantage of *SoapCore* is that it supports dependency injection in services. You can easily request all the dependencies in the constructor, which makes the extraction of the business logic quite easy.

Listing 4-3 shows the equivalent implementation of the service from Listing 4-1.

---

[1] For example, to make several sequential calls for each item in a collection, you must break the foreach loop into a completely unintuitive structure where the event handler needs to invoke the subsequent request or handle the end of the entire process.

[2] See the project repository at https://github.com/DigDes/SoapCore

Listing 4-3. XML Web Service rewritten using SoapCore

```
[ServiceContract]
public class Products
{
    [OperationContract]
    public List<ProductModel> GetProducts()
    {
        ...
    }

    [OperationContract]
    public ProductModel GetProduct(int id)
    {
        ...
    }
    ...
}
```

The last step is the configuration. In `Program.cs` or `Startup.cs` (depending on whether you use the new top-level statement initialization or the classic ASP.NET Core Startup scheme), you need to register SoapCore and all service classes into the service collection and then map the services with corresponding paths into the request pipeline, as shown in Listing 4-4.[3]

---

[3] The cast of the app variable to `IEndpointRouteBuilder` is a workaround for the issue in the library – it declares the same extension method on `IEndpointRouteBuilder` as well as on `IApplicationBuilder` interface, and because app implements both, the compiler is unsure which one to pick. This will probably be solved in a future version of the library.

Listing 4-4. Configuration of SoapCore

```
// register SoapCore
services.AddSoapCore();

// register services
services.AddScoped<Products>();
services.AddScoped<Orders>();

...

// add services in the request pipeline
var endpoints = app as IEndpointRouteBuilder;
endpoints.UseSoapEndpoint<Products>("/Products.asmx",
    new SoapEncoderOptions(), SoapSerializer.XmlSerializer);
endpoints.UseSoapEndpoint<Orders>("/Orders.asmx",
    new SoapEncoderOptions(), SoapSerializer.XmlSerializer);
```

So far, the migration looks quite easy. However, rigorous testing is required to make sure there are no breaking changes in the API. If your API is not covered by integration or end-to-end tests,[4] I recommend doing it before the migration. It allows you to use the same tests to verify the new version behaves correctly. You can see how it can be done in the ModernizationDemo. SoapTests project in the example repository mentioned at the beginning of

---

[4] Depending on whether the API is considered part of a larger solution or an independent application, the tests may be classified as integration tests (ensuring that one part of the system correctly communicates with another one) or as end-to-end tests (ensuring that inputs from the client result in correct outputs). The key objective is to cover the serialization and deserialization of data to be sure that migration does not introduce breaking changes on the API surface. Therefore, the tests should cover building HTTP requests by the client, parsing them by the server, invoking the appropriate action, building HTTP responses by the server, and, finally, parsing the responses by the client. The concrete technology used to build the tests is not important. If both client and server use .NET, writing the tests as C# "unit tests" may be the easiest way. In cases when the API is used by many clients in different languages, tools like Postman can be used.

this chapter. Each test is executed for the old environment as well as for the new one, and the tests compare that the received output is the same. Some effort is needed to ensure the API returns stable outputs (especially when you work with the current date and time). Because I did not want to complicate the sample project by adding a database, I used a nice library called Bogus to generate random but deterministic sample data (see the Data class in the ModernizationDemo.BusinessLogic project).

To verify that the service interface is the same, the natural idea would be to compare the old WSDL definition with the one generated from the new implementation. Unfortunately, this is not as easy as it seems because the emitted XML files use different XML namespace aliases and emit the operation and type definitions in a different order. Using text diffing tools does not help much, and I was not able to find any reasonable tool to make a nice comparison.

From just looking at the definitions in the sample project (visiting /Products.asmx?wsdl in .NET Framework and the new .NET versions and comparing the XML documents), there are several visible differences:

- The old ASP.NET did not treat response messages as nullable; however, SoapCore emits nillable=true. This will probably not cause issues when called from a .NET client,[5] but if you generate the client

---

[5] .NET and C# have a concept of Nullable Reference Types (NRT) which allows you to distinguish between nullable and non-nullable reference types (by declaring a variable as string or string? – the first one cannot contain null; the second one can). When this feature is enabled, the compiler forces you to add checks when casting from nullable to non-nullable type. However, turning this feature on in a large codebase typically produces vast amounts of errors, and thus it is typically not used in modernization projects.

The pull request 771 of the DotVVM project (https://github.com/riganti/dotvvm/pull/771) illustrates nicely how difficult it is to introduce Nullable Reference Types in larger projects. More than 400 files had to be changed to enable NRT just on a small portion of the framework (where it made the greatest sense). Although most of the code changes are trivial and look quite innocent, merging this PR introduced several behavior changes in the framework that had to be fixed later.

code for a language that distinguishes between nullable and non-nullable objects, the generated output may be different.

- The old ASP.NET emitted every service twice – once for SOAP 1.1 and once for SOAP 1.2. SoapCore emits only the SOAP 1.1 endpoint.

- The naming of operations and messages is different. The old ASP.NET names the input and output messages for operations with suffixes SoapIn/SoapOut, while SoapCore uses _InputMessage/_OutputMessage. Also, the names of operations and soapAction namespaces are different. In some languages, these names are used in the generated client code, so this may produce errors.

- You can also experience subtle changes when the service throws an exception. In the old ASP.NET, the fault code[6] is the SOAP response is Server, while in ASP.NET Core, it is Client. The different fault code results in a different exception – SoapHeaderException in the old ASP.NET vs. SoapException in ASP.NET Core. The fault string (textual representation of the error) will also differ, so if your code relies either on the exception type or on its text, you will need to adjust it appropriately.

---

[6] See www.w3.org/TR/2000/NOTE-SOAP-20000508/#_Toc478383510

When the migration is completed, you should try to generate the clients from the WSDL emitted by the new server. The generated code will likely be different (e.g., the order of members in classes). But if everything goes well, you should not experience any compile errors.

SOAP Extensions

Some applications use custom SOAP extensions[7] to customize the serialization and deserialization of messages. These extensions work as interceptors for individual web methods or entire services – you can modify the request and response messages before they are read or after they are written. The API to implement these extensions is a bit uncomfortable to use. It works with streams and does not give you the parsed representation of the SOAP message. Also, it is invoked multiple times for a single request, and hence you must filter out the phases you are not interested in.

In SoapCore, this mechanism is replaced by message processors that you can configure in the endpoint registration code. Like the mechanism of ASP.NET Core middlewares, the message processors also use the Chain of Responsibility pattern – you can decide whether to process the message or pass it to the subsequent processor.

Because message processors are quite low level (they also work with streams and often require you to deserialize the already-serialized message to be able to work with them), there is also a concept of tuners and operation invokers. These allow your code to intercept the actual service method call (after the message has been deserialized or before the result is serialized). For example, you can add your own exception handling, read values from HTTP headers, and so forth.

---

[7] See https://learn.microsoft.com/en-us/dotnet/api/system.web.services. protocols.soapextension?view=netframework-4.8.1

Reimplementing SOAP extensions as message processors is usually easier. Since they also work with streams, fewer changes in the code are needed. Using tuners instead allows you to remove inefficient duplicate serialization, which can improve performance, especially if you apply multiple extensions.

Authentication

The web.config file in old ASP.NET applications allowed the developers to choose a single mode of authentication for the entire application. Most applications used either Forms or Windows authentication. Forms authentication uses authentication tickets (encrypted, digitally signed, and time-restricted values containing the user identifier and other claims about the user). These tickets are stored in cookies and sent to the server with every request. Windows authentication, on the other hand, can use various underlying protocols, such as Kerberos and NTLM, and verifies the user identity against Active Directory or a database of local Windows users on the server. Once the user is verified, an authentication token is generated and sent in the HTTP Authorization header.[8]

There was also a Passport mode which allowed to sign in using an already discontinued .NET Passport technology. A funny fact is that the Obsolete attribute on this type says that this way of authentication was replaced by "Live ID" – a name that has also been discontinued and replaced with "Microsoft Account." The remaining mode is None which means that the application will handle the authentication itself.

---

[8] See https://techcommunity.microsoft.com/t5/iis-support-blog/windows-authentication-http-request-flow-in-iis/ba-p/324645 to learn more about the exact HTTP request flow.

The problem with this single-authentication mode is its lack of flexibility. If you need to utilize multiple ways of authentication in one application, it is not very straightforward. Additionally, since the new .NET is not tightly coupled with IIS and can work with any web server, the authentication is handled solely by the application and does not require any cooperation with the web server.

If your application uses Windows authentication, you can easily configure it in the ASP.NET Core application[9] using the `Microsoft. AspNetCore.Authentication.Negotiate` NuGet package, which is part of the platform. If the application is hosted inside IIS and Windows authentication is installed and enabled, it does not require any further actions. The authentication will be handled by IIS, and the ASP.NET Core Module will forward the tokens to the application.

In different environments, such as Linux or Mac OS, authentication will be handled in Kestrel, the built-in ASP.NET Core web server. An additional configuration is required to be able to obtain user roles and other metadata from the LDAP domain.

Another popular, even though a bit cumbersome, way of authenticating the requests was the WS-Security extension. You had to install the Web Service Enhancements[10] package which extended the configuration model with an option to specify security policies, and you could then apply the policy to selected web services or their methods. Basically, the messages were extended with a custom element that specified the username and password. The framework allowed to implement a custom token manager to let you implement a custom validation of credentials.

---

[9] See `https://learn.microsoft.com/en-us/aspnet/core/security/ authentication/windowsauth`

[10] See `www.microsoft.com/en-us/download/details.aspx?id=14089`

SoapCore contains only basic support for WS-Security with one hard-coded username and password pair, but it is quite easy to implement your own message filter, which checks the credentials any way you need, preferably using a framework like ASP.NET Core Identity. You can use the WsMessageFilter[11] as a starting point and implement custom validation of the username and password values.

The third way of authentication I used to see quite frequently was Basic authentication. It was not supported out of the box in the old ASP. NET. Most developers either configured it in the IIS (for Active Directory or local account verification) or implemented it on its own as an HTTP module[12] (especially when the credential verification involved a custom database of users). ASP.NET Core does not ship with the Basic authentication handler either, as this way of authentication is not recommended. You need to find an existing implementation[13] or write it yourself.

In general, WS-Security suffers from a similar issue as the Basic authentication – the difference between them is only whether the username and password are sent in the Authentication header or in the message body. If you must use any of these methods and cannot upgrade to a safer mechanism, make sure you use HTTPS; otherwise, the credentials will be exposed to anyone. Also, ensure the username and password are unique and not shared between multiple accounts or services. They should be rotated in regular intervals, and a revocation

---

[11] See https://github.com/DigDes/SoapCore/blob/develop/src/SoapCore/WsMessageFilter.cs

[12] See https://learn.microsoft.com/en-us/aspnet/web-api/overview/security/basic-authentication#basic-authentication-with-custom-membership

[13] See https://github.com/blowdart/idunno.Authentication for a sample implementation.

mechanism shall be put in place. To improve security, consider transitioning to API-key authentication,[14] or OAuth client credentials flow with JWT tokens.[15] Unfortunately, this will require changes on the client side.

Migrating to gRPC

If the server and all API clients are under your team's control, moving to gRPC can also be a viable option. It requires switching the technology on both ends of the communication channel, which always increases the risk of introducing breaking changes. However, unlike SoapCore, gRPC is an officially supported technology in ASP.NET Core, so it can be perceived as a more robust and future-proof choice. Additionally, the binary messages used in gRPC offer better performance thanks to faster serialization and smaller payloads that are transferred over the wire. On the other hand, due to the binary nature of messages, debugging is not as straightforward[16] as when using XML or JSON.

---

[14] The API keys are unique random secrets usually sent in the X-Api-Key header. Their validity can be restricted for several months, and they do not usually tend to be used for multiple purposes as classic combinations of usernames and passwords.

[15] Implementing this flow is not trivial, as seen at https://learn.microsoft.com/en-us/entra/identity-platform/v2-oauth2-client-creds-grant-flow, but there are many third-party services and proxy-based solutions which can help. For example, you can deploy the application into Microsoft Azure App Service and turn on the Azure Entra ID authentication, which will make sure that only requests authenticated using valid tokens obtained through the OAuth endpoint of Azure will reach the application.

[16] One of the popular debugging tools is Progress Telerik Fiddler Everywhere. In order to understand the payloads, you will need to provide the .proto file, as explained at https://docs.telerik.com/fiddler-everywhere/knowledge-base/capturing-grpc-traffic

Due to the RPC (Remote Procedure Call) nature of the ASP.NET XML Web Services, the transition to gRPC is not that painful, although it is not possible to achieve the same syntax of the method calls.

In gRPC, the contracts of services and messages are commonly defined using a .proto file. Once you have this file, there are tools to generate client proxies for all the commonly used programming languages.

Listing 4-5 shows a .proto file which defines the service interface and the message types. The syntax is quite self-explanatory, and you will get familiar with the format very quickly. As you can see, the service section defines the service and its methods, including the request and response message. After that, the file contains message definitions. The names of types are quite similar to what we are used to from .NET. Every field specifies the unique number defining its position in the serialized message. This is used for versioning[17] – if you change the service definition but make sure the same fields are using the same numbers, there is a high chance that the clients will survive the change. The repeated keyword is used to indicate arrays – it says that the value may appear in the message any number of times.

Since gRPC is a platform-independent protocol, some .NET-specific types, such as decimal or enums, are not supported. Therefore, I use double in the example as its behavior is the closest to decimal. For enums, I use string. It is also worth mentioning that DateTime and TimeSpan are represented by well-known types timestamp and duration (an import to the "google/protobuf/timestamp.proto" definition is necessary). However, in the case of DateTime, you are limited to transferring the Utc values only. If the Kind of the date is Local, you will get an exception. You can easily run into this issue if you use DateTime.Now or build the date values from the individual parts.

---

[17] See https://learn.microsoft.com/en-us/aspnet/core/grpc/versioning for details on how gRPC service versioning works.

Nullable types are supported via wrappers. For example, the string type that naturally supports nulls is represented by google.protobuf. StringValue in gRPC (notice the import at the top that is required to use this type).

All types, such as decimal, date/time, or enums, work without any special action in ASP.NET XML Web Services. In gRPC, they will require explicit conversions in some places.

Listing 4-5. An example proto file to describe the service contract

```
syntax = "proto3";
import "google/protobuf/wrappers.proto";

service Products {
  rpc GetProducts (GetProductsRequest)
    returns (GetProductsResponse);
  rpc GetProduct (GetProductRequest)
    returns (GetProductResponse);
  rpc AddProduct (AddProductRequest)
    returns (AddProductResponse);
  ...
}

message ProductModel {
  int32 Id = 1;
  string Title = 2;
  string Description = 3;
  google.protobuf.StringValue ImageUrl = 4;
  bool IsOnSale = 5;
  string Unit = 6;
  double UnitPrice = 7;
}
```

```
message GetProductsRequest {
}
message GetProductsResponse {
        repeated ProductModel Products = 1;
}

message GetProductRequest {
        int32 Id = 1;
}
message GetProductResponse {
        ProductModel Product = 1;
}

message AddProductRequest {
        ProductModel Product = 1;
}
message AddProductResponse {
        int32 Id = 1;
}
...
```

Listing 4-6 shows how calling the service looks like in the original ASP. NET XML Web Services and with gRPC. The gRPC client lets you use the standard async/await syntax which is much more comfortable to use than the old event-based asynchronous approach.

Unfortunately, the method signatures are different – gRPC assumes one request and response message for each method. Even methods without arguments must define a single empty message, and void methods must return an empty message.

Some messages may seem unnecessary at first glance. For example, instead of defining GetProductRequest message, we could just use int32 instead because the method accepts just one int parameter – the ID of the product. However, this is not a good strategy from a long-term perspective.

First, you lose information as the message type is just `int32` without any name – it may be unclear what the parameter represents. Second, it hurts the versioning – in the case of adding another parameter to the method, the `int32` would have to be changed for a different message type, which would create a breaking change. The same reason also justifies the empty messages – if you add a field in them in the future, the service will survive it without any problem (you just added a field to a message but did not change the method signature).

However, because of this, switching from ASP.NET XML Web Services requires changing the signature when calling remote methods, as shown in Listing 4-6.

Listing 4-6. Calling the ASP.NET XML Web Service and gRPC service

```
// ASP.NET XML Web Services
var productsClient = new ProductsClient.Products()
{
    Url = "https://url:port/Products.asmx"
};

// calling method without parameters
IEnumerable<ProductModel> products =
    productsClient.GetProducts();

// calling a method with parameters
ProductModel product = productsClient.GetProduct(productId);

// gRPC
var channel = GrpcChannel.ForAddress("https://url:port/");
var productsClient = new Products.ProductsClient(channel);
```

```
// calling method without parameters
GetProductsResponse productsResponse =
    productsClient.GetProducts(new GetProductsRequest());
IEnumerable<ProductModel> products = productsResponse.Products;

// calling a method with parameters
GetProductResponse productResponse =
    productsClient.GetProduct(new GetProductRequest() {
        Id = productId
    });
ProductModel product = productResponse.Product;
```

The service implementation on the server works in a similar manner, as you can see in Listing 4-7. All methods are generated as asynchronous, and they also get an extra parameter, ServerCallContext, with additional information about the method call. gRPC tooling will generate the base class (Products.ProductsBase) for the service automatically – your job is only to override all methods. Same as in the client code, the signatures change because the arguments and the result are wrapped with the message request and response objects.

Listing 4-7. Implementation of the gRPC service

```
public class ProductsImplementation : Products.ProductsBase
{
    public override
        async Task<GetProductsResponse> GetProducts(
            GetProductsRequest request,
            ServerCallContext context)
    {
```

```
    return new GetProductsResponse()
    {
        Products = ...
    };
}

...

}
```

Like in the case of SoapCore, the authentication has also changed with gRPC. You need to migrate the old ASP.NET mechanism to its ASP.NET Core equivalent.

On the client side, there are two ways to pass the authentication metadata such as a bearer token – on a per-call or a per-channel basis. Listing 4-8 shows how to configure the authentication in both ways.

Listing 4-8. Configuring authentication for the gRPC client

```
// per-channel authentication
var credentials = CallCredentials.FromInterceptor(
    (context, metadata) =>
    {
        metadata.Add("Authorization", $"Bearer ...");
    });
var channel = GrpcChannel.ForAddress("https://url:port/",
    new GrpcChannelOptions
    {
        Credentials = ChannelCredentials.Create(
                        new SslCredentials(), credentials)
    });
var productsClient = new Products.ProductsClient(channel);

// per-method authentication
var headers = new Metadata();
```

```
headers.Add("Authorization", $"Bearer ...");
var result = productsClient.GetProducts(
    new GetProductsRequest(), headers);
```

One important limitation is that the HTTP server and all proxies in front of it, if any, must support HTTP/2 and HTTPS. This should not be a problem unless you run on an obscure or very dated infrastructure. However, in some environments (e.g., if you use Cloudflare as a proxy in front of your web application), gRPC is disabled by default and needs to be switched on explicitly.

The error code may be misleading in such cases. I remember spending a couple of hours figuring out why my gRPC service was not called. There was nothing in the application logs (which indicates the request did not get there at all), and all I was getting was a 502 Bad Gateway error. The cause was the Cloudflare default settings which have gRPC disabled (which is reasonable; I was just not aware of that setting).

Rewriting to gRPC can also be a meaningful option for Windows Communication Foundation. It requires more effort, but the benefits it offers in terms of performance, versioning, and wide acceptance across the industry can be interesting to many teams and projects.

Windows Communication Foundation

WCF is my favorite example of a magnificent idea that was killed by excessive complexity. I am fully aware that designing things to be simple and easy to use is an extremely complicated task. This principle reaches far beyond the software development industry. In various circumstances, I heard urban architects, graphics designers, artists, or even music historians sharing a similar experience.

If you look at some works of Mozart, you will find out that he often used relatively simple rhythmic patterns and harmonies with just two or three chords (in contrast to other great composers who came later and whose music was tremendously complicated). For example, in his famous *A Little Night Music*, the viola and violoncello just repeat the same tone again and again, eight times in each measure. To hear these two voices separately would be quite boring, but the clever combination of these simple parts creates an extraordinary experience. Mozart is recognized as the greatest composer of all time. Maybe the magic of his music lies in this kind of simplicity which is so difficult to design.

WCF was built on the idea of abstraction over communication between applications. No matter what underlying communication protocol is going to be used, there is a contract generated from C# interfaces and classes decorated by attributes, and that is the only thing the developer is supposed to care about. The technology supports SOAP and REST and includes its own binary protocol based on TCP/IP, as well as plenty of others, not excluding messaging technologies such as Microsoft Message Queuing (MSMQ) or various dual-channel scenarios where each side of the channel could send requests to the other.

A similar abstraction was built around communication security; you could secure it on the transport level (by using HTTPS or other connection-level encryption methods, such as client certificates), the message level (each message can utilize security mechanisms such as authentication or encryption), or any of the possible combinations.

WCF also had a robust mechanism of tracing and logging. With a tiny configuration change, you could create a diagnostic `.svclog` file that could be analyzed using the Service Trace Viewer tool. Generating service contract metadata was supported by design. You could either generate the client classes at the design time using a command-line tool or Visual Studio or have the client proxies generated at runtime just from the service interface. This helped to avoid various issues caused by forgetting to regenerate the client proxies after the service contract had been changed.

Windows Communication Foundation had several problems: subpar performance (the heavy abstractions do not contribute much to making things fast), various issues with non-.NET clients where many features were not supported, and an overly complex configuration model. The last of the issues got several improvements in later versions of the .NET Framework, but the experience of many developers with WCF was that it was easy to implement the service and make the communication work on the developer machine, but configuring it for reliable operation in production was very tricky.

On the other hand, WCF implemented many features that REST lacked even several years after the rise of its popularity. The service metadata exchange and client proxy generation based on C# interfaces was much more comfortable to use over today's widely used OpenAPI, which requires installing and configuring Swashbuckle, NSwag, or another community-maintained library and setting up some process to generate proxies in order to make everything work.

Today, the tools for that are quite mature, but the experience during the first years of ASP.NET Web API was not that smooth. Still, configuring the generation of client proxies – a thing that used to take minutes with WCF – can still take hours with REST because of the need to do multiple steps and use various tools and libraries for that. For sure, the extra time is worth the flexibility and other benefits REST offers. But is it that much to want both?

Migrating to CoreWCF

When .NET Core was introduced, WCF was not on the list of supported technologies. However, thanks to the initiative of many people, the community-authored project CoreWCF was started. Its primary goal is to implement WCF on the new .NET, excluding just a few features that are tightly coupled to .NET Framework–specific areas. However, the recent versions of this library introduced several new functionalities and integrations, such as support for various messaging technologies like Apache Kafka and RabbitMQ or integration with the Authorize attribute in ASP.NET Core.

In WCF, every service has a contract declared as a .NET interface. Then, there is a class that implements it. In ASP.NET projects, the .svc files were used to define the service endpoint – they contained only one line of code specifying the implementation of the service. All these concepts are shown in Listing 4-9.

Listing 4-9. Anatomy of a WCF service – the interface, the implementation, and the .svc file

```
// interface
[ServiceContract]
public interface IProductService
{
    [OperationContract]
    List<ProductModel> GetProducts();

    ...
}

// implementation
public class ProductService : IProductService
{
    public List<ProductModel> GetProducts()
    {
        return service.GetProducts();
    }

    ...
}

// .svc file
<%@ ServiceHost Service="SomeNamespace.ProductService" %>
```

In the later versions of WCF, the .svc file became optional; it was possible to register the service using the file-less activation.[18]

In CoreWCF, these files are not needed – the services are registered in the Startup routine of the ASP.NET Core application. The code of the service interface and its implementation can remain without changes – the ServiceContract and OperationContract attributes are present in the System.ServiceModel.Primitives NuGet package and are used by CoreWCF. From this point, the migration looks easy.

What has changed significantly is the configuration. In .NET Framework, the configuration of the services was typically specified in the web.config file, as shown in Listing 4-10. Because even developers who used WCF in the past probably do not remember how it is designed, allow me to describe it briefly. In general, it consists of three concepts:

- *Bindings* define the underlying transport protocol. There are several kinds of bindings, and each binding allows to specify parameters of the underlying protocol, such as security, maximum message sizes, and others. Most frequently, the following binding types are used:

- basicHttpBinding represents SOAP communication based on WS-I Basic Profile 1.1 (known as SOAP 1.1). It is compatible with ASP.NET XML Web Services and is typically used when communicating with clients written in different technologies than .NET to achieve maximum compatibility.

- wsHttpBinding uses SOAP 1.2, supports advanced concepts like reliable sessions, and has more security features (such as message-level security using Kerberos).

---

[18] See https://learn.microsoft.com/en-us/previous-versions/dotnet/articles/ee354381(v=msdn.10)?redirectedfrom=MSDN#file-less-activation

- netTcpBinding uses custom binary communication on a TCP connection, which is great for scenarios where WCF is used on both ends.

- netMsmqBinding channels the messages through Message Queuing (MSMQ) technology, a Windows component that provides reliable messaging. The main advantage of using queuing is failure isolation; when the target service is down, the message waits in the queue until the issue is resolved. Additionally, the service cannot be taken down by too many requests at the same time, as it can happen with HTTP or TCP scenarios; the messages will wait in the queue until the service picks them up.

- *Behaviors* can configure various aspects of the services: whether it shall provide the metadata endpoint with WSDL definition, whether it shall return detailed error messages, how the communication will be authenticated and authorized, and what identity store will be used (Windows, ASP.NET Membership, custom provider, and so on), and so on. It also allows configuring tracing, timeouts, throttling, modifying the behavior of serialization, and more.

- *Services* specify the individual services exposed by the application. Each service can reference a specific behavior configuration and have several endpoints, each of them referencing a different binding (communication protocol).

Listing 4-10. An example configuration of a WCF service

```
<system.serviceModel>
  <services>
    <service name="ProductService">
      <host>
        <baseAddresses>
          <add baseAddress="http://localhost:50999/" />
        </baseAddresses>
      </host>
      <endpoint address=""
                binding="basicHttpBinding"
                bindingConfiguration="Basic"
                contract="SomeNamespace.IProductService" />
    </service>
  </services>

  <bindings>
    <basicHttpBinding>
      <binding name="Basic"
               maxReceivedMessageSize="2000000">
        <security mode="None" />
      </binding>
    </basicHttpBinding>
  </bindings>

  <behaviors>
    <serviceBehaviors>
      <behavior>
        <serviceMetadata httpGetEnabled="true" />
        <serviceDebug includeExceptionDetailInFaults="true"/>
```

```
        </behavior>
      </serviceBehaviors>
    </behaviors>
</system.serviceModel>
```

As you can see in the listing, there is one service named
ProductService, with one endpoint using basicHttpBinding named
Basic, and the default behavior configuration. The binding specified no
security (there will be no HTTPS), and the behavior enables the metadata
endpoint to provide WSDL definition, as well as detailed error messages
that are useful for debugging.

In later versions of WCF, it was possible to configure everything using
the C# code, but the structure and semantics remained the same. Even
for the simplest service, you had to configure at least the service, binding,
and endpoint. When the authentication was used, things started to be
complicated.

Every client consuming WCF services also needed a subset of this
configuration. Especially the binding configuration had to match the
server; otherwise, each side would try to communicate using a different
protocol or incompatible means of security.

In CoreWCF, the configuration must be specified in the code. The
structure remains very similar; basically, you can look at the web.config
and transfer the elements and their attributes to the C# code. CoreWCF
works with the built-in ASP.NET Core dependency injection framework,
so its registration looks similar to the registration of any other modern
library. Listing 4-11 shows the previous configuration converted into
CoreWCF. There is one notable difference – in the case of old ASP.NET, the
relative URL of the service in the application defined by the presence of the
ProductService.svc file (which refers to the concrete type of the service).
In the case of CoreWCF, you must specify this path in the code, as the .svc
files are not used.

Listing 4-11. Configuration of a simple service in CoreWCF

```
var builder = WebApplication.CreateBuilder(args);

// Add WSDL support
builder.Services
    .AddServiceModelServices()
    .AddServiceModelMetadata();

var app = builder.Build();

// register WCF services
app.UseServiceModel(options =>
{
    var httpBinding = new BasicHttpBinding();
    options
        .AddService<ProductService>(serviceOptions =>
        {
            serviceOptions.BaseAddresses.Add(
                new Uri("http://localhost:50999/"));
            serviceOptions.DebugBehavior
                .IncludeExceptionDetailInFaults = true;
        })
        .AddServiceEndpoint<ProductService, IProductService>(
            httpBinding, "ProductService.svc");
});

// enable metadata endpoint
var serviceMetadataBehavior =
    app.Services.GetRequiredService<ServiceMetadataBehavior>();
serviceMetadataBehavior.HttpGetEnabled = true;
```

211

The migration to CoreWCF thus involves installing CoreWCF NuGet packages, rewriting the configuration from XML to C#, and finally transferring the services and their interfaces. The namespaces of CoreWCF are the same as in WCF; therefore, there is a high chance you will be able to migrate the services with no code changes at all.

As in the case of ASP.NET XML Web Services, I recommend rigorous testing of all operations to ensure that data is serialized and transferred correctly.

You can find the example tests in the example repository described at the beginning of this chapter. Each test uses the same code to call the .NET Framework and new .NET version and makes sure the output is the same (provided that the server responses are deterministic). Several of the tests try to simulate various error states and check that the same exception is thrown.

Authentication

The matrix of possible combinations of authentication and authorization modes in WCF is quite extensive, so it does not make sense to try to list all of them. The most frequent ones were, for sure, Windows authentication and username-password authentication, which validates the credentials against a custom user store in the database, usually facilitated by ASP.NET Membership or ASP.NET Identity.

CoreWCF also brings support to ASP.NET Core's Authorize attribute,[19] which may be useful to implement modern ways of authentication, such as API keys or JWT (JSON Web Tokens) sent in HTTP request headers. The process will be the same as with ASP.NET Web API. If you think

---

[19] See https://corewcf.github.io/blog/2023/02/19/aspnetcore-authorization-support

about migrating the authentication to these new approaches, refer to the next section about authentication in REST scenarios. The only thing you need to configure on the binding's transport security credential type to HttpClientCredentialType.InheritedFromHost.

In the case of Windows authentication, everything is handled by ASP. NET Core. CoreWCF integrates with its authentication pipeline, which means you do not need to make any extra steps. CoreWCF respects the PrincipalPermission attribute used in WCF which can restrict operations only to particular users or roles.

basicHttpBinding and wsHttpBinding in the old WCF allowed to secure the messages by a combination of username and password – the same mechanism used by ASP.NET XML Web Services extended with WS Security. WCF allowed validation of these credentials either using ASP. NET Membership Provider or by providing a custom token validator. Since ASP.NET Membership Provider is not present in ASP.NET Core, you must migrate to another type of authentication or to a custom validator to check the credentials, ideally using ASP.NET Core Identity.

To validate the username and password, you need to implement your own UserNamePasswordValidator. If you need to work also with user roles, you can implement a custom authorization policy that will detect the roles of the user and build the principal object that will contain them. All this is shown in Listing 4-12.

Listing 4-12. Example of implementing a custom username and password validator and role authorization policy

```
// configuration in startup
app.UseServiceModel(options =>
{
    ...

    options.ConfigureServiceHostBase<ProductService>(
        hostOptions =>
```

213

```
    {
        hostOptions.Credentials.UserNameAuthentication
            .UserNamePasswordValidationMode =
                UserNamePasswordValidationMode.Custom;
        hostOptions.Credentials.UserNameAuthentication
            .CustomUserNamePasswordValidator =
                new CustomUserNamePasswordValidator();

        hostOptions.Authorization.PrincipalPermissionMode =
            PrincipalPermissionMode.Custom;
        hostOptions.Authorization
        .ExternalAuthorizationPolicies =
            new IAuthorizationPolicy[] {
                new CustomRoleAuthorizationPolicy()
            }.AsReadOnly();
    });
});

// custom username and password validator
public class CustomUserNamePasswordValidator
    : UserNamePasswordValidator
{
    public override async ValueTask ValidateAsync(
        string userName, string password)
    {
        // TODO: check the credentials and throw an exception
        // when invalid

    }
}

// custom authorization policy to add roles to the user
public class CustomRoleAuthorizationPolicy
```

```
    : IAuthorizationPolicy
{

    public string Id => "some unique policy name";
    public ClaimSet Issuer => ClaimSet.System;

    public bool Evaluate(EvaluationContext evaluationContext,
        ref object state)
    {
        // extract the GenericIdentity object from properties
        if (!evaluationContext.Properties
            .TryGetValue("Identities",out var identities)
            || identities is not List<IIdentity>
                typedIdentities
            || typedIdentities is not
                [ GenericIdentity identity ])
        {
            return false;
        }

        var userName = identity.FindFirst(ClaimTypes.Name)
            !.Value;
        var roles = GetRolesByUser(userName);
        evaluationContext.Properties["Principal"] =
            new GenericPrincipal(identity, roles);
        return true;
    }

    private string[] GetRolesByUser(string userName)
    {
        // TODO: return the user's roles
    }
}
```

If your application used ASP.NET Membership Providers, see Chapter 6 for more information about migration to ASP.NET Core Identity. Then, you can use UserManager and RoleManager to validate user credentials, as well as retrieve the roles to which the user belongs.

Unsupported Features

Before you start migration to CoreWCF, you should check whether all WCF features that your application uses are supported. Unfortunately, I have not found a road map that is regularly updated and shows what pieces are incomplete. The best source of information is the Release Notes[20] section on the project's GitHub.

Since most of the features have already been ported, I recommend starting the migration and seeing if something is missing. You will discover the blind spots when rewriting the web.config configuration to C# – the API will either not be present in the package at all, or it will throw NotSupportedException.

If you find some missing features, there are several options:

- Find a workaround – for example, use another type of binding or change the API to avoid the unsupported scenario. This will probably require making changes to the client applications as well.

- Look whether the feature is not already in progress and configure your NuGet to use the nightly builds.[21] You can be sure the team will be happy to receive early feedback. Consider contributing to the repository yourself – sometimes, the feature is already ported, but

---

[20] See https://github.com/CoreWCF/CoreWCF/releases

[21] Be aware of the risks of using non-production releases. On the other hand, assuming the migration can take significant time, there is a chance that a stable release containing the feature will be published before the migration is finished.

the API is marked as internal because of missing tests. Helping the team to cover the feature with tests does not have to take much time and will be useful to the .NET community.

- Use the side-by-side approach and migrate at least a portion of the API surface. Use the old project and .NET Framework only for the things that are not supported yet. Also, watch the announcements repo[22] of CoreWCF to be notified when a new version is released.

- Postpone the modernization to a later time. If you use Git, keep the unfinished work in a branch, so you can return to it in the future. Merging the changes from the main branch occasionally is a good idea to prevent too many conflicts.

My last thought for this section is to encourage everyone to participate in open source projects. In my opinion, the .NET community relies too much on official Microsoft solutions, and the maintainers of many open source projects frequently feel nobody really appreciates the work they do. If you are involved in a modernization project in your company and you plan to use an open source project, it makes sense to contribute to it, either by spending some developer effort or via some kind of company sponsorship. If you decide to rely on any technology, you want it to thrive.

Do not be afraid to touch the codebase of a large and publicly visible project. Most maintainers will be happy to provide advice or help, as there are never enough people willing to contribute. Furthermore, a contribution does not have to mean writing the actual feature. Submitting

---

[22] See https://github.com/CoreWCF/announcements

a pull request with a failing test to reproduce the behavior saves significant time for the maintainers and greatly increases the chances of a quick resolution. Writing a blog post or a documentation page is a useful contribution as well.

CoreWCF Improvements over WCF

As I mentioned earlier, it is nice to see that CoreWCF is not only trying to catch up with the feature set of .NET Framework, but it is also adding new features.

CoreWCF is split between several NuGet packages. There is `CoreWCF.Http` for `basicHttpBinding`, `wsHttpBinding`, and `webHttpBinding`, there is `CoreWCF.NetTcp` for `netTcpBinding`, and so on.

Several new packages contain integrations with various messaging technologies, such as Rabbit MQ or Apache Kafka. WCF's abstraction allows for using various communication channels, and the ability to dispatch operations via messaging looks interesting.

Every time I used RabbitMQ or Microsoft Service Bus, I was a bit disappointed by the fact that the messages were just strings or byte arrays with no fixed schema. Since there can be many different types of messages, you must make sure the publisher and consumer sides will use the same structure of the message. In simpler scenarios, there can be a separate queue for each message type, but you often need to transmit various types of messages in the same queue (e.g., to guarantee the processing order). To implement this mechanism, you usually have to make your own format of payloads – some kind of envelope that specifies the message type and wraps the message payload. When reading the message, you need first to determine the type of message and then deserialize the payload into the correct message type, as shown in Listing 4-13. It is not substantially difficult to implement, but a higher-level abstraction would be useful. You can consider using existing formats with the support of versioning, such as Protobuf.

When both ends of the communication are .NET, CoreWCF allows for easy sharing of the service interface and model objects in a class library with the luxury of supporting all .NET-specific types, such as decimal, enums, or generics.

The ReadMessage method in Listing 4-13 also demonstrates how we can efficiently parse the JSON payload using Utf8JsonReader without unnecessary allocations. Instead of deserializing the complete object into a hierarchy of JsonNode objects to read the messageType property and then deserializing from the JsonNode tree, the code reads the byte array containing the JSON sequentially by tokens (such as start object, property name, string value, and so on) and makes sure the structure is correct (the messageType property must come first). Once it advances to the payload property, it already knows the message type, and thus it can call Deserialize with the reader instance. It will continue reading tokens from the reader and build the desired message object.

Listing 4-13. Publisher and subscriber for messages of multiple types

```
// message contracts (shared by both sides)
public record OrderCreated(int OrderId);
public record CustomerCreated(string FirstName,
    string LastName);

// publisher side
public async Task PublishMessage<TMessage>(TMessage message)
{
    // create the envelope
    var envelope = new
    {
        messageType = typeof(TMessage).FullName,
        payload = data
    };
```

219

```
    // send the message
    var json = JsonSerializer.Serialize(envelope);
    await sender.SendMessageAsync(new ServiceBusMessage(json));
}

// subscriber side
// receiver is a Microsoft ServiceBus sender instance
// pointing to a queue
public async Task ProcessMessages()
{
    await foreach (var message in
        receiver.ReceiveMessagesAsync())
    {
        // parse the message
        var messageInstance = ReadMessage(message.Body);

        // process the message based on its type
        // in real-world applications, message handlers can be
        // resolved dynamically, for example using MediatR
        if (messageInstance is OrderCreated orderCreated)
        {
            HandleOrderCreated(orderCreated);
        }
        else if (messageInstance is CustomerCreated
            customerCreated)
        {
            HandleCustomerCreated(customerCreated);
        }
        else
        {
            throw new NotSupportedException(
                "Unknown message type!");
```

```
        }
    }
}

private object ReadMessage(BinaryData body)
{
    var reader = new Utf8JsonReader(body);

    // read start object
    if (!reader.Read()
        || reader.TokenType != JsonTokenType.StartObject)
    {
        throw new JsonException(
            "Message must be JSON object!");
    }

    // read messageType property and make sure it is string
    if (!reader.Read()
        || reader.TokenType != JsonTokenType.PropertyName
        || !reader.ValueTextEquals("messageType")
        || !reader.Read()
        || reader.TokenType != JsonTokenType.String)
    {
        throw new JsonException(
            "Expected messageType string property!");
    }
    var messageType = Type.GetType(reader.GetString(),
        throwOnError: true);

    // read payload property
    if (!reader.Read()
        || reader.TokenType != JsonTokenType.PropertyName
```

```
        || !reader.ValueTextEquals("payload")
        || !reader.Read())
    {
        throw new JsonException("Expected payload property!");
    }

    return JsonSerializer.Deserialize(ref reader, messageType);
}
```

Even though both sender and receiver work with strongly typed messages, the WCF approach with an interface defining all supported service operations is probably more comfortable. Thanks to service metadata endpoints, it is easier to keep the interfaces on both ends in sync.

ASP.NET Web API

REST started being popular even in the days of WCF. However, its webHttpBinding was not easy to use and had too many limitations. That is why Microsoft introduced ASP.NET Web API, a technology specifically designed for implementing HTTP endpoints.

At first glance, the new ASP.NET Core API controllers look very similar to the old ASP.NET Web API. However, there are many subtle differences in routing, JSON serialization, handling of other formats, such as XML or URL-encoded forms, and more.

Like in ASP.NET MVC, the Web APIs are organized in controllers with one or more operations exposed to the users. Which operation will be called is defined by routing specified either by conventions or by attributes on the controller class and its methods. Each operation defines an HTTP method (GET, POST, PUT, DELETE, and others) and specifies binding for its parameters – they can be retrieved from the route, query string, request body, or other sources.

ASP.NET Web API does not support OpenAPI out of the box. However, it provides a metadata layer called API Explorer, which can be used by external libraries to generate OpenAPI documents. Since the birth of ASP.NET Web API, there have been two popular open source libraries for that: *Swashbuckle* and *NSwag*. In .NET 9, Microsoft announced to come up with their own implementation of this standard.[23]

Migrating Controllers

The first step in migrating API applications is to fix API controllers' base classes and namespaces and review attributes on their methods because of slightly different semantics.

In the old ASP.NET Web API, the controllers were inherited from `System.Web.Http.ApiController`. ASP.NET Core uses a different base class – `Microsoft.AspNetCore.Mvc.ControllerBase`. There is also a `Controller` class in the same namespace, but it includes support for views and is designed to be used in MVC web pages.

Optionally, the controllers may be marked with the `ApiController` attribute. This turns on several behaviors:

- Disables the use of conventional routing (generic route pattern for multiple controllers) and requires explicit attribute routes

- Automatically validates input parameters (using the Model Validation framework) and generates an HTTP 400 (Bad Request) response automatically if the `ModelState` is not valid

---

[23] See `https://github.com/dotnet/aspnetcore/issues/54599`

- Automatically infers the binding source for each parameter (whether they come from the query string, route, or body)

- Recognizes IFormFile and IFormFileCollection binding for multipart/form-data requests

- Generates machine-readable JSON responses for failed requests (HTTP code 400 or above)

- Enables support for the Consumes attribute that can specify which content types will be accepted by API operations (e.g., application/json)

I recommend using the ApiController attribute, mainly because of automatic input model validation. It is much easier to mark your model classes with appropriate validation attributes (such as Required, Range, and so on) or implement the IValidatableObject interface to enforce consistency of the data your controller accepts.

Explicit HTTP Methods

The old ASP.NET Web API could infer the HTTP method from the controller action's name. For example, a method named GetProducts was automatically treated as HTTP GET while DeleteProductById was HTTP DELETE by default. This worked when the action name started with a word defining the HTTP method.

This mechanism is not present in ASP.NET Core. Therefore, an explicit specification of HTTP methods is needed. You will need to go through all controllers and add HttpGet, HttpPost, or other attributes to every action. If multiple HTTP methods are supported, you can use the AcceptVerbs attribute same as in the old ASP.NET Web API.

Routing

The first version of ASP.NET Web API supported convention-based routing, which worked quite well in CRUD scenarios, as shown in Listing 4-14. However, when the API surface got more complicated, you had to specify routes for each controller individually. The {controller} placeholder in the route template is substituted automatically with the name inferred from the controller (e.g., Orders standing for OrdersController class), and the {id} parameter is marked as optional because it is not needed in all actions.

Listing 4-14. Convention-based route registration

```
config.Routes.MapHttpRoute(
    name: "DefaultApi",
    routeTemplate: "api/{controller}/{id}",
    defaults: new { id = RouteParameter.Optional }
);
```

Later versions of ASP.NET Web API added support for attribute routing. The controllers could be decorated with the RoutePrefix attributes, and their methods could use the Route attribute. The full route URL of the action was composed by combining the fragments specified in these two attributes, as shown in Listing 4-15. The GetOrder method is mapped to api/Orders/{id}, and the constraint requires the id parameter to be an integer value.[24]

---

[24] The constraint may seem redundant at first glance because the GetOrder method requires the id parameter to be integer anyway. However, with the constraint, the route will not be matched for non-integer values and may potentially be handled by another route (e.g., I could add an action mapped to api/Orders/summary). Without the constraint, an error would be produced as the route would be matched and the parameter parsing would fail when the operation is invoked.

Listing 4-15. Attribute-based routing in the old ASP.NET Web API

```
[RoutePrefix("api/Orders")]
public class OrdersController : ApiController
{
    [Route("{id:int}")]
    public OrderModel GetOrder(int id)
    {
        return service.GetOrder(id);
    }
}
```

The new .NET supports convention routing in MVC and recommends using attribute-based routing for REST APIs as it is the only option for the ApiController attribute. The RoutePrefix attribute is merged with the Route attribute (which can now be used for both controllers and actions). The routes can use tokens (such as [controller] and [action]) that are replaced by the runtime with the inferred names from class and method names. Listing 4-16 shows the equivalent registration in ASP.NET Core.

Listing 4-16. Attribute-based routing in ASP.NET Core

```
[ApiController]
[Route("api/[controller]")]
public class OrdersController : ControllerBase
{
    [HttpGet]
    [Route("{id:int}")]
    public OrderModel GetOrder(int id)
    {
        return service.GetOrder(id);
    }
}
```

Action Results

ASP.NET Web API actions can return plain .NET objects. In such cases, the response is generated automatically and contains the serialized result in JSON, XML, or other formats (based on the incoming message format and the Accept header).

However, you do not have much control over how the response looks like. To return error responses and specify the HTTP status code, you can throw HttpResponseException, but the options are quite limited.

Therefore, ASP.NET Web API offers more options. It supports returning the complete HttpResponseMessage objects, which gives you full control over the response. This is useful when you need to return files or other specific types of content not produced by serialization or when you want to set some response headers.

The last option, a nice compromise between the previous methods, is Web API's IHttpActionResult. This interface is basically a factory for HttpResponseMessage, and it simplifies building HTTP responses for common situations. The controller contains handy methods such as Ok, NotFound, Unauthorized, BadRequest, or Redirect, which make the API very easy to use. These methods are just shorthand for creating common IHttpActionResult objects, and you can easily extend the palette with your own extension methods. Action results also make testing the controllers easier – it is easier to assert that the action returns RedirectResult with a specific location than to dig in the HttpResponseMessage and look at its status code and headers.

Listing 4-17 shows using the action results. The principle of action results is very similar in ASP.NET Core; however, the return type is IActionResult instead of IHttpActionResult. If you implemented custom action results, you would have to change them as well. You can also use ResponseType/ProducesResponseType attributes to provide more information about the returned type. In ASP.NET Core, you can provide multiple variants for each status code.

Listing 4-17. Web API methods returning Action Results

```
// old ASP.NET Web API
[RoutePrefix("api/Orders")]
public class OrdersController : ApiController
{
    [Route("{id:int}")]
    [ResponseType(typeof(OrderModel))]
    public IHttpActionResult GetOrder(int id)
    {
        return Ok(service.GetOrder(id));
    }
}

// ASP.NET Core
[ApiController]
[Route("api/[controller]")]
public class OrdersController : ControllerBase
{
    [HttpGet]
    [Route("{id:int}")]
    [ProducesResponseType<OrderModel>(200)]
    public IActionResult GetOrder(int id)
    {
        return Ok(service.GetOrder(id));
    }
}
```

If your API methods return plain objects instead of action results, you may hit subtle incompatibilities. For example, in the case of void methods (or Task methods without a result), the old ASP.NET Web API returns HTTP 204 (No Content), in contrast to ASP.NET Core which returns

HTTP 200 (OK). This leads to different OpenAPI definitions and can even break clients who are strict about the response status codes (such as client proxies generated by NSwag).

This can be fixed either by changing the methods to return IActionResult and returning NoContentResult explicitly or by an action filter which will fix the response code, as shown in Listing 4-18. It is important to mention that the filter itself changes only the runtime behavior and would get out of sync with the OpenAPI specification. Therefore, you must either add the [ProduceResponseType(204)] attribute to all affected methods or write an operation filter for Swashbuckle or NSwag to reflect the change in metadata documents.

Listing 4-18. Action filter to set the status code to 204 on void action methods

```
public class FixNoContentResponseOnVoidActionsFilter
    : ActionFilterAttribute
{
    public override void OnActionExecuted(
        ActionExecutedContext context)
    {
        if (context.ActionDescriptor
            is ControllerActionDescriptor controllerAction
            // it is a controller action
            && context.Exception is null
            // did not end with exception
            && context.Result is EmptyResult
            // the result is empty
        )
        {
            // if the action returns void or Task,
            // set status code to 204
```

```
        if (controllerAction.MethodInfo.ReturnType
            == typeof(void)
            || controllerAction.MethodInfo.ReturnType
            == typeof(Task))
        {
            context.HttpContext.Response.StatusCode = 204;
        }
    }
    base.OnActionExecuted(context);
}
}
```

Parameter Binding

When action methods specified parameters, ASP.NET Web API used a simple heuristic to infer the source of the value. Primitive types (numbers, boolean, strings, dates, Guid, and more) were by default expected to be in the URL (either in the route parameter or in the query string), while complex types (objects or arrays) came by default from the request body, deserialized using the media-type formatter selected based on the Content-Type header (application/json in the vast majority of cases). You could use the FromUri and FromBody attributes to override this default behavior.

In ASP.NET Core, a similar heuristic is used only when the controller is decorated with the ApiController attribute. Without it, you should explicitly specify where the parameters come from. Also, the set of parameters was extended:

- FromServices tries to obtain the type from ASP.NET Core dependency injection.

- FromBody works the same as in the old ASP.NET Web API.

- • FromForm is usually used with IFormFile and IFormFileCollection objects to bind uploaded files.

- • FromRoute and FromQuery replace the FromUri attribute from the old ASP.NET Web API.

Working with Files

Files are commonly uploaded using the multipart/form-data content type. The old ASP.NET Web API provided the MultiPartFormDataStreamProvider class to access the individual contents in the request. The process of reading the uploaded files was manual. Basically, you had to ensure the request has the expected content type and then iterate through the individual content streams, as shown in Listing 4-19.

Listing 4-19. Working with multipart content in the old ASP. NET Web API

```
[HttpPost]
[Route("api/Products/{id}/image")]
[SwaggerOperationFilter(typeof(AcceptFileOperationFilter))]
public async Task<string> UploadProductImage(int id)
{
    if (!Request.Content.IsMimeMultipartContent())
    {
        throw new HttpResponseException(
            HttpStatusCode.UnsupportedMediaType);
    }

    // store files in the temporary folder
    var storagePath = HostingEnvironment.MapPath("~/images");
```

```
    var provider = new MultipartFormDataStreamProvider(
        storagePath);
    await Request.Content.ReadAsMultipartAsync(provider);

    // process the file
    var file = provider.FileData.Single();

    // generate a unique name for the file
    var uniqueName = $"product{id}.png";

    // save the file
    var targetPath = Path.Combine(storagePath, uniqueName);
    File.Copy(file.LocalFileName, targetPath, overwrite: true);
    File.Delete(file.LocalFileName);

    // return the URL
    return $"images/{uniqueName}";
}
```

Because the method does not define the parameter for the uploaded file, Swashbuckle does not know about it, and the generated OpenAPI metadata will not contain the necessary information. Therefore, you need to implement a Swashbuckle operation filter that enhances the definition of the controller action, as shown in Listing 4-20. The filter is referenced using the SwaggerOperationFilter attribute applied to the method.

Listing 4-20. Implementing an operation filter to indicate the method accepts files

```
public class AcceptFileOperationFilter : IOperationFilter
{
    public void Apply(Operation operation,
        SchemaRegistry schemaRegistry,
        ApiDescription apiDescription)
    {
```

```
    operation.consumes = new List<string>() {
        "multipart/form-data" };
    operation.parameters.Add(new Parameter()
        {
            name = "file",
            required = true,
            type = "file",
            @in = "formData"
        });
    }
}
```

In ASP.NET Core, the process is much easier, thanks to the new
IFormFile and IFormFileCollection types, as shown in Listing 4-21.
Because of the built-in support for dependency injection, you can inject
the IWebHostEnvironment instance, which is used to determine the path
to the web application wwwroot folder. There is no need to fine-tune the
OpenAPI metadata – the IFormFile parameter is handled correctly by ASP.
NET Core API Explorer and Swashbuckle.

Listing 4-21. Working with files in ASP.NET Core

```
[HttpPost]
[Route("{id}/image")]
public async Task<string> UploadProductImage(int id,
    IFormFile file,
    IWebHostEnvironment webHostEnvironment)
{
    var storagePath = Path.Combine(
        webHostEnvironment.WebRootPath, "images");

    // auto-generate unique name
    var uniqueName = $"product{id}.png";
```

```
// save the file
var targetPath = Path.Combine(storagePath, uniqueName);
await using var fs = System.IO.File.OpenWrite(targetPath);
await file.CopyToAsync(fs);

// return the URL
return $"images/{uniqueName}";
}
```

Configuration

The old ASP.NET Web API was configured using the HttpConfiguration class. It was typically invoked from the Global.asax entry point, and there was a convention implemented in Visual Studio project templates to place the startup configuration code in the App_Start/WebApiConfig. cs file. When using Swashbuckle to produce OpenAPI definitions, it was configured in the additional file App_Start/SwaggerConfig.cs.

The ASP.NET Core API configuration model is different, but it takes care of similar things: adjusting serialization settings for JSON and other media type formatters, registering global filters, setting up conventional routes, and so forth.

When you migrate the configuration code, be aware that attribute routing is the default behavior in ASP.NET Core. There is no equivalent to MapHttpAttributeRoutes from the old ASP.NET Web API – you can safely remove it.

As you can see in Listing 4-22, the configuration is split between the general settings of ASP.NET Core API such as global filters, settings for each media type formatter (we configure only JSON), and settings for generating OpenAPI definitions. I also had to register the API Explorer as Swashbuckle needs to get metadata about registered controllers and actions.

Listing 4-22. Configuration of ASP.NET Core Web API

```
var builder = WebApplication.CreateBuilder(args);

// configure Web API
builder.Services.AddControllers(options =>
    {
        // configure global filters and other
        // API-related features
        options.Filters.Add(...);
    })
    .AddJsonOptions(options =>
    {
        // configure JSON serialization
        options.JsonSerializerOptions.Converters.Add(
            new JsonStringEnumConverter());
    });

// add support for Swashbuckle.AspNetCore
builder.Services.AddEndpointsApiExplorer();
builder.Services.AddSwaggerGen(options =>
{
    // configure authentication in Swagger
    options.AddSecurityDefinition(...);
    options.AddSecurityRequirement(...);
});

var app = builder.Build();

// enable Swagger in development mode
if (app.Environment.IsDevelopment())
{
    app.UseSwagger();
```

```
    app.UseSwaggerUI();
}

// default ASP.NET Core pipeline features
app.UseHttpsRedirection();
app.UseRouting();
app.UseAuthentication();
app.UseAuthorization();

// map API controllers
app.MapControllers();

app.Run();
```

Be aware that the security configuration in the AddSwaggerGen method in Listing 4-22 only adds the description of the security mechanism in the OpenAPI document and tells Swagger UI how to authenticate when calling the API. It does not secure the API itself – I will get to it in the "Authentication" section.

Compatibility with Newtonsoft.Json

The default JSON formatter in ASP.NET Core is based on the new System. Text.Json serializer. As I mentioned earlier, there may be some differences in serialization, such as handling polymorphic types or different APIs for custom converters.

Listing 4-23 shows how to enable the Newtonsoft.Json serializer. You will need to install the Microsoft.AspNetCore.Mvc.NewtonsoftJson NuGet package in the project.

Listing 4-23. Using Newtonsoft.Json with ASP.NET Core APIs

```
builder.Services.AddControllers(options =>
    {
```

```
        // configure global filters and other
        // API-related features
        ...
    })
    .AddNewtonsoftJson(options =>
    {
        // configure Newtonsoft.Json serialization settings
        ...
    });
```

I encourage you to try the default serializer and use Newtonsoft.Json only if you have many custom converters or need features the built-in serializer does not support. Review the list of changes between these two libraries in the official documentation.[25] In general, the new serializer is more strict and standard-compliant. Newtonsoft.Json allowed to parse even noncompliant syntax constructs (for instance, JSON property names without double quotes).

Even if you keep using Newtonsoft.Json, I recommend covering both APIs with tests to make sure all actions serialize the results the same way. There might have been subtle breaking changes between the library releases which may cause new incompatibilities.

Authentication

ASP.NET Web API could be hosted in two modes. The classic mode used Global.asax and relied on calling a static method GlobalConfiguration.Configure. A callback passed to this method was called at the right time when the necessary services Web API relied on were initialized. The second option was to use OWIN, a predecessor of the new ASP.NET Core.

---

[25] See https://learn.microsoft.com/en-us/dotnet/standard/serialization/system-text-json/migrate-from-newtonsoft?pivots=dotnet-8-0

OWIN is a universal interface between the web server and web frameworks. It specifies the information that the web server needs to provide to the application frameworks. It also defines the application delegate – a method that receives this input and processes the request. The idea is to chain these delegates, so they can either process the request or pass it to the following delegate in the chain. If this resembles the ASP.NET Core request pipeline to you, you are right – this concept was introduced in the days of OWIN and allows building complex processing pipelines from relatively simple reusable components.

I mention OWIN here because it has unleashed various new authentication methods, mainly OAuth and OpenID Connect. Instead of adding specific support for new authentication models to every ASP.NET framework, thanks to OWIN, the authentication middleware could be implemented just once, and any ASP.NET framework could use it. The only requirement was to register the authentication code in the pipeline before the concrete framework, so the current request's `Principal` object would be populated with the corresponding identity.

Host Authentication

If your application uses cookie-based Forms authentication or Windows authentication, ASP.NET Web API could use it as well – the information about the user identity will be populated by the web server or the ASP. NET infrastructure, and ASP.NET Web API just needs to verify the user is authenticated or has the required role.

However, it is common for APIs to use different ways of authentication than the users who interact with the web application from the web browser. Securing access to REST APIs using cookies or Windows Authentication is not very practical.[26] Instead, API keys or JWT (JSON Web Token) supplied in the request header become widely used, and there are various standards, such as OAuth or OpenID Connect, which facilitate obtaining tokens in various circumstances.

If the application contains both API and the web interface, you often need to combine both approaches. For this, ASP.NET Web API had a method SuppressHostPrincipal, which instructed the framework to ignore the identity provided by the host and use its own means of authenticating the user. The idea was that the application would use Forms or Windows authentication for the web UI, and when the request reaches the ASP.NET Web API layer, the host-provided identity would be ignored in favor of another authentication method used for the API users. This approach solves the frequent problem but is not universal and flexible enough.

ASP.NET Core offers the concept of authentication schemes. You can define any number of authentication methods, and in any area of the application (no matter if it is the web UI, API, or a SignalR hub), you can require authorization using a concrete scheme. This allows more than two parts of the application to be used using different authentication methods. Additionally, ASP.NET Core supports policy-based authentication[27] along with the classic role-based approach.

---

[26] The concept of cookies is meant to keep track of user sessions, offering features like expiration. Most API endpoints are one-time resources that do not use sessions. Sending the authentication token in the Cookie header instead of the Authorization header offers no advantage and can be complicated in client technologies where you cannot manipulate the Cookie header directly (e.g., when the API is called from JavaScript running in the browser). Windows Authentication, on the other hand, is usually available only from internal company networks and is rarely an option for public API endpoints.

[27] See `https://learn.microsoft.com/en-us/aspnet/core/security/authorization/policies?view=aspnetcore-8.0`

In ASP.NET Core, the authentication is completely decoupled from the API controllers. The only thing you need to do is to apply the Authorize attribute to a controller or its action. Optionally, you can specify a policy or a list of allowed roles, as shown in Listing 4-24. One of the parameters is the authentication scheme – you can use it if the application defines multiple schemes and you want to enforce a specific one.

Listing 4-24. Using the Authorize attribute in ASP.NET Core (all parameters are optional)

```
[Authorize(AuthenticationSchemes = "Api", Policy = "MyPolicy",
    Roles = "Role1,Role2")]
```

Custom Authentication Filters

ASP.NET Web API supported providing custom authentication filters by implementing the System.Web.Http.Filters.IAuthenticationFilter interface. This interface contained two methods – AuthenticateAsync and ChallengeAsync.

The first of them was called on every request to determine whether the request was authenticated or not. For authenticated requests, the method creates a principal object and assigns it to the current request. It can also indicate that the user credentials are not valid by setting an error result object. The second method was called when authentication was required to access some controller action, but the principal object was not provided. The method could modify the HTTP response to indicate that the authentication is required, for example, by setting an HTTP header or redirecting to an external identity provider.

These filters were often used to implement API-key or Basic authentication, but their architecture was very universal, and even complex scenarios like OpenID Connect could be implemented in this way.

ASP.NET Core authentication uses the same semantics as the authenticate and challenge actions, but since it is not specific to APIs, you need to implement a different interface, as shown in Listing 4-25. The authentication handler already assumes that it may need some configuration. Therefore, it is a generic type specifying the type of its options. Also, the logger and URL encoder components from the dependency injection are supplied to the constructor. However, you can clearly see the similarities in the highlighted parts of the code.

Listing 4-25. Implementing API key validation in ASP.NET Web API and ASP.NET Core

```
// old ASP.NET Web API
public class ApiKeyAuthenticationFilter : IAuthenticationFilter
{
    // the same instance of the filter can be reused
    // for more requests
    public bool AllowMultiple => true;

    public Task AuthenticateAsync(
        HttpAuthenticationContext context,
        CancellationToken cancellationToken)
    {
        // check if we have the X-Api-Key header
        if (context.Request.Headers.TryGetValues("X-Api-Key",
            out var apiKeys))
        {
            var user = ValidateApiKey(apiKeys.Single());
            if (user == null)
            {
                // invalid API key - set error result
                context.ErrorResult =
```

```
                    new StatusCodeResult(
                        HttpStatusCode.Unauthorized,
                        context.Request);
            }
            else
            {
                // set the current context identity
                context.Principal = new ClaimsPrincipal(user);
            }
        }
        return Task.CompletedTask;
    }

    public Task ChallengeAsync(
        HttpAuthenticationChallengeContext context,
        CancellationToken cancellationToken)
        => return Task.CompletedTask;

    private ClaimsIdentity ValidateApiKey(string apiKey)
    {
        // TODO: validate key
        if (...)
        {
            // valid key - return identity
            return new ClaimsIdentity(new[]
            {
                new Claim(ClaimTypes.Name, userName)
            }, "ApiKey");
        }
        return null;
    }
}
```

```
// ASP.NET Core
public class ApiKeyAuthenticationHandler
    : AuthenticationHandler<ApiKeyAuthenticationOptions>
{
    public ApiKeyAuthenticationHandler(
        IOptionsMonitor<ApiKeyAuthenticationOptions> options,
        ILoggerFactory logger, UrlEncoder encoder)
        : base(options, logger, encoder)
    {
    }

    protected override async
        Task<AuthenticateResult> HandleAuthenticateAsync()
    {
        // check if we have the X-Api-Key header
        if (Request.Headers.TryGetValue("X-Api-Key",
            out var apiKeys))
        {
            var user = ValidateApiKey(apiKeys.Single()!);
            if (user == null)
            {
                // invalid API key
                return AuthenticateResult.Fail(
                    "Invalid API key");
            }
            else
            {
                // create the current context identity
                return AuthenticateResult.Success(
                    new AuthenticationTicket(
                        new ClaimsPrincipal(user),
                        Scheme.Name));
            }
```

```
        }
        return AuthenticateResult.Fail(
            "Missing header X-Api-Key");
    }

    private ClaimsIdentity? ValidateApiKey(string apiKey)
    {
        // TODO: validate key
        if (...)
        {
            // valid key - return identity
            return new ClaimsIdentity(new[]
            {
                new Claim(ClaimTypes.Name, entry.User)
            }, Scheme.Name);
        }
        return null;
    }
}

public class ApiKeyAuthenticationOptions
    : AuthenticationSchemeOptions
{
    // define any configuration parameters for the handler
}
```

JWT and OWIN-Based Authentication

JWT is a popular mechanism of authentication in API applications, and with ASP.NET Web API, it was usually provided by the `Microsoft.Owin.Security.Jwt` NuGet package. When registering this type of authentication, you need to provide several configuration options, such as authority (the address of the authentication server that issues the tokens) and token validation parameters (e.g., valid audiences and issuers specified in the token or even the certificate used to validate the token without the need to contact the issuing server).

The logic of OWIN JWT implementation and ASP.NET Core implementation is very similar, as shown in Listing 4-26, and the most important property TokenValidationParameters comes from the same NuGet package Microsoft.IdentityModel.Tokens, so the transition is relatively seamless.

Listing 4-26. JWT bearer authentication in ASP.NET Web API and ASP.NET Core

```
// OWIN
app.UseJwtBearerAuthentication(
    new JwtBearerAuthenticationOptions
{
    ...
    TokenValidationParameters = new TokenValidationParameters
    {
        ...
    }
});

// ASP.NET Core
builder.Services
    .AddAuthentication(JwtBearerDefaults.AuthenticationScheme)
    .AddJwtBearer(options =>
    {
        ...
        options.TokenValidationParameters =
            new TokenValidationParameters
        {
            ...
```

```
        }
    };
});
```

If you plan to use multiple authentication schemes in your ASP.NET Core application, make sure the JwtBearerDefaults. AuthenticationScheme is the default one (specified as a parameter to the AddAuthorization method), or request it explicitly in the Authorize attributes.

Again, it is recommended practice to have the authentication covered by tests to make sure you do not introduce a security vulnerability.

For development purposes, the new .NET comes with a handy command-line tool dotnet user-jwts, which you can use to generate tokens locally[28] without setting up an identity provider for testing.

Unifying the OpenAPI Metadata

If you generate client proxies using the OpenAPI definitions produced by the application, the last step in the transition is making sure that the OpenAPI definition produced by the new ASP.NET Core application is equivalent and produces the same client classes or at least to some extent. You probably do not want to create breaking changes by unnecessary method renames, but if the previous clients have been using synchronous access, maybe it is a good time to push them to use asynchronous calls. It depends on your priorities – sometimes, the intent is not to create any breaking changes (especially if the generated proxies are distributed to third parties as an SDK), but sometimes it is desirable to clean up the technical debt in client applications.

---

[28] See https://learn.microsoft.com/en-us/aspnet/core/security/ authentication/jwt-authn

Configuring Client Proxy Generation

If you currently do not generate client proxies and want to start, one option to do that is to use the **Add ➤ Connected Service** feature in Visual Studio, as shown in Figure 4-1. Then, select the **Service References** option, choose **OpenAPI**, and enter a URL or a path to the JSON definition as in Figure 4-2. If you have multiple controllers, use the expression {controller}ServiceClient to substitute the actual name of the controller to the generated class. Otherwise, the code generator would produce multiple classes with the same name with the default settings (unless you specify custom NSwag parameters).

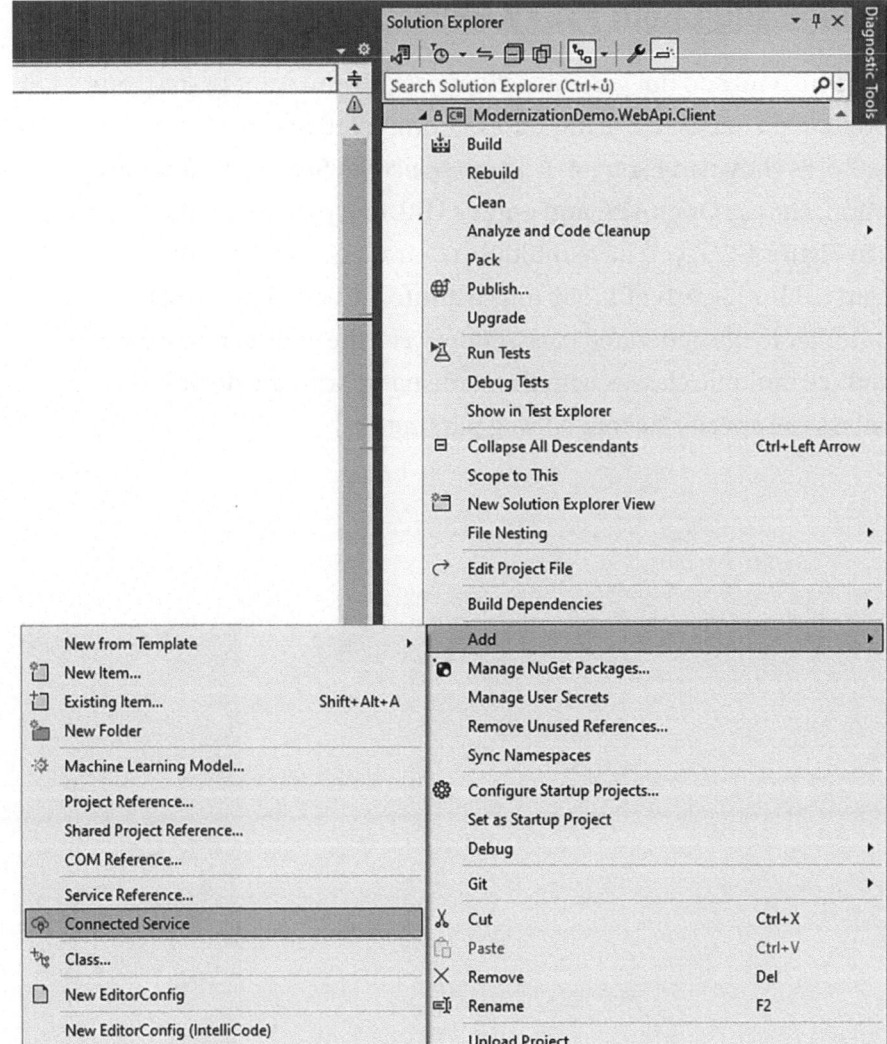

Figure 4-1. *Adding a Connected Service to a project in Visual Studio*

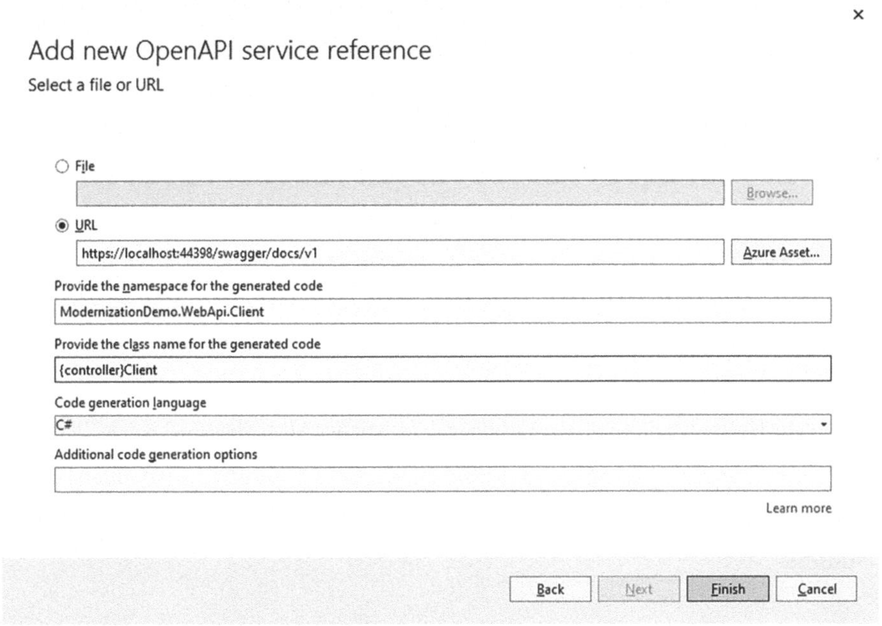

Figure 4-2. *Configuring the OpenAPI Connected Service*

These actions configure the OpenApiReference element in the project file and ensure the client proxies are built when the project is compiled. This is done thanks to the NSwag.MSBuild package, which is added automatically to the project by Visual Studio. If you change the API, you can have the OpenAPI definitions refreshed from the Connected Services window by clicking the **Refresh** context menu action.

Diff Tools

Comparing the OpenAPI documents using regular text diff tools is not very helpful as Swashbuckle for the old ASP.NET Web API emits OpenAPI 2.0 specification, while the ASP.NET Core version of Swashbuckle produces OpenAPI 3.0.

You can use the online Swagger editor[29] to convert the OpenAPI 2.0 file into an OpenAPI 3.0 version. Open the page in your browser, paste the JSON into the left side of the page, and select the **Edit ➤ Convert to OpenAPI 3** option in the top menu. Do not be afraid of pasting JSON in the YAML editor on the page – any JSON document is a valid YAML.

There are several open source tools to compare OpenAPI specifications. One of the popular ones is Oasdiff.[30] You can give it two files (JSON or YAML), and it produces quite nice text output. It can also be used in CI/CD environments to verify that your commit did not introduce breaking changes in the API.

I usually run the tool as a Docker container. All you need to do is place old.json and new.json files in a directory (D:\Temp\api in my case) and run the command in Listing 4-27. Naturally, you will need to have Docker installed.

Listing 4-27. Using the Oasdiff tool through Docker to compare OpenAPI documents

```
docker run --rm -t -v D:/Temp/Api:/data tufin/oasdiff changelog
/data/old.json /data/new.json

73 changes: 28 error, 0 warning, 45 info
error   [response-property-became-nullable] at /data/new.json
        in API GET /api/Orders
                the response property '/items/CanceledAt'
                became nullable
                for the status '200'

error   [response-property-became-nullable] at /data/new.json
        in API GET /api/Orders
```

---

[29] See https://editor.swagger.io/
[30] See https://github.com/tufin/oasdiff

```
                the response property '/items/OrderItems'
                became nullable
                for the status '200'

error    [response-property-became-nullable] at /data/new.json
         in API GET /api/Products
                the response property '/items/Title' became
                nullable for
                the status '200'

info     [api-operation-id-removed] at /data/old.json
         in API GET /api/Orders
                api operation id 'Orders_GetOrders' removed and
                replaced with ''
```

You will have to manually review all errors because not all of them necessarily mean a problem. OpenAPI 2.0 did not have support for nullable types, so the tool complains that some types (nullable DateTime, string, or collections) became nullable – the nullable flag appeared in the 3.0 version and ASP.NET Core started emitting it.

This may also help you to discover properties that are indicated as nullable, and they should not be – such as Title or OrderItems in the preceding example. Decorating them with the Required attribute will remove the nullable flag.

Another issue is that the old version was setting the operationId parameter – the ASP.NET Core version does not use it. These operation names can be specified either explicitly by setting the Name parameter of Http* attributes or by a convention in configuration, as shown in Listing 4-28.

Listing 4-28. Attribute- and convention-based specification of operation IDs

```
// attribute-based setting on a controller action
[HttpGet(Name = "Orders_GetOrders")]
public List<OrderModel> GetOrders()
{
    ...
}

// convention-based setting in startup
builder.Services.AddSwaggerGen(options =>
{
    options.CustomOperationIds(e =>
        e.ActionDescriptor.RouteValues["controller"] + "_" +
        e.ActionDescriptor.RouteValues["action"]);
    ...
}
```

Ensuring the operation IDs are unchanged should resolve most of the differences in generated client codes, as most generators (such as NSwag) rely on them. By default, they use the first segment of the ID to determine the controller and create a class for actions coming from the same controller.

I have found some subtle changes in the names of method arguments representing the request body (e.g., order in the old version and body in the new version), but, hopefully, this should not break the users.

You can always fine-tune the OpenAPI document by adding document or operation filters,[31] and the client generators offer a large set of configuration options to fine-tune the generated client code. NSwag even lets you provide custom Liquid templates to emit the resulting code, but I would recommend it only as the last-resort option.

ASP.NET SignalR

SignalR became a popular way of creating real-time messaging in web applications. All the technologies mentioned earlier in the chapter have one thing in common: communication is always initiated by a client sending a request. With SignalR, both parties can send requests to the other party at any time, which opens plenty of new possibilities.

Today, all commonly used web browsers support WebSockets API – a technology that provides a two-way interactive communication session between the browser and a server. This sounds very similar to SignalR; actually, SignalR uses web sockets internally wherever possible and falls back to other means of transport if needed. However, SignalR provides an RPC-like abstraction over plain messaging web sockets offer and handles various connection life cycle events, such as reconnects. The abstraction allows you to write much simpler code to call a method on the other side, work with groups of clients, and handle scaling to large numbers of clients.

The modernization of SignalR applications is different from previous technologies as it introduces a breaking change for all clients. SignalR on ASP.NET Core is conceptually similar, but the underlying protocols

---

[31] See `https://github.com/domaindrivendev/Swashbuckle.AspNetCore?tab=readme-ov-file#extend-generator-with-operation-schema--document-filters`

and message formats are incompatible. The differences are listed in the documentation page[32] – the most important of them are the different scaling model and removal of persistent connections. The client-side JavaScript libraries do not depend on jQuery anymore.

The new ASP.NET Core SignalR is included as part of ASP.NET Core runtime – therefore, you do not need to list any NuGet packages in projects using `Microsoft.NET.Sdk.Web` SDK explicitly. In .NET client applications, you need to add the `Microsoft.AspNetCore.SignalR.Client` package. The namespace was changed from `Microsoft.AspNet.SignalR` to `Microsoft.AspNetCore.SignalR`.

Migration of SignalR Hubs

The semantics of declaring SignalR hubs remain the same. The class inherits from the `Hub` base class and can define any public methods that clients can call. You can override the `OnConnectedAsync` and `OnDisconnectedAsync` methods to perform actions when a new client connects or disconnects.

In ASP.NET Core SignalR, there is no `OnReconnectedAsync` method. The connection life cycle model was simplified, and reconnecting became just a client-side feature you can opt in for. Therefore, if the network connection drops, your hub will always invoke the `OnDisconnectedAsync` method, and once the connection is restored (no matter how quickly after the disconnection), `OnConnectedAsync` is called again.

This is quite an important change if you assign clients in groups. In the old SignalR, when your connection was added to a group, it was re-added there automatically on reconnect. Since there is no reconnect event on the server in ASP.NET Core SignalR, and the server does not store the group membership information about disconnected clients, you will need to

---

[32] See `https://learn.microsoft.com/en-us/aspnet/core/signalr/version-differences`

add the connection to groups again. In general, you will need to move the logic from the reconnected event to the connected event and treat the connections as a new one.

In ASP.NET Core 8.0, Microsoft added a new feature called stateful reconnects. If enabled on both server and client, it enables data buffering to replay the lost messages once the client reconnects. This is very useful for making the client experience more seamless, but it is not a full replacement for the reconnected event from the old SignalR.

One significant code change you will have to deal with is replacing dynamic method calls when calling the other side by the SendAsync method, as shown in Listing 4-29. There are also some subtle naming changes when interacting with the Clients and Groups APIs to define the recipients of the call.

Listing 4-29. Differences in the Hub implementation in SignalR and SignalR Core

```
// old ASP.NET SignalR
public class ChatHub : Hub
{
    public async Task JoinRoom(string roomId)
    {
        await Groups.Add(Context.ConnectionId, roomId);
        await Clients.Group(roomId).addChatMessage(
            "System",
            $"User {GetUserName()} joined the room.");
    }
    ...
}

// new ASP.NET Core SignalR
public class ChatHub : Hub
{
```

```
public async Task JoinRoom(string roomId)
{
    await Groups.AddToGroupAsync(
        Context.ConnectionId, roomId);
    await Clients.Group(roomId).SendAsync(
        "addChatMessage",
        "System",
        $"User {GetUserName()} joined the room.");
}
...
}
```

Same as in the old SignalR, in order to send messages from outside the hub, you can easily access the IHubContext<THub> Clients object using dependency injection. You should not create hub instances yourself and should not store any state in them, as new instances are created to process each message.

The registration of hubs has changed in ASP.NET Core and follows the patterns used in the other technologies, as you can see in Listing 4-30. The main difference is that you need to list and register hubs to their desired URLs explicitly. This comes from the fact that ASP.NET Core SignalR always uses a separate connection for each hub, in contrast to the old SignalR that shared a single connection for multiple hubs.

Listing 4-30. Registration of ASP.NET Core SignalR hubs

```
// old ASP.NET SignalR (OWIN startup class)
public class Startup
{
    public void Configuration(IAppBuilder app)
    {
        // discovers and maps all hubs to /signalr
```

```
        app.MapSignalR();
    }
}
```

```
// new ASP.NET Core SignalR
var builder = WebApplication.CreateBuilder(args);
```

```
builder.Services.AddSignalR();
```

```
var app = builder.Build();
```

```
// you need to map all hubs explicitly
app.MapHub<ChatHub>("/hubs/ChatHub");
```

```
app.Run();
```

Authentication and Authorization

Since many uses of SignalR involved the client's browser, the authentication model was often the same as for visiting the web interface, such as cookies or Windows authentication. Therefore, no special configuration was required for SignalR.

In a similar fashion as with other ASP.NET communication frameworks, hubs can be marked with the Authorize attribute to limit access to authenticated users or to members of specific roles. The user identity is available through the Context.User object in the Hub class body.

However, some applications need to expose the API client to external users and use, for example, token-based authentication. In such cases, you can take the same approach as with ASP.NET Web API and JWT and OWIN-based authentication. The old ASP.NET SignalR is built on OWIN, which allows plugging the authentication middleware before the registration of hubs. The authentication middleware can check the HTTP request header or a query string parameter, and if a valid token is present, set the request's User object to ClaimsPrincipal. This will allow the SignalR hub to use the Authorize attribute.

In the old SignalR, the header-based authentication could be used only in the .NET client. In JavaScript, there was no way to pass the header when establishing the web socket connection. However, with ASP.NET Core SignalR, it is now possible even in JavaScript. Listing 4-31 shows the implementation in the old SignalR and in the new ASP.NET Core SignalR. As you can see, the ASP.NET Core unifies the authentication infrastructure for all frameworks, so the implementation of the authentication handler is the same in the case of ASP.NET Web API. Being able to reuse the same authentication middleware for various frameworks is one of the architectural improvements of the new .NET.

Listing 4-31. API-key authentication in the old and new SignalR

```
// old ASP.NET SignalR
public class Startup
{
    public void Configuration(IAppBuilder app)
    {
        app.Use<ApiKeyAuthenticationMiddleware>();
        app.MapSignalR();
    }
}

public class ApiKeyAuthenticationMiddleware : OwinMiddleware
{
    public override Task Invoke(IOwinContext context)
    {
        var apiKey = GetApiKeyFromUrlOrHeader(context);
        if (apiKey != null)
        {
            // check the API key
            var user = ValidateApiKey(apiKey);
            if (user != null)
```

```
    {
        // set the current context identity
        context.Authentication.User =
            new ClaimsPrincipal(user);
    }
    else
    {
        // return 401 Unauthorized
        context.Response.StatusCode = 401;
        context.Response.ReasonPhrase =
            "Invalid API Key";
    }
}
return Next.Invoke(context);
}

private static string GetApiKeyFromUrlOrHeader(
    IOwinContext context)
{
    var apiKey = context.Request.Query.Get("auth-token");
    if (!string.IsNullOrEmpty(apiKey))
    {
        return apiKey;
    }
    apiKey = context.Request.Headers.Get("X-Api-Key");
    if (!string.IsNullOrEmpty(apiKey))
    {
        return apiKey;
    }
    return null;
}
```

```
    private ClaimsIdentity ValidateApiKey(string apiKey)
    {
        // TODO: validate key
        if (...)
        {
            // create the API user identity
            return new ClaimsIdentity(new[]
            {
                new Claim(ClaimTypes.Name, user)
            }, "X-Api-Key");
        }
        return null;
    }
}

// new ASP.NET Core SignalR
var builder = WebApplication.CreateBuilder(args);

builder.Services.AddSignalR();
builder.Services.AddAuthentication("ApiKey")
    .AddScheme<
        ApiKeyAuthenticationOptions,
        ApiKeyAuthenticationHandler>(
            "ApiKey", options =>
    {
        builder.Configuration.GetSection("Authentication")
            .Bind(options);
    });

var app = builder.Build();

app.UseAuthentication();
app.UseAuthorization();
```

```
app.MapHub<ChatHub>("/hubs/ChatHub");

app.UseDefaultFiles();
app.UseStaticFiles();

app.Run();

public class ApiKeyAuthenticationHandler
    : AuthenticationHandler<ApiKeyAuthenticationOptions>
{
    public ApiKeyAuthenticationHandler(
        IOptionsMonitor<ApiKeyAuthenticationOptions> options,
        ILoggerFactory logger, UrlEncoder encoder)
        : base(options, logger, encoder)
    {
    }

    protected override async
        Task<AuthenticateResult> HandleAuthenticateAsync()
    {
        // check if we have the X-Api-Key header
        if (Request.Headers.TryGetValue("X-Api-Key",
            out var apiKeys))
        {
            var user = ValidateApiKey(apiKeys.Single()!);
            if (user == null)
            {
                // invalid API key
                return AuthenticateResult.Fail(
                    "Invalid API key");
            }
            else
            {
```

```
            // create the current context identity
            return AuthenticateResult.Success(
                new AuthenticationTicket(
                    new ClaimsPrincipal(user),
                        Scheme.Name));
        }
    }
    return AuthenticateResult.Fail(
        "Missing header X-Api-Key");
}

private ClaimsIdentity? ValidateApiKey(string apiKey)
{
    // TODO: validate key
    if (...)
    {
        // valid key - return identity
        return new ClaimsIdentity(new[]
        {
            new Claim(ClaimTypes.Name, entry.User)
        }, Scheme.Name);
    }
    return null;
}
}

public class ApiKeyAuthenticationOptions
    : AuthenticationSchemeOptions
{
    // define any configuration parameters for the handler
}
```

Persistent Connections

I mentioned earlier in the chapter that persistent connections are not supported in the new ASP.NET Core SignalR. Persistent connections were a low-level communication protocol for exchanging string messages. Along with the connection-level methods known from the hubs (OnConnectedAsync and others), they provided the OnReceived method that was invoked whenever a message was received from the client. You were responsible for deserializing the message and taking appropriate action.

Persistent connections can be quite easily migrated to hubs – for example, you can create a hub method called ProcessMessage which accepts one string parameter. Then you can keep using the same logic as the old code to handle the message. If you use your own message format, I encourage you to convert it to regular hub methods. They provide much more information about the communication interface – what methods are supported, what parameters they have, and so on. You can even use strongly typed hubs, which expose an interface to be used in .NET clients.

ASP.NET Core SignalR supports JSON and MessagePack[33] protocols, and it is possible to implement your own as well. If you want to stick to some format of messages, implementing your own protocol can also be a viable option.

Migration of Client Applications

The old .NET client applications rely on the Microsoft.AspNet.SignalR.Client package. They need to be migrated to Microsoft.AspNetCore.SignalR.Client with appropriate namespace changes. As Listing 4-32 shows, the client-side code is very similar – the most important change is the hub client initialization using HubConnectionBuilder.

---

[33] MessagePack is a binary protocol with similar capabilities to JSON but smaller message sizes. See https://msgpack.org/ for more information.

Because the new SignalR uses a single connection per hub, you need to specify the exact hub URL. In the old code, all hubs shared a single connection – that is why the URL specified only the root of the application (assuming the default /signalr endpoint), and you then had to create a proxy for each hub. You can also notice that the new API is strict about adding the Async suffix to all asynchronous methods.

Listing 4-32. Changes in SignalR .NET client applications

```
// old ASP.NET SignalR
using (var hubConnection =
    new HubConnection("https://localhost:44382/"))
{
    var chat = hubConnection.CreateHubProxy("ChatHub");

    // define client methods
    chat.On<string, string>("addChatMessage",
        (name, message) =>
        {
            Console.WriteLine($"{name}: {message}");
        });
    await hubConnection.Start();

    // join the room
    await chat.Invoke("JoinRoom", roomId);
}

// new ASP.NET Core SignalR
await using var chat = new HubConnectionBuilder()
    .WithUrl("https://localhost:7201/hubs/ChatHub")
    .Build();

// define client methods
chat.On<string, string>("addChatMessage",
    (name, message) =>
```

```
{
    Console.WriteLine($"{name}: {message}");
});
await chat.StartAsync();

// join the room
await chat.InvokeAsync("JoinRoom", roomId);
```

The process of migrating JavaScript client applications is quite similar –
instead of replacing NuGet packages, you need to switch to the new
SignalR libraries. The new library does not depend on jQuery and provides
an initialization API that resembles the .NET version, as you can see in
Listing 4-33.

The JavaScript client library can be obtained from popular CDNs
(Cloudflare, cdnjs, and others) under the name microsoft-signalr. It is
also published as npm package @microsoft/signalr. Many developers
prefer to bundle the script together with other resources. Several ways
of installing ASP.NET Core SignalR client libraries are described in the
documentation.[34] One important difference is that the new SignalR no
longer supports emitting the hub proxies (usually at /signalr/hubs),
which allowed calling methods using proxy.server.methodName(args).
Instead, you need to use the invoke method and pass the hub method
name as the first argument.

Listing 4-33. Changes in JavaScript client applications

```
// old ASP.NET SignalR
const chat = $.connection.chatHub;

// define client methods
chat.client.addChatMessage = function (user, message) {
```

---

[34] See https://learn.microsoft.com/en-us/aspnet/core/signalr/
javascript-client#install-the-signalr-client-package

```
    ...
};

// connect and join the room
$.connection.hub.start().done(function () {
    chat.server.joinRoom(selectedRoomId);

    ...
});

// new ASP.NET Core SignalR
const chat = new signalR.HubConnectionBuilder()
    .withUrl("/hubs/ChatHub")
    .build();

// define client methods
chat.on("addChatMessage", (user, message) => {
    ...
});

// connect and join the room
await chat.start();
await chat.invoke("joinRoom", selectedRoomId);
```

As you can see in the code listings, the changes in both client and server applications are only cosmetic. The patterns of defining hubs and using client proxies remained without changes. However, the new ASP.NET Core SignalR is more flexible and extensible.

Automatic Reconnects

The old SignalR tried to automatically restore the connection when it was interrupted, and the server was involved in the process to prevent messages from being lost due to communication failures.[35] This complex workflow of connection states requires considerable understanding to make your applications bulletproof when running on unreliable networks.

The new ASP.NET Core SignalR has automatic reconnects disabled by default. When you opt in for this feature, the client will try to create a new connection if necessary. You can configure the number of attempts and the timeouts to be used between the attempts. You should watch for the Reconnecting and Reconnected events on the hub client and implement your mechanism of queueing or dropping messages in case the connection is not active. Sending messages during this period will result in exceptions.

The HubConnectionBuilder provides a method called WithAutomaticReconnects. Optionally, you can pass an array of TimeSpan values indicating the delays between connection attempts or an implementation of IRetryPolicy which will decide how long to wait and when to cease further attempts, as shown in Listing 4-34.

Listing 4-34. An infinite retry policy for automatic reconnects

```
await using var chat = new HubConnectionBuilder()
    .WithUrl("https://localhost:7201/hubs/ChatHub")
    .WithAutomaticReconnect(new ForeverRetryPolicy())
    .Build();

public class ForeverRetryPolicy : IRetryPolicy
{
    public TimeSpan? NextRetryDelay(RetryContext retryContext)
    {
        // return a timeout for the next attempt,
        // or null to stop trying
```

---

[35] The complete life cycle is described in the documentation. See https://learn.microsoft.com/en-us/aspnet/signalr/overview/guide-to-the-api/handling-connection-lifetime-events

```
        return TimeSpan.FromSeconds(5);
    }
}
```

Scaling

Web servers can accept only a limited number of TCP connections, which causes issues in high-traffic applications when using SignalR. Even if your application does not hit the maximum number of TCP connections, the other traffic may require running the application on multiple servers. This creates a problem when the SignalR application wants to send messages to a group or to all users – it only knows about its own connections and not about those handled by other servers.

To support scaling, SignalR needs to set up an additional messaging channel between all servers running the application. This channel is used to distribute broadcast or group messages to clients connected to other servers, as shown in Figure 4-3.

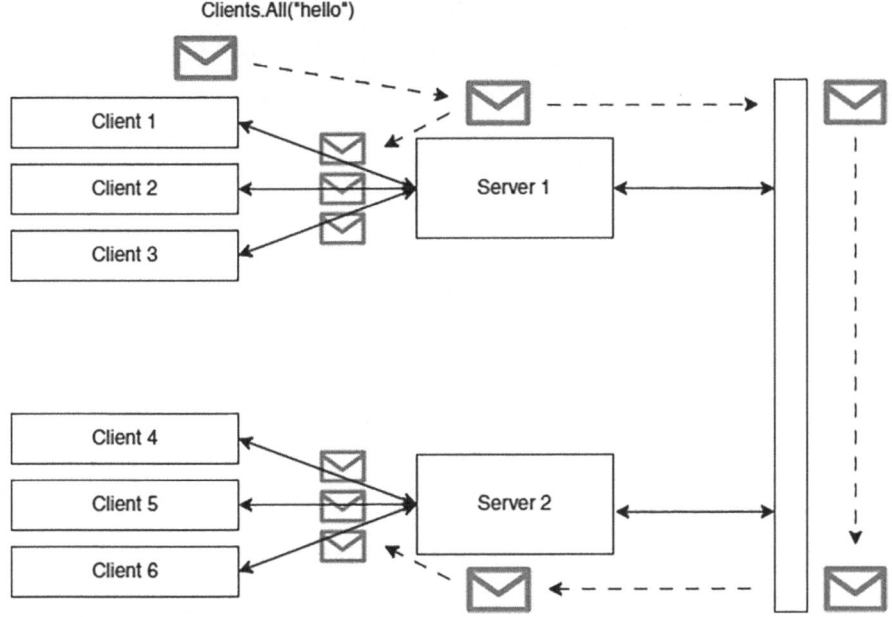

Figure 4-3. *Distribution of a broadcast message in scaled SignalR applications*

The old SignalR supported Azure Service Bus, Redis, and SQL Server (ideally with Service Broker). ASP.NET Core SignalR supports Microsoft's hosted Azure SignalR Service and Redis, but there are third-party providers for NCache, SQL Server, and others.

If you used Redis for scaling previously and have the infrastructure in place, enabling it is just a matter of calling an additional method AddStackExchangeRedis in the startup configuration, as shown in Listing 4-35. You need to add the Microsoft.AspNetCore.SignalR. StackExchangeRedis package and provide a correct connection string. It is also recommended to set a channel prefix in case you want multiple applications to share the same Redis instance.

For other methods, Azure SignalR Service may be the effortless option, but I recommend estimating the costs in Azure Pricing Calculator[36] first. There is a free tier that may be sufficient for your needs. This service can be enabled by calling the AddAzureSignalR extension method from the Microsoft.Azure.SignalR package.

Listing 4-35. Scaling SignalR to multiple servers

```
// adding Azure SignalR Service
builder.Services.AddSignalR()
    .AddAzureSignalR(connectionString);

// adding Redis backplane
builder.Services.AddSignalR()
    .AddStackExchangeRedis(connectionString,
        options => {
            options.Configuration.ChannelPrefix =
                RedisChannel.Literal("YourApp");
    });
```

If the application runs on multiple servers and uses protocols other than web sockets, sticky sessions (Application Request Routing Affinity in Azure) must be enabled for the scaling to work properly. These techniques tell the load balancer to send all HTTP requests from the same client to the same server instance. Without them, SignalR cannot function properly because other servers may not know anything about the client.

---

[36] See https://azure.microsoft.com/en-us/pricing/calculator/

Summary

This chapter covered all communication frameworks available in the old ASP.NET and provided guidance on how to replace them with their modern equivalents. Naturally, it is not feasible to cover every scenario and every API. Each framework has numerous features and configuration options, and the number of possible combinations is extremely high.

I recommend modernizing the application incrementally using the side-by-side approach, especially in larger projects or when the API communication is bundled with the user interface. This allows you to avoid large chunks of work and deploy the new implementation early. However, as you will see in Chapter 8, this method can get complicated to set up when it comes to authentication, caching, or other advanced concepts.

CHAPTER 5

Migrating Data Access

The majority of .NET applications heavily interact with a database. Despite the rising popularity of NoSQL databases, Microsoft SQL Server is the first choice (and sometimes the only one) for many .NET developers.

NoSQL ("Not only SQL" or "Non-SQL") is a bit confusing term that refers to any non-relational database, even though there are non-relational databases that use the SQL language (e.g., Azure Cosmos DB, which is a document database). In the early days of .NET, most developers did not even consider using a database other than a relational one. The "NoSQL movement" called for including other approaches in the decision matrix, as the classic relational design is not always the best fit.

The popularity of non-relational databases started as a response to the rising complexity of software applications and decreasing costs of storage. Relational models were designed in the 1970s and quickly became popular. One of the reasons was normalization – a technique of structuring data in the database by creating tables and establishing relationships according to sets of rules (called normal forms) to prevent data duplication. Modifying any field, for example, a customer's name, was a relatively easy operation, no matter how complex the model was. In most cases, the name was stored only in one place on disk, and other entities used relations to refer to the concrete customer instead of having a copy of the customer's name as part of their own data.

© Tomáš Herceg 2024
T. Herceg, *Modernizing .NET Web Applications*,
https://doi.org/10.1007/979-8-8688-0617-9_5

However, many applications read or query data way more often than write or modify them, and the data storage costs nowadays are one of the cheapest things on the infrastructure bill (compared to computational power, operation memory, or costs of license for the operation system and database engine). It is not unusual to see complex SQL queries with many JOIN clauses, accessing data from dozens of tables at the same time, and such queries are often orders of magnitude more frequent than simple write queries for adding or updating a single row.

This is the completely opposite usage of what the relational databases are optimized for, and that is why document databases have become so popular in recent years. They allow you to store a complex entity as a single document instead of requiring you to navigate through a tree of relationships to obtain all necessary data. This approach may introduce data duplication (the customer's name is embedded as part of every order of that customer) and complicate data updates (the customer's name will have to be changed in many places, and it is quite difficult to do it as a single transaction), but since write operations are not that common, it may be an acceptable trade-off.

This issue became even more visible when using ORMs such as Entity Framework. I saw many queries containing dozens of Include clauses, which severely hurt the query performance. Storing the entities as single documents with no relationships would certainly be much faster.

CODE SAMPLES FOR THIS CHAPTER

The migration of data access code is demonstrated in the GitHub repository available via the book's product page at `https://github.com/Apress/Modernizing-.NET-Web-Applications`. You can find the entire solution in the `chapter05` folder.

For each technology mentioned in this chapter, there is a collection of projects:

- `AdoNetTests` shows the same ADO.NET code running in .NET Framework as well as in the new .NET.

- `LinqToSqlTests` shows a simple LINQ to SQL model, and `LinqToSqlToEfCoreTests` demonstrates the code changes required to migrate to Entity Framework Core.

- `EfLegacyTests` shows the old `ObjectContext` API used in Entity Framework 3.5 and 4.0.

- `EfTests` uses the Database First approach, and `EfCodeFirstTests` uses the Code First approach in .NET Framework.

- `EfCoreTests` shows the Code First approach, and `EfCoreEdmxTests` uses the Database First approach in the new .NET.

If you want to run the projects, follow the instructions in the `Readme` file in the `chapter05` folder.

Migrating ADO.NET Primitives

The oldest way of accessing data in the .NET Framework is a technology called ADO.NET. It is a collection of APIs that allows you to access various data sources – either through database-specific providers (such as System. Data.SqlClient for Microsoft SQL Server, third-party ODP.NET's Oracle. ManagedDataAccess for Oracle, and others) or through database-agnostic protocols such as ODBC or OLE DB.

Later, other data access technologies, such as LINQ to SQL and Entity Framework, were added. Technically, they are also considered to be part of ADO.NET, but because of their complexity, they will be covered in the subsequent sections. For now, I want to focus on the low-level API: connections, commands, data readers, and others.

Table 5-1 shows the popular data providers in the old .NET Framework and the new .NET. As you can see, some of them are the same for both branches of .NET (their NuGet packages are either built against .NET Standard or use multi-targeting), but the others have undergone some evolution. The most important changes happened to SQL Server and SQLite providers.

SQL Server

The new .NET offers two versions of SqlClient for Microsoft SQL Server. In recent years, many new features have been added to Microsoft SQL Server and its cloud version, Azure SQL Database, and thus there is a need to enhance and evolve this API.

However, in .NET Framework, the System.Data.SqlClient assembly is installed globally in Windows and depends on the version of .NET Framework. In order to not break existing applications, the API must remain compatible. In the new .NET, the same assembly is distributed as a NuGet package, and the applications are free to pick a specific version to be used. However, using new SqlClient's features, such as new models of authentication (e.g., integration with Azure Entra ID) in the old .NET Framework's applications would be very useful, and, therefore, Microsoft decided to introduce a new package[1] – Microsoft.Data.SqlClient.

The idea is that the old System.Data.SqlClient package remains supported (it cannot be changed or removed from .NET Framework anyway), but it will only receive important bug fixes and security patches. All the new features will be added to the new Microsoft.Data.SqlClient, versioned and distributed through NuGet.

Since both versions came from the same codebase, and the new version does not change the old concepts, the migration is mostly about changing the package and the namespace.

Table 5-1. *Common ADO.NET providers for .NET Framework and the new .NET*

Database	.NET Framework	.NET Core/.NET
SQL Server	System.Data.SqlClient	System.Data.SqlClient Microsoft.Data. SqlClient
SQL Server Compact	System.Data.SqlServerCe	Not supported[2]

(continued)

---

[1]You can find a more detailed description of the reasons in the official blog post at https://devblogs.microsoft.com/dotnet/introducing-the-new-microsoftdatasqlclient/

[2]SQL Server Compact Edition was an embedded database developed by Microsoft. The technology became unsupported in 2021, and there is no official support in the new .NET.

Table 5-1. (*continued*)

Database	.NET Framework	.NET Core/.NET
OLE DB	System.Data.OleDb	
ODBC	System.Data.Odbc	
Oracle	System.Data.Oracle (deprecated) Oracle.ManagedAccess (third party)	Oracle.ManagedAccess. Core (third party)
PostgreSQL	Npgsql (third party)	
MySQL	MySQL.Data (third party)	
Firebird	FirebirdSql.Data.FirebirdClient (third party)	
SQLite	System.Data.SQLite (third party)	System.Data.SQLite (third party) Microsoft.Data.Sqlite

As you can see in the ModernizationDemo.AdoNetTests project in the example repository, the code using SQL Server ADO.NET primitives is the same. The test project is configured to target both .NET Framework 4.8.1 and .NET 8.0, just with different references and a different using statement for each version, as shown in Listing 5-1. For the old .NET Framework, there is an assembly reference to System.Data.SqlClient, while in the new .NET, there is a package reference to Microsoft.Data.SqlClient. I have the new global usings feature in place (see the Using element), so I do not have to add the corresponding namespace imports in the code files. If you prefer to avoid this feature, you can use conditional compilation symbols to import the correct namespace, as demonstrated in Listing 5-2.

Listing 5-1. Multi-targeted project with SqlClient package reference for the new .NET and assembly reference for the old .NET Framework

```
<Project Sdk="Microsoft.NET.Sdk">
  <PropertyGroup>
    <TargetFrameworks>net8.0;net481</TargetFrameworks>
    <ImplicitUsings>enable</ImplicitUsings>
    <LangVersion>latest</LangVersion>

    ...
  </PropertyGroup>

  <ItemGroup Condition="$(TargetFramework) == 'net8.0'">
    <PackageReference Include="Microsoft.Data.SqlClient"
    Version="5.2.0" />
    <Using Include="Microsoft.Data.SqlClient" />
  </ItemGroup>

  <ItemGroup Condition="$(TargetFramework) == 'net481'">
    <Assembly Include="System.Data.SqlClient" />
    <Using Include="System.Data.SqlClient" />
  </ItemGroup>
</Project>
```

Listing 5-2. Conditional symbols to import namespace based on the target framework (when avoiding the global usings)

```
#if DOTNETCORE
using Microsoft.Data.SqlClient;
#else
using System.Data.SqlClient
#endif
```

The example project uses the standard ADO.NET objects such as SqlConnection, SqlCommand, SqlDataReader, SqlDataAdapter, and DataTable. All of them work as expected without further code changes.

There have been a few differences in less-frequently used types, and there are some subtle functional changes described in the porting cheat sheet.[3] The official repository also publishes release notes[4] for every version of the library.

Here are the most interesting features of the new Microsoft.Data. SqlClient:

- New Azure Active Directory (Azure Entra ID) authentication modes allow, for example, to display a pop-up dialog box where the user can sign in using Azure Entra ID, including the support for various multifactor verification options. There is also a mode that supports using Azure Entra ID integrated authentication or using service principal credentials (client ID and client secret).

- The Data Classification API allows access to column sensitivity classification when using SqlDataReader (e.g., you can access information about whether a specific column in the result set carries any personally identifiable information).

- Configurable Retry Logic allows automatic retries for transient errors. It includes several configuration options, such as specifying the number of attempts and waiting intervals between them.

---

[3] See https://github.com/dotnet/SqlClient/blob/main/porting-cheat-sheet.md

[4] See https://github.com/dotnet/SqlClient/tree/main/release-notes

- Always Encrypted is an SQL Server feature that performs sensitive data encryption on the client without revealing the key to the database engine. This ensures complete confidentiality of stored information – the database administrators or cloud providers cannot decrypt the values. This setting cannot be used for the entire database because querying on encrypted columns has numerous limitations. For example, the database engine has no way to sort by an encrypted column or filter values from a certain range because it cannot decipher the values. It can only look for an exact match.

- The `GetFieldValueAsync` method of `SqlDataReader` supports `Stream`, `XmlReader`, or `TextReader`, which is very useful for efficiently loading long values.

Connection Encryption by Default

One important change you will probably run into when migrating your code to the new .NET is the connection encryption – it has been enabled by default. When you connect to a server that presents itself with an untrusted certificate (it typically happens on a developer machine or in on-premises environments where the self-signed certificate is used), you will see the following exception:

A connection was successfully established with the server, but then an error occurred during the login process. (provider: SSL Provider, error: 0 - The certificate chain was issued by an authority that is not trusted.)

To fix the error, you have several options:

1. Configure the SQL Server to use a certificate issued by a trusted certification authority. This is the best solution for non-development, on-premises

installations. If the server does not have a fully qualified domain name (FQDN), for example, if you access it using a local network hostname or an IP address, you can set the `HostNameInCertificate` property in the connection string to accept the certificate stating a different name.

2. Export the self-signed certificate from the SQL Server, and install it on the client machine, or reference the certificate file in the connection string using the `ServerCertificate` property. This property specifies the path to the certificate (public key) that will be used to verify the server identity. This is a good enough solution for many scenarios, but you will need to regularly re-export the new certificate from the SQL Server once the current one expires.

3. Add `TrustServerCertificate=true` in the connection string. This is recommended only in development scenarios where the SQL Server runs on your machine; do not use it when the traffic goes over the local network or the Internet.

4. Note that the SQL Server administrator may turn on the `Force Strict Encryption` option. In this case, you will not be able to connect to the server without the proper certificate validation.

SQLite

When using SQLite with the new .NET, you have two choices. There is an official System.Data.SQLite provider managed directly by the SQLite team. It already existed in the days of .NET Framework. Its recent versions support .NET Standard 2.0 and 2.1 – therefore, the migration should be quite simple.

Along with .NET Core 1.0, Microsoft has released its own alternative provider for SQLite. The motivation for bringing a new implementation instead of porting the existing one was that .NET Core 1.0 was missing quite a lot of APIs (DataSet, for instance), and Microsoft aimed to have a lightweight provider for this popular database.

For example, the System.Data.SQLite provider contains quite a complex logic for handling .NET's rich family of data types. SQLite itself has only four primitive types, and the provider extends the SQL syntax with its own TYPES statement to specify additional type information to the provider. The provider needs to parse the command SQL and remove the metadata before passing it to the native driver.

Microsoft.Data.SQLite provider is much closer to the SQLite native behavior and does not attempt to hide the implementation details. In .NET Core 1.0, it was the only available provider for SQLite. With subsequent versions of .NET Core, the initial motivation of the .NET team shifted a bit. Most of the missing APIs were re-introduced to simplify migration to the new .NET. This allowed for porting the System.Data.SQLite provider, so now there are two options, each having its pros and cons.[5]

Since Microsoft.Data.SQLite did not exist in .NET Framework and System.Data.SQLite is supported in the new .NET, you can keep using it when modernizing legacy applications. However, if you plan to use Entity Framework Core for SQLite, please note that it depends on Microsoft's provider.

---

[5] The key differences are described in the documentation at https://learn. microsoft.com/en-us/dotnet/standard/data/sqlite/compare

Oracle

The .NET Framework's built-in provider for Oracle (System.Data. OracleClient) was deprecated in 2009, long before the new .NET appeared.

If you have already been using ODP.NET (the official provider developed by Oracle), you will need to change the NuGet package to Oracle.ManagedDataAccess.Client. The namespaces and most of the API should remain untouched.

If your code still depends on the unsupported Microsoft client, you will need to change the namespace to Oracle.ManagedDataAccess.Client, and you can expect more breaking changes in the API.

However, since the ADO.NET API is quite strictly tied to shared abstract classes (DbConnection, DbCommand, and others), the number of required code changes, except for the namespaces, is usually close to zero.

LINQ to SQL

It is not a big exaggeration to say that LINQ (Language Integrated Query), introduced with .NET Framework 3.5 in 2007, was a revolution in .NET. It brought concepts known from functional programming into object-oriented C# and VB.NET languages, unleashing numerous possibilities for writing more readable and expressive code.

With LINQ being around for so long, it is sometimes hard to think how we used to do things like searching an array for an object with a minimum value of some property. Today, it feels completely natural to use the OrderBy and First extension methods and pass lambda expressions to declare the intent, but as shown in Listing 5-3, it took several lines of code before LINQ.

Listing 5-3. Searching an array with and without LINQ

```
// find the customer with the oldest order date without LINQ
Customer oldestCustomer = null;
foreach (var customer in customers)
{
    if (oldestCustomer == null
        || customer.FirstOrderDate <
            oldestCustomer.FirstOrderDate)
    {
        oldestCustomer = customer;
    }
}

// the same thing using LINQ
oldestCustomer = customers
    .OrderBy(c => c.FirstOrderDate)
    .First();

// the same thing using LINQ after .NET 6.0
oldestCustomer = customers
    .MinBy(c => c.FirstOrderDate);
```

It is worth mentioning that the second solution with OrderBy and First methods is slower. I do not mean the overall small performance penalty that LINQ adds, because of requiring more virtual method invocations.

In this case, the problem is with the algorithm's time complexity. The non-LINQ version is $O(N)$ because it iterates the entire array exactly once. The second method uses OrderBy, which contains the Quick Sort algorithm inside,[6] increasing the time complexity to $O(N^2)$ in the worst case.

---

[6] It is implemented in the EnumerableSorter class of the .NET: https://source.dot.net/#System.Linq/System/Linq/OrderedEnumerable.cs,6079633a8b8fc091,references

The third method with MinBy (introduced in .NET 6) is again *O(N)*, because the internal implementation of the MinBy function is very similar to the non-LINQ version.

LINQ changed dramatically how we, .NET developers, write code. My personal experience is that it removed about 90% of for and foreach loops from the code, replacing them with calls to LINQ extension methods. In fact, I never got accustomed to the SQL-like syntax of LINQ, with the only exception of the occasional use of the let statement, which I found quite useful. However, in the preceding example, you can see that it is crucial to understand what the LINQ methods do under the hood and think about the implications. If the collection has only 50 items and the code is not invoked a million times every hour, using the slower method may not be a big deal. LINQ greatly improves the code readability and saves the developer's time which may often be preferred. However, when implementing performance-critical sections of the application, you should probably focus on choosing the best-performing option. Or better, use a profiler to measure the real impact and make decisions based on data rather than intuition.

Still, the real game-changers coming with LINQ were not the fancy new syntax for searching collections and support of lambda functions. It was the Expression Trees feature – a way of representing application code in a tree-like data structure that can be either compiled to IL or interacted with using the API in the System.Linq.Expressions namespace. As shown in Listing 5-4, you can look inside and explore the structure of the expression.

Listing 5-4. Inspecting the structure of a lambda expression

```
// define a lambda function (you cannot inspect its structure)
Func<Customer[], Customer> oldestCustomersMethod =
    x => x.MinBy(c => c.FirstOrderDate);

// define a lambda expression (you can inspect its structure)
Expression<Func<Customer[], Customer>> oldestCustomers =
    x => x.MinBy(c => c.FirstOrderDate);
```

```
// you can compile the expression to method
Func<Customer[], Customer> method = oldestCustomers.Compile();

// inspect the structure of the expression
// body represents "x.MinBy(c => c.FirstOrderDate)"
var body = (MethodCallExpression)oldestCustomers.Body;

Console.WriteLine(body.Method.Name);
// writes MinBy

Console.WriteLine(body.Arguments[0].Type);
// writes Customer[]

// Arguments[0] is the object on which the method is called
// Arguments[1] is the lambda expression passed to the method

// lambda represents "c => c.FirstOrderDate"
var lambda = (LambdaExpression)body.Arguments[1];

Console.WriteLine(lambda.Parameters[0].Name);
// writes c

// lambdaBody represents "c.FirstOrderDate"
var lambdaBody = (MemberExpression)lambda.Body;

Console.WriteLine(lambdaBody.Member.Name);
// writes FirstOrderDate
```

This brought the LINQ revolution, allowing ORM libraries, such as LINQ to SQL, Entity Framework, nHibernate, and others, to translate code expressions to SQL or other query languages. The API also allows to build such expressions dynamically at runtime and compile them, which is useful for libraries that need to generate code, such as AutoMapper, mocking frameworks, or numerous dependency injection containers.

LINQ to SQL was the first ORM introduced in .NET Framework 3.5 and provided an easy way of working with database rows without writing SQL commands. Its popularity declined quite quickly in favor of the more powerful Entity Framework, but there are still applications using it out in the world.

LINQ to SQL uses a .dbml file to represent the database model. Usually, it was edited by the designer in Visual Studio, which could display a visual diagram of all included tables and their relationships. In contrast to Entity Framework's .edmx files, the structure of the .dbml is much simpler and quite understandable, as shown in Listing 5-5. This file was the source of truth for generating C# classes representing the database context and entities for included tables. There was no Code First approach available – you always had to generate the context from a real database schema.

Listing 5-5. An excerpt from the LINQ to SQL context definition file

```
<Database Name="dotnetcollege"
    Class="DotNetCollegeContextDataContext"
    xmlns="http://schemas.microsoft.com/linqtosql/dbml/2007">
  <Connection Mode="AppSettings" ConnectionString="..."
              Provider="System.Data.SqlClient" />
  <Table Name="dbo.Courses" Member="Courses">
    <Type Name="Course">
      <Column Name="Id"
              Type="System.Int32"
              DbType="Int NOT NULL IDENTITY"
              IsPrimaryKey="true"
              IsDbGenerated="true"
              CanBeNull="false" />
      <Column Name="BeginDate"
              Type="System.DateTime"
              DbType="DateTime2 NOT NULL"
              CanBeNull="false" />
```

```
    ...
    <Association Name="Course_CourseDate"
                Member="CourseDates"
                ThisKey="Id"
                OtherKey="CourseId"
                Type="CourseDate" />
    ...
  </Type>
</Table>
```

Listing 5-6 shows the code interacting with the model using the LINQ to SQL API. As you can see, it is very similar to Entity Framework.

Listing 5-6. Accessing the database in LINQ to SQL

```csharp
using (var context = new DotNetCollegeDataContext())
{
    // load recent courses
    // (the filtering and ordering is reflected
    // in the generated SQL query)
    var courses = context.Courses
        .Where(c => !c.IsDeleted)
        .OrderByDescending(c => c.BeginDate)
        .Take(20)
        .ToList();
    // iterating over the IQueryable will trigger
    // generating the SQL command and fetching the data

    // you can use lazy-loading to access related data
    Console.WriteLine(
        courses[0].CourseDates.First().BeginDate);

    // you can update the course by modifying
    // the retrieved objects
```

```
courses[0].Price = 10000;
courses[0].IsApproved = true;

// you can delete a course
context.Courses.DeleteOnSubmit(courses[1]);

// or you can add a new course
var newCourse = new Course()
{
    IsApproved = true,
    AllowCashPayments = false,
    ...
};

// you can use navigation properties to
// add related entities without the need
// to link the objects by their foreign keys
newCourse.CourseDates.Add(new CourseDate()
{
    BeginDate = new DateTime(2024, 8, 1, 9, 0, 0),
    EndDate = new DateTime(2024, 8, 1, 17, 0, 0)
});
newCourse.CourseDates.Add(new CourseDate()
{
    BeginDate = new DateTime(2024, 8, 2, 9, 0, 0),
    EndDate = new DateTime(2024, 8, 2, 17, 0, 0)
});
context.Courses.InsertOnSubmit(newCourse);

// save all changes made to the model to the database
context.SubmitChanges();
}
```

The context object represents a database connection and exposes database tables for querying and data manipulation. It tracks all objects loaded through querying or added into any table by calling InsertOnSubmit. When calling SubmitChanges, all tracked object properties are compared with their original values, and appropriate UPDATE statements are generated. Similarly, INSERT and DELETE commands are generated for objects passed to InsertOnSubmit or DeleteOnSubmit. LINQ to SQL respects the relationships between objects. For example, the Course entity from Listing 5-6 must be inserted first by LINQ to SQL, and its Id (assigned by the database) must be fetched and set to the CourseId property of CourseDate entities before they can be saved. Otherwise, the referential integrity would be violated, and the SQL Server would reject the command.

Entity Framework and Entity Framework Core work the same way. Table 5-2 shows the naming changes when converting LINQ to SQL to Entity Framework Core (using the synchronous API).

Table 5-2. *Entity Framework Core replacements for the LINQ to SQL common API*

LINQ to SQL Method	Entity Framework Core Method
context.SubmitChanges()	context.SaveChanges()
context.SomeTable.InsertOnSubmit(...)	context.SomeTable.Add(...)
context.SomeTable.InsertAllOnSubmit(...)	context.SomeTable.AddRange(...)
context.SomeTable.DeleteOnSubmit(...)	context.SomeTable.Remove(...)
context.SomeTable.DeleteAllOnSubmit(...)	context.SomeTable.RemoveRange(...)

(continued)

Table 5-2. (*continued*)

LINQ to SQL Method	Entity Framework Core Method
context. ObjectTrackingEnabled = false	context.SomeTable.AsNoTracking()
context.GetTable<T>()	context.Set<T>()
context.LoadOptions = ...	context.SomeTable.Include(...)
context.ExecuteCommand(...)	context.Database.ExecuteSql(...)
context.ExecuteQuery(...)	context.Database.SqlQuery(...)

Lazy and Eager Loading

As you could see earlier, the most frequently used API remained, just with subtle naming changes. A notable difference between LINQ to SQL and Entity Framework Core is how they work when loading related objects. Both technologies offer eager loading and lazy loading approaches. However, the second one is not recommended as it often leads to performance issues.

Entity Framework Core provides Include and ThenInclude extension methods on its DbSet<T> objects (collections that represent database tables). These methods can instruct the ORM to load related entities together with the main entity within a single query. This approach is referred to as eager loading. It also has its problems (it sometimes fetches more data than necessary), but it performs better in the majority of cases. The inefficiency is caused by the database relational model which can only return the results shaped as rectangular tables.

In Listing 5-7, I am loading the MainCategories table, where each main category has a collection of second-level categories. The problem here lies in how the SQL database can return the data. I want to retrieve a list of records, but each of them carries multiple related records.

The SQL database needs to shape the result set as a single rectangular table, as shown in Table 5-3. Because of this, the same values from the first table must be repeated many times. If any column in the MainCategories table contains long values (e.g., a description or an image), there may be a substantial share of redundant data retrieved from the database.

Listing 5-7. Eager loading in LINQ to SQL and Entity Framework Core

```
// LINQ to SQL - eager loading
var loadOptions = new DataLoadOptions();
loadOptions.LoadWith<MainCategory>(c => c.Categories);
context.LoadOptions = loadOptions;

var mainCategories = context.MainCategories.ToList();

// EF Core - eager loading
var mainCategories = context.MainCategories
    .Include(mc => mc.Categories)
    .ToList();
```

Table 5-3. *Data duplication (cells in italics) in eager loading queries*

MainCategory Table			Category Table		
Id	Name	Other columns	Id	Name	Other columns
1	Developers and software architects	...	1	Web applications	...
1	*Developers and software architects*	...	2	Database development	...
1	*Developers and software architects*	...	3	Desktop applications	...

(continued)

293

Table 5-3. (*continued*)

MainCategory Table			Category Table		
Id	Name	Other columns	Id	Name	Other columns
1	*Developers and software architects*	...	4	Testing and team development	...
1	*Developers and software architects*	...	5	Software architecture and design patterns	...
2	IT professionals	...	10	Microsoft Business Solutions	...
2	*IT professionals*	...	10	Server Administration	...
2	*IT professionals*	...	10	Security	...

This problem can be addressed by avoiding eager loading. Instead, you can use the Select method to return a custom "projection," as demonstrated in Listing 5-8. Both LINQ to SQL and Entity Framework Core can translate it to a single SQL query. The query will also return a rectangular table with the same duplicities, but because you specify only the columns you are interested in instead of retrieving full entities (which can have way more columns than you need), the redundancy is not that large.

Listing 5-8. Custom projection to avoid eager loading

```
var categoryTree = context.MainCategories
    .Select(c => new
    {
        Id = c.Id,
        Name = c.Name,
        Categories = c.Categories.Select(sc => new
```

```
    {
        Id = sc.Id,
        Name = sc.Name
    })
  })
  .ToList();
```

Entity Framework Core also offers a method called AsSplitQuery which instructs it not to load everything as one SQL query. It loads MainCategories as the first query, and subsequently, it retrieves a subset of the Categories table joined to the results of the first query. You can see the queries emitted by Entity Framework Core in Listing 5-9.

Listing 5-9. Split queries produced by Entity Framework Core

```
-- load MainCategories first
SELECT [m].[Id], [m].[Name]
  FROM [MainCategories] AS [m]
  ORDER BY [m].[Id]

-- load Categories related to MainCategories
SELECT [c].[Id], [c].[Name], [m].[Id]
  FROM [MainCategories] AS [m]
  INNER JOIN [Categories] AS [c] ON [m].[Id] = [c].
  [MainCategoryId]
  ORDER BY [m].[Id]
```

Please note that there are some drawbacks to the solution. If the first query is paged using Skip/Take and the sort criteria do not produce unique results, the second query may join on a different set of records obtained from the MainCategories table, and some data can be missing. For example, it can happen when the table is sorted by a date column, and there are multiple records with the same date. If you are unlucky, the first page of records may return a slightly different (but still valid) set of results in the first and second queries because the rows may be ordered in multiple ways. Additionally, if the data are modified in the short moment between these two sequential queries, it may also lead to inconsistent results with potentially missing data. Wrapping the code in a transaction with the Serializable isolation level can solve this issue, but it usually increases the chances for deadlocks. Unfortunately, there is no silver bullet for all situations.

Lazy loading, an alternative approach to load related data, was enabled by default in LINQ to SQL. You can turn it off by setting `DeferredLoadingEnabled` to `false`, but since not many developers did, it is the largest migration issue. With lazy loading enabled, any time you load an entity from the database and access any of its navigation properties for the first time, the related entity or a collection gets loaded automatically. There are several problems with this feature. First, all modern application frameworks assume that any operation that can lead to waiting should be done asynchronously. However, property getters are synchronous, and there is no reasonable way around it. Second, the problem is when lazy loading is invoked repeatedly, especially when iterating through a collection of records. This is known as the SELECT N+1 problem, and I mentioned it already in Chapter 3.

The first version of Entity Framework Core did not support lazy loading at all, and the subsequent releases added support for this feature through a separate package called `Microsoft.EntityFrameworkCore.Proxies`. Although rewriting the code to use eager loading or projections instead of lazy loading increases the effort of modernization, I recommend at least considering this option, especially if you already struggle with performance issues. It can be quite a fruitful way to get an interesting performance benefit from the migration.

Scaffolding Entity Framework Core Model

I have not found any good tool to convert .dbml files to an Entity Framework Core model. However, since LINQ to SQL did not allow for many model customizations, the actual database schema is usually a 1:1 representation of the model used in the application. Therefore, you should start with generating the EF Core model from the database using the standard tooling that comes with .NET.

First, you need to install the dotnet ef command-line tool. You can either install it as a global tool[7] or use it only in the migrated project, as shown in Listing 5-10. Make sure you run it in the root folder of an empty Class Library project that targets a recent version of the new .NET. The project needs to have the following packages installed:

- Microsoft.EntityFrameworkCore.SqlServer

- Microsoft.EntityFrameworkCore.Design

Also, do not forget to replace the connection string in the script with the correct one pointing to your database. I also added the --output-dir argument to tell the generator to place the classes in the Model folder. Feel free to adjust the model path so it fits your conventions. There are additional options[8] you can use to fine-tune the scaffolding, for example, to select only some tables or schemas you want to import.

---

[7] See https://learn.microsoft.com/en-us/ef/core/cli/dotnet#installing-the-tools

[8] See https://learn.microsoft.com/en-us/ef/core/managing-schemas/scaffolding/?tabs=dotnet-core-cli#command-line-options

Listing 5-10. Installing dotnet-ef tool locally and scaffolding the EF Core model from the database

cd **YOUR_NEW_PROJECT_FOLDER**

```
dotnet new tool-manifest
dotnet tool install dotnet-ef
```

```
dotnet ef dbcontext scaffold "YOUR_CONNECTION_STRING" ↵
  Microsoft.EntityFrameworkCore.SqlServer --output-dir Model
```

After the model is generated, you can start porting the code. Both LINQ to SQL and Entity Framework used pluralization algorithms to make collection names in plural (Courses) and entity names singular (Course). This often created very funny results when database objects were named in other languages – I remember one consulting gig where the customer complained that their table KontaktniOsoba (contact person in Czech) was generated as KontaktniOsobies (instead of KontaktniOsoby). Naturally, the pluralized did not expect any other language than English.

Unfortunately, the algorithm implementation is different in both libraries, so you can expect some subtle differences.

Other Differences

Since the query translator in LINQ to SQL did not offer many features and model mapping could not be customized much, the migration should not be very difficult as you are probably using a subset of Entity Framework Core features.

The Entity Framework Core scaffolder can detect many-to-many relationships. In such cases, it omits the joining table when generating the code, which results in a slightly different code from the original LINQ to SQL model. You need to modify the application code or manually add the joining table in the model.[9]

After you resolve all compile errors caused by the differences, you will need to test the entire codebase to ensure the queries and data manipulation operations work the same way. In more complex applications, you can find numerous subtle differences, for example, in null or date handling.

The largest difference is in the lazy loading. It cannot be revealed at the compile time – you need to run the actual code to see whether it works or not. If you use this feature in LINQ to SQL frequently, you can install the NuGet package called `Microsoft.EntityFrameworkCore.Proxies` and add call `UseLazyLoadingProxies` in the `OnConfiguring` method of the generated Entity Framework Core context, as shown in Listing 5-11.

Listing 5-11. Turning on the lazy loading in Entity Framework Core

```
protected override void OnConfiguring(
    DbContextOptionsBuilder optionsBuilder)
{
    optionsBuilder

        ...

        .UseLazyLoadingProxies();
}
```

---

[9] See `https://learn.microsoft.com/en-us/ef/core/modeling/relationships#many-to-many`

I have found only one feature that LINQ to SQL supports and Entity Framework Core does not – the Delay-loaded properties. It was quite useful for properties with long values, such as descriptions, images, or other binary content. These properties were not fetched automatically when the entity was loaded. Instead, they were loaded using a separate SQL query only after their get accessor was called for the first time. In the .dbml designer, you could select a property and set Delay Loaded to true, as demonstrated in Figure 5-1.

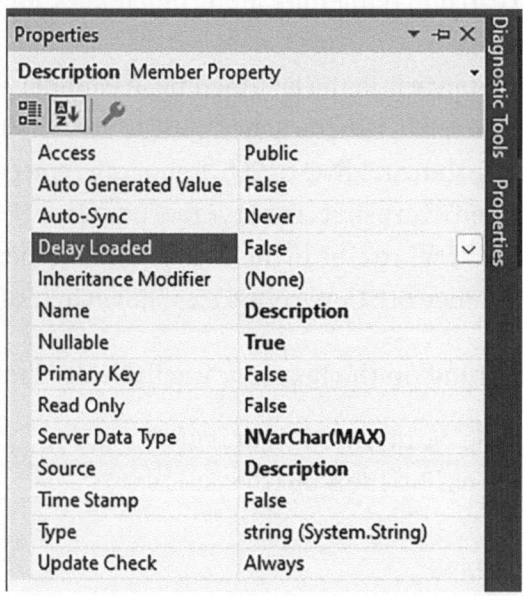

Figure 5-1. *Setting Delay Loaded flag on LINQ to SQL entity properties*

Entity Framework Core does not support this concept. The solution is to move such properties to a separate table with the one-to-one relationship, as shown in Listing 5-12. Then, you can load them manually or via lazy loading (if you have it turned on).

Listing 5-12. Moving long values to a separate 1:1 entity

```
public class CourseTemplate
{
    public int Id { get; set; }

    [MaxLength(100)]
    public string Name { get; set; }

    ...

    public virtual CourseTemplateAssets? Assets { get; set; }
}

// a new entity with long values
public class CourseTemplateAssets
{
    public int Id { get; set; }

    public int CourseTemplateId { get; set; }

    public virtual CourseTemplate CourseTemplate { get; set; }

    public string Description { get; set; }

    public byte[] ImageData { get; set; }
}
```

Entity Framework

Entity Framework was released in 2008, shortly after LINQ to SQL was
introduced. It was included in .NET Framework 3.5 Service Pack 1 (yes, a
Service Pack of .NET Framework added such a significant feature, but the
version number remained almost the same).

Entity Framework was one of the first parts of the .NET Framework, which was separated and shipped as a stand-alone NuGet package (starting with version 4.1). Thanks to this, it could have a different release cycle and did not depend on releases of .NET Framework. Soon, other official parts of the .NET platform adopted the same approach. It lets them deliver new features more quickly and without the risk of breaking existing applications. You could easily have several .NET applications, each using a different version of Entity Framework. Even if Microsoft released a new version of Entity Framework, nothing could happen to your application unless you explicitly upgraded to the new package.

Choose Between Entity Framework and Entity Framework Core

If your application uses Entity Framework, the important decision you should make is whether to migrate to Entity Framework Core or keep using Entity Framework with the new .NET. The new EF Core has many benefits, but switching to it may introduce many breaking changes, especially in more complex queries.

Entity Framework 6.4 targets .NET Framework 4.5 (and all subsequent releases of .NET Framework) as well as .NET Standard 2.1 (all versions of the new .NET since .NET Core 3.0). Thanks to this, you can upgrade the version of Entity Framework used in your application to 6.4 and keep using it. In most cases, this is just a question of upgrading the corresponding NuGet package and fixing some startup code (supplying the connection string from the new configuration system).

In the long term, it makes great sense to migrate to EF Core, as all new stunning features and improvements happen here. But if your modernization project involves migrating many frameworks and libraries, you can consider splitting the process into multiple stages. In the first stage, you will need to focus on migrating libraries that are not supported on the new .NET at all. Migration of Entity Framework to Entity Framework Core can wait until the project is already running on the new stack.

Additionally, you may face various issues when it comes to other libraries that somehow interact with Entity Framework. Using EF 6 on the new .NET is not a frequent use case, and some library authors do not even know about this option or have no plans to support it. Even Microsoft's old ASP.NET Identity library, which is closely coupled with Entity Framework 6, targets neither .NET Standard nor the new .NET. You need to port it yourself if you plan to use it.[10] I have also experienced several issues with newer versions of AutoMapper that started producing LINQ expressions which the old Entity Framework could not translate. The issue was reported on GitHub to the AutoMapper authors, but it was closed because the team no longer has any plans to support Entity Framework 6. I had to implement a simple expression rewriter[11] which fixes the generated expressions before executing the query.

In the previous chapters, I already described the differences between Entity Framework and Entity Framework Core. Check the official list of changes[12] in the documentation if you are unsure whether EF Core supports everything you need.

---

[10] I ported the codebase to .NET Standard 2.1, including all tests. It is submitted as a pull request in the official GitHub repository (`https://github.com/aspnet/AspNetIdentity/pull/62`), but since the library has not been updated recently, I do not believe the PR will be merged.

If you want to clone the branch and use it in your migration project, note that **the ported version did not undergo any serious security review and was not extensively tested. Thus, I do not recommend using it in any production scenario. Use it at your own risk.**

[11] See `https://stackoverflow.com/a/78384513/1482195`

[12] See `https://learn.microsoft.com/en-us/ef/efcore-and-ef6/`

In general, EF Core is already a mature ORM that offers plenty of new features the old Entity Framework does not provide. However, EF 6 has a very strong query translator engine and can often translate complex queries that do not work in EF Core. You will most probably reach some limitations when using EF Core in large applications. On the other hand, all issues I encountered always had some solution or a workaround. The last resort option, which is always available, is to implement the functionality directly in SQL.

Migrate ObjectContext to DbContext API

Entity Framework 3.5 and 4.0 used the ObjectContext class to represent the database model. It imposed a significant level of abstraction in order to support multiple database providers and offered quite exotic features, such as self-tracking entities.[13]

Together with the introduction of the Code First approach in Entity Framework 4.1, the new DbContext API was introduced. It was a wrapper over ObjectContext which still lived somewhere inside, but it exposed just a subset of the ORM features, and in a more convenient way. On the other hand, it added a crucial feature necessary for the Code First approach – support for POCO[14] entities. With ObjectContext, the entity classes must

---

[13] The context object usually tracks all entities that pass through it. For example, it remembers their initial property values and information about the entity state (whether it was added, marked for deletion, and so on). Thanks to this, you can call SaveChanges and have all changes of the in-memory objects reflected in the database. Self-tracking entities do not rely on the context object. Instead, they track their state and property changes themselves. This was useful in some scenarios when the entities were sent through an API to a client-side application (e.g., a framework called WCF RIA Services used this concept). However, this approach is no longer recommended.

[14] POCO stands for Plain-Old CLR Objects. The term refers to plain C# classes with auto-generated properties and no logic in getters and setters.

inherit from a base class and contain code in all get and set accessors of every property in order to make the change tracking work, as shown in Listing 5-13. DbContext can work with entities with auto-generated properties.

The Visual Studio designer for Entity Data Model (.edmx) files was soon updated to generate DbContext entities, so if your application used Entity Framework 5 or 6, you are probably already using the new DbContext API. If the application still uses the old version of Entity Framework, it may still use the old ObjectContext API. In this case, the number of code changes will be higher because you will technically need to go through two migrations.

Listing 5-13. Example of a generated ObjectContext entity class and the equivalent DbContext entity

```
// ObjectContext API
[EdmEntityTypeAttribute(NamespaceName="MTSModel",
    Name="AddressGPSLocation")]
[Serializable()]
[DataContractAttribute(IsReference=true)]
public partial class AddressGPSLocation : EntityObject
{
    [EdmScalarPropertyAttribute(
      EntityKeyProperty=true, IsNullable=false)]
    [DataMemberAttribute()]
    public global::System.Int32 Id
    {
        get
        {
            return _Id;
        }
```

```
        set
        {
            if (_Id != value)
            {
                OnIdChanging(value);
                ReportPropertyChanging("Id");
                _Id = StructuralObject.SetValidValue(value);
                ReportPropertyChanged("Id");
                OnIdChanged();
            }
        }
    }
    private global::System.Int32 _Id;
    partial void OnIdChanging(global::System.Int32 value);
    partial void OnIdChanged();

    ...
}

// DbContext API
public class AddressGPSLocation
{
    // [Key] attribute is optional - EF can infer it
    // from the property name
    public int Id { get; set; }

    ...
}
```

To migrate to the DbContext API, you need to open the .edmx file, click the empty space in the diagram, and press F4 to display the *Properties* window. Then, change the Code Generation Strategy to *T4*, as shown in Figure 5-2. It will stop the generation of the legacy ObjectContext class.

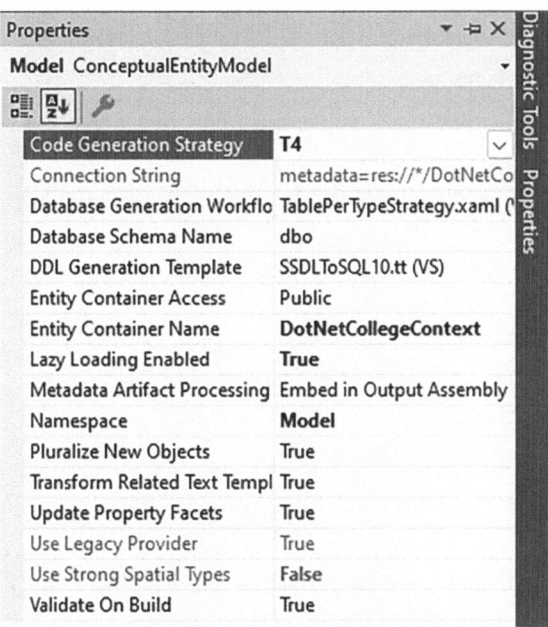

Figure 5-2. *Switching the Code Generation Strategy in the Entity Data Model*

Next, you will need to right-click the empty space in the diagram and select the Add Code Generation Item like in Figure 5-3. After that, select the *EF 6.x DbContext generator* to enable the generation of DbContext-based model classes.

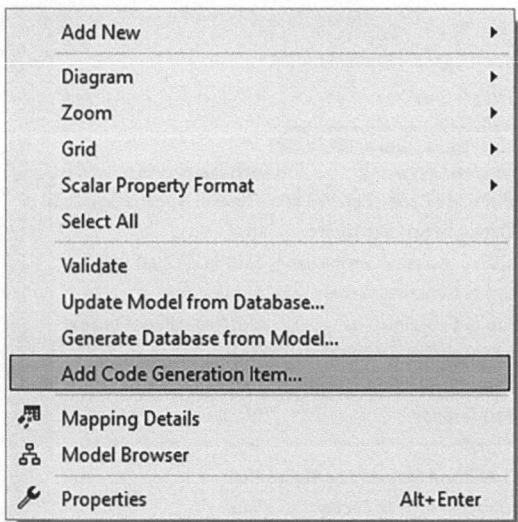

Figure 5-3. *Adding a code generation item to the Entity Data Model*

The new API is quite different – you will need to make several changes in your code, as shown in Table 5-4. The good news is that there should be no changes in LINQ queries – there is the same underlying query translator.

Table 5-4. *Code changes when migrating from ObjectContext to DbContext API*

ObjectContext API	DbContext API
context.DatabaseExists()	context.Database.Exists()
context.CreateDatabase()	context.Database.Create()
context.SomeTable.AddObject(...)	context.SomeTable.Add(...)
context.AddToSomeTable(...)	context.SomeTable.Add(...)
context.SomeTable.DeleteObject(...)	context.SomeTable.Remove(...)
context.DeleteObject(...)	context.SomeTable.Remove(...)

Database First Approach with Entity Framework and the New .NET

In Entity Framework Core, the only supported approach is to define the database model using the C# code – the Code First approach. To define the model in code does not necessarily mean that you cannot start with designing the SQL database. As you already saw in the "LINQ to SQL" section, you can – there is a command-line tool to scaffold the model from the database schema (I will get back to it again in the following sections). If you already have the database, you do not need to manually write its code representation.

However, if you plan to set up your development workflow to update the database schema and then re-scaffold the model every time, you will lose many opportunities to adjust the model to be convenient to use from the code. Any manual change to the code would be overwritten by the next re-scaffold.

Therefore, most teams that do not start with an empty database prefer to scaffold the model just once at the beginning and then make all changes in the C# code. It is quite common to use Entity Framework Core Migrations to update the database schema based on the model changes. Once you change the model, you can use command-line tooling to generate a database migration. Then, there are several ways to apply it to the database – you can either generate SQL scripts to be executed manually by the database administrator, run the migrations using the command-line tool during deployment, or invoke them from the code on application startup.

If you plan to keep using Entity Framework 6.4, you can even keep using the Database First approach. EF 6.4 supports .edmx files when used in the new .NET. However, you may be facing issues with the designer in Visual Studio, which does not work inside SDK-based projects. To make it work, you will have to host the model in a .NET Framework project.

This project is not going to be deployed; it is used only for editing the model using Visual Studio. The new .NET project will link the .edmx file and generated .cs files in the .csproj file from the old project. It needs to use the EntityDeploy build action to correctly pack it as an embedded resource in the resulting assembly, as you can see in Listing 5-14.

You can see how to configure it in the ModernizationDemo. EfCoreEdmxTests project in this chapter's example repository. The only thing that feels a bit unnatural is the presence of the app.config file with the connection string. To get rid of it, you can create a partial class for the context and add a second constructor that accepts the connection string as a parameter. This way, the old configuration file will not be needed.

Listing 5-14. Linking the Entity Data Model file from .NET Framework host project

```
<ItemGroup>
  <EntityDeploy
    Include="..\HostProject\Model\DotNetCollegeContext.edmx"
    Link="Model\DotNetCollegeContext.edmx" />
  <Compile Include="..\HostProject\Model\*.cs"
    LinkBase="Model" />
</ItemGroup>
```

When migrating to Entity Framework Core, you will need to migrate to the Code First approach, which is covered in the next section.

Migrate to Entity Framework Core

If you decided to migrate to Entity Framework Core, you have two options based on what approach you use in the application:

- Use the Entity Framework model classes and port the model configuration code in the OnModelCreating method. This option is feasible if you already use the

Code First approach with Entity Framework. If you use the Database First approach, you can use the generated context and entity classes, but a substantial part of the metadata (such as field lengths, precisions, names of columns in the original database, and so on) is stored only in the .edmx file. Therefore, I would not recommend this option for Database First models.

- Scaffold the model from the database schema using EF Core command-line tool. This will probably result in a number of small differences in the model, but resolving them is often easier than porting the model configuration from EF to EF Core.

Scaffolding

Entity Framework Core comes with a command-line tool called dotnet-ef which can be used for various tasks, such as generating the migrations or scaffolding the model (Microsoft documentation also refers to it as reverse engineering the model). If you are used to the PowerShell commands Add-Migration and Update-Database, the good news is that you can use them as well.

To use the tool, you need to install several NuGet packages in the project:

- Microsoft.EntityFrameworkCore.SqlServer (or other provider-specific package for the database of your choice)

- Microsoft.EntityFrameworkCore.Design

To use the command-line tool, you need to install it either globally for the entire machine or locally for the project, as shown in Listing 5-15. The local installation offers an advantage to sticking to a concrete version of the tool.

Listing 5-15. Installing the dotnet-ef command-line tool

```
# option 1: install the tool globally
dotnet tool install --global dotnet-ef

# option 2: install the tool locally
cd YOUR_PROJECT_FOLDER
dotnet new tool-manifest
dotnet tool install dotnet-ef
```

If you prefer to use the PowerShell version, you can add the Microsoft.EntityFrameworkCore.Tools NuGet package in the project instead and use the Package Manager Console to invoke the Scaffold-DbContext command.[15]

To scaffold the code, you can use the command shown in Listing 5-16. There are several options[16] to fine-tune the code generation. You need to specify the connection string and the database provider (named the same as the NuGet package containing its implementation). The MODEL_FOLDER parameter is a relative path to a folder in which you want the context class and model classes stored (if you prefer to have the context somewhere else, use the --context-dir or -ContextDir option). I am also used to enabling the data annotation option, which tells the scaffolder to use attributes on entities and their properties where possible. It makes the OnModelCreating method short and easier to work with.

---

[15] See the full PowerShell command reference: https://learn.microsoft.com/en-us/ef/core/cli/powershell#scaffold-dbcontext

[16] See the full CLI command reference: https://learn.microsoft.com/en-us/ef/core/cli/dotnet#dotnet-ef-dbcontext-scaffold

Listing 5-16. Scaffolding the code using the CLI tool and
PowerShell command

```
# CLI command
dotnet ef dbcontext scaffold "YOUR_CONNECTION_STRING" ⏎
  Microsoft.EntityFrameworkCore.SqlServer ⏎
  --output-dir MODEL_FOLDER ⏎
  --data-annotations

# Package Manager Console command
Scaffold-DbContext -Connection "YOUR_CONNECTION_STRING" ⏎
  -Provider Microsoft.EntityFrameworkCore.SqlServer ⏎
  -OutputDir MODEL_FOLDER ⏎
  -DataAnnotations
```

After the model is scaffolded and you try to use it from the application,
the compiler will probably complain about some incompatibilities in
the model. It largely depends on how much the original model was
different from the database schema, but even if you did not change it,
the naming conventions the scaffolder uses are a bit different in Entity
Framework Core.

In my applications, I usually had to fight with the following constructs:

- Properties with abbreviations have a different casing.
  For example, a column named DIC (Czech abbreviation
  for Tax Identification Number) was generated as DIC
  by Entity Framework 6. However, EF Core names the
  property Dic and annotates it with a [Column("DIC")]
  attribute (because some databases are case-sensitive
  when referring to table and column names). I had to
  rename the property in the generated model to remove
  compile errors in my application code.

313

- The pluralization algorithm produces different results in some cases. In the example project, I have a table called Courses which Entity Framework 6 incorrectly singularizes to Cours. EF Core has fixed this issue and singularizes it correctly as Course, but since the incorrect name was used in the original application for some navigation properties, this produces a new inconsistency. In this case, I preferred fixing the application code rather than reproducing the same bug in the new model.

- The inference of navigation property names is smarter in EF Core. In the example repository, there is the CourseTemplateRelation entity, which expresses the relationship between two CourseTemplate entities (e.g., if you attend one course, we recommend attending another one, and this pair is represented by the CourseTemplateRelation). EF 6 names the navigation properties CourseTemplate and CourseTemplate1, while EF Core can recognize the prefix in the foreign key properties (CourseTemplateId and RelatedCourseTemplateId) and produce CourseTemplate and RelatedCourseTemplate properties, as shown in Listing 5-17.

Listing 5-17. Differences in inferring navigation property names between EF and EF Core (data annotation attributes omitted for clarity)

```
# EF 6
public class CourseTemplateRelation
{
    public int Id { get; set; }
    public int CourseTemplateId { get; set; }
```

```
    public int RelatedCourseTemplateId { get; set; }
    public virtual CourseTemplate CourseTemplate { get; set; }
    public virtual CourseTemplate CourseTemplate1 { get; set; }
}

# EF Core
public class CourseTemplateRelation
{
    public int Id { get; set; }
    public int CourseTemplateId { get; set; }
    public int RelatedCourseTemplateId { get; set; }
    public virtual CourseTemplate CourseTemplate { get; set; }
    public virtual CourseTemplate RelatedCourseTemplate
        { get; set; }
}
```

- The scaffolder has no way to recognize properties mapped to enums, as they are represented by number or string columns in the database. You will have to manually review the generated model classes and change the types of such properties.

- The scaffolder often does not recognize inheritance and other mapping changes that are not visible from the database schema. For example, when using Table Per Type inheritance, the scaffolder can see several tables with one-to-one relationships but has no way to infer that their entities have a common base class. The same applies to different naming of model objects from the name in the database, complex types, table splitting, and other features.

Porting the Code First Model

If you have been using the Code First approach with Entity Framework 6, you already have the functional model classes and the context object. Nothing prevents you from using the scaffolding, but you will probably lose many manual changes you made to the model to be more convenient to use. Therefore, porting the data annotation attributes and the OnModelCreating method, which uses a different model builder API, is usually easier.

Let us start with the OnModelCreating method. Its name in both DbContext classes is the same, but the model builder object has changed. The old API uses System.Data.Entity.DbModelBuilder, while the new one uses Microsoft.EntityFrameworkCore.ModelBuilder. The comparison of the API is shown in Table 5-5.

Table 5-5. *Examples of differences in the ModelBuilder API*

EF DbModelBuilder	EF Core ModelBuilder

.Entity<T>()
  .HasRequired(...)
  ...
	.Entity<T>(e => {
	  .HasOne(...)
	
	  ...
	  .IsRequired()
	})

.Entity<T>()
  .HasOptional(...)
  ...
	.Entity<T>(e => {
	  .HasOne(...)
	
	  ...
	  .IsRequired(false)
	})

(continued)

Table 5-5. (*continued*)

EF DbModelBuilder	EF Core ModelBuilder
| ```
.Entity<T>()
 .HasMany(...)
 .WithRequired(...)
``` | ```
.Entity<T>(e => {
  .HasMany(...)
  .WithOne(...)
  .IsRequired()
})
``` |
| ```
.Entity<T>()
 .HasMany(...)
 .WithOptional(...)
``` | ```
.Entity<T>(e => {
  .HasMany(...)
  .WithOne(...)
  .IsRequired(false)
})
``` |
| ```
.Entity<T>()
 .HasMany(...)
 .WithMany(...)
 .Map(m => m.ToTable(...)
   .MapLeftKey(...)
   .MapRightKey(...))
``` | ```
.Entity<T>(e => {
  .HasMany(...)
  .WithMany(...)
  .UsingEntity(
    "table",
    ...,   // right key
    ...   // left key
  )
})
``` |
| ```
.Entity<T>()
 ...
 .WillCascadeOnDelete()
``` | ```
.Entity<T>(e => {
  ...
  .OnDelete(DeleteBehavior.Cascade)
})
``` |
| ```
.Entity<T>()
 .Property(e => ...)
 .HasDatabaseGeneratedOption(...)
``` | ```
.Entity<T>(e => {
  .Property(e => ...)
  .ValueGeneratedOnAdd()
  // or .ValueGeneratedNever()
  // or .UseIdentityColumn()
})
``` |

317

Instead of placing everything into the OnModelCreating method, which can get very long and hard to maintain, I recommend splitting the configuration and moving it to separate classes, a feature that is new to Entity Framework Core. You can declare a class implementing IEntityTypeConfiguration<T> and omit the modelBuilder. Entity<T>(...) wrapper call. Instead, you can just configure the single entity based on the type parameter of T. I found it quite convenient to place these configurations in the same files as the entities, as shown in Listing 5-18. I use nested classes – thanks to that, they can all be named just EntityConfiguration.

Listing 5-18. Moving entity type configuration in separate classes

```
public class Lector
{
    public int Id { get; set; }
    ...

    class EntityConfiguration
      : IEntityTypeConfiguration<Lector>
    {
        public void Configure(EntityTypeBuilder<Lector> entity)
        {
            entity.Property(
              e => e.DefaultSupplierId).HasDefaultValue(4);
            ...
        }
    }
}

// register entity type configurations in the DbContext
public class DotNetCollegeContext : DbContext
{
    ...
```

```
protected override void OnModelCreating(
  ModelBuilder modelBuilder)
{
    modelBuilder.ApplyConfigurationsFromAssembly(
        typeof(DotNetCollegeContext).Assembly);

    ...

}
}
```

After you port the configuration and resolve all compile errors, you will face the most annoying part of the process – making sure that the database schema emitted by the model has not changed.

Entity Framework Core tries to infer names for indexes, primary, and foreign key constraints (e.g., IX_Lectors_DefaultSupplierId). If you did not have these names explicitly stated in the old model and had them generated by Entity Framework automatically, Entity Framework Core will also have to auto-generate them, and it uses different naming conventions. Making these names synchronized is especially important when you plan to use Entity Framework Core Migrations. If you alter any relationship, the generated migration code will not work because of referencing non-existing indexes or constraints.

Visual Studio's SSDT (SQL Server Data Tools) component has a nice feature to compare database schemas. You can find it in the *Tools* ➤ *SQL Server* ➤ *New Schema Comparison*. Select the current database on the left and the newly generated database on the right. It will create a report like in Figure 5-4.

In applications I have migrated, I mostly experienced the following differences in the schemas:

- Relationships have indexes named by a different convention. EF 6 names the indexes IX_LectorId, while EF Core uses IX_Accounts_LectorId.

- Primary keys are named `PK_Accounts` instead of `PK_dbo.Accounts`.

- Foreign keys are named `FK_Accounts_Suppliers_SupplierId` instead of `FK_dbo.Accounts_dbo.Suppliers_SupplierId`.

- The `DateTime` properties produce `DATETIME` SQL data type with Entity Framework, but EF Core uses `DATETIME2` (with higher precision and support of earlier dates than `1753-01-01`).

Specifying the constraint and index names manually in the configuration using the model builder API is possible, but copying and pasting hundreds of names like this is dull work. The recent versions of Entity Framework Core allow registering conventions which you can use to adjust the configured model. They are quite useful for making global changes to the configuration, as you can see in Listing 5-19. Be careful that this convention overrides the names of all keys and indexes. If you configure these names manually for several entities, update the code to omit them.

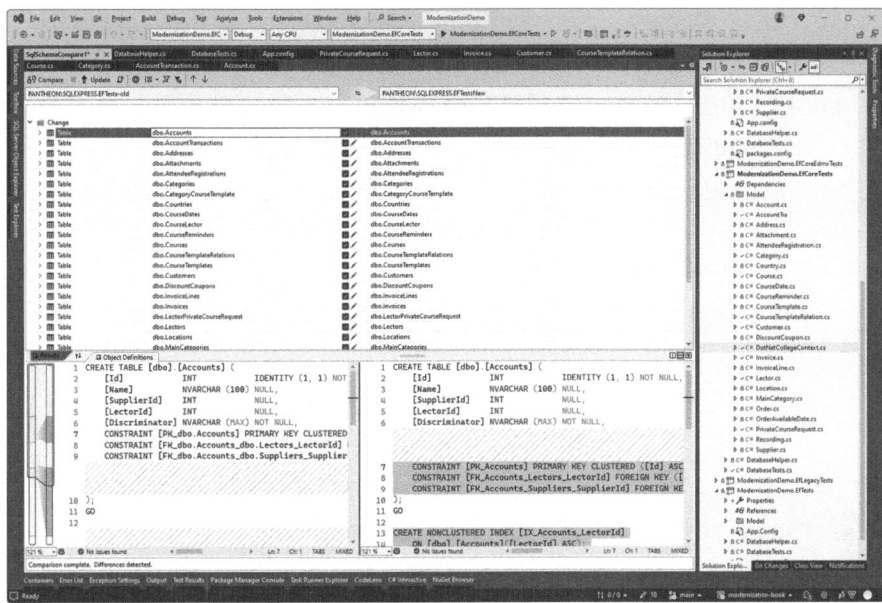

Figure 5-4. *Schema compare tool in SQL Server Data Tools in Visual Studio*

Listing 5-19. A model convention to fix the names of indexes and constraints

```
public class DotNetCollegeContext : DbContext
{
    ...

    protected override void ConfigureConventions(
        ModelConfigurationBuilder configurationBuilder)
    {
        configurationBuilder.Conventions.Add(
            _ => new KeyNamingConvention());
        base.ConfigureConventions(configurationBuilder);
    }
}
```

```
public class KeyNamingConvention : IModelFinalizingConvention
{
    public void ProcessModelFinalizing(
        IConventionModelBuilder modelBuilder,
        IConventionContext<IConventionModelBuilder> context)
    {
        foreach (var entity in
           modelBuilder.Metadata.GetEntityTypes())
        {
            foreach (var index in entity.GetDeclaredIndexes())
            {
                index.SetDatabaseName($"IX_{string.Join("_", ↵
index.Properties.Select(p => p.GetColumnName()))}");
            }
            foreach (var key in entity.GetDeclaredKeys()
                .Where(k => k.IsPrimaryKey()))
            {
                if (key.IsPrimaryKey())
                {
                    key.SetName(
                        $"PK_dbo.{entity.GetTableName()}");
                }
            }
            foreach (var key in
                entity.GetDeclaredReferencingForeignKeys())
            {
                key.SetConstraintName($"FK↵
_dbo.{key.DeclaringEntityType.GetTableName()}↵
_dbo.{key.PrincipalEntityType.GetTableName()}↵
```

```
_{string.Join("_", key.Properties.Select(↵
p => p.GetColumnName()))}");
            }
        }
    }
}
```

After you achieve having the same database schema from the migrated model, you are ready to go testing whether the application behaves the same.

Lazy Loading

Like LINQ to SQL, Entity Framework enabled lazy loading by default, and many developers were using this feature. However, for new applications, I strongly advocate not enabling it or maybe even forgetting that this feature exists. The usefulness of lazy loading comes at a very high price – the risk of significant performance issues that are often hard to discover and fix. However, removing it would require extreme effort if you have a large codebase relying on it.

To make this unfortunate feature work, you need to install the `Microsoft.EntityFrameworkCore.Proxies` NuGet package and call the `UseLazyLoadingProxies()` method in the `OnConfiguring` method of your context, as shown in Listing 5-11 in the "LINQ to SQL" section.

Remember to declare all navigation properties as `virtual`. Lazy loading generates proxy classes that are inherited from the entity classes, and without this keyword, the proxies would not have a chance to override the property getters to inject the loading code.

Configuration and Connection Strings

A tiny but important bit of the migration is how to supply the connection string to the context object.

In Entity Framework Core, the context declares a constructor that accepts an object of type DbContextOptions<TContext>. Also, the context has its own OnConfiguring method to provide an additional or default configuration. Because the modernization of the database layer often takes place before dependency injection is configured, you may need to build the options object yourself, as shown in Listing 5-20.

Listing 5-20. Building the DbContextOptions manually

```
var optionsBuilder =
    new DbContextOptionsBuilder<DotNetCollegeContext>()
    .UseSqlServer(connectionString)
    .UseLazyLoadingProxies();
context = new DotNetCollegeContext(optionsBuilder.Options);
```

In the case of keeping the old Entity Framework in place, the situation is a bit different. By default, the DbContext object has only the default constructor without parameters which loads the connection string from the app.config or web.config file. Technically, it is possible to use these files in the new .NET, but I recommend migrating away from them. These files do not work well with the new configuration model of .NET, which supports features like User Secrets, overriding the configuration using environment variables, and other concepts. The tooling also does not expect these files to be used, and you may run into various complications, for example, when creating automated build or release pipelines:

- If you use the Code First approach, you can easily add a constructor to your DbContext to be able to supply your own connection string.

- If you generate the DbContext from the .edmx file, you can do the same thing. However, instead of manually editing the generated file (it could get rewritten by the designer), add a partial class next to it, as demonstrated in Listing 5-21.

Listing 5-21. Partial class adding a constructor to the generated DbContext object (make sure it is in the same namespace)

```
public partial class DotNetCollegeContext : DbContext
{
    public DotNetCollegeContext(string connectionString)
        : base(connectionString)
    {
    }
}
```

ASP.NET Identity Tables

One notable complication you can run into when migrating to Entity Framework Core is ASP.NET Identity. This library can store information about users and roles in the database using Entity Framework, and in such cases, the Entity Framework context is inherited from `IdentityDbContext`.

Because the official ASP.NET Identity libraries are not compatible with .NET Standard and the new .NET, the base type of the context is not available in the new .NET, which will produce compilation errors.

Ideally, the library should be replaced by the new ASP.NET Core Identity. If you plan to keep using Entity Framework 6 with the old ASP.NET Identity, you will have to maintain its .NET Standard unofficial port yourself.

When migrating to Entity Framework Core, you must migrate the identity tables to ASP.NET Core Identity, which involves migrating user accounts to the new schema. The next chapter will cover this in detail.

If you do not want to migrate user stores now, you can temporarily add the `Users`, `Roles`, and other necessary tables and entities to your context and change its base type to `DbContext`. This will help you to resolve compilation errors in your data model. However, other ASP.NET Identity artifacts, such as usages of the `UserManager` class, will remain in the codebase. These will have to be replaced or temporarily commented out.

Testing

When you succeed in compiling the project without errors, you will need to verify that all data queries done through Entity Framework will work. If your application is at least partially covered by integration tests, you already have tools in place to see potential problems quickly. However, I have met a substantial number of applications with no tests at all.

Working in a company that builds tailor-made applications that usually have just one customer, I am the last person on the planet who would criticize insufficient test coverage in any project. It is a completely different situation than running a productized solution for thousands of customers, where the costs of having proper testing infrastructure are shared by many. The return on investment in testing in such cases is usually reasonably short. But when there is only one customer, many companies need to carefully consider which areas are critical and thus worth spending extra effort on. I insist that there should be at least some tests covering the most important parts of the application (sometimes referred to as smoke testing), but I deeply understand the situation of many developer teams that never had the time or budget to put tests in place. However, it is important to emphasize that not having any tests is a severe risk, and in numerous cases, "not having time for tests" is more an excuse.[17]

---

[17] In my consulting engagements, I have seen multiple projects where the time required to implement a reasonable number of tests would certainly be orders of magnitude lower than the time the team spent on fixing issues in production, not speaking about potential financial losses originating from these issues. The argument of insufficient time for tests was not valid, and my advice was to implement the "add a test for every bug" strategy. This allowed the team to gradually cover the most problematic parts of the code with tests.

Modernization is an opportunity to introduce various improvements to tackle technical debt, and the testing infrastructure may be one of the valuable outcomes. The concepts introduced in the new .NET, such as dependency injection, abstraction over configuration, and logging, remove most obstacles to introducing tests. Furthermore, adding the next one is much easier once the test project is set up and the first few tests are already in place. You can agree on a policy that every bug you discover and fix from now on will have to be covered by a test. This helps to increase the test coverage continuously and slowly improves the overall code quality.

Feel free to look in the example repository described at the beginning of this chapter to see how to use Entity Framework in test projects. For example, there is a helper class that recreates the database before every test which you can use as a quick start. Be ready to invest some time in preparing good test data – you will need them to write meaningful tests.

Differences in Complex Queries

You should be quite safe if you make only simple database queries in Entity Framework Core. All the basic methods, such as `Where`, `OrderBy`, `OrderByDescending`, `ThenBy`, `ThenByDescending`, `Skip`, `Take`, `Min`, `Max`, `Average`, `Sum`, and `Count`, should not break anything.

The `Select` clause may behave a bit differently when returning complex objects, such as child collections, as you can see in Listing 5-22. For example, if you build the nested collection of categories and use *OrderBy* on it, you have to add `ToList()`, because EF Core can translate the query only when the property type is `IEnumerable<T>` or `List<T>`. `OrderBy` returns `IOrderedEnumerable<T>` and is not recognized by Entity Framework Core as a supported type. Using `ToList()` inside the query looks counterintuitive – you would expect that it will try to run a SQL query for every returned *MainCategory*. Luckily, this is not true – the entire code snippet will produce only a single SQL query with the appropriate `JOIN` clause, and inner `ToList` is just a way to "cast" the property of the supported type.

Listing 5-22. Difference in Select queries loading child collections

```
var categoryTree = context.MainCategories
    .Select(c => new
    {
        Id = c.Id,
        Name = c.Name,
        Categories = c.Categories
            .Select(sc => new
            {
                Id = sc.Id,
                Name = sc.Name
            })
            .OrderBy(sc => sc.Name)
            // in EF Core, we have to add ToList() here
            .ToList(),
        CategoryCount = c.Categories.Count
    })
    .ToList();
```

If you use mapping libraries like AutoMapper, they sometimes auto-generate Select clauses for you based on the mapping configuration. In AutoMapper, there is the ProjectTo<TResult> extension method on IQueryable<T> which does exactly that. You may run into various issues if the dynamically generated Select clause contains something that EF Core does not support.

Be extra careful when using the following advanced query operators:

- Join

- GroupJoin

- SelectMany

- GroupBy

These operators are supported in Entity Framework Core, but certain combinations of them are not. The error messages improve with every major release of Entity Framework Core to better explain which part of the query is not supported. However, I sometimes had to randomly remove various parts of the query to determine which part was breaking it.

I recommend turning on console logging of the SQL queries the EF Core produces to make sure they are not overly complicated. If you do not have the logging infrastructure set up in the target project, you can use the LogTo method when building the options to emit the queries to the console, as shown in Listing 5-23.

Listing 5-23. Enabling console logging for SQL queries in DbContext

```
protected override void OnConfiguring(
    DbContextOptionsBuilder optionsBuilder)
{
    optionsBuilder.LogTo(Console.WriteLine,
        LogLevel.Information);

    ...
}
```

You may run into scenarios that are not supported yet in Entity Framework Core. Although this is becoming quite rare, you sometimes need to fall back to the good old SQL. In fact, doing it is easier in EF Core than in the old Entity Framework, which tried hard to abstract you from SQL. It is possible to call stored procedures or functions in Entity Framework, but there is no simple API that can take the result as IQueryable and continue working with it in the Entity Framework way. For me, this Entity Framework limitation was always very annoying. When I needed to use raw SQL to do even a simple task that could not be done with the means of EF, I could not just write the one problematic bit that was missing and use the ORM for the rest. I had to rewrite the entire query (often a very complex one), including sorting, paging, and other things.

This is much easier with Entity Framework Core, as you can see in Listing 5-24. GetMenuCategoryTree is a table-valued function with one parameter. It returns the tree of menu categories which uses the SQL type HierarchyId[18] internally. The rest of the query is built on top of IQueryable<T> the FromSql method returns. Entity Framework Core will use the supplied SQL fragment as a subquery and wrap it with its own SQL expression into a single query.

The important thing here is to use the string interpolation feature to substitute parameters in the query in a safe way. Although it looks like a concatenation of strings, the FromSql method, in fact, examines the interpolated string and emits SQL parameters for every placeholder. Be cautious and always prefer this way over FromSqlRaw, which does not do this for you. Otherwise, you can introduce a SQL injection vulnerability[19] into your code.

Listing 5-24. Calling a stored procedure and applying query operators on its result

```
var menuCategories = context.MenuCategories
    .FromSql(
      $"SELECT * FROM dbo.GetMenuCategoryTree({userId})")
    .Select(c => new {
        Id = c.Id,
```

---

[18] Entity Framework Core has already added support for the HierarchyId type in SQL Server. The purpose of the example is only to demonstrate the principle. See https://learn.microsoft.com/en-us/ef/core/providers/sql-server/hierarchyid?tabs=netcore-cli for more information.

[19] See https://learn.microsoft.com/en-us/sql/relational-databases/security/sql-injection

```
    Text = c.Text,
    Level = c.Level
    NumberOfCourses = c.Courses.Count
})
.ToList();
```

Migrations

Both Entity Framework and Entity Framework Core allow the developers to modify the database schema indirectly – through modifications made to the Code First model. This method has become quite popular in most developer teams that do not have dedicated database architects. Although the principles of migrations remained unchanged, the inner workings of migrations were redesigned with EF Core to suit team environments better.

When using the Database First approach, the process is the exact opposite. The schema is updated first in the SQL database, and subsequently the .edmx model is updated in Visual Studio by choosing the *Update Model from Database* option. This will apply the changes of database objects to the model.

The way of changing the database schema with Database First greatly varies. Some developer teams use Database Projects – a special type of project in Visual Studio, which is part of the SQL Server Data Tools component. This type of project holds the definition of the database schema and can generate change scripts for deployment. I have also seen several implementations of "custom migrations" where the SQL scripts were written manually or generated using SQL Management Studio. The convention was to add them to a specific folder in the project to be included as embedded resources. When the application started, these scripts were executed automatically, using a special table in the database to track which had already been applied. However, the process was usually manual and sometimes a bit error-prone.[20]

The developer workflow when using migrations consists of the following steps:

1. Modify the entity classes or the DbContext object.

2. Run Add-Migration migration_name in Package Manager Console or dotnet ef migrations add migration_name in the command line. The command will auto-generate the migration: a C# class with Up and Down methods. The first method upgrades the database schema to the new version; the second reverts the changes to the previous version.

3. Review the migration and make manual changes to it if needed.

4. Run Update-Database or dotnet ef database update. This will apply the migration to the database (using the development connection string, which the tooling infers from the configuration or from the context class).

---

[20] If the change scripts are authored manually by the developers or architects, it can lead to subtle mistakes or differences in the resulting database schema (for instance, if you do not specify defaults explicitly and the change script is executed in an environment with a different configuration). On the other hand, if these change scripts are generated automatically, some database changes (such as renaming tables or columns) may not be understood by the schema comparison tools, and data loss may occur. Automated testing of the entire process of building the database by applying all change scripts is recommended.

Because the tooling needs to compare the previous model to the new one to detect the changes, it stores the new version of the model as part of step 2. The old Entity Framework serializes the model and stores it in a `.resx` file in a Base64-encoded format, which proved quite impractical. That is why Entity Framework Core generates a C# class with a model snapshot, which works much better in team environments.

If more developers make changes to the model on their machines and push the changes to the repository, the C# model snapshot produced by EF Core is quite easy to merge, and in most cases, Git will combine the changes automatically. A conflict that needs to be resolved manually is quite rare. When the same situation happened with the old Entity Framework, resolving the problem was more complicated. The model snapshot was a single long Base64-encoded value, and the only thing you could do was regenerate the migrations again and hope. In fact, it took a long documentation page with a "grab-a-coffee" disclaimer[21] to describe the problem and explain how to solve it.

Migrating the Entity Framework Migrations

There is no reasonable way of converting or migrating Entity Framework migrations to Entity Framework Core. The migration builder API was changed, and EF Core stores the model snapshot in a completely new way.

To proceed, you will need to delete the old Entity Framework migrations folder to get rid of compilation errors.

Afterward, you will need to create the initial Entity Framework Core migration and remove all its contents. Because EF Core does not have a model snapshot, it thinks that the database does not exist, so it tries to create all database objects within the Up method. Run one of the commands in Listing 5-25 to generate the migration.

---

[21] See `https://learn.microsoft.com/en-us/ef/ef6/modeling/code-first/migrations/teams`

Listing 5-25. Creating an initial migration with Entity
Framework Core

```
# Option 1: Package Manager Console
# (make sure the Default project and Startup project is correct)
Add-Migration InitialSchema

# Option 2: Command-line tool
dotnet ef migrations add InitialSchema
```

If the tools complain that they cannot find the Entity Framework Core DbContext class or a connection string, make sure you run it in the correct project context (the Package Manager Console looks at the Startup project in your solution as well as the Default project selector; the CLI command should be invoked in the project root folder). The DbContext class can have a default constructor and supply the development-time connection string specified in its OnConfiguring method. Alternatively, the tooling can try to infer the development-time connection string from the service collection by examining the startup project. Refer to the documentation[22] for more options.

Once the migration is generated, you have to remove all code from its Up and Down methods. Optionally, you can let the first migration delete the __MigrationHistory table the old Entity Framework used to track which migrations have been applied, as shown in Listing 5-26. Entity Framework Core uses a different name for the migrations table (__EFMigrationsHistory), and since you removed the old EF migrations, the old table is not used anymore.

---

[22] See https://learn.microsoft.com/en-us/ef/core/cli/dbcontext-creation?tabs=dotnet-core-cli

Listing 5-26. Initial migration for Entity Framework Core

```
public partial class InitialSchema : Migration
{
    protected override void Up(
        MigrationBuilder migrationBuilder)
    {
        // remove everything - database already contains
        // all objects

        // optional step
        migrationBuilder.DropTable(
            name: "__MigrationHistory");
    }

    protected override void Down(
        MigrationBuilder migrationBuilder)
    {
        // remove everything - database already contains
        // all objects
    }
}
```

When ready, apply the initial empty migration to the database using one of the commands from Listing 5-27. It will do nothing to the database schema except remove the old migrations table and create the new EF Core one. Generating the migration also created the model snapshot (in my case, `Migrations/DotNetCollegeContextModelSnapshot.cs`). If you look in the file, you will see the complete description of the database schema that Entity Framework tooling uses to detect model changes.

Listing 5-27. Applying the migration to the development database

```
# Option 1: Package Manager Console
# (make sure the Default project and Startup project is
# correct)
Update-Database

# Option 2: Command-line tool
dotnet ef database update
```

The project should now be ready for new development. Any time you need to change the model, just generate the migration and update the database. The last piece of the puzzle is to set up a process on how to run the migrations when the application is deployed. There are multiple ways of doing that, and you should pick the option that is the best fit for your team and environment.

- Generating SQL scripts using the CLI command with the names of starting and ending migration:

  dotnet ef migrations script **from_migration to_migration**

  The resulting scripts should be reviewed and potentially optimized.[23] You can run them in the database manually or set up an automated workflow to apply them during the deployment.

---

[23] There are many schema changes which may take a long time when applied on large tables, for example, adding a column to a table with tens of millions of records. However, when developing the application, the path to the new schema might not have been the shortest possible. For example, the developer might have first added an INT NOT NULL column to the database and found out later that the column should have been nullable. Because of that, there are two migrations (add column and alter column) that can potentially take a long time when applied. Merging them in just one (add column) can save a significant amount of time and minimize the application downtime.

If you do not know which version your database is (or when it differs across various environments), you can add the `--idempotent` option. This will generate an SQL script with IF statements, applying only the migrations that are not present in the database.

- Running the tool directly against the database, for example, from the Continuous Deployment pipeline:

```
dotnet ef database update --connection
"connection_string"
```

  This assumes that the database is accessible from the CD environment (at least for the moment of applying the migration).

- Generating a migrations bundle (a single-file executable that will apply the migrations):

```
dotnet ef migrations bundle
```

  The generated bundle can be deployed to the production server and launched without requiring to have any SQL tools installed.

- Applying the migrations by calling `context.Database.Migrate()` on application startup. This is the easiest option in single-instance environments but is not ideal from a security perspective.

If multiple instances of the application are launched at the same time and attempt to perform the migrations, the process may fail and leave the database in an inconsistent state. Additionally, the application must have elevated permissions to make schema changes in the database, which is not recommended. It is better when the application can only read and write data, and the elevated access is given only to the migrations bundle that is launched separately.

If your application has used the `MigrateDatabaseToLatestVersion` database initializer with the old Entity Framework and you want to keep using the process of automatic applying of migrations, update the code to use the `Migrate` method as shown in Listing 5-28. The example also shows how to register the new Entity Framework context in the service collection. I provide the context with a connection string obtained from the configuration file. Since the context is registered in the service collection as a scoped service by default, I request a new scope by calling `CreateScope()` on the service provider. The scope needs to be disposed when the migration is completed.

Listing 5-28. Applying the migrations on application startup

```
var builder = WebApplication.CreateBuilder(args);
builder.Services.AddDbContext<DotNetCollegeContext>(options =>
{
    options.UseSqlServer(
      builder.Configuration.GetConnectionString("DB"));
});

var app = builder.Build();
...

// apply the migrations
using (var scope = app.Services.CreateScope())
{
    var db = scope.ServiceProvider
        .GetRequiredService<DotNetCollegeContext>();
    db.Database.Migrate();
}

app.Run();
```

Summary

In this chapter, I have shown how to migrate from `System.Data.SqlClient` to the new `Microsoft.Data.SqlClient`, what to do with the LINQ to SQL model, and how to migrate from Entity Framework to Entity Framework Core.

Especially in the case of Entity Framework, the migration may not be an easy task, and even resolving all compile errors may take days. The different behavior of query translator in Entity Framework Core will probably introduce many runtime errors you will need to fix. On the other hand, EF Core's benefits are becoming more fruitful with every major release, and the number of new features and possibilities makes the migration increasingly worthwhile. Even if you decide to stay with good old Entity Framework 6, I recommend checking out the new features of EF Core regularly.

CHAPTER 6

Migrating Identity Stores

.NET has always been a favorite choice for building "line of business" applications. It was not impossible to build a public-facing website in .NET, but in the first years of .NET Framework, the experience was quite subpar. ASP.NET Web Forms, the only web UI framework until the introduction of ASP.NET MVC in 2009, often generated HTML that was hard to ingest by search engines. Thus, it required a significant effort to make the pages SEO-friendly.

The infamous __VIEWSTATE hidden field, which could reach hundreds of kilobytes or even small megabytes in size, had to be rendered in the page's <head> section – but because of that, it increased the time to load and render the page. Most web browsers try to render the page content as soon as possible, even while the page HTML is still being downloaded. Because the hidden field was at the beginning, the browser had to download more bytes to be able to render at least some meaningful content (in page speed diagnostic tools, it is often referred to as the First Contentful Paint metric[1]). I have seen several tricks ASP.NET developers used to move the hidden field value to the session or render it at the end of the page, but all of these solutions had many drawbacks and could

---

[1] See https://developer.chrome.com/docs/lighthouse/performance/first-contentful-paint

© Tomáš Herceg 2024
T. Herceg, *Modernizing .NET Web Applications*,
https://doi.org/10.1007/979-8-8688-0617-9_6

not be deployed universally. When comparing Web Forms to other web frameworks, it was extremely difficult to achieve the same results in terms of page load speed. This did not get much better until ASP.NET MVC was introduced.

However, when it came to business applications, it was a completely different story. Such applications were often accessible only within the company's internal network and required Windows Authentication. It was possible because all of their users were company employees or contractors in possession of an Active Directory account. This simplified many things for the developers as they did not have to implement the login page, the process of password recovery, blocking access to the removed users or users with too many failed sign-in attempts, and so forth. All these features were already implemented in Active Directory, and the only thing you had to do was to enable Windows Authentication.

Another large group of business applications was used by both internal employees and external partners. The only public-facing page of such applications was the login screen with an option to sign in or recover forgotten passwords. Everything else required the users to authenticate, and because of the presence of external users, the AD integration was much less common. Instead, the user accounts were managed by the application itself, and the corresponding data usually ended up in an SQL database. This is not trivial to implement – and even less trivial if you want to implement it correctly.

Microsoft was well aware of the risk coming from requiring every company to implement their custom user management solution. Therefore, an infrastructure for storing application user accounts in a secure way, along with an API for verification and resetting the credentials, was added to .NET Framework 2.0. Over the years, the security mechanisms involved in it were becoming increasingly weak, and at the same time, applications required more features such as authenticating through external identity providers. That is why ASP.NET Identity and its successor, ASP.NET Core Identity, were introduced. In this chapter, I will explain the migration paths from ASP.NET Membership Providers, ASP. NET Universal Providers, and ASP.NET Identity to the most up-to-date implementation – ASP.NET Core Identity.

In general, the number of changes required in the application code will be quite small. The largest changes will be in the database, as every library has a different implementation of identity object storage. The trickiest part is definitely verifying passwords hashed by older methods.

CODE SAMPLES FOR THIS CHAPTER

The migration of data access code is demonstrated in the GitHub repository available via the book's product page at `https://github.com/Apress/ Modernizing-.NET-Web-Applications`. You can find the entire solution in the `chapter06` folder.

For each technology mentioned in this chapter, there is a collection of projects:

- `MembershipTests` and `MembershipCoreIdentityTests` projects show how to migrate from ASP.NET Membership Providers.

- `UniversalTests` and `UniversalCoreIdentityTests` projects show the process of migrating from ASP.NET Universal Providers.

- `IdentityTests` and `IdentityCoreIdentityTests` projects show the way of migration from ASP.NET Identity.

If you want to run the projects, follow the instructions in the `Readme` file in the `chapter06` folder.

ASP.NET Membership Providers

As I already mentioned, ASP.NET Membership Providers were introduced in .NET Framework 2.0. Their main components were called Membership, Roles, and Profile:

- The Membership provider was responsible for operations with application users, including creating, updating, deleting, validating, and resetting the password, as well as locking the user out after several failed attempts.

- The Role provider was used to create and delete roles. It also kept track of which user belonged to which role.

- The Profile provider was able to store additional information about every user, such as names, profile pictures, and so on.

When configured properly in the web.config file, you could just use static methods on Membership, Roles, and ProfileManager classes to access all functionality of these providers. You could implement your own providers – all you had to do was inherit from the default base classes and override a decent number of methods. Thanks to this, many implementations storing the data in other databases than Microsoft SQL Server emerged.

ASP.NET Web Forms also shipped with high-level UI components that relied on the providers, such as Login, CreateUserWizard, and more. If you did not handle the control events yourself, the configured default membership provider was used.

The components were also integrated with Forms authentication. The Login component called FormsAuthentication.SetAuthCookie after it verified that the credentials were correct (using Membership. ValidateUser). It also retrieved the list of user's roles and added them to the authentication ticket.

The default providers were using Microsoft SQL Server as the data store and could create the database automatically (if you used the User Instance=true parameter in the connection string). In the ideal case, you did not have to do anything – it just worked. If not, the common cause was that the tables and stored procedures used by the providers were not created automatically. There was a tool called aspnet_regsql.exe that could do this for you.[2]

Listing 6-1 shows how you could choose the concrete implementation of the provider and configure its parameters.

Listing 6-1. Configuration of ASP.NET Membership and Role providers

```
<configuration>
  <connectionStrings>
    <add name="DB"
         connectionString="..."
         providerName="System.Data.SqlClient"/>
  </connectionStrings>
  <system.web>
    <membership defaultProvider="MembershipDB">
      <providers>
        <clear />
        <add
          name="MembershipDB"
          type="System.Web.Security.SqlMembershipProvider"
          connectionStringName="DB"
          applicationName="ModernizationDemo"
          enablePasswordRetrieval="false"
```

---

[2] See https://learn.microsoft.com/en-us/previous-versions/aspnet/x28wfk74(v=vs.100)

```
          enablePasswordReset="true"
          requiresQuestionAndAnswer="false"
          requiresUniqueEmail="true"
          passwordFormat="Hashed" />
      </providers>
    </membership>
    <roleManager enabled="true" defaultProvider="RoleDB">
      <providers>
        <clear />
        <add
          name="RoleDB"
          type="System.Web.Security.SqlRoleProvider"
          connectionStringName="DB"
          applicationName="ModernizationDemo" />
      </providers>
    </roleManager>
  </system.web>
</configuration>
```

Listing 6-2 shows how the static methods of the Membership and Role providers can be used. As you can see, the API is easy to use but far from ideal from today's perspective. For example, when creating the user, you must specify the security question and answer, which is no longer a recommended practice.[3] On the other hand, commonly requested features, such as two-factor authentication or authentication using a third-party identity provider, are not supported.

---

[3] See the warning at the top of the page at https://cheatsheetseries.owasp.org/cheatsheets/Choosing_and_Using_Security_Questions_Cheat_Sheet.html

Listing 6-2. Basic functionality of the Membership provider

```
// create a user
Membership.CreateUser(
    "username", "password", "email",
    "security question", "security answer",
    isApproved: true, out var createStatus);

// check the validity of user credentials
// (respects the user lockout after several failed attempts)
var valid = Membership.ValidateUser(username, password);

// change password
var user = Membership.GetUser("username");
user.ChangePassword("old password", "new password");

// determine whether the user is a member
var isMember = Roles.IsUserInRole("username", "some role");
```

Insecure Passwords

The way the Membership provider stored the password could be configured – the options were Clear, Encrypted, and Hashed. The official documentation starts the description of all options except for the last one with "Not secure, do not use." The Hashed format uses the SHA1 algorithm by default, which is problematic because of the computing power we have today. The documentation mentions that Microsoft recommends switching to SHA-256, but even that is not enough considering the password hashing method being used.

The user credentials are stored in the aspnet_Membership table in the PasswordHash column, which is accompanied by PasswordSalt – a randomly generated binary value.

To calculate the `PasswordHash` from a password, the following formula is used (plus meaning concatenation of byte arrays):

```
Sha1(salt + unicode(password))
```

The purpose of salt is to make the input for the hashing function longer. If you would hash only the password (which is often less than ten characters long), there are already precomputed lists of hashes (called rainbow tables). For example, a list of precomputed hashes for alphanumeric strings of one to nine characters is only about 690 GB.[4] If the database file leaks, the attacker can simply look up the hash in the rainbow table and obtain most of the passwords immediately.

The salt in the Membership provider is 16 bytes long, which efficiently removes the option of using the rainbow table. However, another type of attack (dictionary attack) is still possible. You can easily download a list of the most frequently used passwords[5] that contains billions of entries. With it, you can take the salt of any user in the database and calculate the hash for each password from the list. If you find a match, you have the password for the particular user account.

On today's graphics cards, you can generate tens of billions of SHA-1 hashes[6] per second. I tried to make a very naïve implementation in .NET just to verify I implemented the salting algorithm of the Membership provider correctly. My code did not use GPU, ran on a single thread, and caused unnecessary allocations of arrays and strings that could be eliminated. Still, I was able to compute over seven million password hashes per second on a tenth-generation Intel i9 CPU (released in 2020). I believe you already have an idea why such a trivial algorithm is not secure

---

[4] See http://project-rainbowcrack.com/table.htm for sizes of various rainbow tables and their success rates.

[5] See a website with publicly available password datasets: https://weakpass.com/download

[6] See the SHA-1 benchmark results: https://openbenchmarking.org/test/pts/hashcat&eval=306f31f896ee6afac758df6db7589b6a2a232723#metrics

enough today. Using the weakpass_3a[5] database with 8.7 billion passwords and my very inefficient algorithm, it would take only 20 minutes to try all of them to crack a single user account. Of course, whether you find the password depends on its presence in the list, but you can surely expect a high success rate – only a small percentage of people use randomly generated passwords that are unique for every site.

Migration to ASP.NET Core Identity

ASP.NET Core Identity is a modern implementation of a framework to take care of application users and roles. It integrates well with the new ASP.NET Core authentication model and is extensible to support various data stores. Because Entity Framework Core is a popular choice for many .NET developers, it is no wonder that ASP.NET Core Identity provides a nice support for it. Thanks to this, it works out of the box with any database EF Core supports.

In the previous chapter, I discussed how to migrate your data access code to Entity Framework Core. If you want to store the users and roles in the database along with other application data, your DbContext can inherit from the ASP.NET Core Identity's IdentityDbContext class. This will add the AspNetUsers, AspNetRoles, and other tables to the database, and you will be able to create relationships to ASP.NET Core Identity objects from your entities, which is often very useful.

By default, the users and roles in ASP.NET Core Identity are represented by the IdentityUser and IdentityRole classes. However, it is very common to inherit from them to add other properties. Many developers are used to extending the IdentityUser class with properties that would be handled by the Profile provider in the old days because it is easier than having a separate database entity for user profiles. Listing 6-3 shows how to define a DbContext with extended user and role entities. I am used to redefining the primary key to Guid instead of string that is used by default.

Listing 6-3. Defining the DbContext and extending IdentityUser and IdentityRole entities

```
public class AppDbContext
    : IdentityDbContext<AppUser, AppRole, Guid>
{
    public AppDbContext(DbContextOptions<AppDbContext> options)
        : base(options)
    {
    }

    ...
}

public class AppUser : IdentityUser<Guid>
{
    public DateTime CreatedDate { get; set; }
    ...
}

public class AppRole : IdentityRole<Guid>
{
}
```

The structure and names of database tables used by ASP.NET Core Identity are different from the ASP.NET Membership provider. Therefore, you need to migrate data from the old tables to the new ones. Although it should be possible to write a SQL script to transfer the data, I recommend implementing it in C#. You will have more options for handling error states or implementing any special rules, but, most importantly, you will need to store the password using ASP.NET Core Identity hashing mechanisms, which would be very difficult to replicate in SQL.

The example repository mentioned at the beginning of the chapter contains a project called ModernizationDemo.MembershipCoreIdentity Tests. There is a class named MembershipMigrator, which is responsible for the entire transfer of the user accounts and roles. Listing 6-4 shows the transformation of user accounts (without handling the password, to which I will get back later).

Listing 6-4. Migrating the user account information

```
var command = new SqlCommand(
    """

    SELECT m.*, u.*
      FROM dbo.aspnet_Users u
      JOIN dbo.aspnet_Membership m ON m.UserId = u.UserId
      JOIN dbo.aspnet_Applications a
        ON a.ApplicationId = u.ApplicationId
      WHERE a.ApplicationName = @applicationName
        AND u.IsAnonymous = 0
    """, connection);
command.Parameters.AddWithValue(
    "@applicationName", ApplicationName);

using var reader = command.ExecuteReader();
while (reader.Read())
{
    var migratedUser = new AppUser()
    {
        Id = (Guid)reader["UserId"],
        UserName = (string)reader["UserName"],
        Email = (string)reader["Email"],
        EmailConfirmed = true,
        TwoFactorEnabled = false,
        LockoutEnabled = true,
```

```
        LockoutEnd = (bool)reader["IsApproved"]
            ? null : new DateTime(9999, 12, 31),
        CreatedDate = (DateTime)reader["CreateDate"]
    };

    // save the user
    var result = await userManager.CreateAsync(migratedUser);
    if (!result.Succeeded)
    {
        throw new Exception(
            $"Failed to migrate {reader["UserName"]}");
    }
}
```

As you can see, the code just reads the original aspnet_Memberships and aspnet_Users table (the accounts have rows in both tables and need to be joined together by the UserId column). Membership providers support hosting accounts for multiple applications in the same database – that is why I am filtering the records by the application name.

When the column values are transferred to my AppUser entity, I pass it to the ASP.NET Core Identity object UserManager<AppUser> and have the account created. Be careful – when using ASP.NET Core Identity, most of its methods do not throw exceptions. Instead, they return a result object you need to check explicitly. Usually, the object provides more details than just success or failure.

There are some notable differences between ASP.NET Membership and ASP.NET Core Identity:

- ASP.NET Core Identity has the EmailConfirmed field which has no equivalent in the old database. You need to decide whether the users will be required to verify their email on the first sign-in or whether it will be treated as verified by default.

- ASP.NET Core Identity does not use the IsApproved field to block user access. I migrated the data using a similar feature – lockout after several unsuccessful attempts. The LockoutEnabled property specifies whether the user account can be locked out after multiple sign-in failures (always set it to true), and LockoutEnd says until when the account is actually locked out. I passed December 31, 9999, which I believe is far enough in the future, and it is the maximum value SQL Server can store. Feel free to adjust this to any other strategy.

- ASP.NET Core Identity does not use the MobileAlias, Comment, LastActivityDate, and LastPasswordChangeDate fields. To keep them, simply add them to the AppUser entity.

- ASP.NET Core Identity does not support the mechanism of security questions and answers.

- The code ignores whether the user was locked out in the old system. I use the lockout fields for the IsApproved scenario, and I wanted to avoid the potential need to merge these two situations. Since lockouts are only temporary and get reset after a few minutes, I believe ignoring them is not an issue.

The MembershipMigrator class in the example repository contains a similar routine to migrate the aspnet_Roles table to ASP.NET Core Identity using the RoleManager<AppRole> object. You can also find the migration of role memberships from the old database. ASP.NET Core Identity does not allow providing just the ID of the user and the role – the AddToRoleAsync method on the UserManager requires the AppUser object and the role name, which requires loading plenty of unnecessary information. If your aspnet_UsersInRoles table has a large number of entries, consider doing this part in raw SQL.

Migration of Passwords

If you leave the code as is, the new database structure will not contain user passwords. Before the users can sign in, they need to use the forgotten password feature, which is present in the vast majority of applications. This may be annoying for some users, and you may expect a minority of users to experience problems during the process. For example, their email address might have changed, and the password reset link will not reach them.

There are situations where this annoyance to the users may be better than a silent migration of accounts. It can be useful if you have many inactive accounts and want to remove them if the users do not sign in within some time window. Maybe the new version of the application has a new branding, and the users would be informed of switching to the new system anyway. Maybe you implemented new ways of authentication, such as integration with social media accounts, and you want your users to consider switching to these services. Finally, I have participated in several modernization projects that were done as part of a merger of two companies. In this case, the users had to be asked whether they accepted the new terms and conditions and agreed with the processing of their personal information by the new legal entity. If the users disagreed, their accounts would not be migrated at all.

If none of that is your case and you want to make a seamless migration, it is possible, albeit a bit complicated. The problem is that ASP.NET Core Identity uses a different (more secure) method of hashing the passwords, but at the time of account migration, the password is not available in an unencoded form. Therefore, we cannot pass the actual user's password to the `userManager.AddPasswordAsync` method to have it encoded the normal way.

Do Not Keep Passwords in the Original Format

A naïve idea is to take the passwords in the old format (values from the `Password` and `PasswordSalt` columns) and move them to the new database structure as they are. When the user tries to sign in, we can verify the password using the old method. If the attempt is successful and we still have the unencoded password in the memory, we can store it in the new secure format through ASP.NET Core Identity and clear the legacy salt and hash.

ASP.NET Core Identity uses a class called `Microsoft.AspNetCore.Identity.PasswordHasher` for password verification. It is designed to expect the password format is going to be updated in the future. Therefore, the first byte in the new `PasswordHash` column is either 0x00 or 0x01 – the first represents the algorithm used by ASP.NET Identity v2 (the .NET Framework version), while the second represents the new algorithm used in ASP.NET Core Identity. You could just use a different value of the first byte to indicate that it is the legacy algorithm, and the following bytes would represent the salt and the legacy password hash.

However, I discourage doing that because you will not get rid of the insecure hashes this way – at least until the particular user signs in. If there are inactive accounts in the database, their old hashes will remain there forever.

Storing the Old Password Hashes Securely

A more secure way to migrate the legacy password hashes is to protect them as if they were normal passwords. Technically, you can call `userManager.AddPasswordAsync` and give it the legacy password hash (Base64 encoded). ASP.NET Core Identity will hash it using the up-to-date algorithm (the actual user's password would be hashed twice – first by the insecure SHA-1 and then using the up-to-date algorithm). However, you will need to keep the legacy salt somewhere until the user's first sign-in. Otherwise, you will not be able to calculate the SHA-1 hash from it.

When the user enters valid credentials, and we still hold the unencoded password in memory, we can ask ASP.NET Core Identity to rehash the password using the up-to-date algorithm. Thanks to that, we will get rid of double-hashed passwords. But even if this never occurs for some users, their legacy hashes will be protected.

The problem is where to store the salt. The AspNetUsers table has only one column, which is meant to store the password, salt, and additional metadata, such as the algorithm being used. As I mentioned earlier, the first byte in it indicates the version of the password format. We can create our own format, which will contain both legacy salt and the double-hashed password, as shown in Figure 6-1.

1 byte 0xFF	4 bytes length of the salt	legacy salt	legacy password hash hashed using ASP.NET Core Identity

Figure 6-1. *Custom format for hashing legacy passwords*

In order to build the last segment of this structure, we will need the ASP.NET Code Identity's PasswordHasher instance to call the HashPassword method on it. Because we will need to override the password verification procedure as well, I have created my own implementation of a password hasher, which inherits from the default one. Listing 6-5 shows how to update the migration code.

Listing 6-5. Storing legacy password hashes and salts in ASP.NET Core Identity

```
...
while (reader.Read())
{
    var migratedUser = new AppUser()
    {
        ...
    };
```

```
// encode the legacy password hash as a new password
// this will protect it using the new stronger format
var hasher = (MembershipAwarePasswordHasher)
    userManager.PasswordHasher;
migratedUser.PasswordHash =
    hasher.BuildDoubleHashedPassword(
        migratedUser,
        (string)user["PasswordSalt"],
        (string)user["Password"]);

// save the user
var result = await userManager.CreateAsync(migratedUser);
...
}
...

public class MembershipAwarePasswordHasher
  : PasswordHasher<AppUser>
{
    public string BuildDoubleHashedPassword(
        AppUser user, string legacySalt,
        string legacyPasswordHash)
    {
        // encode the legacy hash using ASP.NET Code Identity
        var encodedPassword = base.HashPassword(
            user, legacyPasswordHash);

        // build the password data structure
        var legacySaltBytes = Convert.FromBase64String(
            legacySalt);
        var passwordBytes = Convert.FromBase64String(
            encodedPassword);
```

```
    return Convert.ToBase64String(
    [
        0xFF,
        ..BitConverter.GetBytes(
            legacySaltBytes.Length),
        ..legacySaltBytes,
        ..passwordBytes
    ]);
    }
}
```

As you can see, I took the original password hash in a Base64-encoded form as it was in the Membership database (e.g., qw3V4ky6P1z7mSxkAG2lEbC6cOM=) and passed it to the base.HashPassword method defined in the default ASP.NET Core Identity password hasher. Thanks to this, I do not store the weak hash in the database unprotected – it gets additional protection from the modern ASP.NET Core Identity algorithm. The reason for introducing the custom format is that I need to store also the old password salt. Figure 6-2 shows how the resulting byte array is composed.

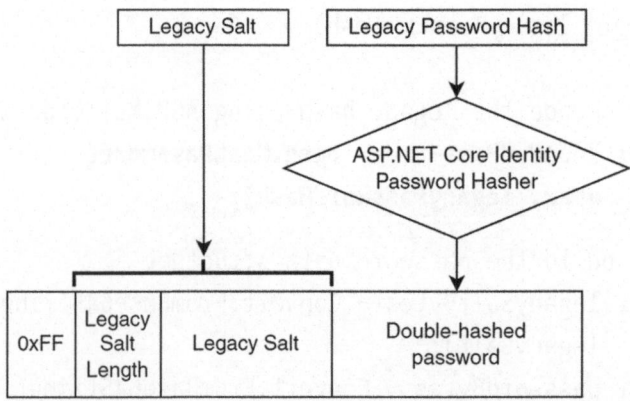

Figure 6-2. *Custom format of storing the legacy salt and double-hashed password*

On sign-in, we have to check if the password is stored in our custom format. In that case, I calculate the legacy hash from the legacy salt and the password provided by the user. Then, I verified this calculated legacy hash as it was the password using standard ASP.NET Core Identity's password hasher. To do that, I need to override the VerifyHashedPassword method in my hasher implementation, as in Listing 6-6.

Listing 6-6. ASP.NET Core Identity implementation PasswordHasher which supports old ASP.NET Membership password hashes

```
public class MembershipAwarePasswordHasher
    : PasswordHasher<AppUser>
{
    public override
        PasswordVerificationResult VerifyHashedPassword(
            AppUser user, string hashedPassword,
                string providedPassword)
    {
        // is the password in the old format?
        var passwordData = Convert.FromBase64String(
            hashedPassword);
        if (passwordData[0] == 0xFF)
        {
            // extract the legacy salt
            // and double hashed password
            ExtractSaltAndDoubleHashedPassword(
                passwordData, out var legacySalt,
                out var doubleHashedPassword);

            // calculate original PasswordHash
            // using the legacy algorithm
```

```
            // and use it as it was the user provided password
            providedPassword =
                HashPasswordUsingLegacyAlgorithm(
                    providedPassword, legacySalt);

            // use the double-hashed password as the value
            // for verification
            hashedPassword = Convert.ToBase64String(
                doubleHashedPassword);
        }

        // use the default algorithm to verify the password
        var result = base.VerifyHashedPassword(
            user, hashedPassword, providedPassword);

        // if the old format was used and credentials
        // were valid, rehash
        if (result == PasswordVerificationResult.Success
            && passwordData[0] == 0xFF)
        {
            return
                PasswordVerificationResult.SuccessRehashNeeded;
        }

        return result;
    }

    public void ExtractSaltAndDoubleHashedPassword(
        byte[] passwordData,
        out byte[] legacySalt, out byte[] encodedPassword)
    {
        var legacySaltLength = BitConverter.ToInt32(
            passwordData, 1);
        var passwordStartIndex = 5 + legacySaltLength;
```

```
        legacySalt = passwordData[5..passwordStartIndex];
        encodedPassword = passwordData[passwordStartIndex..];
    }

    private string HashPasswordUsingLegacyAlgorithm(
        string providedPassword, byte[] legacyPasswordSalt)
    {
        var hashAlgorithm = SHA1.Create();
        var hashData = legacyPasswordSalt
            .Concat(
                Encoding.Unicode.GetBytes(providedPassword))
            .ToArray();
        var result = hashAlgorithm.ComputeHash(hashData);
        return Convert.ToBase64String(result);
    }

    ...
}
```

Let us go through what the code does when the user tries to sign in:

- First, the code checks if the password format is ours (it starts with 0xFF). If it is, we extract the legacy salt and the double-hashed password by calling the ExtractLegacySaltAndEncodedPassword method.

- Then, we calculate the legacy password hash using the HashPasswordUsingLegacyAlgorithm method. This method does the same thing as ASP.NET Membership did – concatenates the salt with the password and calculates the SHA-1 hash. If the entered password was correct, the result should be exactly the same as the value we passed to the HashPassword during the user account migration.

- Next, the calculated legacy hash is passed to the default implementation of ASP.NET Core Identity's password hasher as if it were the password. The hashedPassword variable is replaced with the last chunk of our byte array – it is the double-hashed value that will be used for verification.

The entire process is illustrated in Figure 6-3. It looks complicated, but the only thing we did was treat the legacy password hash as if it were the user's password. Before we pass it to the ASP.NET Core Identity password hasher, we will apply the first (insecure) hashing. ASP.NET Core hasher will then apply its up-to-date hashing and compare the result with the provided double-hashed value we created during the account migration. If the values are equal, it means that the credentials are correct.

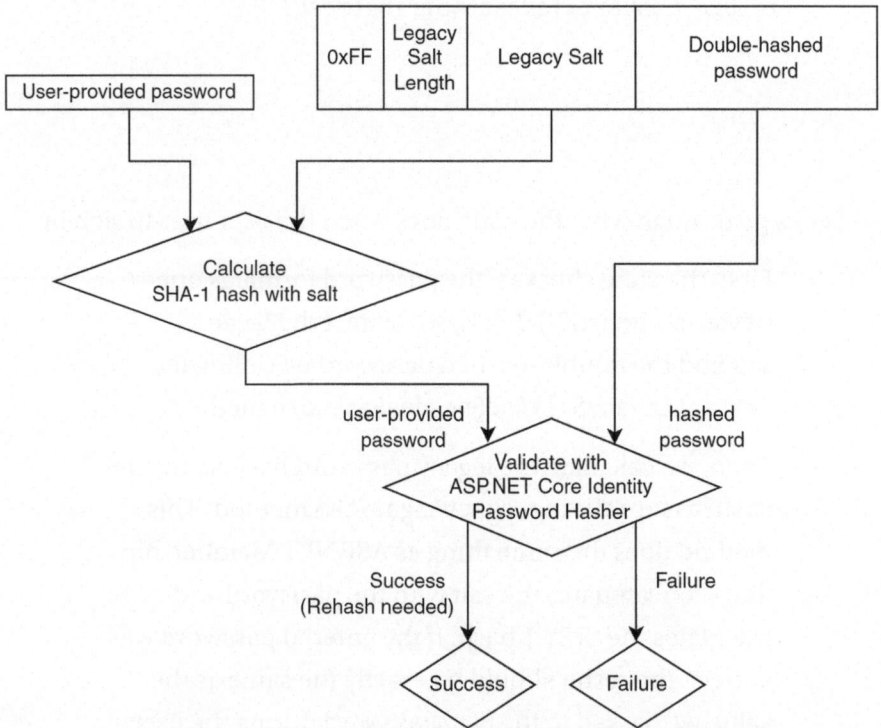

Figure 6-3. *The process of password verification using double-hashing*

The last piece of the puzzle is to upgrade the password to the standard ASP.NET Core Identity format. That is why the method does not return the Success result when our own password format was used. Instead, it returns the third option – SuccessRehashNeeded. This tells ASP.NET Core Identity that the password was correct but was encoded using an older version of the algorithm. ASP.NET Core Identity, still having the user's password in an unencoded form in memory, will hash it using the newest version of the algorithm. ASP.NET Core Identity will save the AppUser entity automatically in the routine, which invokes the password hasher.

Before following these steps, make sure that your application is not configured to use a different algorithm. If you migrate from some very old .NET Framework versions, there is a chance that MD5 was used instead of SHA-1. Additionally, the algorithm might have been changed in the web. config file or in the application code.

You can find a test for this behavior in the example repository – it is called ValidateCredentialsAndTestRehashing. You can try to migrate your user database by running the test to see whether the algorithm and its parameters are correct. Be careful when setting the connection strings. The oldConnectionString should point to your database, while the newConnectionString should point to an empty or, better, nonexistent database. The tests drop and create the database specified by newConnectionString when they are run, so be sure there is no important data.

The last thing you need to do in order to start using the password hasher is to register ASP.NET Core Identity in the IServiceCollection and replace the default password hasher with your own, as demonstrated in Listing 6-7.

Listing 6-7. Registering ASP.NET Core Identity and replacing the password hasher

```
// register Entity Framework Core
services.AddDbContext<AppDbContext>(options =>
{
    options.UseSqlServer(connectionString);
});

// register ASP.NET Core Identity
services
    .AddIdentityCore<AppUser>()
    .AddRoles<AppRole>()
    .AddUserManager<UserManager<AppUser>>()
    .AddRoleManager<RoleManager<AppRole>>()
    .AddEntityFrameworkStores<AppDbContext>();

services.Replace(
    ServiceDescriptor.Scoped<IPasswordHasher<AppUser>,
        MembershipAwarePasswordHasher>());
```

Other Password Formats

If your application uses the plaintext format of the passwords, the situation is easier – you just call AddPasswordAsync and do not need the custom password hasher.

In the case of reversibly encrypted passwords, you will have to decrypt them using the machine key from the server on which the application was running. The easiest way is probably to write a .NET Framework console application that will decrypt all passwords using the Membership provider API and store them in a secure place somewhere, so they can be migrated. The DecryptPassword method of the SqlMembershipProvider is virtual, so you will have to create a class that inherits from it to be able to call it.

ASP.NET Universal Providers

A small evolution to ASP.NET Membership Providers was a library called ASP.NET Universal Providers released in 2011. Their concepts remained quite similar, and the integration with the provider model of ASP.NET did not change, but the implementation using Entity Framework allowed supporting databases other than Microsoft SQL Server.

Because the new providers had to fit the old API, they have many similar properties – for example, the password questions and answers. Also, their database structure was simplified and does not rely on stored procedures and views. Like ASP.NET Membership Providers, Universal Providers also support reusing the same tables for multiple applications.

What has changed is the algorithm used for hashing the passwords. Universal Providers use the HMAC SHA-256 algorithm. In contrast to the primitive approach of just concatenating the salt and password and computing a hash of it, HMAC uses a more sophisticated approach to "combine" the key (salt) and the message.[7] SHA-256 is used as the underlying hash function (which is better than SHA-1). The length of the salt is still 16 bytes, but the algorithm key size is 64 bytes. In this case, the implementation in ASP.NET Universal Providers just repeats the salt until the key array is filled. If you look in the database, you can see that the hashes are longer than with the classic Membership provider. However, in terms of security, this algorithm is not much better and is not considered safe by today's standards. The problem, same as with the old membership, is that calculating a single hash from a given password is not sufficiently expensive, and you will be able to calculate at least millions of HMAC SHA-256 hashes per second on a common CPU.

---

[7] See `https://learn.microsoft.com/en-us/dotnet/api/system.security.cryptography.hmacsha256#remarks`

All the similarities make the process of moving to ASP.NET Core Identity very similar to what I have shown in the "ASP.NET Membership Providers" section. Therefore, this section will just highlight the differences.

The providers are distributed in the Microsoft.AspNet.Providers NuGet package and registered in web.config as shown in Listing 6-8. The difference is mainly in the namespaces in which the providers reside.

Listing 6-8. Registration of ASP.NET Universal Providers

```
<membership defaultProvider="MembershipDB">
  <providers>
    <clear />
    <add
      name="MembershipDB"
      type="System.Web.Providers.DefaultMembershipProvider,↵
System.Web.Providers"
      connectionStringName="DB"
      ...
      passwordFormat="Hashed" />
  </providers>
</membership>
<roleManager enabled="true" defaultProvider="RoleDB">
  <providers>
    <clear />
    <add
      name="RoleDB"
      type="System.Web.Providers.DefaultRoleProvider,↵
System.Web.Providers"
      connectionStringName="DB"
      applicationName="ModernizationDemo" />
  </providers>
</roleManager>
```

Migration to ASP.NET Core Identity

The code to migrate users from the old table structure to ASP.NET Core Identity tables is practically the same. The database tables lost the prefix aspnet_, and the aspnet_Membership was changed to the plural name Memberships.

The MobileAlias column and a few others are missing, but 90% of the schema is unchanged. In contrast to ASP.NET Membership Providers, there is not a single stored procedure or view.

If you inspect the UniversalMigrator class in the example repository and compare it with MembershipMigrator, you will see that there are no significant changes.

The principle of migrating user passwords is again the same. You will need to replace the ASP.NET Core Identity's default PasswordHasher with the implementation from Listing 6-6. The only change is in the HashPasswordUsingLegacyAlgorithm method, which is shown in Listing 6-9. Notice that the salt is repeated four times – HMAC SHA-256 uses a 64-byte key, but the salt is only 16 bytes.

Listing 6-9. The HashPasswordUsingLegacyAlgorithm method for Universal Providers

```
private string HashPasswordUsingLegacyAlgorithm(
    string providedPassword, byte[] legacyPasswordSalt)
{
    byte[] key = [..legacyPasswordSalt, ..legacyPasswordSalt,
                  ..legacyPasswordSalt, ..legacyPasswordSalt];
    var hashData = Encoding.Unicode.GetBytes(providedPassword);

    var hashAlgorithm = new HMACSHA256(key);
    var result = hashAlgorithm.ComputeHash(hashData);
    return Convert.ToBase64String(result);
}
```

367

The rest of the process is the same. To configure the custom password hasher, use the code shown in Listing 6-7; just change the name to `UniversalAwarePasswordHasher`.

Migrating User Profiles

The sections about ASP.NET Membership Providers and Universal Providers did not mention migrating user profiles. They work on the same principles, but since not all developers used them, I decided to separate them into a separate section. Trying to migrate the profile data when preparing the example repository was a hilarious chain of obstacles I had to deal with, including fixing a bug and submitting a pull request to an open source project. However, I was able to successfully read the ASP. NET Profile data from a .NET 8.0 application and migrate them as native properties of the `AppUser` entity.

The Profile API allowed the storage of additional information about users, such as names or profile pictures. You could define a list of properties in `web.config`, as shown in Listing 6-10, and then use the auto-generated `Profile` class to access the current user's profile information. There was also the `ProfileManager` class for listing and managing all user profiles.

Listing 6-10. Configuring the ASP.NET Profile provider and its properties in the web.config file

```
<system.web>
  ...
  <profile enabled="true" defaultProvider="ProfileDB">
    <providers>
      <clear />
```

```xml
    <add
      name="ProfileDB"
      type="System.Web.Profile.SqlProfileProvider"
      connectionStringName="DB"
      applicationName="ModernizationDemo" />
  </providers>
  <properties>
    <add name="FirstName" />
    <add name="LastName" />
    <add name="FavoriteNumber" type="System.Int32" />
    <add name="BirthDate" type="System.DateTime" />
    <add name="ImageUrls"
         type="System.Collections.Specialized.StringCollection,↵
System, Version=4.0.0.0, Culture=neutral,↵
PublicKeyToken=b77a5c561934e089" />
    <add name="ShoppingCart"
      type="ModernizationDemo.MembershipTests.ShoppingCart,↵
ModernizationDemo.MembershipTests"
         serializeAs="Binary"/>
  </properties>
  </profile>
</system.web>
```

The properties could be of primitive types (string, numbers, dates, and so on). Complex objects such as StringCollection or a custom ShoppingCart class could be serialized. You could choose whether you want to use XML or a binary serialization.

I would naturally expect that every property would be stored in its own column in the SQL database, but since the database structure supported multiple applications (which could use different properties), ASP.NET Profiles used a custom way of serializing the property values in three database columns, as shown in Listing 6-11. The first column contained colon-separated entries defining property name, serialization format (S for string, B for binary), offset, and value length. Based on the format, the value was stored either in the PropertyValuesString or PropertyValuesBinary.

Listing 6-11. Example of serialized profile properties in the Profile table

PropertyNames column:
ShoppingCart:B:0:2274:FirstName:S:0:10:LastName:S:10:9:⏎
FavoriteNumber:S:19:2:BirthDate:S:21:81:ImageUrls:S:102:280:

PropertyValuesString column:
First NameLast Name42<?xml version="1.0" encoding="utf-16"?>
<dateTime>2000-01-01T00:00:00</dateTime><?xml version="1.0"⏎
encoding="utf-16"?>
<ArrayOfString xmlns:xsd="http://www.w3.org/2001/XMLSchema"⏎
xmlns:xsi="http://www.w3.org/2001/XMLSchema-instance">
  <string>https://picsum.photos/200/300</string>
  <string>https://picsum.photos/id/237/200/300</string>
</ArrayOfString>

PropertyValuesBinary column (binary data converted to HEX):
0x0001000000FFFFFFFF01000000000000000C02000000584D6
F6465726...

To represent the profile in ASP.NET Core Identity, I decided to add the profile properties directly into the AppUser class, as demonstrated in Listing 6-12. An alternative way would be to create the UserProfile table and use a one-to-one relationship – this would be better if the profile contains non-essential properties that are likely not needed in most situations.

Because the list of image URLs and the shopping cart objects are more complex, I used the Entity Framework Core 7.0 feature to serialize them in string columns as JSON. To do that, you have to configure the child objects as owned entities (using OwnsOne or OwnsMany) and then tell Entity Framework to map them as JSON instead of creating tables for them. Unfortunately, I could not use just an array of strings for the ImageUrls property – instead, I had to define AppUserImage entity with a single property for the URL. This is because of the concept of owned entities – a string cannot be treated as an entity by EF Core.

Listing 6-12. Adding the profile properties in the user entity and configuring JSON serialization of complex objects

```
public class AppUser : IdentityUser<Guid>
{
    ...
    public string? FirstName { get; set; }
    public string? LastName { get; set; }
    public int? FavoriteNumber { get; set; }
    public DateTime? BirthDate { get; set; }
    public List<AppUserImage>? ImageUrls { get; set; }
    public ShoppingCart? ShoppingCart { get; set; }
}

public class AppUserImage
{
    public string Url { get; set; }
}
```

```
public class ShoppingCart
{
    public DateTime Created { get; set; }
    public DateTime LastUpdated { get; set; }
    public List<CartItem> Items { get; set; } = new();
}

public class CartItem
{
    public string Item { get; set; }
    public int Quantity { get; set; }
    public double Price { get; set; }
}

public class AppDbContext
    : IdentityDbContext<AppUser, AppRole, Guid>
{
    ...
    protected override void OnModelCreating(
        ModelBuilder builder)
    {
        ...

        builder.Entity<AppUser>(entity =>
        {
            entity.OwnsMany(u => u.ImageUrls,
                relationship => relationship.ToJson());

            entity.OwnsOne(u => u.ShoppingCart,
                relationship => relationship.ToJson()
                                    .OwnsMany(c => c.Items));
        });
    }
}
```

Now, you can iterate through database rows from the old table and transfer the data into the AppUser entities. To parse the PropertyNames and extract the correct ranges from PropertyValuesString and PropertyValuesBinary columns is not difficult. For non-string values, you will need to convert the data or use XmlSerializer to deserialize the value, as shown in Listing 6-13. The ParseProperties method was omitted – there is nothing sophisticated inside. You can find it in the ProfileParser class in the example repository.

Listing 6-13. Parsing profile information and converting the values

```
// load user
var user = await userManager.FindByIdAsync(
    profile["UserId"].ToString());

// parse properties
var properties = ParseProperties(
    (string)profile["PropertyNames"],
    (string)profile["PropertyValuesString"],
    (byte[])profile["PropertyValuesBinary"]);
foreach (var property in properties)
{
    switch (property.Name)
    {
        case "FavoriteNumber":
            user.FavoriteNumber = int.Parse(
                property.StringValue!,
                CultureInfo.InvariantCulture);
            break;
```

373

```
    case "ImageUrls":
        user.ImageUrls = XmlDeserialize<StringCollection>(
                property.StringValue!)
            .Select(u => new AppUserImage()
            {
                Url = (string)u
            })
            .ToList();
        break;
    ...
  }
}

// save changes
await userManager.UpdateAsync(user);

public static T XmlDeserialize<T>(string value)
{
    var serializer = new XmlSerializer(typeof(T));
    using var reader = new StringReader(value);
    return (T)serializer.Deserialize(reader)!;
}
```

The most complicated thing was the binary serialization used for the ShoppingCart custom class. Binary serialization was a way to capture an object graph and serialize it, including references between objects (even circular ones). However useful this may sound, it opens a wide variety of security issues when you accept binary payloads from an untrusted source. Check out the readme of the YSoSerial.Net project[8] to see how many types of malicious payloads are known.

---

[8] See https://github.com/pwntester/ysoserial.net

When deserializing, the BinaryFormatter can create an instance of any class specified in the message and set its fields (not properties). This allows, for example, to call a deserialization constructor of the PSObject class with a specially crafted XML that could invoke the XamlReader.Parse method and launch any process on the machine (by providing XAML with ObjectDataProvider calling the Start method on System.Diagnostics. Process). There are so many possible (and still unknown) ways to invoke something malicious that securing BinaryFormatter is virtually impossible, and that is why it became obsolete in .NET 5 and started throwing exceptions in .NET 8. For .NET 9, Microsoft plans to remove the API completely.

Please note that even JSON deserialization in Newtonsoft.Json is not saved from such issues. For example, there is a setting that allows using the $type property to specify what type shall be created. However, if you have a property of type object in a class, the deserializer can create an instance of the attacker-requested class and call setters on specific properties. With these settings, you can allow instantiating, for example, System.Configuration.Install.AssemblyInstaller and setting its Path property, which triggers the loading and executing of an attacker-specified local assembly in the memory, or the famous System.Windows.Data. ObjectDataProvider, which can be used to call any method by setting its ObjectType and MethodName properties.

To prevent issues like that, the new System.Text.Json requires you to whitelist derived types for any property where you expect them. However, make sure you allow and use only objects with no arbitrary logic in their setters. The JSON deserializer calls them in random, or worse, attacker-specified order.

This leads to the question of how to read the binary serialized data from .NET 8 (which disallows using the BinaryFormatter). In our case, the serialized profile properties are under our control, and unless you use polymorphism (which is not very likely), you know the exact types appearing in the payloads. They are generated by your old application, and hopefully no attacker can inject their serialized payloads into the database.

The format used by binary serialization (MS-NRBF) is documented,[9] and there are open source libraries that you can use to read the payloads manually (without actually building the objects), for example, BinaryFormatDataStructure.[10]

Its API is quite simple – the NRBFReader.ReadStream method will either return a deserialized primitive value (string, numbers, dates, and so forth) or a BinaryObject, which contains a dictionary of field names and their values (again either a primitive value or BinaryObject). To read out the ShoppingCart object from the legacy application and build the representation (slightly modified to use List instead of Dictionary to work with Entity Framework Core) is not that complicated, provided you know the field names and exact object types, as shown in Listing 6-14. Notice how weird the field names are – it is because they are auto-generated by the compiler for properties with automatic getters and setters.

Listing 6-14. Reading a binary-serialized object using the BinaryFormatDataStructure library

```
public ShoppingCart DeserializeShoppingCart(Stream stream)
{
    var document = (BinaryObject)NRBFReader.ReadStream(stream);

    var cart = new ShoppingCart();
    cart.Created =
        (DateTime?)document["<Created>k__BackingField"];
    cart.LastUpdated =
        (DateTime?)document["<LastUpdated>k__BackingField"];
```

---

[9] See https://learn.microsoft.com/en-us/openspecs/windows_protocols/ms-nrbf/75b9fe09-be15-475f-85b8-ae7b7558cfe5

[10] See https://github.com/bbowyersmyth/BinaryFormatDataStructure

```csharp
    var itemsDictionary =
        (BinaryObject)document["<Items>k__BackingField"];

    // Dictionary<K, V> contains a field named KeyValuePairs
    // (array of KeyValuePair<K, V>)
    var keyValuePairs =
        (object[])itemsDictionary["KeyValuePairs"];
    foreach (var pair in pairs.Cast<BinaryObject>())
    {
        var cartItem = new CartItem();

        // KeyValuePair<K, V> has fields named key and value
        cartItem.Item = (string)pair["key"];

        var value = (BinaryObject)pair["value"];
        cartItem.Quantity =
            (int)value["<Quantity>k__BackingField"];
        cartItem.Price =
            (double)value["<Price>k__BackingField"];

        cart.Items.Add(cartItem);
    }
    return cart;
}

// the original serialized classes
[Serializable]
public class ShoppingCart
{
    public DateTime Created { get; set; }
    public DateTime LastUpdated { get; set; }
    public Dictionary<string, CartItem> Items { get; set; }
        = new();
}
```

[Serializable]
```
public class CartItem
{
    public int Quantity { get; set; }
    public double Price { get; set; }
}
```

At the beginning of the section, I promised a funny anecdote. When I tried to deserialize the payloads using the library, I was getting an exception from `BinaryReader.ReadDecimal()`. After looking at the library code, which seemed fine, I opened the specification of the NRBF format to find out that `decimal` is serialized in its string representation and not as the actual bits used while in memory.

I guessed that the code should probably be `BinaryReader.ReadString()` followed by parsing the value as decimal using `InvariantCulture`. After validating this thought in the .NET Framework reference source code,[11] I fixed the routine and submitted a pull request,[12] including some tests to cover this behavior. I mention this story mainly to show that resolving tiny issues in open source libraries does not have to be difficult and time-consuming (in my case, it took no more than 20 minutes).

The database structure of the `Profiles` table in ASP.NET Universal Providers looks very similar, so it would be natural to expect the implementation to be the same. Unfortunately, it is not. The column with binary property values remained in the database, but it was actually never used. All properties configured with the `serializeAs="Binary"` option in the `web.config` are serialized using `NetDataContractSerializer`. It uses

---

[11] See https://referencesource.microsoft.com/#mscorlib/system/runtime/serialization/formatters/binary/binaryformatterwriter.cs,98

[12] See https://github.com/bbowyersmyth/BinaryFormatDataStructure/pull/9/files

quite a complicated XML format with fully qualified type and assembly names. To make it look binary,[13] the result is Base64-encoded and stored in the PropertyValueStrings.

Deserialization from this format proved to be even more painful than binary serialization. The NetDataContractSerializer is not present in the new .NET as it also suffers security issues. There is, however, DataContractSerializer. The main difference between the two is that NetDataContractSerializer uses full .NET type names, while DataContractSerializer uses only names specified in the DataContract attribute and allows the whitelisting of known types. This makes it secure enough to get its way into the new .NET. However, the XML formats are not compatible, so I decided to parse the XML manually.

I found an open source port of NetDataContractSerializer for .NET Standard, but in order to use it, I would have to extract the types used in the ASP.NET Profile into a separate assembly (with the same fully qualified name and namespaces) and hope that the types will match during the deserialization. This seems to be quite difficult for many modernization projects.

As you can see in the example repository, the code parsing the XML is very ugly as the document changes XML namespaces in the structure to match .NET namespaces. However, since it is just a one-time operation and I do not expect many people to store complicated objects in the profile, using such a method seems as least painful.

You may ask why on Earth I tried to migrate the profile data in the new .NET instead of dumping it in the old project where I could read the information through the Profile class and .NET Framework would do the deserialization automatically. There are two reasons for this. First, the old

---

[13] I cannot find any reason for Base64-encoding the value and storing it as string, when it already was a string. The encoding only increases its size by 33%. I believe implementing it like this was unintended.

code cannot move the data into ASP.NET Core Identity because they do not exist yet. You would have to dump the profiles to some other place and migrate them to the final structure later. Second, it is good when the data migration process is implemented in a repeatable way. You will likely need to migrate the users and profiles several times to ensure the data is migrated correctly and completely. If you manage to do everything in one single application (or a test project, as I did in the example repository), it is much easier to orchestrate. However, feel free to use any way that suits your environment.

ASP.NET Identity

ASP.NET Identity was the answer to new requirements for authentication and user management in web applications. With the rising popularity of Internet services, such as social media platforms, many users have started to interact with more and more web applications. However, the security of password-based authentication relies on having a different password for every service, which introduces a significant obstacle for common users.

Using third-party identity providers to sign in to many web applications using a single Google, Microsoft, or Facebook account helps to improve security. Adding a second factor to the authentication began a recommended practice – in fact, it is often mandatory in some highly regulated industries such as banking or healthcare. The global players have the advantage of offering various implementations of the second factor because they operate multiple services, and there is a high chance you are using more than one. For example, when I try to sign in to my Google account, one of the ways for additional identity verification is by using YouTube or any other Google-authored application on my phone. I do not have to install and configure any special authenticator application.

Similarly, when I sign in to the tax portal operated by the Czech government, I can verify my identity using an application I use to access my bank account because the government identity provider is integrated with the banking systems, and most people already have some banking application installed in their phones. It is more secure than using text messages (SMS) which carry a risk of message interception or phone number hijacking.[14]

The old ASP.NET Membership providers were not prepared for any of these use cases. They assumed that every user possesses a password. Neither the database structure nor the API of the providers allowed for storing additional claims with the users, such as their identifiers used by external providers.

ASP.NET Identity was a new set of libraries that tried to address this issue. It dropped some features of the providers, such as the special API around user profiles, and focused on a good representation of the user's identity.

If you used this library with Entity Framework store implementation, which was the most popular method, you could find the `AspNetUsers` and `AspNetUserLogins` tables in the database. The first table contained basic information about the user (username, email address, phone number) as well as several important flags (whether the two-factor authentication was enabled or whether the user account was locked). The password hash field was optional, as not every user must have the password.

There was a new field called `SecurityStamp`, which allows the invalidation of any security token derived from the user identity, such as the token used in authentication cookies or the token used for resetting the user's password. ASP.NET Identity changes this stamp in various

---

[14] NIST (National Institute of Standards and Technology) does not consider authentication methods leveraging PSTN (Public Switched Telephone Network) as secure, and they define them as restricted, meaning that you have to assess and understand the risk associated with the authenticator. See `https://pages.nist.gov/800-63-FAQ/#authentication`

situations, for example, when the user changes the password or removes a login method. Because all security tokens are derived from this stamp, it will automatically invalidate all issued tokens and sign out the user from every device.

The AspNetUserLogins table allows storing user identifiers for third-party authentication providers, such as Microsoft or Google accounts, social media platforms, and others. To implement this authentication method, the application needs to redirect the user to the provider's sign-in page, and after the user passes through the authentication, they are redirected back to your application with a token carrying the user identifier for the corresponding platform. If the token is valid (the library verifies that the token is signed by the authentication provider), you can use ASP.NET Identity API to find the user account with the specified user identifier.

Migration to ASP.NET Core Identity

If you compare the tables created by ASP.NET Identity and ASP.NET Core Identity, you will see numerous similarities. In ASP.NET Core Identity tables, there are some additional columns, such as NormalizedUserName and NormalizedEmail, that are used for case-insensitive matching. There is an additional table called AspNetUserTokens to store any number of arbitrary tokens for a particular user.

If passwords are used, the format used in ASP.NET Identity is supported by ASP.NET Core Identity. The first byte of the PasswordHash column specifies the version of the hash algorithm (0x00 for ASP.NET Identity format, 0x01 for ASP.NET Core Identity format). Therefore, you do not need to introduce your own password hasher to support the legacy password hashing format as we had to do in the case of ASP.NET Membership or ASP.NET Universal Providers. When the user signs in for the first time after the data is migrated, the password will be rehashed to the new format automatically.

Instead of hashing the salt and password just once, ASP.NET Identity used the HMAC SHA-1 algorithm, but it repeated it 1000 times by using another algorithm – PBKDF2. Basically, the salt, password, and number of iterations are given to PBKDF2, which produces a derived key by iteratively calling the underlying function (HMAC SHA-1). The first iteration is computed from the salt and the password; every other iteration uses the result of the previous one as the input. Thanks to this, computing the hash for any given password is more computationally expensive, effectively slowing down the brute-force attacks the attacker can do by orders of magnitude. Same as in previous sections, the number of iterations is unfortunately too low by today's standards.

ASP.NET Core Identity also uses PBKDF2, but the number of iterations and other parameters of the algorithm are stored in the `PasswordHash` field instead of being hardcoded in the library. Furthermore, with some major releases of ASP.NET Core, the number of iterations gets increased so the passwords can be rehashed to increase security. The first byte of the value stored in the column is the version format (`0x01`). It is followed by 4 bytes defining the hashing algorithm (e.g., HMAC SHA-256) and another 4 bytes specifying the number of iterations. Then, the size of the salt (4 bytes) and the salt itself follow, finishing with the PBKDF2-produced result.

When inspecting the actual value in .NET 8, the algorithm is HMAC SHA-512, and the number of iterations is 100,000.[15] It is interesting that the number of iterations is lower than 210,000 (a value recommended by OWASP[16]), and the same value was used in .NET 7, which means that it did not increase in .NET 8. I asked the ASP.NET team at GitHub[17] and the answer was that following an internal discussion, they decided to keep the lower value to avoid excessive delay. If you prefer to follow the OWASP

---

[15] It corresponds to what you can find in ASP.NET Core source code: `https://github.com/dotnet/aspnetcore/blob/v8.0.4/src/Identity/Extensions.Core/src/PasswordHasher.cs#L134`

[16] See `https://cheatsheetseries.owasp.org/cheatsheets/Password_Storage_Cheat_Sheet.html#pbkdf2`

[17] See `https://github.com/dotnet/aspnetcore/issues/55690`

recommendation, increase the number of iterations to the recommended value by configuring PasswordHasherOptions, as shown in Listing 6-15. Remember that the ultimate reason for using such complex algorithms with many iterations is to slow down the attacker in the case of a database leak. Being able to compute hashes for billions of passwords must be slow.[18]

Listing 6-15. Configuring the iteration count for PBKDF2 in ASP. NET Core Identity

```
services.Configure<PasswordHasherOptions>(options =>
{
    opt.IterationCount = 210000;
});
```

By default, the IdentityUser and other ASP.NET Identity entities use string properties for the primary keys. Because many developers preferred to use a different type, such as Guid, ASP.NET Identity provided generic classes for its entities and allowed you to declare the set of classes to specify your desired type of the primary key, as shown in Listing 6-16. The inconvenient aspect of this is that you had to define classes for all five entities in order to redefine the primary key. You could not use generic types (such as IdentityUser<Guid>) as Entity Framework would not know how to map them. It is also useful to make custom classes for the UserManager and RoleManager that inherit from the generic ones, supplying all of their generic parameters and providing the correct type of identity store (Entity Framework in my case). After doing this, you can use just the AppUserManager class or the AppUser entity in the application code instead of using the base types and providing all the generic arguments.

---

[18] Please note that there is also a risk of DOS attack (Denial of Service) if the password verification is too slow – the attackers may be able to easily exhaust server CPU resources by sending just thousands of passwords. Instead of relying just on the security of a stored password, consider implementing multifactor authentication.

Listing 6-16. Using Guid as a primary key in ASP.NET Identity entities

```
// context
public class AppDbContext
    : IdentityDbContext<AppUser, AppRole, Guid,
        AppUserLogin, AppUserRole, AppUserClaim>
{
    ...
}

// entities
public class AppUser
    : IdentityUser<Guid, AppUserLogin, AppUserRole,
        AppUserClaim>
{
}

public class AppRole : IdentityRole<Guid, AppUserRole>
{
}

public class AppUserLogin : IdentityUserLogin<Guid>
{
}

public class AppUserRole : IdentityUserRole<Guid>
{
}

public class AppUserClaim : IdentityUserClaim<Guid>
{
}
```

```
// managers
public class AppUserManager : UserManager<AppUser, Guid>
{
    public AppUserManager() : base(
        new UserStore<AppUser, AppRole, Guid,
            AppUserLogin, AppUserRole, AppUserClaim>(
                new AppDbContext()
            )
        )
    {
    }
}

public class AppRoleManager : RoleManager<AppRole, Guid>
{
    public AppRoleManager() : base(
        new RoleStore<AppRole, Guid, AppUserRole>(
            new AppDbContext()
        )
    )
    {
    }
}
```

ASP.NET Core Identity offers a very similar concept, but there are generic versions of IdentityDbContext with fewer arguments that allow providing just the class for the user, role, and the type of primary key, which is the most frequent scenario. Also, the ASP.NET team has made changes to reduce the coupling of the classes. For example, the role entity no longer needs to know the type of the user-role relationship. Redefining the primary key to Guid in ASP.NET Core Identity is shown in Listing 6-17.

Like in ASP.NET Identity, I could also "redefine" the UserManager and RoleManager types here, but since they have only one generic parameter and do not need to specify anything in their constructor, I can use directly UserManager<AppUser> in my application.

Listing 6-17. Using Guid as the primary key in ASP.NET Core Identity entities

```
// context
public class AppDbContext
    : IdentityDbContext<AppUser, AppRole, Guid>
{
}

// entities
public class AppUser : IdentityUser<Guid>
{
}

public class AppRole : IdentityRole<Guid>
{
}
```

The migration of ASP.NET Identity to ASP.NET Core Identity tables is not difficult as the schema is almost equal. The only problem may arise if you want to do the migration within the same database – the tables use the same names. You either need to rename the old tables, create the new ones, and move all data or alter the existing tables and add some new ones (including the relationships) to exactly match the schema used by ASP. NET Core Identity.

In the example repository, I preferred to migrate from one database to another to avoid this issue. Even though the data are copied without any transformation (even the PasswordHash is just copied as is), I decided to create the users using a C# code through the ASP.NET Core Identity API, as you can see in Listing 6-18. The main reason is that the ASP.NET Core entities have some new properties, such as NormalizedUserName and NormalizedEmail (username and email address in the uppercase form), which are calculated when the entity is saved.

You may object that it is not difficult to calculate the NormalizedUserName and other columns using the UPPER() function directly in SQL. However, I did not want to risk hitting some edge cases where the SQL result might differ from the .NET result.[19]

Listing 6-18. Migration of the AspNetUsers table to ASP.NET Core Identity

```
var migratedUser = new AppUser
{
    Id = (Guid)user["Id"],
    UserName = (string)user["UserName"],
    Email = (string)user["Email"],
    EmailConfirmed = (bool)user["EmailConfirmed"],
    TwoFactorEnabled = (bool)user["TwoFactorEnabled"],
    LockoutEnabled = (bool)user["LockoutEnabled"],
    LockoutEnd = (DateTime?)user["LockoutEndDateUtc"]
        .HandleDbNull(),
    PasswordHash = (string)user["PasswordHash"],
    SecurityStamp = (string)user["SecurityStamp"],
    PhoneNumber = (string?)user["PhoneNumber"].HandleDbNull(),
    PhoneNumberConfirmed = (bool)user["PhoneNumberConfirmed"],
    AccessFailedCount = (int)user["AccessFailedCount"]
};
```

---

[19] My favorite example of this is the Turkish language which uses both i and ı letters (yes, i, but without the dot). Converting i to uppercase results in İ instead of I when using Turkish locale.

```
// save the user
var result = await userManager.CreateAsync(migratedUser);
if (!result.Succeeded)
{
    Assert.Fail($"Failed to migrate user {user["UserName"]}");
}
```

In contrast to Membership and Universal providers, there is no Profile API in ASP.NET Core. I expect most developers to store the user profile properties directly in the user entity or in a separate table with a one-to-one relationship. You need to adjust the code to transfer this data yourself based on the schema you use.

If you used AspNetUserClaims or AspNetUserLogins tables, you need to move them to the new database as well. Except for adding an optional ProviderDisplayName column to AspNetUserLogins table, the tables did not change at all.

As I mentioned earlier, the passwords are rehashed automatically from the old format to the new one once the user signs in. To make sure it works this way, I have a test in the example repository, as shown in Listing 6-19.

Listing 6-19. Testing that the password is rehashed in ASP.NET Core Identity on first sign-in

```
[TestMethod]
public async Task ValidateCredentialsAndTestRehashing()
{
    // get the user and remember the original password hash
    var user = await userManager.FindByNameAsync("testuser");
    Assert.IsNotNull(user);
    var originalPasswordHash = user.PasswordHash;
```

```csharp
// check the password for the first time
// it must start with 0x00 - ASP.NET Identity version
var result = await userManager.CheckPasswordAsync(
    user, "TestPassword1234+");
Assert.IsTrue(result);
Assert.AreEqual((byte)0,
    Convert.FromBase64String(originalPasswordHash)[0]);

// reload the user
var user2 = await userManager.FindByNameAsync("testuser");
Assert.IsNotNull(user2);

// verify that the password hash has changed
// it must not start with 0x00 indicating it uses
// a newer algorithm
Assert.AreNotEqual(originalPasswordHash,
    user2.PasswordHash);
Assert.AreNotEqual((byte)0,
    Convert.FromBase64String(user2.PasswordHash)[0]);

// verify the new password works
result = await userManager.CheckPasswordAsync(
    user, "TestPassword1234+");
Assert.IsTrue(result);
}
```

Authentication in ASP.NET Core

So far, I have discussed how to store user information and verify their credentials. This is only one part of the process. What has also changed is how to tell the web application to sign the user in or out and how to work with authentication cookies.

Before I get to the details, let me just briefly explain how authentication works in ASP.NET Core. One big limitation of the old ASP.NET was that the web.config file allowed for configuring only one type of authentication per application, and the list was not extensible. This was the most visible when using ASP.NET Web API along with MVC or Web Forms in the same application. A different way of authentication was needed for the web users and for the API consumers. Therefore, the configuration of the Web API allowed to call SuppressDefaultHostAuthentication to ignore the user identity provided from the outside of the ASP.NET Web API. This allowed for using a different means of authentication, such as a bearer token, but only in the Web API. The rest of the application used what was configured in web.config. This is far from a universal solution that would work in complex scenarios.

ASP.NET Core solves this limitation by introducing the concept of authentication handlers and schemes. The authentication handler defines how the authentication is performed – for example, reading a ticket from an authentication cookie or validating a bearer token sent in the HTTP request header. You have already met the authentication handlers in Chapter 4 when implementing custom username and password authentication for CoreWCF.

The authentication scheme is a unique string constant that defines a particular authentication handler and its configuration. Every authentication scheme defines a constant with the scheme's default name, which you can use (e.g., CookieAuthenticationDefaults. AuthenticationScheme).

Multiple schemes can use the same handler but use their own options – for example, you can have two different configurations for the bearer token validation used in various parts of the application REST API. If you use more than one authentication scheme, you must specify which is the default one, as shown in Listing 6-20.

Listing 6-20. Configuring multiple authentication schemes

```
Services
    .AddAuthentication(
        defaultScheme:
            CookieAuthenticationDefaults.AuthenticationScheme)
    .AddJwtBearer(
        JwtBearerDefaults.AuthenticationScheme,
        options =>
    {
        options.Audience = "https://your-identity-provider/";
        options.Authority = "https://your-identity-provider/";
    })
    .AddCookie(
        CookieAuthenticationDefaults.AuthenticationScheme,
        options =>
    {
        options.LoginPath = "/Account/Unauthorized/";
        options.AccessDeniedPath = "/Account/Forbidden/";
    });
```

The authentication handlers in ASP.NET Core are responsible for the following functionality:

- AuthenticateAsync validates the incoming request and tries to authenticate it. If successful, it returns an AuthenticationTicket – an object containing the name of the authentication scheme and the ClaimsPrincipal object carrying one or more user identities. It can also return a failure result (the credentials were provided, but incorrect) or an empty result (the credentials were not provided).

- `ChallengeAsync` is called when a restricted resource is accessed and the request is not authenticated (e.g., when you try to access a page that requires an authentication cookie). This method can modify the response, for example, redirect the user to the login page, or add some HTTP headers indicating which methods of authentication are accepted, such as `www-authenticate: bearer`.

- `ForbidAsync` is called when a restricted resource is accessed and the request is authenticated, but the user lacks permissions for the resource. Again, this method can modify the response before it is sent out, for example, set the status code to 403 Forbidden.

In most cases, application frameworks in ASP.NET Core use the `Authorize` attribute to mark resources that require authentication. This attribute may specify a concrete authentication scheme, as shown in Listing 6-21. If no authentication scheme is specified in the attribute, the default scheme is used. Optionally, you can restrict access only to members of a particular role.

Listing 6-21. Using the Authorize attribute with a particular scheme

```
[Authorize(AuthenticationSchemes = "myscheme")]
```

Once the user is authenticated, the `ClaimsPrincipal` object is set to the current `HttpContext`. This principal object can carry one or more user identities, each defining a set of claims about the user (such as user identifier, name, email address, or any other key-value pair). By default, the `AuthenticateAsync` method is called only on the default authentication scheme. If you want to obtain the `ClaimsPrincipal` for a non-default scheme, you can invoke the authentication explicitly, as shown in Listing 6-22.

Listing 6-22. Authenticating the user using a non-default scheme

```
var result = await context.AuthenticateAsync(
    CookieAuthenticationDefaults.AuthenticationScheme);
if (result.Succeeded)
{
    var principal = result.Principal;
    ...
}
```

In the old ASP.NET, we were used to working only with a role-based access mechanism (any user can be assigned to one or more roles). ASP. NET Core brings an additional concept of authorization policies.[20] A policy is a set of requirements that must be satisfied to comply with it. It is quite easy to define custom authorization policies and enforce them either using the Authorize attribute or by an explicit call to IAuthorizationService. AuthorizeAsync.

Using ASP.NET Core Identity

ASP.NET Core Identity can do many things out of the box. For example, if you register it in the service collection, it will configure the cookie authentication for you, as demonstrated in Listing 6-23. Make sure the ConfigureAuthenticationCookie is called after AddIdentity. Otherwise, your explicit changes to cookie configuration can be overwritten by ASP. NET Core Identity defaults.

---

[20] See https://learn.microsoft.com/en-us/aspnet/core/security/ authorization/policies

Listing 6-23. Adding ASP.NET Core Identity to the application

```
builder.Services.AddIdentity<AppUser, AppRole>(options =>
    {
        // ASP.NET Core Identity settings
        options.SignIn.RequireConfirmedAccount = true;

        options.Lockout.DefaultLockoutTimeSpan =
            TimeSpan.FromMinutes(5);
        options.Lockout.MaxFailedAccessAttempts = 5;
        options.Lockout.AllowedForNewUsers = true;
    })
    .AddEntityFrameworkStores<AppDbContext>();

builder.Services.ConfigureApplicationCookie(options =>
{
    // cookie settings
    options.Cookie.HttpOnly = true;
    options.ExpireTimeSpan = TimeSpan.FromMinutes(20);
    options.LoginPath = "/Identity/Account/Login";
    options.AccessDeniedPath =
        "/Identity/Account/AccessDenied";
    options.SlidingExpiration = true;
});
```

Once you have ASP.NET Core Identity configured, you can use the **SignInManager<AppUser>**, **UserManager<AppUser>**, and other services, which are automatically registered in the dependency injection. Most operations you will need to do with the user accounts are exposed as a single method in one of these services, as shown in Listing 6-24.

Listing 6-24. Typical operations using ASP.NET Core Identity

```
// sign the user in
// (using the IdentityConstants.ApplicationScheme by default)
var result = await signInManager.PasswordSignInAsync(
   "username", "password",
   isPersistent: true, lockoutOnFailure: true);

// sign the user using social media provider
result = await signInManager.ExternalLoginSignInAsync(
    loginProvider, providerUserIdentifier, isPersistent: true);

// verify user's e-mail
result = await userManager.GenerateEmailConfirmationTokenAsync(
    user);
...
result = await userManager.ConfirmEmailAsync(user,
    providedToken);

// change the user's password
result = await userManager.ChangePasswordAsync(
    user, "old-password", "new-password");

// generate a password reset token
result = await userManager.GeneratePasswordResetTokenAsync(
    user);
...
result = await userManager.ResetPasswordAsync(
    user, providedToken, "new-password");
```

For example, the PasswordSignInAsync of the SignInManager method handles the entire logic of user sign-in. Not only does it verify the provided credentials, it also checks whether the user is not locked out (and records a failed sign-in attempt in case the credentials were not correct). If configured, it will also check that the account's email address is confirmed. Finally, if the credentials are correct, the method will automatically generate the application cookie by calling HttpContext.SignInAsync with the user principal and configured authentication scheme.

It can also handle two-factor authentication. If it is required for the user, the result object will indicate this fact, so you can redirect the user to a page that performs the verification. The authentication cookie will be set already, but the identity's amr claim (Authentication Method Reference) will contain the value pwd. Once the second factor is verified (e.g., by calling the SignInManager.TwoFactorSignInAsync method for that), the claim will be updated to the value of mfa.

Similarly, the process of recovering a forgotten password is handled by two easy-to-use methods – GeneratePasswordResetTokenAsync and ResetPasswordAsync. They are implemented to follow the best practices. When the user enters the username of an email address in the forgotten password form, you need just to find the user and call GeneratePasswordResetTokenAsync. The method will produce a time-restricted token which you can use to generate the recovery link to be emailed to the user. When the user receives the email, opens the link, and enters the new password on the password reset page, you just call the ResetPasswordAsync with the token generated by the first method and the new user's password. ASP.NET Core Identity will validate the token for you (whether it belongs to the specified user and did not expire), and if it is legitimate, it will save the new password.

Summary

In this chapter, I described how to migrate from old authentication and user management frameworks to the most up-to-date implementation – ASP.NET Core Identity. This library can do much more than what was described in this chapter. Feel free to review the documentation[21] and see all the possibilities you can add to your application. If your application does not support two-factor authentication, consider adding it after the migration is completed. It can greatly improve the security of your solution.

---

[21] See https://learn.microsoft.com/en-us/aspnet/core/security/

CHAPTER 7

In-Place Migration of Web UI Applications

In the previous chapters, we have dealt with modernizing API applications and the portions of code that access the database or handle application user management. However, we have not yet explored frameworks used to build user interfaces. In fact, this part of the migration often represents most of the effort.

As I already explained in the first chapter, all web UI frameworks present in the .NET Framework have undergone substantial changes. ASP.NET Web Forms are completely missing from the new .NET, while ASP. NET MVC has evolved to ASP.NET Core MVC. Its simpler variant – ASP. NET Web Pages – was redesigned to Razor Pages. Blazor, a new application framework, was introduced in 2018, and it receives most of the attention and investments of the ASP.NET team. It shares some aspects with ASP. NET MVC (mainly the Razor-based view engine), but the underlying principles are completely different. Thus, no matter which framework your application uses, most of the code cannot remain as is.

Because of these differences, the migration requires code changes practically in every page and UI component of the application, as well as in all code-behind files (in the case of ASP.NET Web Forms) or controllers (in the case of ASP.NET MVC or Web Pages). If you try to upgrade the project to target the new .NET and new UI frameworks, hundreds or even thousands of compilation errors will probably appear. To resolve them

© Tomáš Herceg 2024
T. Herceg, *Modernizing .NET Web Applications*,
https://doi.org/10.1007/979-8-8688-0617-9_7

quickly is impossible – the estimates we have seen earlier in this book showed an effort of hundreds of hours for quite a simple application (that was not even very old).

In projects with a long history, where some parts were implemented by developers who are no longer part of the team, rewriting all pages and components usually takes months.

Despite the fact that many code changes you will experience are rather trivial (such as namespace changes, different naming of components for the same purpose, and so on), there is always a chance of introducing new bugs and breaking changes. For any larger project, you will need to pick an approach that allows migrating the pages or application parts incrementally. This includes the ability to deploy the already migrated functionality to get early user feedback, which will help significantly reduce the number of newly introduced issues.

Without this incremental approach, doing the migration as a single big step would mean that the code will not be buildable for a very long time, and the team will not want or even be able to focus on anything else than finishing the modernization as quickly as possible. The longer the codebase is in an uncompilable state, the higher the risk of introducing new errors.

This can create huge problems for company management, as they will probably need the application to get new features and functionality during migration. In most companies, it is quite difficult to imagine that the developer team would be gifted with one year to modernize the entire application and would not be pushed to ship new features, fix production issues, and respond to ever-changing business requirements.

I have not seen a "feature freeze" lasting one or two months; it is quite usual in ecommerce companies because their sales can increase by orders of magnitude every holiday season. But even during these periods, the developer teams were under constant pressure to plan and prepare new features so that they could start implementing them as soon as the freeze was over.

Trivial Applications

There is a special category of web applications where you can afford to do a single-step rewrite without aspiring to be able to deploy the application during the process. I call these applications "trivial" because I do not have a better name for them. The word "trivial" refers primarily to the size of the UI surface – the applications that belong to this category usually have just several uncomplicated web pages.

A typical example of this category is a public company website (built without using a CMS[1]). There will probably be many static pages, and only a few of them will involve more sophisticated functionality. There is often a search feature, which can involve substantial business logic, but its UI surface is pretty simple. There may be various forms for submitting inquiries, calculating prices, and so on, but they usually do not appear on every page.

Some applications in this category involve complex business logic underneath the thin UI layer, but it can usually be migrated as a separate step, as shown in the previous chapters. Thus, in these applications, the effort of rewriting all UI pages and components is relatively small and can be done in days or within the boundary of one sprint.[2]

---

[1] Content Management System – a software or a framework that provides a user-friendly interface to manage the website content, often including the functionality to define the layout of individual pages or compose them from ready-made blocks. If the website is built using a CMS, its UI is usually generated by the CMS. Therefore, the process depends primarily on the migration of the CMS.

[2] Many developer teams use Scrum or some kind of agile approach. Even if they do not follow these methodologies to the full extent, they usually plan their work in sprints – time intervals of a fixed length (from one to four weeks). If the entire application can be migrated and deployed in less than one sprint, it quite nicely fits in the standard flow of these methodologies. Involving the incremental modernization approach is not of much value – it would only add unnecessary complexity. However, if you estimate the migration will take more than one sprint, you will be forced to split this large task in smaller items that would fit into the sprint. Then the incremental approach makes sense.

In-Place and Side-by-Side Migration

If you look in the Microsoft documentation, you will find the entire section[3] about migrating web UIs to the new .NET. Although the concrete steps are not covered in much detail (which is understandable as every legacy application is different, and there are an unimaginably high number of possible combinations), the process described there is what I refer to as side-by-side migration.

Side-by-side migration involves creating a new empty ASP.NET Core application, which is put in front of the original application and acts as a proxy (it uses the YARP reverse proxy NuGet package to implement this functionality). At the beginning of the migration, all requests coming to the new application are just sent to the old application to be handled, and their responses are sent back to the client. The migration involves taking parts of the old application and moving or reimplementing them in the new application. This can be done in reasonably small steps, and when everything is migrated to the new application, you can just discard the old application and remove YARP. The entire process is illustrated in Figure 7-1.

---

[3] See https://learn.microsoft.com/en-us/aspnet/core/migration/inc/overview

Initial state: All traffic is sent to the old application

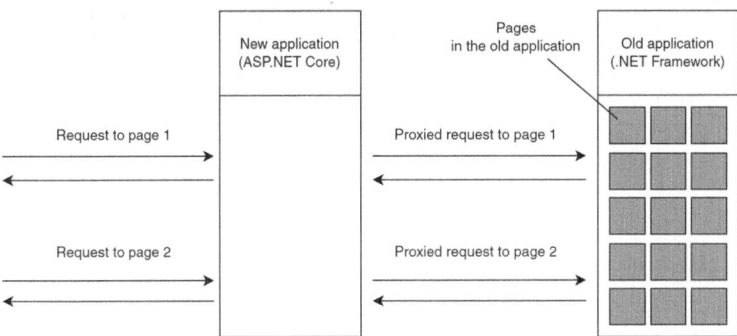

Migration process: Pages and business logic are moved to the new application

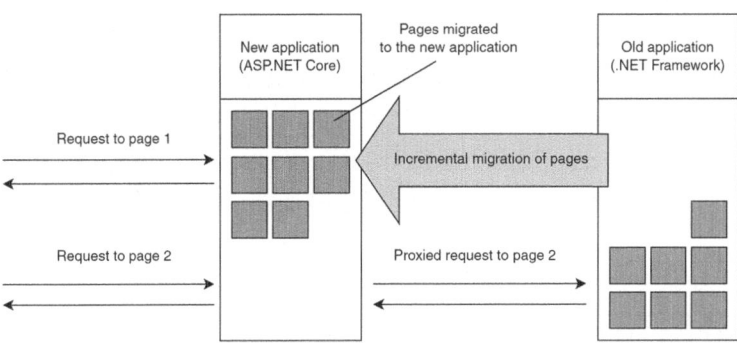

Final state: All pages are migrated

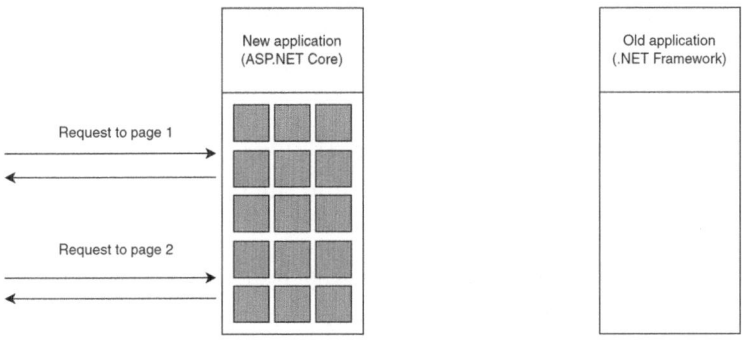

Figure 7-1. *Visualization of the side-by-side migration process*

This method of migration will be described in detail in Chapters 8 and 9. At first sight, it looks quite easy, but there are various challenges originating from the fact that your business logic is spanned across two applications. For example, you will need to make a single sign-on experience between these applications. If the code uses a session state, you will need to ensure that it is accessible from both applications or replace it with some other concept of managing the temporary state. There are also various complexities when it comes to caching, accessing local resources or the filesystem, concurrency, locking, and so on.

There is an easier way that I call the in-place migration. Instead of moving the functionality from one application to another and running two applications at the same time, the migration may be done within the same project. Because everything will run in the same process, the challenges I described earlier are not present. There is, however, one strong requirement to leverage this method – it requires the use of a UI framework that supports the old .NET Framework and the new .NET versions.

Modernization Using DotVVM

Earlier in this chapter, I mentioned that every UI framework in the old .NET Framework has been changed in some way. However, I listed only the official frameworks developed and maintained by Microsoft as parts of the standard .NET distribution.

If I relax this restriction, there is at least one web UI framework that is compatible with both .NET Framework and the new .NET and can be used for this purpose – it is called DotVVM.[4]

Before I continue any further, I shall disclaim that I have been involved in the development of this project since its early days. The original raison d'être of the framework was not to allow modernization of legacy

---

[4] The project is hosted on GitHub at https://github.com/riganti/dotvvm

applications – its development started before .NET Core was announced, and this use case did not come to our mind at the beginning. The framework was meant as a modern replacement for ASP.NET Web Forms to allow building interactive web UIs easily and approachable – without the need to learn JavaScript and frameworks like React or Angular. Because we liked the Model-View-ViewModel approach used in WPF and other XAML-based technologies, we decided to use this approach in a web-based framework. The modernization use case appeared as a side effect in 2015 because we decided to support the new version of .NET Core and keep the support for the .NET Framework as well.

I dedicate most of this chapter to showing the modernization using DotVVM, not because I am one of its authors and contributors. I believe it is worth describing as it demonstrates a unique modernization method that is not possible with other ASP.NET frameworks. At RIGANTI, we used DotVVM many times for incremental modernization of (mostly) ASP.NET Web Forms applications, and thanks to the fact the migration could be made in place, it was considerably easier than the side-by-side method described in Chapters 8 and 9.

As I already mentioned, the main restriction of this in-place modernization is that you have to use a framework that supports both .NET worlds, and there are not many choices. I wish Microsoft had introduced a solution such as DotVVM back in the early days of .NET Core – it would simplify the migration for many companies and make the transition to the new .NET much more seamless.

On the other hand, I understand the reasons why they did not – technically, it would be possible to port these frameworks to the new platform, but it would be hard to take advantage of the new platform concepts, such as the new configuration model, dependency injection, logging stack, and more, without introducing too many tiny breaking changes.

A Brief History

To understand how in-place modernization works, it is useful to discuss how the first version of DotVVM was built. I already discussed OWIN, a universal interface defining the communication interface between web frameworks and web servers. Earlier in this book, I used OWIN to add SignalR to the web application. The same principle was leveraged in DotVVM to allow running it within an ASP.NET application.

DotVVM has its own syntax for defining the web pages, as you can see in Listing 7-1. It is based on HTML, but it enhances its syntax with the following constructs:

- *Directives*: They provide metadata for the page, such as namespace imports, the full name of the associated viewmodel class, and so on. They are always at the top of the file.

- *Server controls*: They are similar to ASP.NET Web Forms components or ASP.NET MVC Tag Helpers. It is a special HTML-like element that is translated to actual HTML elements before the page is sent to the browser. In DotVVM, components have some prefix, for example, dot: (in dot:TextBox).

- *Data-binding expressions*: They define relationships between UI components and viewmodel properties. DotVVM uses single or double curly braces to define the expressions – for example:

```
{value: FirstName}
```

Listing 7-1. Example of DotVVM syntax

```
@viewmodel DotvvmApp.ViewModels.DefaultViewModel

<p>
    <dot:TextBox Text="{value: FirstName}"
        placeholder="Enter your name" />
</p>
```

Because of the custom syntax, DotVVM does not rely on much of the ASP.NET infrastructure. It uses neither the Razor view engine nor the Web Forms one – it has its own. The implementation of routing in .NET Framework[5] was not to be extensible enough to be used by DotVVM, so DotVVM implements its own routing mechanism.

Luckily, the entire authentication stack is handled by the ASP.NET platform. Therefore, DotVVM does not have to deal with it on its own. Instead, it just looks at `HttpContext.Current.User` to access the user's identity and in which roles the user is assigned in.

DotVVM is implemented as an OWIN middleware on .NET Framework. When the application receives an HTTP request, DotVVM looks at the URL and searches its own route table. If a corresponding route is found, DotVVM takes care of the request and generates the response. If no route is registered to match the request URL, it passes the request to the next middleware in the pipeline. Thanks to this, it can live in the same application with any other frameworks or technologies.

The 1.0 version of DotVVM (with only .NET Framework support) was just one NuGet package called `DotVVM`. When .NET Core was released, we moved the code that relied on the old ASP.NET and OWIN to a separate package called `DotVVM.Owin` and introduced a new package called `DotVVM.AspNetCore`. If you look in the corresponding folders in the project's

---

[5] One was in ASP.NET Web Forms, another one in ASP.NET MVC, and the third one was in ASP.NET Web API.

GitHub repository,[6] you can see that there is not much code in these packages. Most of the files are implementations of IHttpContext or other universal interfaces we added to the framework – we use them everywhere we need to access the ASP.NET's or the ASP.NET Core's infrastructure classes such as HttpContext, Data Protection API, and others. ASP.NET Core also has a concept of middlewares, and although the interfaces and namespaces are different, the principles did not change much. Therefore, porting DotVVM 1.1 to .NET Core was not that difficult.

Both host-specific packages depend on the DotVVM main NuGet package that contains the entire framework. This way, we can offer the same syntax for pages and the viewmodels for the old .NET Framework and the new .NET. The TargetFrameworks of DotVVM are net472;netstan dard2.1;net6.0.

You may wonder why anyone would write their own full-featured web framework (except for having fun – I do not deny it was an important driver of our motivation). The idea started in 2014. At RIGANTI, we stopped using ASP.NET Web Forms as it was not catching up with the customer requirements in terms of the complexity and interactivity of the web pages. Even simple tasks like hiding a text field when a checkbox is checked by the user required either writing JavaScript (or jQuery) code snippets, which was quite an annoying activity,[7] or making a postback, which made a poor

---

[6] See https://github.com/riganti/dotvvm/tree/v4.2.0/src/Framework/ Hosting.Owin and https://github.com/riganti/dotvvm/tree/v4.2.0/src/ Framework/Hosting.AspNetCore

[7] The reason we did not like the experience was not because we, as .NET developers, did not like JavaScript. The reasons were that the solution was not very elegant. You had to reference the components from JavaScript to be able to determine their states and control their visibility. ASP.NET Web Forms auto-generated component IDs that you would have to pass to the JS code or use some other way of looking up the control, such as CSS classes or custom data attributes. However, it was annoying when you had to move such code as the JavaScript was usually in a different file, and it was too easy to tear these two parts of the code apart or break them.

user experience – it was slow even when the `UpdatePanel` component was used. The same situation was with C# code-behind files. If the page UI was a bit more complicated, you often had to search for components dynamically by calling `FindControl` and using control ID to identify the control. This was error-prone and could break easily when you moved the code to another place.

There was no .NET Core or Blazor at that time. We tried all three popular JavaScript frameworks of that time: Angular JS,[8] React, and Knockout JS. At that time, most RIGANTI developers had a deep .NET experience, but it seemed too hard to learn JavaScript and get the same level of experience in another language and ecosystem. Not that it would be impossible – today, there are many "full stack" developers, but it is still far from being the mainstream. Most developers prefer to specialize in one language and ecosystem.

From the three choices, we decided to use Knockout JS for several projects. We got enthusiastic about the idea of using the Model-View-ViewModel approach we knew from WPF to build web UIs. Many things that annoyed us in Web Forms (such as hiding the text box based on the checkbox state I already mentioned) were so easy to do with the MVVM approach, as shown in Listing 7-2.

Listing 7-2. Using MVVM binding attributes in Knockout JS

```
<input type="text"
    data-bind="visible: IsChecked, value: FirstName" />
<input type="checkbox" data-bind="checked: IsChecked" />

<script type="text/javascript">
var viewModel = {
    IsChecked: ko.observable(false),
```

---

[8] Angular JS was the first version of Angular. It is quite different from the following versions which are named just Angular.

```
    FirstName: ko.observable("")
};
ko.applyBindings(viewModel);
</script>
```

However, we found out that building API controllers on the server, writing many lines of JavaScript code to call the API, and building the JavaScript viewmodel for Knockout still required quite a lot of effort. Most of the JavaScript code we had to write was actually dull – it just took data from the API and passed it to the UI or back. We tried TypeScript and proxies generated from OpenAPI definitions, which helped us to get at least some compile-time checking of the client-side code, but it was still far from our expectations of building web UI applications in an efficient way.

After several projects, we tried to eliminate writing JavaScript code. What if the Knockout viewmodels were defined as C# classes, and the framework would send them to the client and generate all that Knockout JS ceremony? That was the key question that started the entire DotVVM project.

Was it worth implementing our own framework? I believe it was. Today, Blazor is the most popular .NET web UI framework. Its selling point is that you do not have to learn and write JavaScript – just use C# and HTML. We got this experience with DotVVM as early as 2014 – four years before Blazor was introduced (and five years before it was production-ready). We were able to migrate all .NET Framework projects started before the release of .NET Core quite easily because of the DotVVM support for both .NET Framework and .NET Core. And finally, we got a tremendous share of experience with writing frameworks, compilers, and running an open source project in general. This is not what most developers learn as part of their day-to-day job. The development of DotVVM has continued since 2014, and every year, we publish a new major or minor release with new features and bug fixes.

Even today, with Blazor being the natural choice for many .NET developers, we use DotVVM for many new projects in RIGANTI. We believe it offers a similar level of efficiency and productivity. With its JavaScript part having less than 100 kB, it is more lightweight than Blazor WebAssembly, and compared to Blazor Server, DotVVM works better on high-latency or unreliable networks as it does not require holding a SignalR connection with the server.

Model-View-ViewModel on the Web

The purpose of modern client-side web UI frameworks is to allow manipulating the page DOM[9] through some abstraction.

In React, you work with components, which are basically functions that generate a piece of HTML from its properties and state object. Whenever the state changes, a new HTML is generated by calling the component render function. React will compare the actual DOM with the desired one and make appropriate changes.

Angular and Knockout JS have a model object that also represents the state of the page, and you can manipulate the UI indirectly by changing this model object.

DotVVM is a hybrid framework that runs on both the server and the client. On the server, it is responsible for rendering pages, creating C# viewmodels, and calling methods on them. On the client, it draws and updates the UI based on the changing state of the viewmodel object. Both parts of the framework communicate using classic HTTP requests, exchanging JSON-serialized viewmodels (or, more precisely, only the subsets of the viewmodel that were changed).

Every DotVVM page consists of two files – a `.dothtml` file (MVVM view) defining the page contents and structure (using the syntax I was

---

[9] Document Object Model – the hierarchy of HTML elements and other nodes that define the contents of the page.

411

showing earlier) and a C# class (MVVM viewmodel). The model (from the MVVM perspective) is the code called from the viewmodel to invoke business logic or exchange data with the underlying layers. You can think of the model as of the top of your business layer – the methods you can call and the data these methods accept or return.

The view defines how the page looks like. As demonstrated in Listing 7-1, it can contain data-binding expressions which mark all "moving" parts of the page. Everything that can be changed while the page is loaded and displayed to the user should be connected to the viewmodel using data-binding expressions.

The viewmodel is responsible for maintaining the state of the view (it holds all dynamic values that appear on the page). It also handles all interactions with the user. If the user clicks something or changes some value in a form field, the viewmodel may respond to this, for example, by using the model (e.g., invoking some method in the business layer), by changing its own state, or both. The viewmodel can also decide whether the user shall be navigated to some other part of the application – it can make a redirect. You can see a more detailed example in Listing 7-3.

Listing 7-3. Simple page in DotVVM

```
<!-- View: Search.dothtml -->

@viewModel DotvvmApp.ViewModels.SearchViewModel
<p>
    Enter search query:
    <dot:TextBox Text="{value: SearchQuery}" />
    <dot:Button Text="Search" Click="{command: Search()}" />
</p>

<dot:Repeater DataSource="{value: Results}">
    <div class="result">
        <a href="{value: Url}">
```

```
    <big>{{value: Title}}</big>
    <br />
    {{value: Description}}
  </a>
</div>
</dot:Repeater>

// ViewModel: SearchViewModel.cs

public class SearchViewModel : DotvvmViewModelBase
{
    private readonly SearchService searchService;

    public string SearchQuery { get; set; }
    public List<SearchResultModel> Results { get; set; }

    public SearchViewModel(SearchService searchService)
    {
        this.searchService = searchService;
    }

    public async Task Search()
    {
        Results = await searchService.Search(SearchQuery);
    }
}
```

As you can see, the view defines three components:

- TextBox is bound to the SearchQuery string property
  in the viewmodel. The data binding in DotVVM works
  in two ways – if you set the SearchQuery property from
  the C# code, the value will appear in TextBox, and if the
  user changes the text in the control, it will get written
  back to the viewmodel.

- Button is set to call the Search() function in the viewmodel.

- Repeater is bound to the SearchResults collection (List of model objects). Whenever the collection is updated (e.g., by assigning to it in the Search() function), the Repeater will update the UI to match the contents of the collection. For every item in the collection, the template specified in the control will be instantiated on the page, evaluating the inner data-binding expressions on the particular collection item.

If you look at the viewmodel, you will see a couple of concepts there:

- The SearchService is passed in the constructor and stored as a private field in the class. At some point (I will get to it later), DotVVM needs to serialize the viewmodel in JSON and send it to the browser; therefore, these injected dependencies should be fields and not properties. That way, they are excluded from the serialization.

- In contrast, SearchQuery and Results are declared as public properties with auto-generated getters and setters. This is intentional as they represent the state of the page – we want them to be included in the payload sent to the browser.

- The Search() method passes some data from the viewmodel to the service (calling the model) and updates the viewmodel state with the results obtained from this call. Thanks to the data-binding expression on the Repeater's DataSource property, the new contents of the Results collection will appear in the UI.

This is the basics of how the MVVM approach is implemented in DotVVM. If you ever used MVVM in WPF, .NET MAUI, or any other XAML-based framework, you might have noticed that we do not implement INotifyPropertyChanged in DotVVM. It is not necessary to do so because the MVVM data bindings are evaluated on the client, where the change tracking is done in Knockout JS observables.[10] This part is handled by DotVVM, and unless you want to extend the framework or build more complex components, you do not need to do anything special to make the MVVM experience work.

Communication with the Server

The last bit we need to cover before we get to the actual process of modernization is how DotVVM client and server parts communicate with each other.

1. When the user navigates to the page, an HTTP GET request is sent to the server. DotVVM looks in its route table and finds the corresponding .dothtml file. At the top of the file, there is always the @viewModel directive telling the framework which class is the viewmodel. DotVVM will create an instance of this class (injecting all dependencies registered in IServiceCollection in the constructor) and build the control tree for the HTML in the .dothtml file. The sequence of

---

[10] Knockout JS wraps every viewmodel property in an observable object. Knockout observable is basically a function that behaves like a property with getter and setter. Calling an observable function without arguments returns the value stored inside, while calling it with one argument changes the value of the observable and triggers notifications to all subscribers. This is basically what INotifyPropertyChanged does in C#, only it is implemented in a different way.

Init, Load, and PreRender methods are called on the viewmodel, and after that, the controls are rendered, producing a final HTML to be sent to the browser. The viewmodel is JSON-serialized and included in this HTML output, which is then sent as the response to the HTTP GET request. The viewmodel instance is discarded and will be later collected by GC, but you can imagine that the viewmodel continues its life in the browser in the form of a JavaScript object (a hierarchy of Knockout JS observables).

2. The user can now see the page and interact with its components. For example, they can modify the value in the TextBox control. If they do so, the new value is written in the corresponding property in the JavaScript viewmodel (we are still in the browser). It is also possible to change the JavaScript viewmodel from JavaScript code – if such a thing happens, the UI is automatically updated to match the viewmodel state by Knockout JS. As I mentioned, the data binding works in two ways.

3. At some point, the user will make an action that triggers a command binding (data-binding expression starting with the command prefix), for example, by clicking a button. Because the command references a method on the server, the execution cannot continue on the client. DotVVM will take the JavaScript viewmodel, serialize it as JSON, and send it to the server in an HTTP POST request (asynchronously, using a JavaScript fetch call, so the page remains loaded in the browser

and the user may keep using it). Once this request reaches the server, DotVVM will create an instance of the viewmodel again, call its `Init` method, and then populate the viewmodel with values received from the client. At this point, the state of the viewmodel should be the same as it was before the first HTTP GET request ended. Afterward, the `Load` method is called, and after it finishes, the command the user requests is invoked (in our example, the `Search()` method will be called, and its asynchronous result will be awaited). Then, the `PreRender` method on the viewmodel is called, and finally the changes made to the viewmodel are JSON-serialized and sent as the response. As you can see, DotVVM tries not to transmit the entire viewmodel in order to reduce the traffic between the server and the client.

4. When the response reaches the client, the changes to the viewmodel are applied to the existing JavaScript viewmodel, which instructs Knockout JS to update the UI accordingly. The page is not reloaded as it was in ASP.NET Web Forms, and the user may continue interacting with it.

The entire process is illustrated in Figure 7-2. If this resembles the ASP. NET Web Forms life cycle to you, you are right. Many things in DotVVM, including the naming of `Init`, `Load`, and `PreRender` methods (which is quite unpleasant – they could be named to express better what they really do), were inspired by this technology. As I mentioned earlier, the modernization of ASP.NET Web Forms applications was not the primary intent of DotVVM, and on several occasions, we often regretted taking inspiration from Web Forms. However, the closeness of these frameworks makes modernization easier. As you will see later, refactoring Web Forms code-behind files to DotVVM viewmodels is pretty straightforward.

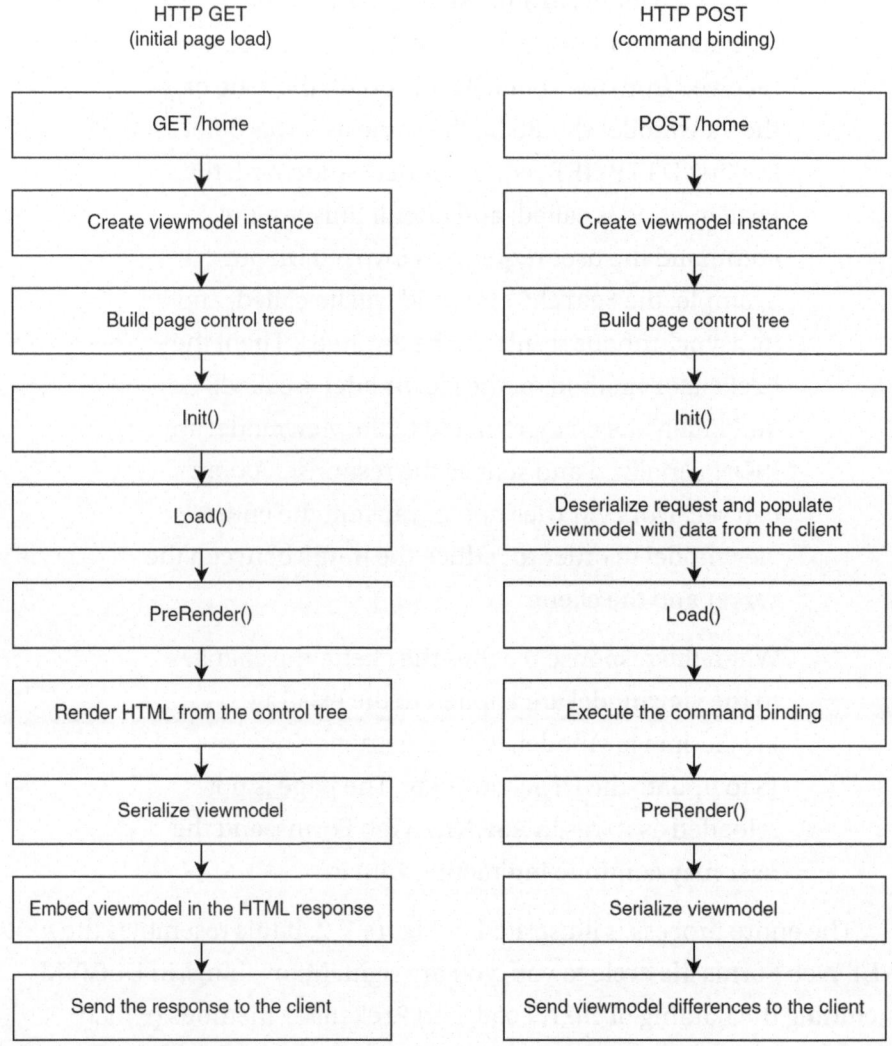

Figure 7-2. *The life cycle of the page in DotVVM*

Sending serialized viewmodels to the server back is not the only way of communication that is possible in DotVVM. Even though it is very easy to use, the amount of data transmitted over the wire may be suboptimal (especially when the page contains more components, such as GridView with a large number of rows). Still, the viewmodels are usually much smaller than the infamous cryptic view state field in ASP.NET Web Forms, and HTTP compression that is enabled by default in many environments can get their size to a fraction. Also, you can directly influence what properties will be part of your viewmodel, which makes it easy to optimize the page for speed. However, sometimes you only need to "patch" a small porting of the viewmodel with the rest remaining untouched.

Therefore, DotVVM offers a concept of static commands that do not transfer the entire viewmodel (unless you explicitly decide to send it to the server). Static commands can assign values to viewmodel properties directly. Sometimes, they do not even need to call the server. DotVVM can translate some of the constructs to JavaScript, for example, basic manipulation with viewmodel properties, some LINQ methods or operations on collections, and so forth. If you call a server method from a static command binding, only its arguments are sent to the server, and the response contains only the serialized return value of the method. This way, you can usually save kilobytes of data transferred between the server and the client. DotVVM can also call REST APIs directly, but this feature is not as popular because of its numerous limitations. How to use static commands is shown in Listing 7-4. The @inject directive allows you to inject the service to be used in data-binding expressions.

Listing 7-4. Using static commands in DotVVM

```
...
@inject DotvvmApp.Services.SearchService searchService

<!-- will be translated to JS - no communication
with the server needed -->
<dot:Button Text="Reset form"
    Click="{staticCommand: Results = null; SearchQuery = ""}" />
```

```
<!-- will call server and send
only the SearchQuery property -->
<dot:Button Text="Search"
    Click="{staticCommand: Results =
        searchService.Search(SearchQuery)}" />
```

Before You Start

I could continue explaining other concepts of DotVVM, but it is far beyond the scope of this book. DotVVM is a full-featured framework that can be used to build any web application. It is open source, developed on GitHub, and it became a member of the .NET Foundation.[11] Its development started in 2014 and has continued since then. Every year, a major or minor version is released, introducing new features and bug fixes. The framework includes about 30 UI components, from simple ones like TextBox to complex components like GridView. There are also free Visual Studio and Visual Studio Code extensions you can download from Visual Studio Marketplace.[12] As you will see later in this chapter, any React component can be used in DotVVM pages, which allows you to use third-party controls authored by popular component vendors.

The long-term sustainability of the DotVVM project is ensured by offering commercial packages that extend the framework functionality. They bring more powerful components with custom CSS themes and more features in the Visual Studio extension, such as IntelliSense in data-binding expressions. However, everything I am going to show in this book

---

[11] Although the .NET Foundation membership does not guarantee the project will be actively developed forever, the foundation has means to help in case the maintainers stop working on the project – for example, they can find new maintainers and give them access to the project's repository, package publishing infrastructure, and so on. Also, the .NET Foundation helps the projects follow best practices and meet standards of how they are maintained and developed.

[12] See https://marketplace.visualstudio.com/items?itemName=TomasHerceg. DotVVM-VSExtension2022

can be done with the free version of the Visual Studio extension and the open source framework. More than half of the DotVVM community uses only the framework without the commercial offerings.

Prerequisites

There are three considerations you should be aware of before you start.

The lowest .NET Framework version supported by DotVVM is 4.7.2. It is because of using .NET Standard 2.0 in shared parts of the framework. If your application uses an older version of .NET Framework, you must first move it to .NET Framework 4.7.2. This is usually quite easy, but I recommend reading the release notes[13] and checking there are no breaking changes that may affect you.

If you use Visual Basic .NET, be aware that the DotVVM for Visual Studio extension has no support for it. Although there are no reasons why VB.NET should not work with DotVVM, this scenario has not been tested, and some issues are likely to occur. You can create a new DotVVM .NET Framework project aside from the Web Forms project and reference it from the Web Forms project.[14] This case is technically not an in-place migration – you will be moving pages from the old project to the new one and moving the VB.NET business logic to a shared class library project. However, since both projects will run as a single process, it is still more similar to the in-place modernization approach than to the side-by-side method.

Finally, if the old application is an ASP.NET Web Site project (a special type of project without the `.csproj` or `.vbproj` file), again, the DotVVM for Visual Studio extension does not support this scenario. The project-less

---

[13] See https://learn.microsoft.com/en-us/dotnet/framework/migration-guide/versions-and-dependencies

[14] See https://github.com/riganti/dotvvm-samples-webforms-migration-vbnet

experience is not supported in ASP.NET Core; therefore, I recommend converting the Web Site project to a web application project first.[15]

Coexistence of DotVVM and Web Forms

You can use DotVVM to modernize any ASP.NET web application, not only if it is using ASP.NET Web Forms. On the other hand, in the case of ASP. NET MVC, it is probably more reasonable to move to ASP.NET Core MVC or Blazor, as these technologies are conceptually closer. The same applies to ASP.NET Web Pages – it will probably involve less friction to migrate to ASP.NET Core Razor Pages. However, as I mentioned at the beginning of the chapter, migration to ASP.NET Core frameworks cannot be done in place, and the side-by-side approach needs to be used in such cases.

DotVVM can run in any .NET Framework web application thanks to the `Microsoft.Owin.Host.SystemWeb` package. If you use ASP.NET SignalR or another OWIN-based framework in your application, you may already have this package installed in the project. Basically, the package plugs the OWIN pipeline in front of the ASP.NET runtime, allowing DotVVM to handle some HTTP requests. If the request is not handled by any OWIN middleware, it is sent to the default ASP.NET pipeline.

To install DotVVM in your ASP.NET application, you can use the *Add DotVVM* feature that is added by the DotVVM for Visual Studio extension, as shown in Figure 7-3.

---

[15] See `https://learn.microsoft.com/en-us/previous-versions/aspnet/ aa983476(v=vs.100)`

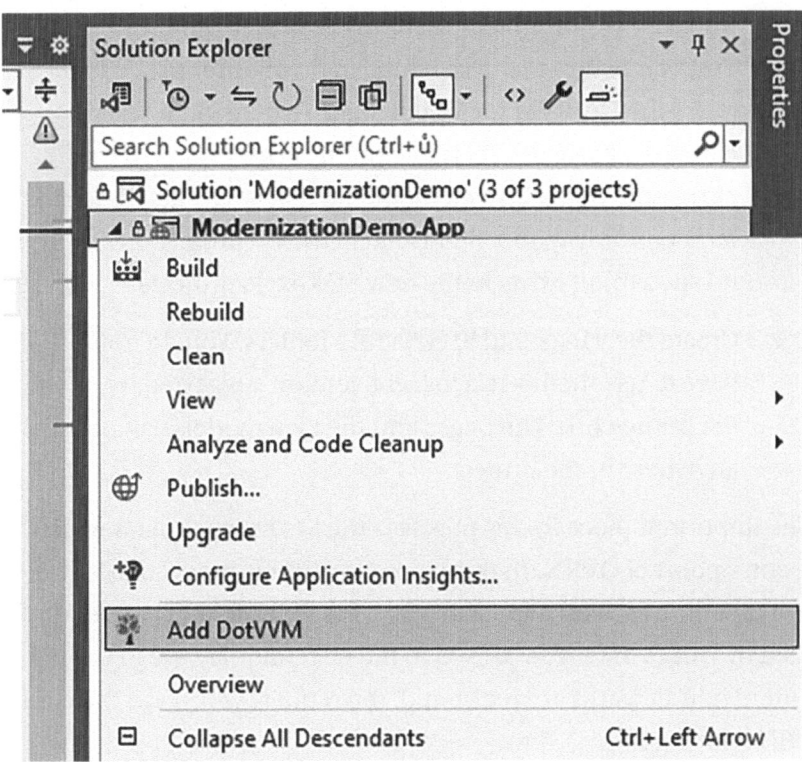

Figure 7-3. *Adding DotVVM in the project from DotVVM for Visual Studio*

The feature will make the following actions in your project:

- Install the Microsoft.Owin.Host.SystemWeb package.

- Add the OWIN Startup class (Startup.cs) to the project.

- Install the DotVVM.Owin package.

- Add the DotvvmStartup.cs file that contains the DotVVM configuration.

- Add a DotVVM project flavor in the project file.
  This is mostly a technical thing to do in order to
  make the DotVVM for Visual Studio extension work
  correctly. Basically, it is just adding a Guid value in the
  `<ProjectTypeGuids>` element in the `.csproj` file. This
  happens only in the old format of the C# project files –
  no such thing exists in the new SDK-style projects.

- Create the `Views` and `ViewModels` folders. You do not
  have to use them – it is just convention suggested by
  the framework. The pages and the viewmodels can be
  anywhere in the project.

The important piece in this puzzle is the `Startup.cs` class which
is the entry point of OWIN. In this class, DotVVM is plugged into the
request pipeline, as shown in Listing 7-5. Please note that any requests not
handled by DotVVM will be passed to the next middleware in the pipeline.
If no more middlewares are registered, the request will get to the classic
ASP.NET runtime.

This is very useful in modernization projects – you can "override" Web
Forms pages with DotVVM pages by registering a DotVVM route to match
the same URL, but the old Web Forms page can remain in the project. If
anything goes wrong with the new implementation, you can easily unregister
the DotVVM route, and the traffic will return to the original version.

Listing 7-5. Example OWIN Startup class

```
[assembly: OwinStartup(typeof(Startup))]
public class Startup
{
    public void Configuration(IAppBuilder app)
    {
        var path = HostingEnvironment.ApplicationPhysicalPath;
```

```
    var dotvvmConfiguration =
        app.UseDotVVM<DotvvmStartup>(path);
    dotvvmConfiguration.AssertConfigurationIsValid();
    }
}
```

The configuration of DotVVM is defined in DotvvmStartup.cs class, as you can see in Listing 7-6. There are two main methods: Configure is responsible for setting the DotvvmConfiguration object, while ConfigureServices can register services in IServiceCollection.

It is worth mentioning that the Microsoft.Extensions. DependencyInjection package works even on the old .NET Framework because it targets .NET Standard – that is why DotVVM can use it. This makes the transition to the new .NET smooth because you can use the same dependency injection framework with the same configuration.

Listing 7-6. Example configuration of DotVVM

```
public class DotvvmStartup
    : IDotvvmStartup, IDotvvmServiceConfigurator
{
    public void Configure(DotvvmConfiguration config,
        string applicationPath)
    {
        ConfigureRoutes(config, applicationPath);
        ...
    }

    private void ConfigureRoutes(DotvvmConfiguration config,
        string applicationPath)
    {
        // register routes
```

425

```
        config.RouteTable.Add("Search", "search",
            "Views/Search.dothtml");
    }
    ...

    public void ConfigureServices(
        IDotvvmServiceCollection options)
    {
        ...
        options.Services.AddSingleton<SearchService>();
    }
}
```

After installing DotVVM in the project, the application should work as before. Occasionally, you might run into classic .NET Framework's problems with incompatible assembly versions. DotVVM depends on Newtonsoft.Json, which you may already use in a different version, and it also needs some NuGet packages that depend on .NET Standard libraries, bringing many additional NuGet dependencies (several System.* packages will likely be added to the project). It can take some time to resolve the assembly version conflicts. Usually, it is sufficient either to upgrade NuGet packages to the highest versions required by the libraries you use or to fix the assemblyBinding section in the web.config file. There is one neat trick in Visual Studio that worked for me in most cases – delete the assemblyBinding section from the web.config file entirely and rebuild the project. Visual Studio will emit a warning listing all the assembly version conflicts, and if you double-click it, the assembly bindings section will be generated automatically.

If the application still does not start and complains about assembly load issues, please note that DotVVM needs to scan the referenced assemblies in the project. Sometimes, there are unused libraries in the bin directory DotVVM will try to load. You can delete the bin directory and have it recreated by rebuilding the project. This will ensure there are no historical artifacts that would confuse DotVVM.

Migrating the Master Page

Once DotVVM is installed in the project, you can start modernizing. Most ASP.NET Web Forms applications have at least one master page – a template that defines a common layout and structure for all pages and contains one or more placeholders where the content from the concrete page will be placed.

DotVVM offers the concept of master pages that is very similar to Web Forms, so preparing the master page is the first task you will need to do.

Master pages usually contain menus and links to the application pages. In ASP.NET Web Forms, you could generate the URLs from route definitions by using expression builders `<%$ RouteUrl: RouteName=Search %>` or by calling the `GetRouteUrl` method on the page. The problem is that now we have two route tables. The Web Forms route table contains all routes in the application, but the DotVVM route table will contain only the pages that have already been migrated. In the beginning, it is going to be empty; therefore, you cannot use the `<dot:RouteLink RouteName=Search />` – this would produce an exception as the DotVVM's `RouteLink` component looks for the route in the DotVVM route table, and there is no such route yet.

There is a useful package called `DotVVM.Adapters.WebForms` you can add to the project. To initialize it, you will have to call `config.AddWebFormsAdapters()` in `DotvvmStartup.cs` to register this package. Then, you can use a special control called `<webforms:HybridRouteLink>` with the same properties as DotVVM `RouteLink` control. This control can look up the route URLs in the DotVVM route table as well as in the ASP. NET Web Forms route table.

Now, it is all about rewriting from the `.aspx` syntax to `.dothtml` and refactoring the code-behind files to DotVVM viewmodels.

The syntax of the pages is slightly different, but many components have the same names (TextBox, Repeater, GridView, and others), and we often use the same names for their properties. Because this is going to be the most mundane part of the process, there is a tool called the ASPX to DotVVM Converter[16] you can use to perform most common transformations (e.g., removing runat="server"). The tool is open source[17] and can be extended with additional rules. I encourage anyone to contribute to the repository – writing additional transforms is not that difficult, as shown in Listing 7-7. Basically, the tool parses the pasted .aspx markup and runs "matchers," which can recognize patterns in the code and provide suggestions for code edits. In the example, there is a matcher that looks for ToolTip attributes (that is how the property was named in ASP.NET Web Forms) and transforms them to title attributes (standard attribute name in HTML). There are also tests set up, so you can easily ensure the transform rule you implemented works as expected.

Listing 7-7. Example transform in the ASPX to DotVVM Converter

```
public class ToolTipAttributeMatcher : AttributeMatcher
{
    public override string MatchedAttributeName => "ToolTip";

    protected override
        IEnumerable<Suggestion> TryProvideSuggestions
        (BeginTagToken tagToken, AttributeToken attributeToken)
    {
        yield return new Suggestion()
        {
            Description = "Change ToolTip to title",
            Fixes = new FixAction[]
```

---

[16] See https://dotvvm.com/webforms/convert
[17] See https://github.com/riganti/dotvvm-webforms

```
        {
            new RenameAttributeFix(attributeToken, "title")
        }
    };
}
}
```

After the markup is migrated, you will need to refactor the code-behind file to the viewmodel. In Web Forms, the code-behind file could reference the UI components by their IDs – either statically generated in the Designer class or dynamically looked up by using the FindControl method. Usually, you will have to do the following edits:

- All places that reference component properties should be replaced by data-binding expressions and properties in the viewmodel. Instead of accessing the search query through SearchTextBox.Text, you will just use the SearchQuery viewmodel property and have it bound to the TextBox in the view by a data-binding expression.

- Event handlers of components will need to be changed to DotVVM commands. Instead of declaring SearchButton_OnClick(object sender, EventArgs e), you will have the Search() method. DotVVM supports asynchronous methods – you can return Task from it. DotVVM commands can also pass any arguments to the methods.

- The Init, Load, and PreRender events of the code-behind should be changed to the corresponding (equally named) methods of the viewmodel. They have different signatures and are asynchronous.

- Calls to Request, Response, and other HttpContext objects need to be changed to Context.HttpContext. The IsPostBack property is available as Context. IsPostBack in DotVVM (yes, we kept even this name). Redirects can be done by the Context.Redirect* methods – there are options to redirect to a route or an arbitrary URL.

- If you used ViewState to store values between postbacks without giving the user the ability to read or modify the value,[18] use the viewmodel properties decorated with [Protect(ProtectMode.Encrypt)] to ensure the value is not sent to the browser in clear-text form.

This should cover most of the changes. If you interact with any ASP.NET API that is not present in ASP.NET Core (e.g., calling FormsAuthentication, accessing the HttpContext properties, accessing the request headers or manipulating the response, and so on), I recommend extracting such mechanisms to specialized classes to minimize the number of places you will have to make changes in the last step of the migration – switching to the new .NET.

Migrating the Pages

Once the master pages and their viewmodels are migrated, you will need to take all .aspx pages one by one and repeat the same process with them. Again, you can use the ASPX to DotVVM Converter to perform the most frequent transforms and do the rest manually or by leveraging AI-powered tools such as GitHub Copilot or ChatGPT.

---

[18] The viewstate in ASP.NET Web Forms was encrypted.

If the pages use a master page, their viewmodels must inherit from the viewmodel of its master page. If the viewmodel starts getting too complicated, consider splitting them into multiple classes and nesting them in the page's viewmodel as properties. This is especially useful when the page contains several independent parts, such as multistep wizards, modal dialogs, and so on. DotVVM works with nested viewmodels quite nicely,[19] and you can use events to send signals from the nested viewmodels to the root. If the child viewmodels inherit from DotvvmViewModelBase, the Init, Load, and PreRender methods will be invoked on them automatically.

Once the page is rewritten in DotVVM syntax, remember to register its route in DotvvmStartup. Otherwise, the traffic would still go to the old page. You can always look at the page source in the browser to ensure there is no viewstate hidden field.

Migrating Components

A very similar process applies to all .ascx components – they can be represented as DotVVM markup controls;[20] however, the concept of DotVVM components is quite different from ASP.NET Web Forms. In DotVVM, the components are just a presentation concern and should not contain any logic or manipulate their own state. I have seen many Web Forms components that involved a significant amount of business logic. In such cases, their code-behind should be transformed into a viewmodel of the component and nested in the page's viewmodel. When using the component, its DataContext property will need to be bound to this child viewmodel. This will allow encapsulating parts of the business logic for the controls into their own viewmodels.

---

[19] See www.dotvvm.com/docs/4.0/pages/concepts/viewmodels/work-with-data/best-practices#use-nested-viewmodels

[20] See www.dotvvm.com/docs/4.0/pages/concepts/control-development/markup-controls

DotVVM also supports other types of components – code-only controls and composite controls.[21] Especially the latter one can be used in many scenarios where you need to emit a certain hierarchy of HTML elements and substitute passed property values or bindings, as shown in Listing 7-8. In the example, we render a box with a title, image, and inner content. The parameters of the GetContents method are treated as control properties. The imageUrl parameter is declared as string – it means that the user can set the value in the markup, but it cannot be a data-binding expression. The title parameter, on the other hand, is defined as ValueOrBinding<string>, which means that the property supports both static value and data-binding expression. The last parameter is TextOrContentCapability – this allows the control to set the content as an attribute (Text="some content") or as an HTML placed inside the control element. The control capabilities are another concept of DotVVM that helps to share functionality between multiple controls without the need for using inheritance.

Listing 7-8. An example of DotVVM composite control

```
public class ImageTextPanel : CompositeControl
{
    public static DotvvmControl GetContents(
        ValueOrBinding<string> title,
        TextOrContentCapability content,
        string imageUrl
    )
    {
        return new HtmlGenericControl("div")
            .AddCssClass("image-text-panel")
```

---

[21] See www.dotvvm.com/docs/4.0/pages/concepts/control-development/composite-controls

432

```
    .AppendChildren(
        new HtmlGenericControl("h2")
            .SetProperty(c => c.InnerText, title),
        new HtmlGenericControl("div")
            .AddCssClass("content")
            .SetCapability(content),
        new HtmlGenericControl("img")
            .SetAttribute("src", imageUrl)
            .SetAttribute("alt", title)
    );
    }
}
```

DotVVM also allows hosting React components. This is especially useful if your application utilizes component packs by Telerik, DevExpress, or other popular vendors. Most of them offer their components implemented for React, and DotVVM can host these components on the page, give them data from the viewmodel, and respond to events that occur inside. It requires writing a bit of JavaScript, but it is very powerful.

The component needs to be registered in a JavaScript module linked to the page using the @js directive. Then, you can use the component as <js:RegisteredComponentName> and give it parameters from the viewmodels, including commands or static commands that the control can invoke. You only need to write a short piece of JavaScript code that wraps the React component and provides the default values of its properties in case they are not set in the markup. You can see it in Listing 7-9.

Listing 7-9. An example of a React component hosted on a DotVVM page

```
<!-- Page -->
@js ReactAppModule

<js:recharts data={value: ChartData}
    series={value: SerieNames}
    onSeriesClick={staticCommand:
        (string s) => CurrentSeries = s}/>
<p>Selected series: {{value: CurrentSeries}}</p>

// JS module
import * as React from 'react';
import * as ReactDOM from 'react-dom';
import { registerReactControl }
    from 'dotvvm-jscomponent-react';
import { LineChart, Line } from 'recharts';

// the React component
function RechartComponent(props: any) {
    return (
        <LineChart
            data={props.data}, ...
            {
                series.map((s, i) =>
                    <Line dataKey={s} yAxisId={i} ...
                        onMouseEnter={
                            _ => props.onMouse(s)
                        } />
                )
            }
        </LineChart>
    );
}
```

434

```
export default (context: any) => ({
    $controls: {
        recharts: registerReactControl(RechartComponent, {
            context,
                // if the user does not set onSeriesClick
                // in the markup, use empty function as the default
                onSeriesClick() { }
        })
    }
});
```

As you can see, the example uses a popular charting library called Recharts.[22] In the viewmodel, I have the SerieNames and ChartData properties which contain a collection of entries (in the format the component expects them). I handle the onSeriesClick event which is called when the user clicks any element in the chart. The argument passed to the event will be the name of the series the user clicked.

In the JavaScript code, I declare the component – it is a function that gets the props argument with all properties passed to the control. Based on this argument, it will render the React component with appropriate data. Whenever any of the control properties change, React will call the method again to reflect the changes in the UI.

At the end of the file, I pass the component to the registerReactControl, which will create an integration bridge between DotVVM and React, and export it as the $controls.recharts property of the JS module – this will tell DotVVM under which name the component can be used in the page.

Thanks to this, you do not need to worry about what happens if you find a use case for which DotVVM does not have appropriate control. You can always find a React component and host it on the page. What is more, the component hosting mechanism is quite universal and can support other frameworks in the future.

---

[22] See https://recharts.org/en-US/

Handlers

Many ASP.NET Web Forms applications define HTTP handlers for various use cases, such as generating custom XML or JSON responses. Handlers are usually defined using .ashx files, which point to a class implementing the IHttpHandler interface. Alternatively, they can be registered in the web.config file or in the route table.

I have also seen cases where pages were "abused" to behave as handlers. They contained no user interface, and in the code-behind file, they wrote a custom output in the Response.Output stream and called Response.End. I recommend transforming such pages to IDotvvmPresenter objects, which is a replacement for HTTP handlers. Converting the IHttpHandler to IDotvvmPresenter is very easy as the interface is almost equal, as you can see in Listing 7-10.

Listing 7-10. HTTP handler to generate an RSS feed and its DotVVM equivalent

```
// HTTP handler in the old ASP.NET
public class ProductsRssHandler : IHttpHandler
{
    public bool IsReusable => true;

    public void ProcessRequest(HttpContext context)
    {
        context.Response.ContentType = "application/atom+xml";

        var feed = new SyndicationFeed()
        {
            Title = new TextSyndicationContent("Contoso Shop"),
            Description = new TextSyndicationContent(
                "All products"),
            Items = GetFeedItems(baseUri)
        };
```

```
    using (var xw = new XmlTextWriter(
        context.Response.Output))
    {

        xw.Formatting = Formatting.Indented;
        var ff = new Atom10FeedFormatter(feed);
        ff.WriteTo(xw);
    }
}

private IEnumerable<SyndicationItem> GetFeedItems()
{

    ...

}
}

// DotVVM equivalent of an HTTP handler
public class ProductsRssPresenter : IDotvvmPresenter
{
    public Task ProcessRequest(IDotvvmRequestContext context)
    {
        context.HttpContext.Response.ContentType =
            "application/atom+xml";

        var feed = new SyndicationFeed()
        {

            ...

        };
        using (var xw = new XmlTextWriter(
            context.HttpContext.Response.Body))
        {

            xw.Formatting = Formatting.Indented;
            var ff = new Atom10FeedFormatter(feed);
            ff.WriteTo(xw);
```

```
        }
        return Task.CompletedTask;
    }
    ...
}
```

The presenter can be registered in the DotVVM route table in
DotvvmStartup.cs, as shown in Listing 7-11. Because the presenters
can use dependency injection, they also need to be added to the
IServiceCollection.

Listing 7-11. Registering the DotVVM presenter in the route table

```
public void Configure(
    DotvvmConfiguration config, string applicationPath)
{
    ...
    config.RouteTable.Add("ProductsRss", "products/rss",
        presenterType: typeof(ProductsRssPresenter));
}
public void ConfigureServices(IDotvvmServiceCollection options)
{
    ...
    options.Services.AddScoped<ProductsRssPresenter>();
}
```

The Final Step

Using the steps mentioned earlier, you can rewrite all ASP.NET Web Forms
pages and handlers to use the DotVVM API, which works in the new .NET
without any changes. Once you succeed in having everything running in
DotVVM, it is time to remove all Web Forms artifacts from the project and
switch the target framework.

As always, it is not a single action but a sequence of steps you will need to take:

- Remove all .aspx, .master, .ascx, .ashx, and other Web Forms files, including their code-behind files.

- Create the wwwroot directory and move all files that should be served as static files (scripts, stylesheets, images, and others) into this folder. In contrast to the old ASP.NET that would serve any file from the web application folder (provided it was not in the App_Data folder and its extension was registered in the MIME map configuration section), ASP.NET Core serves only the files from the wwwroot folder.

- Remove the web.config file, App_Data, and other ASP. NET Web Forms folders.

- Upgrade the project file to the SDK-style project (you can use the .NET Upgrade Assistant extension as discussed in Chapter 1 or remove the file contents and start from scratch, as shown later in Listing 7-19). Make sure the target framework is the latest version of the new .NET.

- Substitute the DotVVM.Owin package with DotVVM. AspNetCore.

- Add the Program.cs class and register all services required by the application there. Configure the authentication, logging, application configuration, and database connection strings using the new .NET configuration model.

- Resolve all remaining compile errors. If some code was
  using the API from System.Web, either reimplement
  it to utilize the new ASP.NET Core API or use the
  Microsoft.AspNetCore.SystemWebAdapters package,
  which reimplements a significant portion of the old API
  using the means of ASP.NET Core.

This list may not be exhaustive as there can be other things
incompatible with the new .NET. However, after reading this and the
previous chapters, you should already have quite a good idea of what is
supported and what is not and how to proceed with the migration.

This last step may take a few days to complete based on the number of
required changes. Naturally, rigorous testing is required as this switch of
frameworks may uncover subtle breaking changes. Even though the code
will compile, you may get runtime exceptions, for example, if you try to
write to the ASP.NET Core response stream synchronously. On the other
hand, this last big step is the only problematic place in the entire process
of migration. All the previous steps could be split into very small tasks and
span across a longer period.

Practical Example

The previous sections briefly walk you through the process to illustrate
what you can expect. Naturally, there are a lot of steps involved. I believe
that a substantial complexity comes from the fact that most developers are
not familiar with DotVVM, and the migration process will require learning
the framework.

In my experience from projects I have participated in, it typically
takes one to two weeks to get familiar with most of the DotVVM concepts
needed for the migration. Knowledge of ASP.NET Web Forms is helpful
because DotVVM is inspired by this framework in many ways.

In this section, I will show the migration of a small ASP.NET Web Forms application to DotVVM. It is not a real-world application; it has been crafted to be as small and simple as possible but to demonstrate common concepts used in Web Forms applications – components like GridView, FormView, and ListView, using forms, validation, working with nested records, using model binding, caching, session, authentication, and more.

The only part that feels unnatural is the business logic. I did not want to complicate the example by adding the need to migrate database access as well. Therefore, the application business logic is embedded in a separate ASP.NET Core project exposing a REST API, which is called by the Web Forms application. I wanted to focus the example on migrating the user interface, not the business logic. Therefore, the code-behind files only call an external REST API through a generated client – this will not change when we migrate to the new .NET. Thanks to this, the changes required in the application will be related only to replacing Web Forms with another presentation technology – DotVVM.

CODE SAMPLES FOR THIS CHAPTER

The in-place migration of ASP.NET Web Forms application is demonstrated in the GitHub repository available via the book's product page at https://github.com/Apress/Modernizing-.NET-Web-Applications. You can find the entire solution in the chapter07 folder.

There are several folders showing the project in various stages:

- 01-initial-state shows the original ASP.NET Web Forms application running on .NET Framework 4.7.2.

- 02-add-dotvvm shows the project after adding DotVVM.

- `03-master-page-and-first-page` shows the project after migrating the master page and one of the application pages.

- `04-all-pages-and-handler` shows the project after all DotVVM pages and handlers have been migrated.

- `05-complete-migration` shows the project switched to the new .NET.

If you want to run the projects, follow the instructions in the `Readme` file in the `chapter07` folder.

Since all five solutions are configured to use the same ports, please make sure you are not running multiple versions simultaneously.

Running the Project

If you clone the repository and open the folder `01-initial-state`, you can open the solution file in Visual Studio.

The connection string in `ModernizationDemo.BackendApi/appsettings.json` is configured for a local instance of SQL Server Express. If you plan to use SQL Server LocalDB or any other SQL Server instance, change the connection string and ensure the user has permission to create the database.

Next, run the `ModernizationDemo.BackendApi` project by right-clicking it in the *Solution Explorer* window and selecting *View in Browser*. This way, Visual Studio will not attach the debugger and keep the project running in the background. If you look at the console window that appears, you should see how the application seeds data in the database.

Now you can run the `ModernizationDemo.App` project by setting it as a startup project and running it normally (e.g., by pressing F5). If the application does not run and reports a problem connecting to the API, make sure the port in the `web.config` `appSettings` entry corresponds to the port on which the API is running.

If everything works, you should see the home page of the application, as shown in Figure 7-4.

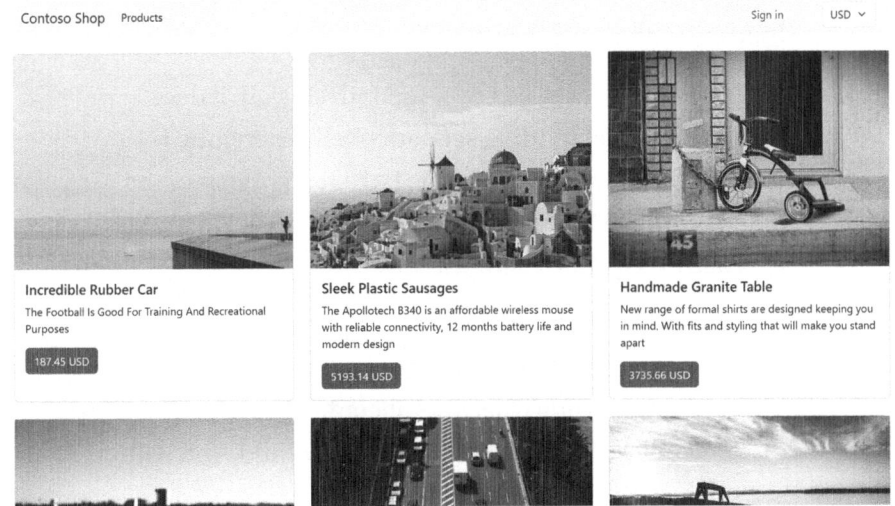

Figure 7-4. *Home page of the sample application*

Feel free to examine the application. Here is a short list of interesting things you can find there:

- The API which returns products does not return prices. Instead, for each product, you need to make a separate API call to obtain a price in a specified currency. This is intentional to simulate a real-world scenario that requires caching. Once the application obtains a price for a particular product, it stores it in an in-memory cache to avoid hitting the API rate limit. The cache is invalidated when the product price is changed in the admin area. You can find the caching logic in the Utils class.

- The master page contains a currency selector component that stores its value in the ASP.NET session. You can find it in the PageBase class – a base class for all ASP.NET Web Forms pages in the application.

- All pages accessing the data use the model binding approach. The older ASP.NET applications will probably use `ObjectDataSource` or manual data binding in the code-behind files.

- Since the price is loaded by a second API call, it does not fit the model binding scenario well. Therefore, I make the second request in the `DataBound` event of the data controls. This will have to be changed in DotVVM as it has no equivalent for this event.

- The `Admin/ProductDetail.aspx` page contains `GridView` and `FormView` nested in another `FormView`. This requires several calls to `FindControl` to dynamically look for controls in code-behind. You will see how much this is easier in DotVVM where all data are contained in the viewmodel. The page also uses validation, including validation groups, as there are multiple independent forms the user may interact with.

- The `Login.aspx` page contains the `Login` control. Instead of using the Membership providers, the control signs the user in in the `Authenticating` event by verifying the credentials using an API endpoint.

- The access to the administration is restricted by a rule in the `web.config` file.

- The application contains a handler that generates an RSS feed with all products. You can find it in the `Handlers` folder.

Adding DotVVM

The folder 02-add-dotvvm contains a copy of the solution in which I used the *Add DotVVM* option in Visual Studio. You need to install the *DotVVM for Visual Studio* extension to see this option in the context menu.

The main difference is in the packages.config file. You can see that there are DotVVM.Owin, Microsoft.Owin.Host.SystemWeb, and all their dependent packages. You can also notice the Startup.cs and DotvvmStartup.cs files that were added during the process.

Master Page and the First Page

The 03-master-page-and-first-page folder shows the project after the master page was migrated, and the first page was migrated to DotVVM.

Once DotVVM is present in the project, you can right-click the *Views* folder and choose *Add ➤ New Item*. From the list of templates, select *DotVVM Master Page*, as shown in Figure 7-5. I prefer to name it the same way as it was in the Web Forms project – Site.dotmaster. Because every DotVVM page needs its viewmodel, once you confirm your selection, another window, as in Figure 7-6, will appear to ask you where the viewmodel shall be placed. By default, it goes to the ViewModels folder.

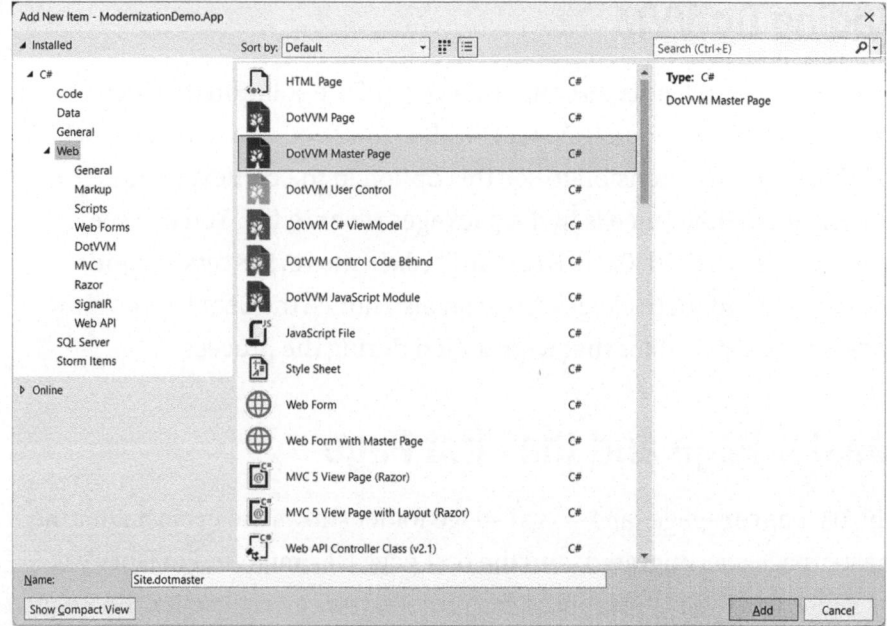

Figure 7-5. *Adding a DotVVM master page in the project*

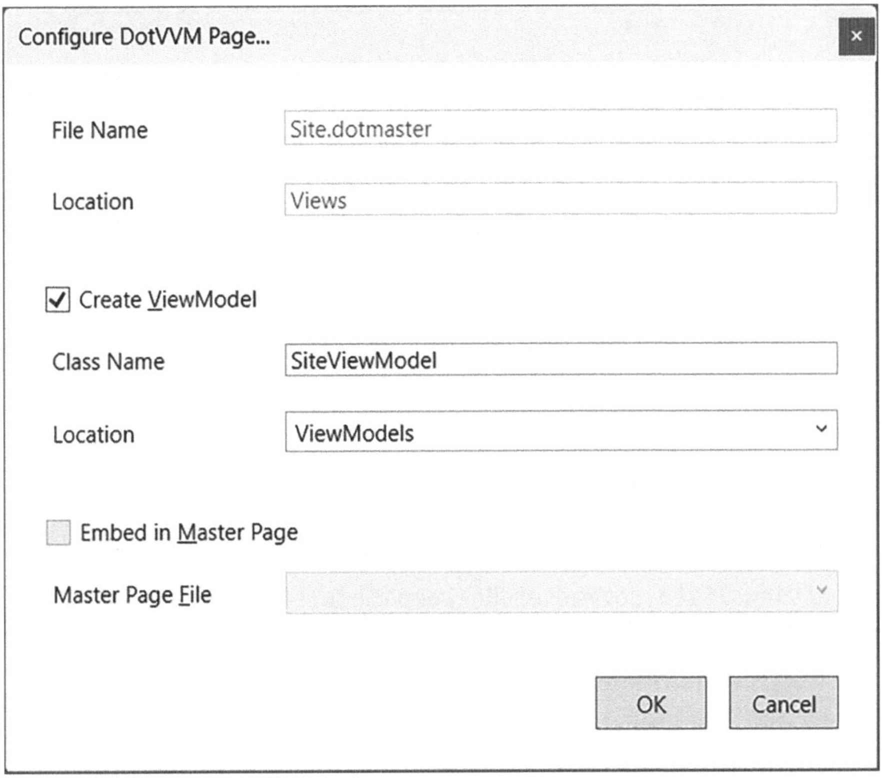

Figure 7-6. *Selecting where the viewmodel shall be created*

The goal is to make a master page that will look the same as the Web Forms one, so the users will not be able to tell the difference. It will have the same layout and use the same CSS styles.

As the first step, you can open the ASPX to DotVVM Converter[23] and paste there the contents of the Pages/Site.master (I recommend omitting the first line as the converter does not modify it). Click *Continue*, review the suggested fixes, and apply them, as illustrated in Figure 7-7.

---

[23] See https://dotvvm.com/webforms/convert

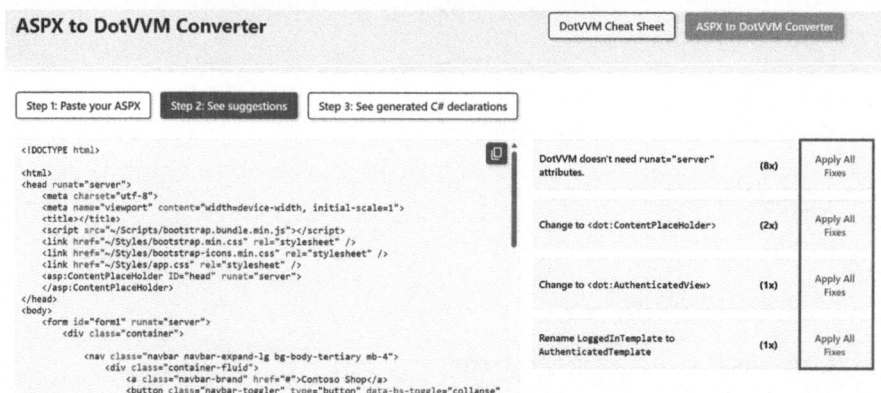

Figure 7-7. *Using the ASPX to DotVVM Converter to apply most common fixes*

After that, you can copy the updated markup and paste it in the newly created Views/Site.dotmaster file (keep the first line with the @viewModel directive).

We will need to handle a few things manually, as the converter covers only the most common code changes.

First, the <asp:LoginStatus> component is not supported by the converter because there is no equivalent control in DotVVM. Based on whether the user is authenticated, the component displays either a link to the login page or a button that signs the user out. We can implement it on our own using the snippet shown in Listing 7-12. The sign-out button requires adding a method in the master page's viewmodel.

Listing 7-12. Replacing the ASP.NET Web Forms LoginStatus component

```
<dot:AuthenticatedView>
    <NotAuthenticatedTemplate>
        <webforms:HybridRouteLink RouteName="Login"
                                  Text="Sign in"
                                  class="nav-link" />
```

```
    </NotAuthenticatedTemplate>
    <AuthenticatedTemplate>
        <dot:LinkButton Text="Sign out"
                        Click="{command: SignOut()}"
                        Validation.Enabled="false"
                        class="nav-link" />
    </AuthenticatedTemplate>
</dot:AuthenticatedView>

// SiteViewModel.cs
public void SignOut()
{
    FormsAuthentication.SignOut();
    Context.RedirectToRouteHybrid("Products");
}
```

Second, the converter does not support handling the
<asp:DropDownList> control as its usage is significantly different in
DotVVM. We can implement it using DotVVM's ComboBox component, as
shown in Listing 7-13. The list of available currencies must be moved in
the viewmodel, as DotVVM requires providing the list of items using data-
binding expressions.

Listing 7-13. Replacing the DropDownList with ComboBox

```
<dot:ComboBox class="form-select me-2"
        Validation.Enabled="false"
        SelectedValue="{value: SelectedCurrency}"
        DataSource="{value: Currencies}"
        SelectionChanged="{command: OnCurrencyChanged()}"
        />

// SiteViewModel.cs
```

```
[Bind(Direction.ServerToClientFirstRequest)]
public List<string> Currencies { get; set; } =
    ["USD", "EUR", "JPY", "GBP"];

public string SelectedCurrency { get; set; } = "USD";

public override Task Init()
{
    if (HttpContext.Current.Session["SelectedCurrency"]
        is string currency)
    {
        SelectedCurrency = currency;
    }
    return base.Init();
}

public void OnCurrencyChanged()
{
    HttpContext.Current.Session["SelectedCurrency"]
        = SelectedCurrency;
    Context.RedirectToLocalUrl(
        Context.HttpContext.Request.Url.PathAndQuery);
}
```

Notice the [Bind] attribute that decorates the Currencies property. Because the list of currencies never changes, this attribute tells DotVVM that it needs to be transferred only when the page is loaded the first time (using HTTP GET request) and does not need to be transferred to the server on postbacks. This helps to reduce the amount of data exchanged between the server and the client. There are more options for the Bind attribute to allow fine-tuning the viewmodel serialization.

Also, notice that I did not use the PageBase class (a base page I defined for all my Web Forms pages) to access the SelectedCurrency property which used session in its getter and setter. Instead, I have reimplemented this functionality in `SiteViewModel` because it will now be the base class for all viewmodels. Also, because the viewmodel gets JSON-serialized, it is not recommended to place anything in the getters and setters, as there is no guarantee in which order the properties will be accessed by the serializer. That is why I explicitly obtain the value from the session in the `Init` phase and set it directly when the user selects another currency in the `ComboBox`.

Finally, because the viewmodel code uses the new collection expression feature of C#, you need to manually edit the project file and add `<LangVersion>12</LangVersion>` in it. I recommend trying to upgrade to new C# language concepts as you modernize the pages – it can make the code shorter and more understandable. Although not all C# language features are available when targeting the old .NET Framework, some of them are, and there are not many reasons for avoiding them.

Third, the Web Forms master page used the `<%$ RouteUrl: ... %>` expression builder to build the link for the RSS feed in the page footer. We can convert it to the `HybridRouteLink` control, which I already mentioned before. Listing 7-14 shows what it looks like.

Listing 7-14. Replacing the Web Forms hyperlink with HybridRouteLink

```
<webforms:HybridRouteLink RouteName="ProductsRss" Text="RSS" />
```

Now, the master page should be ready to use. Let us continue with migrating the `Pages/ProductDetail.aspx` page as it is the easiest one. Right-click the `Views` folder again and select *Add* ➤ *New Item*. This time, add a new item of type *DotVVM Page* called `ProductDetail.dothtml`. In the dialog window that appears, make sure the *Embed this page in master page* is checked and the proper master page file is selected, as shown in Figure 7-8.

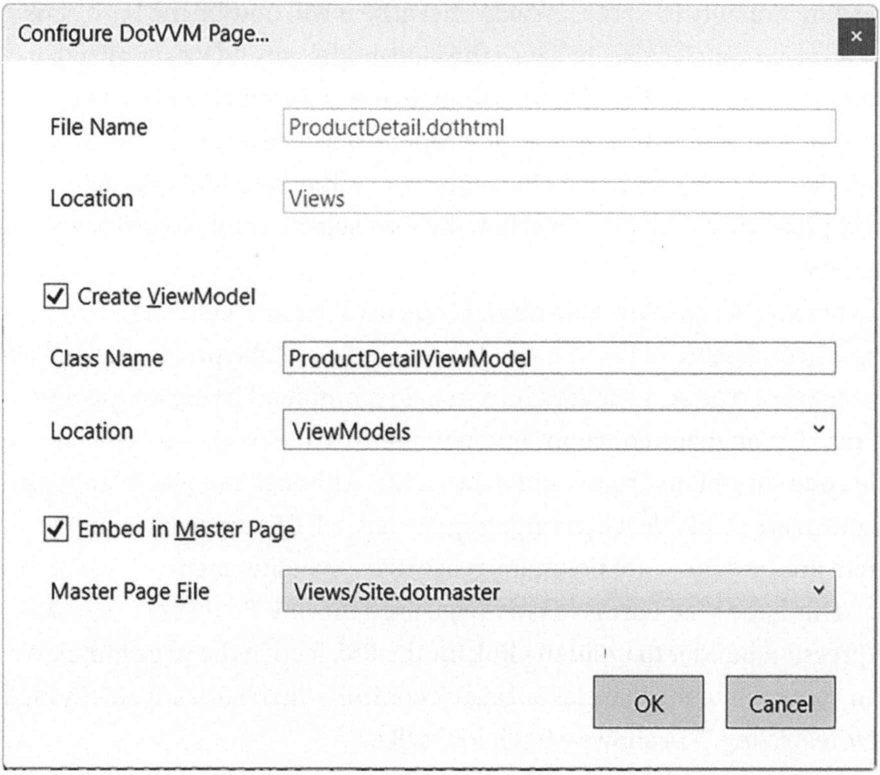

Figure 7-8. *Embedding the DotVVM page in a master page*

You can repeat the same process of pasting the Pages/ProductDetail.
aspx code (except for the first line) into the converter and using the output
in the Views/ProductDetail.dothtml.

Same as in the case of the master page, the migration will require
manual finishing touches. First, the <asp:FormView> control is not
present in DotVVM. You can replace it with <div DataContext="{value:
Product}"> and remove the <ItemTemplate> element. Instead of data-
binding the form control as we did in Web Forms, we will declare a
property of type ProductModel in the viewmodel and load data in it in the
PreRender phase, as shown in Listing 7-15.

Binding the product model object to the DataContext tells DotVVM to evaluate all data-binding expressions inside the <div> element in the context of this Product property – therefore, we will be able to use just {value: Title} instead of {value: Product.Title}.

Notice that I have also declared the Id property in the viewmodel and bound it to the route's Id parameter using the FromRoute attribute. DotVVM will automatically set the value in this property based on the request URL.

Instead of reusing the GetData method from ASP.NET Web Forms, I have updated the code to call the asynchronous version of the GetProducts method on the API client.

Also, instead of using a static factory to obtain the ApiClient instance, I have it injected into the viewmodel using dependency injection. Notice how I use the new C# language feature, primary class constructor, to save the field declaration as well as define an explicit constructor to set the field.

Listing 7-15. Loading the product detail in the viewmodel

```
<!-- Views/ProductDetail.dothtml -->
<asp:FormView ID="ProductForm"
                SelectMethod="GetData"
                OnDataBound="ProductForm_OnDataBound">
    <ItemTemplate>

<div DataContext="{value: Product}">
    <div class="row">
        ...
    </div>
</div>

    </ItemTemplate>
</asp:FormView>

// ViewModels/ProductDetailViewModel.cs
```

```
public class ProductDetailViewModel(ApiClient apiClient)
    : SiteViewModel
{

    [FromRoute("Id")]
    public Guid Id { get; set; }

    public ProductModel Product { get; set; }

    public override async Task PreRender()
    {
        if (!Context.IsPostBack)
        {
            Product = await apiClient.GetProductAsync(Id);
        }
        await base.PreRender();
    }
}
```

The second thing I have to update on the page is the <asp:Literal ID="PriceLiteral"> control that shows the price. Its value was set in the DataBound event handler of the FormView.

The price is not a part of the ProductModel class, but we can declare it aside, as shown in Listing 7-16. The ASP.NET Web Forms literal control is replaced just by the DotVVM data-binding expression. Notice that I use the _root variable to access the page's viewmodel context (otherwise, DotVVM would try to look for the property in the ProductModel as it is the current data context).

Listing 7-16. Replacing the PriceLiteral and loading the price

```
<!-- Views/ProductDetail.dothtml -->
{{value: _root.Price}}

// ViewModels/ProductDetailViewModel.cs
```

454

...

public string Price { get; set; }

```
public override async Task PreRender()
{
    if (!Context.IsPostBack)
    {
        ...
        Price = Utils.GetProductPriceWithCaching(
            Id, SelectedCurrency);
    }
    ...
}
```

The last thing we will have to change on the product detail page is the form fields composed of <asp:Label> and <asp:TextBox>. The converter successfully changed the TextBox controls to their DotVVM equivalents, but it does not know what to do with the labels as there are no components for that in DotVVM. We have to change the form fields to use plain HTML label elements. Also, I have added the Quantity property in the viewmodel and bound the second TextBox to it, as you can see in Listing 7-17.

Listing 7-17. Replacing the ASP.NET Web Forms label controls with HTML labels

```
<!-- Views/ProductDetail.dothtml -->
<div class="col">
    <div class="mb-3">
        <label for="StockLiteral"
            class="form-label">Availability</label>
        <dot:TextBox ID="StockLiteral"
            readonly
```

```
                    class="form-control-plaintext
                        fw-bold text-success"
                    Text="In stock"/>
        </div>
    </div>
    <div class="col">
        <div class="mb-3">
            <label for="QuantityTextBox"
                class="form-label">Quantity</label>
            <dot:TextBox Text="{value: _root.Quantity}"
                ID="QuantityTextBox"
                TextMode="Number"
                class="form-control"
                style="width: 5em" />
        </div>
    </div>

// ViewModels/ProductDetailViewModel.cs
...
public int Quantity { get; set; }
```

Here, you can see that DotVVM components do not try to have
properties for every feature – the strategy is only to provide properties
for things that have some special behavior in data-binding expressions
or other aspects. However, you can add classic HTML attributes to
most DotVVM controls, and they will just be rendered along the HTML
produced by the control. You can see how I add the readonly attribute to
the <dot:TextBox> control.

DotVVM tries to render as simple HTML as possible to allow easy
styling of components using CSS. This is quite different from the way most
ASP.NET Web Forms controls work.

There are two final steps to take:

- You have to register the page route in DotvvmStartup.cs.

- Since we want the page to get the ApiClient parameter using dependency injection, we have to register it in the IServiceCollection. Again, this can be done in DotvvmStartup.cs.

Both steps are shown in Listing 7-18.

Listing 7-18. Registering the page route and adding ApiClient to the service collection

```
private void ConfigureRoutes(
    DotvvmConfiguration config, string applicationPath)
{
    config.RouteTable.AutoDiscoverRoutes(
        new DefaultRouteStrategy(config));
    config.RouteTable.Add("ProductDetail", "product/{id}",
        "Views/ProductDetail.dothtml");
}

public void ConfigureServices(IDotvvmServiceCollection options)
{
    ...
    options.Services.AddScoped(_ => Global.GetApiClient());
}
```

If you followed all the steps, the product detail page should now replace the corresponding ASP.NET Web Forms page. The old page still remains in the project, but because OWIN was placed in front of the classic ASP.NET pipeline and we have registered the new page for the same URL pattern, the request will never reach the Web Forms version of the page.

I recommend keeping the page in the project until the very end of the migration process because you might need to fall back to the original implementation in case of any issues or breaking changes. It is also useful to be able to compare both versions to ensure they behave the same.

You can verify that the DotVVM version of the product detail page is being used by running the project, opening any product and looking at the page source. As you can see in Figure 7-9, the code does not contain the viewstate hidden field and references several scripts starting with / dotvvmResource – this is typical for DotVVM pages.

```
←   C   ⌂   ①   view-source:localhost:52477/product/dfd483a5-f4ca-8312-1d70-01f56fc4446e

Line wrap ☐
1
2  <!DOCTYPE html>
3
4  <html>
5  <head>
6      <meta charset=utf-8 />
7      <meta name=viewport content="width=device-width, initial-scale=1" />
8      <title></title>
9      <script src=/Scripts/bootstrap.bundle.min.js></script>
10     <link rel=stylesheet href=/Styles/bootstrap.min.css />
11     <link rel=stylesheet href=/Styles/bootstrap-icons.min.css />
12     <link rel=stylesheet href=/Styles/app.css />
13
14
15
16     <!-- Resource knockout of type ScriptResource. Pointing to EmbeddedResourceLocation. -->
17     <script src=/dotvvmResource/knockout/knockout defer></script>
18     <!-- Resource dotvvm.internal of type ScriptModuleResource. Pointing to EmbeddedResourceLocation. -->
19     <script src=/dotvvmResource/dotvvm--internal/dotvvm--internal type=module defer></script>
20     <!-- Resource dotvvm of type InlineScriptResource. -->
21
22     <!-- Resource dotvvm.debug of type ScriptResource. Pointing to EmbeddedResourceLocation. -->
23     <script src=/dotvvmResource/dotvvm--debug/dotvvm--debug defer></script>
24     <!-- Resource globalize of type ScriptResource. Pointing to EmbeddedResourceLocation. -->
25     <script src=/dotvvmResource/globalize/globalize defer></script>
26     <!-- Resource globalize:en-US of type ScriptResource. Pointing to JQueryGlobalizeResourceLocation. -->
27     <script src="/dotvvmResource/globalize---en-US/globalize---en-US" defer></script>
28  </head>
29  <body>
```

Figure 7-9. *Source code of the new product detail page*

Migrating the Other Pages

The process of migrating the remaining application pages is very similar. Create a new page, use the converter to perform the basic code edits, and resolve the remaining issues. In most cases, you can copy-paste most of the business logic from the code-behind files. It is wise to make refactoring on the way, move to asynchronous methods if possible, and involve the dependency injection instead of creating instances of services on your own.

You can see all migrated pages in the 04-all-pages-and-handler chapter. The ASP.NET Web Forms pages and the RSS generating handler are still there, so you can compare both versions. However, the DotVVM route table now specifies all the routes – no request can pass through to the Web Forms engine except for the request pointing to static files, such as scripts or stylesheets.

There are a few differences worth noting:

- The home page uses paging on the list of products, which is done by specifying startRowIndex, maximumRows, and totalRowCount parameters in the GetData method used for model binding. DotVVM uses another approach – instead of using List<T> in the viewmodel, you can use GridViewDataSet<T>, which is basically List<T> accompanied with metadata for sorting and paging. For example, there is the PagingOptions property holding the index of the current page, page size, and the total number of records in the data set. Data sets in DotVVM can be loaded from IQueryable by a useful LoadFromQueryable helper method, or you can fill their contents manually. In our case, I assigned the results to the Items collection and set the PagingOptions. TotalRecordsCount property manually, because I am not able to obtain IQueryable from the API.

- DotVVM has a component called DataPager, which has a similar usage as the Web Forms DataPager. However, in the current version of DotVVM, it is not customizable enough to be able to render just the previous and

459

next buttons as we do in Web Forms.[24] However, the GridViewDataSet contains all the properties required for building the experience ourselves. In the example application, you can find a <cc:CustomDataPager> component that renders a similar UI as the Web Forms DataPager. Notice it declares one property of type IPageableGridViewDataSet (without the generic parameter), which makes it pretty universal – it will work with a data set of anything.

- DotVVM does not have the <asp:Login> component. However, it is quite easy to define the form yourself. Because the project still runs on .NET Framework, we can continue signing the user in by calling FormsAuthentication.SetAuthCookie. This will have to be changed in the final step when we switch the project to ASP.NET Core.

- Notice the data annotation attributes and the ValidationSummary components in Views/Login. dothtml used to perform validation. It is easier than using RequiredFieldValidator controls in ASP.NET Web Forms. Also, you do not have to manually check Page.IsValid in commands. DotVVM will not invoke the command when the viewmodel does not pass validation.

---

[24] This feature is planned for DotVVM 5.0 release. You can find more information at www.dotvvm.com/blog/114/What-is-coming-to-DotVVM-5-0-Extensible-GridViewDataSet

- Redirecting to other pages can be done by using
  `Context.RedirectToRoute`. Since we can suffer from
  the same issue as with the `RouteLink` control (some
  routes are not yet present in the DotVVM routing table),
  you can use the `RedirectToRouteHybrid` extension
  method, which is also added by the `DotVVM.Adapters.`
  `WebForms` NuGet package.

- The `Views/Admin/Products.dothtml` page uses
  `GridView`, and like the home page, it is easy to use
  `GridViewDataSet` to handle sorting and paging.
  To delete a product, you can call a command and
  give it parameters from the current data context.
  Notice the command binding `{command: _root.`
  `DeleteProduct(Id)}`, which calls the `DeleteProduct`
  method declared on the page viewmodel and gives
  it the current record's `Id`. After deleting the product,
  you need to call `Products.RequestRefresh()` to
  indicate the data set shall be reloaded. In ASP.NET
  Web Forms, the delete method was invoked by the
  `GridView` control itself, and because of that, it knew
  that the data had to be reloaded afterward. In our case,
  the deletion is invoked by an arbitrary button, which
  is not aware of the situation. Notice that we load the
  data in the `PreRender` method only when `Products.`
  `IsRefreshRequested`. This pattern helps to make the
  page more efficient by not reloading the data every
  time, for example, in postbacks that do not manipulate
  the data set.

- As was already mentioned, the validation in DotVVM
  works differently than in Web Forms. Instead of
  validating controls, which was the case in Web
  Forms (the validator controls had a property named
  `ControlToValidate`), DotVVM validates the viewmodel
  (or its part). To define the validation rules, you can
  use either data annotation attributes on viewmodel
  properties or implement the `IValidatableObject`
  interface to perform the validation in code.
  Additionally, you can add custom errors into the
  model state by calling `viewModel.AddModelError(vm
  => vm.Property, message)`. Validation controls in
  DotVVM only display the errors from the `ModelState`
  object – for instance, by showing the error message,
  applying a CSS class to a particular element, and so on.

- Instead of validation groups (groups of controls that
  were validated together), DotVVM uses the viewmodel
  hierarchy. If you bind the control's `Validation.Target`
  property to a particular object in the viewmodel, you tell
  DotVVM that any postback coming from that control
  will validate only the specific object instead of validating
  the entire viewmodel. You can also turn the validation
  off completely by setting `Validation.Enabled=false`
  on a control that makes postbacks. In the `Views/Admin/`
  `ProductDetail.dothtml` page, you can see that the
  insert row for the new prices has the validation target set
  to the `NewPrice` object, but the main *Save* button for the
  entire page sets the target to the `Product` object. If you
  add the new price for the product, the product itself may
  not be valid at that moment. Similarly, the new price
  row does not have to be valid when saving the product.

Switching to the New .NET

We have successfully reached the point where all business logic is accessed through DotVVM pages or the DotVVM presenter. Now, it is time to remove all ASP.NET Web Forms artifacts and all other dependencies that prevent us from switching the target framework to the new .NET.

You can see the result of the migration in the 05-complete-migration folder. Before touching the project file, I performed the following steps:

- Removed the entire Pages folder.

- Removed Global.asax, ProductsRssHandler.cs, PageBase.cs, and GenericRouteHandler.cs.

- The Scripts and Styles folders were moved under the wwwroot.

- Removed the web.config file.

- Removed Properties/AssemblyInfo.cs as it will be auto-generated by the new project system.

After cleaning up these obvious artifacts, you can right-click the project file and choose the *Unload project* option. Then, you can remove all XML code in this file and replace it with the code shown in Listing 7-19. Before reloading the project, I recommend deleting the bin and obj directories, as they contain files in a different structure than the new project system expects, which can sometimes produce unexpected build errors (Visual Studio reuses the MSBuild processes, which often cache various information in order to speed up the compilation process).

Listing 7-19. New SDK-style project file

```
<Project Sdk="Microsoft.NET.Sdk.Web">
    <PropertyGroup>
        <TargetFramework>net8.0</TargetFramework>
```

```
  </PropertyGroup>
  <ItemGroup>
    <Content Include="**/*.dothtml;**/*.dotmaster;↵
**/*.dotcontrol"
              Exclude="obj/**/*.*;bin/**/*.*"
              CopyToPublishDirectory="Always" />
    <None Remove="**/*.dothtml;**/*.dotmaster;↵
**/*.dotcontrol" />
  </ItemGroup>
  <ItemGroup>
    <None Remove="dotvvm_serialized_config.json.tmp" />
  </ItemGroup>
  <ItemGroup>
    <PackageReference Include="DotVVM.Adapters.WebForms"
        Version="4.2.6" />
    <PackageReference Include="DotVVM.AspNetCore"
        Version="4.2.6" />
  </ItemGroup>
</Project>
```

As you can see, the new project file is very simple. It targets .NET 8, references only two NuGet packages (DotVVM.AspNetCore and DotVVM. Adapters.WebForms), and contains conventions for treating DotVVM-specific files. I believe it is better to start with a minimalistic project file and add only the things that are necessary than trying to adopt all references from the previous version.

Next, we have to change the Startup.cs class. To follow the current conventions, I recommend renaming it to Program.cs and using the code in Listing 7-20 to initialize DotVVM.

Listing 7-20. New Program.cs file with DotVVM and static files

```
using Microsoft.AspNetCore.Builder;
using Microsoft.Extensions.DependencyInjection;

var builder = WebApplication.CreateBuilder(args);

builder.Services.AddDotVVM<DotvvmStartup>();

var app = builder.Build();

app.UseAuthentication();
app.UseAuthorization();

app.UseDotVVM<DotvvmStartup>();
app.UseStaticFiles();

app.Run();
```

Naturally, there will be compile errors, and definitely some NuGet packages will be missing. For example, in the example application, there is a missing project reference to ModernizationDemo.BackendClient that must be re-added. Also, I had to add the System.ServiceModel. Syndication NuGet package because the objects I use to generate the RSS feed are no longer part of .NET and are distributed separately.

It is quite probable that you will also find unnecessary using statements that are no longer valid – for example, System.Web.UI, and so on. You will have to remove them.

Authentication and Authorization

If you use the Forms authentication, you will need to modify the places where you handle sign-in and sign-out of the users, as shown in Listing 7-21. The DotVVM Context object has an extension method called GetAuthentication, which gives you access to the SignInAsync and SignOutAsync methods.

Feel free to add more claims to the ClaimsIdentity object. For example, the roles can be represented by adding a claim of type ClaimTypes.Role for each role.

Listing 7-21. The new authentication code using DotVVM

```
// sign in code in LoginViewModel.cs
var identity = new ClaimsIdentity(
    [ new Claim(ClaimTypes.Name, UserName) ],
    CookieAuthenticationDefaults.AuthenticationScheme);

await Context.GetAuthentication().SignInAsync(
    CookieAuthenticationDefaults.AuthenticationScheme,
    new ClaimsPrincipal(identity));

// sign out code in SiteViewModel.cs
await Context.GetAuthentication()
    .SignOutAsync(
        CookieAuthenticationDefaults.AuthenticationScheme);
```

An important thing is that we need to re-add the authorization to the individual pages. In the example application, the access rules for the Admin folder were defined in the Pages/Admin/web.config file.

You can ensure the page can be accessed only by authenticated users by calling the Context.Authorize method in the Init phase of the viewmodel, as shown in Listing 7-22. You can specify a concrete authentication scheme or roles you require the users to be assigned to.

Alternatively, you may use the Authorize attribute (defined in DotVVM. Framework.Runtime.Filters namespace), but it produces a warning as it is not always obvious in which cases it works (e.g., it does not work when it is applied on an interface implemented by the page, and so on). Explicit authorization seems to be a better choice.

Listing 7-22. Defining authorization rules in DotVVM pages

```
public override async Task Init()
{
    await Context.Authorize();
    await base.Init();
}
```

In order to make the cookie authentication work, it must be configured in Program.cs, as demonstrated in Listing 7-23.

Listing 7-23. DotVVM-specific configuration of cookie authentication

```
builder.Services
    .AddAuthentication(
        CookieAuthenticationDefaults.AuthenticationScheme)
    .AddCookie(
        CookieAuthenticationDefaults.AuthenticationScheme,
        options =>
        {
            options.Events = new CookieAuthenticationEvents
            {
                OnRedirectToReturnUrl = c =>
                    DotvvmAuthenticationHelper
                        .ApplyRedirectResponse(
                            c.HttpContext, c.RedirectUri),
                OnRedirectToAccessDenied = c =>
                    DotvvmAuthenticationHelper
                        .ApplyStatusCodeResponse(
                            c.HttpContext, 403),
                OnRedirectToLogin = c =>
                    DotvvmAuthenticationHelper
                        .ApplyRedirectResponse(
```

```
                                c.HttpContext, c.RedirectUri),
                    OnRedirectToLogout = c =>
                        DotvvmAuthenticationHelper
                            .ApplyRedirectResponse(
                                c.HttpContext, c.RedirectUri)
        };

        options.LoginPath = "/login";
    });
```

The reason for overriding the redirect action in the Events object is
that DotVVM handles HTTP redirects differently than classic server-side
frameworks. When you make a postback in DotVVM, the HTTP POST
request is called from JavaScript, and a JSON-serialized viewmodel is
sent to the server. However, if the server responds with the redirect, the
JavaScript fetch function will automatically follow it and obtain the HTML
of the page the server redirected to. Since there is no way around that,
DotVVM makes redirects by sending special JSON results with a status
code of 200. This is exactly what the ApplyRedirectResponse helper
method does.

Other Changes

Several other things had to be changed in our example application.
Because the old application uses the session state, I had to reimplement
the code in SiteViewModel.cs to use the new ASP.NET Core Session
API. First, you need to call LoadAsync for the session to be loaded, and if
you make any changes, you need to call CommitAsync. Also, the session
values are byte arrays in ASP.NET Core, so you need to serialize your values
to fit into this format. Since I only store string values, I used a plain ASCII
encoding.

You also need to register the session in Program.cs, as shown in Listing 7-24. The session requires the distributed cache – that is why I register the distributed memory cache (which is in fact not distributed but implements the asynchronous interface IDistributedCache).

Listing 7-24. Registration and code changes for ASP.NET Core Session

```
// Program.cs
...
builder.Services.AddSession();
builder.Services.AddDistributedMemoryCache();

var app = builder.Build();

app.UseSession();
...

// SiteViewModel.cs
public override async Task Init()
{
    var session = Context.GetAspNetCoreContext().Session;
    await session.LoadAsync();

    if (session.TryGetValue("SelectedCurrency",
        out var currency))
    {
        SelectedCurrency = Encoding.ASCII.GetString(currency);
    }
    ...
}

public async Task OnCurrencyChanged()
{
    var session = Context.GetAspNetCoreContext().Session;
```

```
await session.LoadAsync();

session.Set("SelectedCurrency",
    Encoding.ASCII.GetBytes(SelectedCurrency));
await session.CommitAsync();
...
}
```

Similar changes had to be made to the Utils class, which used caching. The new .NET memory cache is not available as a static member, so I had to change the static methods to instance ones and change the access of HttpRuntime.Cache to IMemoryCache. I registered the Utils class in the service collection, so I can inject it in all the places I need it. A different name (for instance, PriceCache), would be more appropriate for this class.

In general, it is a good idea to avoid static methods that include more complex functionality – not only for the sake of testing but also to allow for mocking the dependencies such as the memory cache implementation.

Finally, I had to add the appsettings.json file in the project and specify the URL of the back-end API in order to register the ApiClient in the services. In all places where the client was obtained by calling a static factory method, I had to change it to the dependency injection approach.

Wrapping Up

After resolving the compilation errors, you can try to run the project. In most cases, it will not start successfully on the first attempt. I always made some mistakes during this step, such as missing configuration entries or registrations in IServiceCollection. However, the exception messages are quite clear and will inform you which dependencies could not be resolved.

It is necessary to test the entire application to ensure that the framework switch has not broken anything. Please be aware that there were eight years of work between .NET Framework 4.7.2 and .NET 8, and the number of changes is enormous. "If it compiles, it works" is not a good assumption.

Summary

In this chapter, I have shown how to migrate an ASP.NET Web Forms application in place. In several incremental steps that could be done in parallel with other development tasks, we replaced portions of code that are not supported on the new .NET with equivalent functionality built using an open source DotVVM framework, which has the unique feature of supporting both .NET Framework and the new .NET.

In the next two chapters, you will see how to do a similar process when there is no common ground between the two .NET worlds. It will be more complicated than this in-place method, but it has one significant advantage – you will be able to use .NET 8 from the first day, at least in the new part of the application.

CHAPTER 8

Side-by-Side Migration of UI Applications

In the previous chapter, I showcased an easier method of in-place modernization, which was made possible because we used a framework with a unique property – the ability to run in both .NET Framework and the latest .NET versions.

As explained earlier, the side-by-side approach brings several complications because of running two processes simultaneously. Although some larger applications were designed to support horizontal scaling by using database-persisted sessions, distributed caching, and other necessary concepts, this is certainly not true for all projects. Furthermore, the old application will be running behind a reverse proxy in our scenario, which can bring additional issues we must deal with.

How the side-by-side modernization works was briefly explained in the previous chapter. Feel free to return to Figure 7-1, which illustrates the process in three stages. In this section, we will examine them in detail.

© Tomáš Herceg 2024
T. Herceg, *Modernizing .NET Web Applications*,
https://doi.org/10.1007/979-8-8688-0617-9_8

Initial Setup

At the beginning, we will create an empty ASP.NET Core application running on the new .NET. This new application will use a reverse proxy to forward HTTP traffic to the old one. The recommended solution is to use YARP,[1] a Microsoft-developed reverse proxy built with .NET, but if you prefer using another proxy, it should work as well. However, YARP is a proven solution that is used at a considerably large scale, for example, by the Azure App Service team.[2]

> *YARP is a key component as it takes over from IIS as the router. YARP is special sauce since it can run on any OS using Kestrel, but with the magic of being built on ASP.NET primitives, it can also run natively on IIS or HTTP.sys directly.*
>
> *This means you can use YARP as an efficient router since it has a multitude of transports (Unix domain sockets, HTTP.sys fast delegation, HTTP/1.1/2).*
>
> —David Fowler[3]

Depending on your environment and company policies or conventions, you may prefer to use a long-term support (LTS) release or the latest stable version of .NET. Please note that the new .NET support policy[4] is stricter than the .NET Framework one[5] in terms of requiring you to keep your application up to date. Even the new .NET LTS releases offer only three years of support, which means that keeping the project without

---

[1] See https://microsoft.github.io/reverse-proxy/index.html

[2] See https://devblogs.microsoft.com/dotnet/bringing-kestrel-and-yarp-to-azure-app-services/

[3] See https://x.com/davidfowl/status/1801855504177893474

[4] See https://dotnet.microsoft.com/en-us/platform/support/policy/dotnet-core

[5] See https://learn.microsoft.com/en-us/lifecycle/faq/dotnet-framework

updates for years is not a good idea. I stopped counting how many legacy .NET Framework applications I encountered still used some ancient and unsupported version of .NET Framework.

I recommend going to the highest version of .NET possible to eliminate as much technical debt as possible. Although version upgrades between the recent versions of .NET (especially since .NET Core 3.1) were usually smooth and required only to upgrade some NuGet packages, there is always a small but nonzero possibility of hitting some breaking change. You should check out the documentation[6] that lists all known issues for the new .NET versions since .NET Core 2.1.

CODE SAMPLES FOR THIS CHAPTER

The migration of data access code is demonstrated in the GitHub repository available via the book's product page at `https://github.com/Apress/Modernizing-.NET-Web-Applications`. You can find the entire solution in the `chapter08` folder.

There are several folders showing the project in various stages:

- `01-initial-state` shows the original ASP.NET Web Forms application running on .NET Framework 4.7.2.

- `02-add-second-app` shows the project after adding the new ASP.NET Core application and configuring YARP.

- `03-master-page-and-first-page` shows the project after migrating the master page and one of the application pages. It contains the configuration for remote sessions, remote authentication, and cache invalidation.

---

[6] See `https://learn.microsoft.com/en-us/dotnet/core/compatibility/breaking-changes`

- `04-all-pages-and-handler` shows the project after all pages and handlers have been migrated.
- `05-complete-migration` shows the final application migrated into ASP.NET Core.

If you want to run the projects, follow the instructions in the `Readme` file in the `chapter08` folder.

Since all five solutions are configured to use the same ports, please make sure you are not running multiple versions simultaneously.

Create the New ASP.NET Core Application

The easiest way to start is to use the .NET Upgrade Assistant[7] extension for Visual Studio. If you have it installed, you will see a new menu item called *Upgrade* when you right-click a legacy project in the *Solution Explorer* window, as shown in Figure 8-1.

---

[7] See `https://learn.microsoft.com/en-us/dotnet/core/porting/upgrade-assistant-install#install-the-visual-studio-extension`

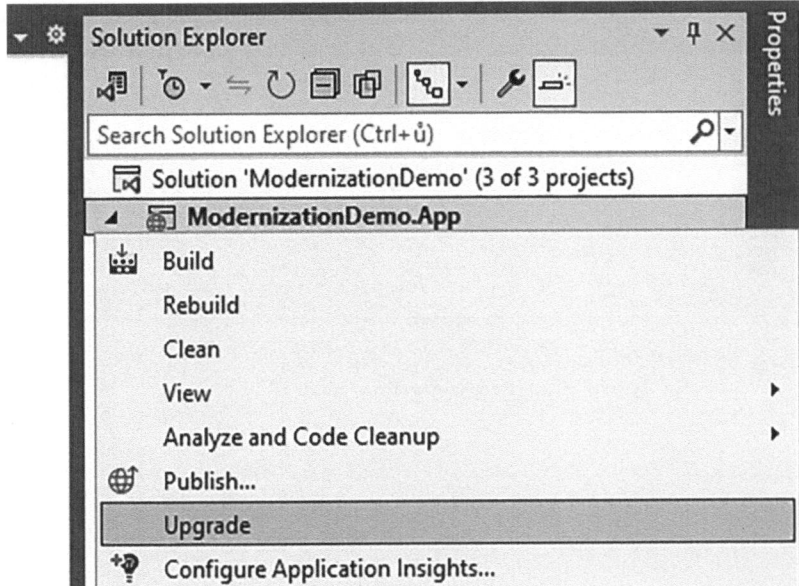

Figure 8-1. *Starting the .NET Upgrade Assistant by right-clicking a project*

Once you use this menu item, another window will appear, asking you whether you want to upgrade your project to a newer version of .NET or whether you want to upgrade project features while keeping the current .NET version. The latter option is useful for converting projects from the old format to the new SDK-style syntax. Select the *Upgrade project to a newer .NET version* option, as shown in Figure 8-2.

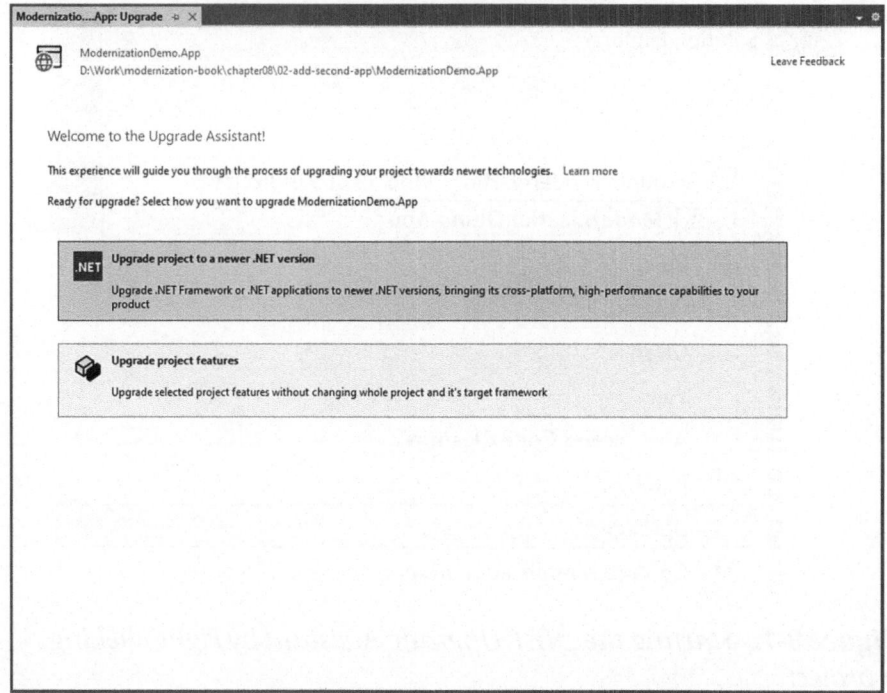

Figure 8-2. *Choosing the upgrade strategy (upgrading to a newer .NET version)*

Because we are dealing with ASP.NET projects, the next step offers only one path: our side-by-side migration method using YARP. Proceed, as demonstrated in Figure 8-3.

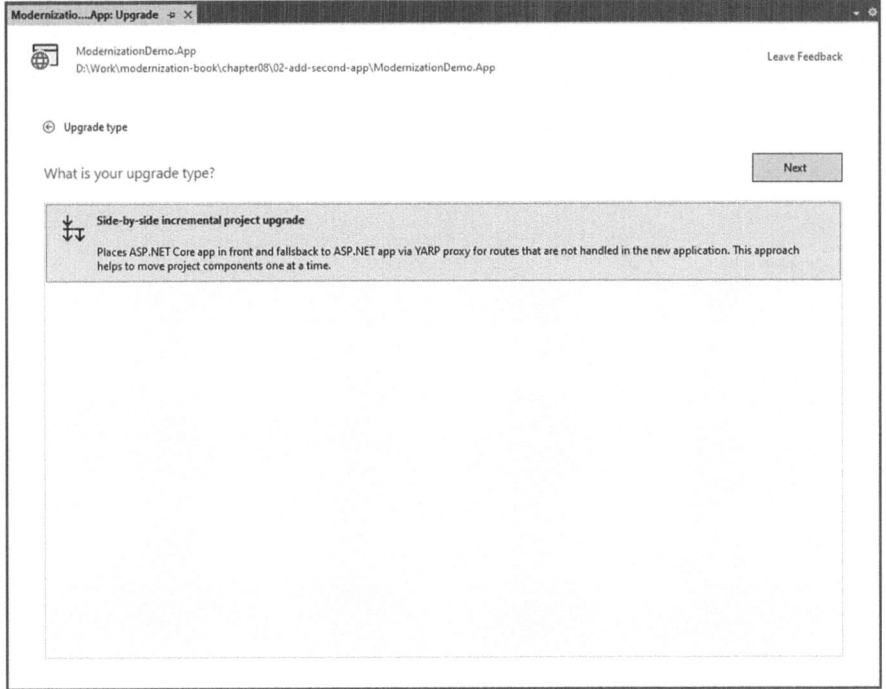

Figure 8-3. *Choosing the side-by-side migration method*

In the following step, we have an option to create a new application or select an existing ASP.NET Core application. I will continue with selecting the first option, as shown in Figure 8-4. The second option may be useful if you have already started migrating functionality to a stand-alone application.

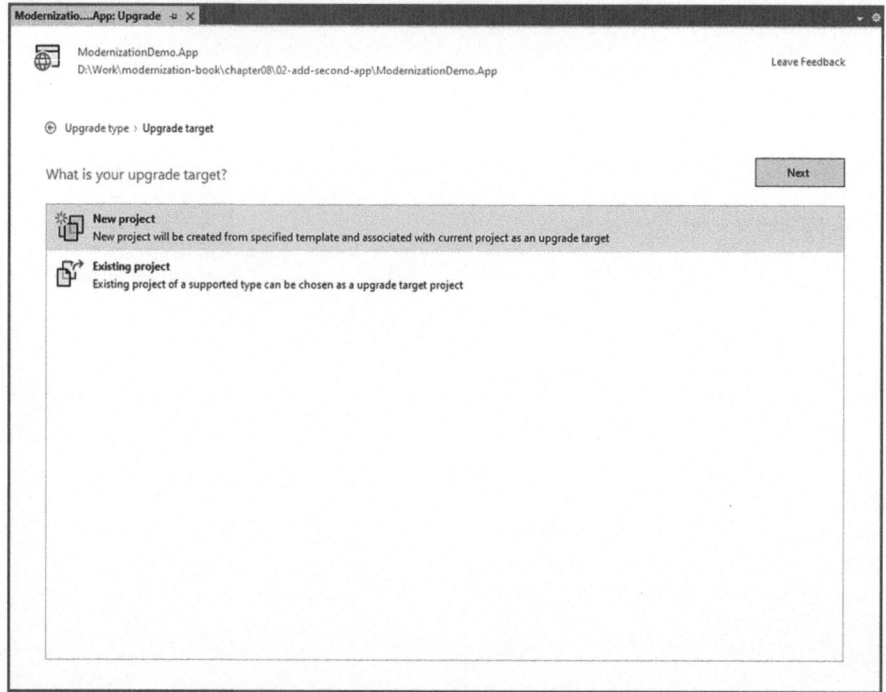

Figure 8-4. *Choosing to create a new empty ASP.NET Core project*

After this screen, the wizard will ask for the project name (I used ModernizationDemo.AppNew) and the version of .NET we want to target. A nice feature is that the upgrade assistant shows the actual end-of-support dates. If you do not have all the information to make a decision, select the newest long-term support version (the most conservative choice). You will be able to upgrade to a newer version quite any time later. After proceeding, you will see the summary as illustrated in Figure 8-5.

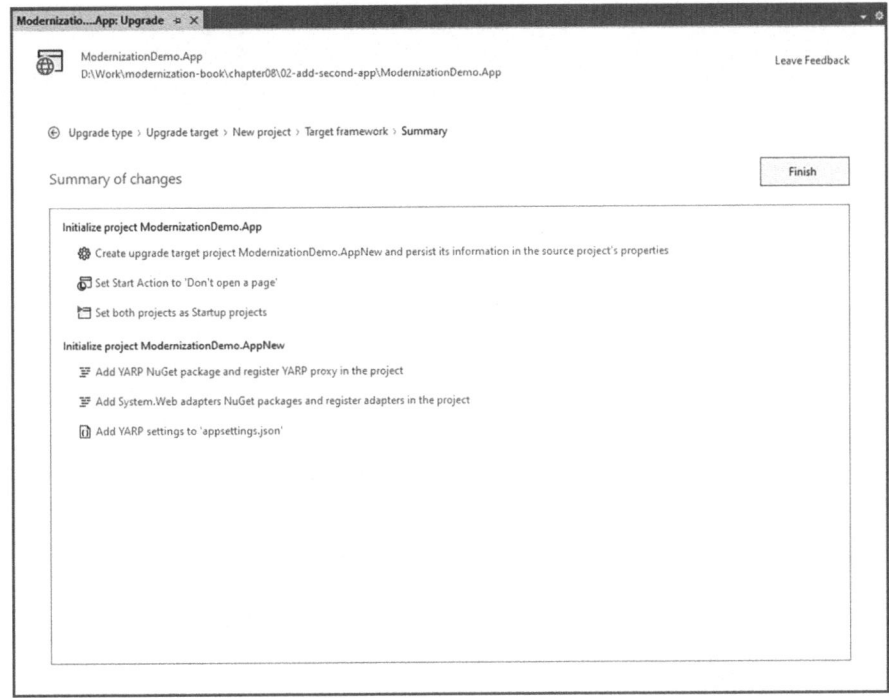

Figure 8-5. *Summary of the migration plan*

Once you click the *Finish* button, the .NET Upgrade Assistant will take all necessary steps and create a new ASP.NET Core application aside from the legacy one, as shown in Figure 8-6.

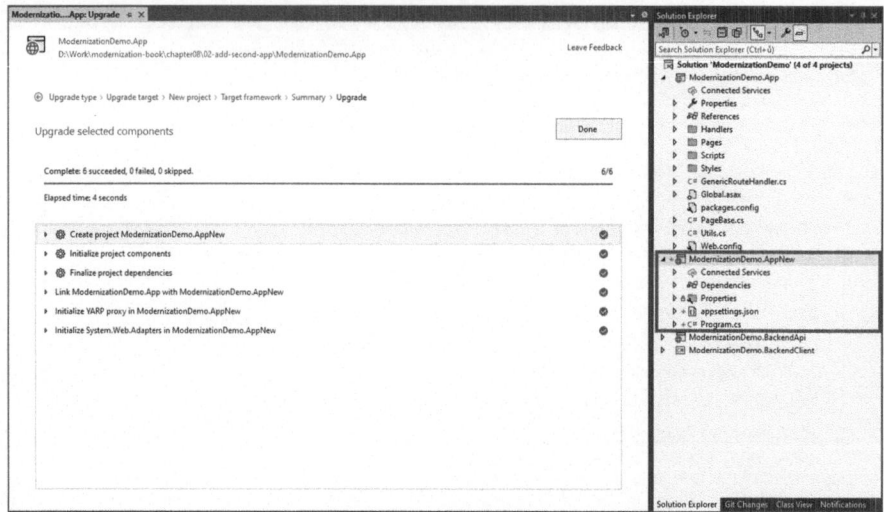

Figure 8-6. *The newly created ASP.NET Core application*

You can notice that the wizard configured the solution to have multiple startup projects. If you right-click the solution file, there is the *Configure Startup Projects* option. Because our example application has the back-end API project, configure it to start the ModernizationDemo.BackendApi project together with both web applications, as shown in Figure 8-7.

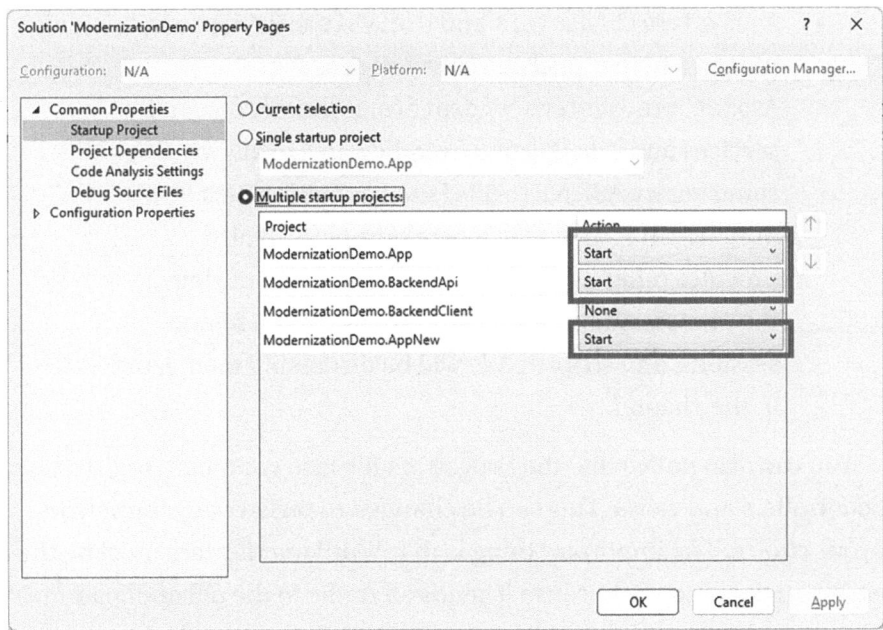

Figure 8-7. *Configuring the solution startup projects*

If you look in the Program.cs, the only code present in the newly created project, it follows the usual structure of any ASP.NET Core application, as Listing 8-1 shows. There are two specific components:

- AddHttpForwarder and MapForwarder calls are configuring YARP. You can see that it forwards the traffic to an address specified by the ProxyTo key in the configuration. The actual value is not in the appsettings.json file – Visual Studio configured the Properties/launchSettings.json file to supply it to the process as an environment variable. When deploying the application to a server, do not forget to configure it correctly.

- AddSystemWebAdapters and UseSystemWebAdapters plug in a helper package called Microsoft. AspNetCore.SystemWebAdapters. It registers several services and sets up some middlewares to allow some legacy ASP.NET APIs (such as System.Web. HttpContext.Current) to work properly. It also provides other useful features we will need during the process, such as remote authentication, remote sessions, and so forth. We will be discussing them later in the chapter.

You can also notice that the Progam.cs file also contains a registration of controllers and views. This can be changed to register any framework of your choice. The important thing is that YARP middleware must be the last one in the pipeline because it sends all traffic to the old application. No request would reach any middleware after YARP.

Listing 8-1. YARP configuration in the new ASP.NET Core application

```
var builder = WebApplication.CreateBuilder(args);
builder.Services.AddSystemWebAdapters();
builder.Services.AddHttpForwarder();

builder.Services.AddControllersWithViews();
var app = builder.Build();

if (!app.Environment.IsDevelopment())
{
    app.UseHsts();
}

app.UseHttpsRedirection();
app.UseStaticFiles();
```

```
app.UseRouting();
app.UseAuthorization();
app.UseSystemWebAdapters();

app.MapDefaultControllerRoute();
app.MapForwarder(
    "/{**catch-all}", app.Configuration["ProxyTo"])
    .Add(static builder => ((RouteEndpointBuilder)builder)
                    .Order = int.MaxValue);
app.Run();
```

After this initial procedure, you should be able to run the application. As you will see shortly, some things may not work properly. Therefore, it is crucial to test the application locally before trying to deploy it on the server for the first time.

Here are the common issues you should focus on when testing the application:

- The old application will be moved to a different URL, and the traffic will be proxied through YARP. This will hide the client's actual IP address, and if the application generates absolute URLs based on the request addresses, it will see a different Url in the Request object.

- If the old application stores any temporary state in ASP. NET Session, the new application will not see this data automatically.

- If the old application uses Forms authentication or some other type of cookie authentication, the authentication cookie will not be readable by the new ASP.NET Core application as it uses a different format. The user will appear as not authenticated. Windows Authentication will probably not work either.

485

- If the old application uses an in-memory cache, the new application will not be aware of it, and you may experience various data concurrency issues. When the new application changes any data, the old application may still use previously cached values, and vice versa.

- Any in-process or in-memory locking and synchronization, or any objects assumed to be singletons, will cease to work reliably because they are not shared between the two application instances.

This list of issues is not exhaustive, but I believe the preceding items represent the most frequent cases. We will deal with each of the items in the following sections.

Forwarded Headers

The first problem you may discover when testing the new setup locally is that the old application suddenly receives requests for a different domain.

For example, the old application may now be effectively running at `https://localhost:50433`, but the client's browser accesses it through the new application at `https://www.my-awesome-app.com:433`.

If the old application needs to know the real URL (for instance, to be able to compose an absolute URL for hyperlinks), it can no longer infer its public URL from the `Request.Url` property.

You can see this behavior in our example application when you scroll down and click the *RSS Feed* link. You will see the `<link>` and `<id>` elements reporting the wrong URL in the XML document that appears. It will show `http://localhost:52477` instead of `https://localhost:7220`, which you can see in the browser address bar. The code builds the absolute URL from the current request URL. You can see it in the `GetApplicationBaseUri` method in the `ProductsRssHandler` class.

A similar problem occurs when the legacy application needs to know the client's IP address. Because it now receives all traffic through the new application, which probably runs on the same server, the IP address you will find in the Request.UserHostAddress property will be 127.0.0.1 or ::1 (for IPv6).

Luckily, most web proxies can add HTTP headers called X-Forwarded-Proto, X-Forwarded-Host, and X-Forwarded-Prefix to the requests to provide information about the original request before it was reissued by the proxy.

The actual client's IP address will be sent in the X-Forwarded-For HTTP header, along with the IP addresses of proxies on the way. Similarly, the X-Forwarded-Proto and X-Forwarded-Host will contain the protocol and hostname the clients see in their browsers.

Instead of updating the application code to use these headers, the SystemWebAdapters project has a NuGet package called Microsoft. AspNetCore.SystemWebAdapters.FrameworkServices. It can be installed in the old application and handle this behavior for us, so you may keep using Request.Url and Request.UserHostAddress properties.

The package is configured in the Global.asax class, as shown in Listing 8-2.

Listing 8-2. Handling forwarded headers using a SystemWebAdapters proxy module

```
...
protected void Application_Start(object sender, EventArgs e)
{
    ...

    SystemWebAdapterConfiguration.AddSystemWebAdapters(this)
        .AddProxySupport(
            options => options.UseForwardedHeaders = true);
}
```

When you install the NuGet package in the project, it registers an HTTP module in the web.config file automatically, as you can see in Listing 8-3. Make sure you test the setup before deploying the application. YARP sends the forwarded headers by default, but the actual behavior depends on the proxy configuration.

Listing 8-3. Registering the HTTP module in the web.config file

```
<system.webServer>
  ...
    <modules runAllManagedModulesForAllRequests="true">
      <remove name="SystemWebAdapterModule" />
      <add name="SystemWebAdapterModule"
          type="Microsoft.AspNetCore.SystemWebAdapters.⏎
SystemWebAdapterModule,Microsoft.AspNetCore.SystemWebAdapters.⏎
FrameworkServices"
          preCondition="managedHandler" />
    </modules>
</system.webServer>
```

You will need to ensure that the legacy application is not accessible without going through the proxy. Otherwise, it may be vulnerable to various header spoofing attacks.[8] For example, if your application applies rate limits to certain actions or blocks potentially malicious activities based on the client IP addresses, it would be trivial for the attacker to send millions of requests with unique IP addresses in the X-Forwarded-For header directly to the old application. In the default configuration, YARP ignores incoming forwarded headers and generates them from scratch, so the attacker-provided values are never used.

---

[8] See https://owasp.org/www-community/pages/attacks/ip_spoofing_via_http_headers

If you apply this change to the example application, you will see that the RSS feed will not report the correct URL (it would match the hostname and port you can see in the browser's address bar).

Server Configuration

This is the earliest point where you can start thinking about making the configuration changes on the server and deploying the first version of the application. The issues I mentioned earlier will probably not appear yet, as all business logic is still contained in the old application. We will have to resolve them, but only once you start migrating the first page.

However, you should be prepared to make deployments during the entire process of side-by-side modernization, so you can deliver the new versions of pages to the users and get early feedback. Many developer teams have already adopted continuous integration and continuous deployment practices. If this is not the case for your legacy application, I recommend investing time into it. Although we will try making as small changes as possible, there is always a chance of introducing bugs. Therefore, it is crucial to have a way to resolve them as quickly as possible.

When you look at the server, only the legacy application is currently deployed. It is exposed to the users and receives all web traffic. In order to place the new proxy application in front of it, the old application needs to be moved to a new local-only URL, and the new application needs to take its place, as shown in Figure 8-8.

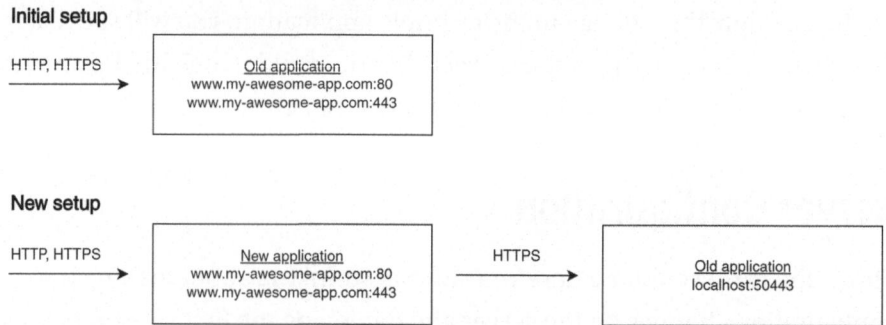

Figure 8-8. *Configuration changes after creating the new application*

Do not forget to set the ProxyTo configuration key in the new application to the URL of the old application. You can do this either in the appsettings.json file (or ideally, in appsettings.Production.json) or by setting the site's environment variable in the web server configuration.

You must secure the old application to accept only traffic from the local IP (127.0.0.1 or ::1 for IPv6). If you are running on IIS, you can use the *Address and Domain Restrictions* feature. Alternatively, you can achieve a similar effect by adding a firewall configuration rule.

Sharing Code Between the Applications

In the previous migration method, it was easy to share the business logic in both old and new code, as everything was in the same project, targeting the same set of NuGet packages and using the same version of .NET.

In side-by-side migration, it is a bit more complicated. Let us first try to split the code into several "virtual groups," as shown in Figure 8-9.

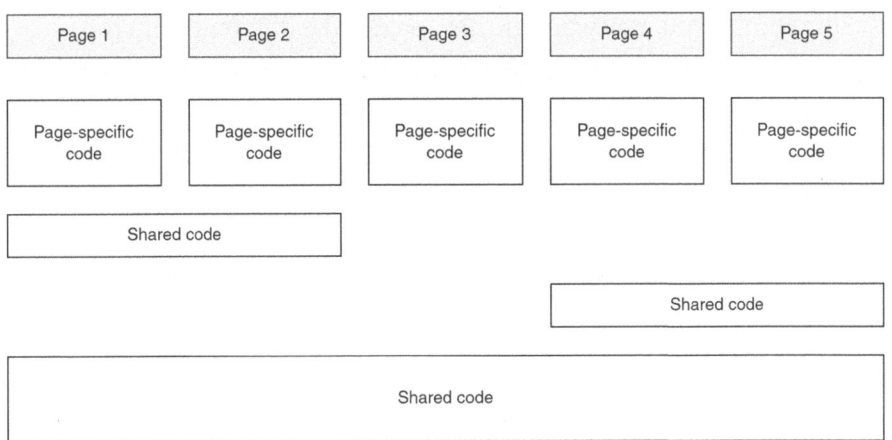

Figure 8-9. Shared and page-specific code

Please note that these boxes in the picture do not need to correspond to namespaces or projects in the solution. Sometimes, they do not correspond even to classes – you would have to go down to the method level to be able to identify which code belongs to which box. The edges of these boxes may not be sharp and precise – in some projects, they are quite blurry.

The first type of box in the picture is page-specific code. You can think of it as a collection of methods, classes, and other parts of the codebase used exclusively by a single page. For example, in the case of ASP.NET Web Forms, these boxes will probably include most of the code-behind files. In the case of ASP.NET MVC, the same can be said about controllers. Technically, it is possible to call methods declared in these files from other places in the code, but it does not happen frequently.

The page-specific code must be migrated together with the page (otherwise, the page could not work), but since the other pages in the old application do not need it, you can simply *move it* from the old project to the new one. This will probably include some code changes or refactoring. I strongly recommend cleaning up the code – you do not want to have a mess in the new project from the first day.

Sometimes, you may want the new page to be different from the original one. The old page-specific code can be removed completely, and a new implementation is added to the new project.

When dealing with the shared code boxes, the situation is slightly more complicated. First, it is good to inspect whether the code is shared by all pages or parts of the application or at least by a majority of them. It is not always the case – often, the code is shared only by small "clusters" of pages. For example, there may be just a few pages in the application that work with the product catalog, and, therefore, there will probably be parts of the code related to the product catalog that are called only from these few pages. If the cluster is not too large, you can decide to move it as a single piece. Thus, this code can be approached the same way as it is page-specific code – you will be able to move it instead of sharing it in both applications.

The most complicated situation occurs when the shared code is used from many pages that are not possible to move in a single step. Such parts of code are often perceived as "infrastructure code," and because of their wide utilization, we need to make them available in both applications – often for a considerably long time. There are several options. As usual, there is no silver bullet.

1. The cleanest and most elegant choice is to move the code to a shared class library that targets either .NET Standard or uses the `<TargetFrameworks>` element to be compiled separately for both platforms. Sometimes, it is not entirely straightforward to find a combination of NuGet packages that work for both platform targets, as was shown in previous chapters, for example, in Listing 3-1. Also, there is a risk of introducing issues to the old application, as you will be moving (and probably slightly editing) significant parts of its code to a separate project.

492

Furthermore, if the code contains many references to an API that is unsupported on the new .NET, this method will not be easily applicable as you will need to use preprocessor directives to adjust the code to compile on both platforms, as shown in Listing 3-2. On the other hand, if the code uses only the concepts supported on both platforms, the risks of breaking changes will be much lower as the code will be just moved to another place.

2. If you are afraid of making any changes to the old application, you can link the relevant C# files to the new project instead. This can be done by using the *Add* ➤ *Existing Item* option in Visual Studio and selecting *Add as Link* from the drop-down menu in the dialog box, as shown in Figure 8-10. Alternatively, you can add the entry in the `.csproj` file manually, as shown in Listing 8-4. This latter method can be especially useful if you need to include entire folders because you can use wildcards to match multiple files. Please note that this only tells the compiler to include the files in the compilation, but it will not copy them to the new project's folder. Same as in the previous case, you can use the preprocessor directives to use a different code for the new .NET. Be aware that linking files only includes the "text contents" but not any references from the project the files originate from. Therefore, the linked code will be compiled with the packages and the target framework configured in the new project.

3. The last option is copying the code from the old project to the new project. Use this method only if there is a need for so many preprocessor directives that the file would be hard to work with. Any code duplication always increases the risk of inconsistencies and "returning bugs." If you fix any problem in one instance of the code and forget to apply the same changes in the other places, the issue is not resolved completely, and when it reappears, it is usually more difficult to track and fix its real cause.

Listing 8-4. Adding an existing file in the new project as a link manually in the project file

```
<ItemGroup>
  <Compile Include="..\ModernizationDemo.App\Utils.cs"
      Link="Utils.cs" />
</ItemGroup>
```

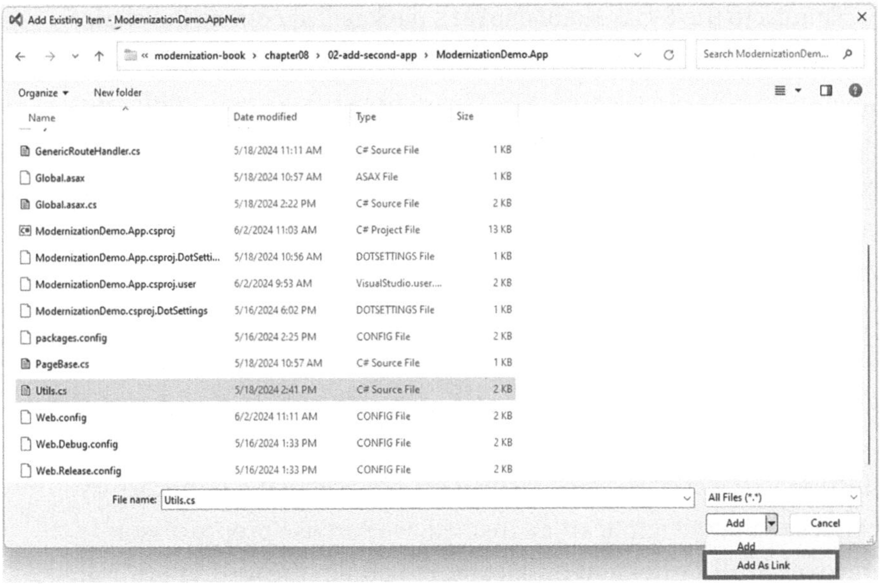

Figure 8-10. *Adding an existing file in the new project as a link*

In our example Web Forms application, the distinction between the shared and page-specific code is quite clear. Having the business logic already extracted in a separate project (the back-end API) makes the situation very straightforward. The entire `ModernizationDemo.BackendClient` project containing the API client and model classes is shared code that is already prepared to be used from the new project, as it is a .NET Standard class library. You just need to add a reference to this project in the new application.

The `Utils` class is another example of a shared code that we need to make available to the new application. I decided to add it as a link to demonstrate how this method works.

Thanks to the SystemWebAdapters package, accessing the static System.Web.HttpRuntime.Cache property will work – the package implements this old caching API. Please note that it uses a different implementation of cache than the new Microsoft.Extensions.Caching. Memory package, so you may want to migrate the code to use IMemoryCache eventually, but thanks to the package, you can leave this step for a later time.

There will be one compile error caused by calling the Global. GetApiClient() static method we had in the Web Forms application to create an instance of the API client. Because the Utils class is static and is used in the old application, we cannot change it to use dependency injection in the constructor – we want to avoid making unnecessary changes to the old application. Instead, we can use preprocessor directives to allow the new application to obtain the ApiClient from IServiceProvider scoped to the current request. In ASP.NET Core, we can use the IHttpContextAccessor interface, but it also requires dependency injection we do not have in a static method.

However, the SystemWebAdapters package implements the HttpContext.Current static property, which has an extension method called AsAspNetCore(). This will give us an option to access the current ASP.NET Core context and obtain our API client explicitly from the service provider, as shown in Listing 8-5. Please note that this extension method is available only in the adapters package, and thus the corresponding using statement must be included only for the new .NET project. I also used the preprocessor directive here.

Please note that this is not the final solution. Once we discard the old application, we should refactor the Utils class to remove the static methods to allow for the proper use of dependency injection. Additionally, we should update the code to use the async version of the GetProductPrice method. You probably remember I was suggesting the same thing in the previous chapter.

Listing 8-5. Obtaining the ApiClient instance in the ASP.NET Core project

```
...

#if NET
using Microsoft.AspNetCore.SystemWebAdapters;
#endif

...

private static ApiClient GetApiClient()
{
#if !NET
    return Global.GetApiClient();
#else
    return System.Web.HttpContext.Current!.AsAspNetCore()
        .RequestServices.GetRequiredService<ApiClient>();
#endif
}
```

To make the class work, we need to register the ApiClient in the Program.cs file like we did in the last step of the in-place migration. Listing 8-6 shows how to do that. Do not forget to add the corresponding key with the URL of the back-end API to the appsettings.json file.

Listing 8-6. Registering ApiClient in the IServiceCollection

```
builder.Services.AddSingleton(_ => new ApiClient(
    builder.Configuration["Api:Url"], new HttpClient()));
```

There is also some shared code in the PageBase class, but since this class inherits from ASP.NET Web Forms Page class, we cannot use the file as is. In this case, I decided not to reuse this file – we will eventually copy and modify the code. You can take it as an example of code that would be hard or impossible to migrate as is. Copying the functionality is the only option.

As you can see, I combined all three approaches to dealing with shared code. I recommend using a shared class library project wherever possible, as it is the most maintainable approach. Linking files can be a good option to share several individual files that would be difficult to extract into separate projects. The remaining cases can be solved by copying the functionality and adjusting it for the new project.

Migrating the First Page

From now on, the process is quite straightforward and, to some extent, similar to the previous in-place modernization method. We will reimplement individual pages of the ASP.NET Web Forms application using a different UI framework, reusing parts of HTML and page-specific back-end code.

After every page is migrated, we will register a route for it in the new application. This will allow the request to be handled within the new application instead of being forwarded to the old application through YARP.

Eventually, when we migrate all pages, handlers, static files, and other possible request handlers, no traffic will reach the legacy application, which will allow us to remove it completely.

However, the SystemWebAdapters package will still remain in the application and may be heavily used. You may eventually want to update the code to use the native ASP.NET Core API, but this can be done incrementally afterward. This will almost certainly require some refactoring, especially converting static methods to instance ones to allow for use of dependency injection.

Choosing the UI Framework

The strongest benefit of the side-by-side modernization method is its universality. You can use any UI framework to rewrite the pages – Blazor, Razor Pages, React, Angular, and so on.

Naturally, it makes sense to consider how close the selected framework is to the one used in the legacy application. In the case of ASP.NET Web Forms, the choice is not that important, as the syntax is not close to any of the new Microsoft ASP.NET Core frameworks. There is a popular NuGet package `BlazorWebFormsComponents`[9] that helps migrating ASP.NET Web Forms pages to Blazor by providing components similar to what Web Forms had. Naturally, it is by far not feature-complete, but since today's requirements on web applications are quite different, I believe the goal of this package is not to bring a complete one-to-one reimplementation of the components. Its intent is to simplify the process of rewriting pages, and having components based on similar concepts and with the same property names is very helpful.

If your application was written in ASP.NET MVC, migration to ASP.NET Core MVC will probably be the easiest option. Similarly, ASP.NET Web Pages can be converted to Razor Pages. I will cover the choices in detail in Chapter 9.

Another aspect is whether you want just to move the application with as few changes as possible or make larger changes and improvements to the user interface on the fly. The side-by-side migration method allows for both approaches.

---

[9] See `https://github.com/FritzAndFriends/BlazorWebFormsComponents`

Adding Blazor Server

In the example application, I decided to migrate it to Blazor Server. Using Blazor WebAssembly would be possible and maybe easier because we already have our business logic packed as a REST API. However, this is not the usual case in most modernization projects. Although many projects expose some part of the business logic as an API, the UI of the application often requires many features the API does not offer.

I believe that migration to Blazor Server will be the most frequent scenario, especially for ASP.NET Web Forms applications, as most of the code-behind code interacts with server-side resources such as a database. Porting this code to run in the browser would probably require much more effort.

The `Program.cs` file generated by Visual Studio assumes that we will use ASP.NET Core MVC. Listing 8-7 shows how to replace it with Blazor registration.

Listing 8-7. Registration of Blazor Server in the new ASP.NET Core project

```
var builder = WebApplication.CreateBuilder(args);
...

builder.Services.AddControllersWithViews();
builder.Services.AddRazorComponents()
    .AddInteractiveServerComponents();

var app = builder.Build();
...
app.UseRouting();
app.UseAuthorization();
app.UseAntiforgery();
...
```

```
app.MapDefaultControllerRoute();
app.MapRazorComponents<App>()
    .AddInteractiveServerRenderMode();

app.MapForwarder(...);


app.Run();
```

The code references the App component, which needs to be added to the project. I created the Components folder and added the App.razor file containing the page's main structure. It uses the same CSS styles and scripts as the ASP.NET Web Forms master page, combined with a Blazor-generated CSS file, as shown in Listing 8-8.

You do not need to create this file from scratch – if you create an empty Blazor project, you can just take the Components folder from it and adapt it to your needs. That is exactly how I got to this file. There are also the Routes.razor and _Imports.razor files in the example project. They define the Router component and the default imported namespaces. I did not make any changes in the files, except for wrapping the Router component with the CascadingAuthenticationState helper to be able to use components that depend on the authentication data, such as AuthorizeView. Since these files do not contain anything specific to the modernization process, I have not listed them in the book.

Listing 8-8. Blazor main component

```
<!DOCTYPE html>
<html lang="en">
<head>
    <meta charset="utf-8" />
    <meta name="viewport"
        content="width=device-width,initial-scale=1.0" />
    <base href="/" />
```

```
<script src="Scripts/bootstrap.bundle.min.js"></script>
<link href="Styles/bootstrap.min.css" rel="stylesheet" />
<link href="Styles/bootstrap-icons.min.css"
    rel="stylesheet" />
<link href="Styles/app.css" rel="stylesheet" />
<link rel="stylesheet"
    href="ModernizationDemo.AppNew.styles.css"/>
<HeadOutlet />
</head>
<body>
    <Routes @rendermode="new InteractiveServerRenderMode(↵
prerender: false)"/>
    <script src="_framework/blazor.web.js"></script>
</body>
</html>
```

There is one point worth mentioning. In .NET 8, Blazor introduced a new feature that allows combining multiple rendering modes[10] in the same application. Some components can be rendered on the server and use the SignalR communication channel to provide client-side interactivity, while others are rendered on the client using the WebAssembly infrastructure. There is also an automatic mode – on the first visit, it renders the component on the server, but it starts downloading the WebAssembly bundle in the background. When the component is visited the second time, it is rendered on the client.

In the example application, I decided to use the interactive server mode with disabled prerendering. By default, the interactive mode renders the HTML on the server, so the content can be displayed more

---

[10] See https://learn.microsoft.com/en-us/aspnet/core/blazor/components/render-modes?view=aspnetcore-8.0

quickly in the browser, and after that, the classic Blazor Server approach is established, allowing the UI to be interacted with and updated whenever the state changes. However, the prerendering causes the `OnInitialized` methods in components to be called twice – first in the server prerendering stage and subsequently when the UI switches to the interactive mode.

I expect most modernized applications to be rather business applications or intranet portals than public-facing sites where the time to content is crucial for achieving a good search engine ranking. That is why I think the server rendering is not crucial in our case, but feel free to change the mode to your preferences.

Migrating Layout Page

Before migrating the first page, we must build the layout page. As you can see in Figure 8-11, the menu of our example application contains the sign-in button and the currency selection component. Like in the previous chapter, the selected currency is stored in the session.

Basically, we are rewriting the `Pages/Site.master` file and its code-behind class. Instead of quoting the entire file here, I will focus only on the important parts. Most of the menu structure is built using pure HTML elements with Bootstrap CSS classes – you can copy them from the Web Forms master page. You can safely remove the `<form>` element that wraps the entire page and clean any other parts of the HTML file.

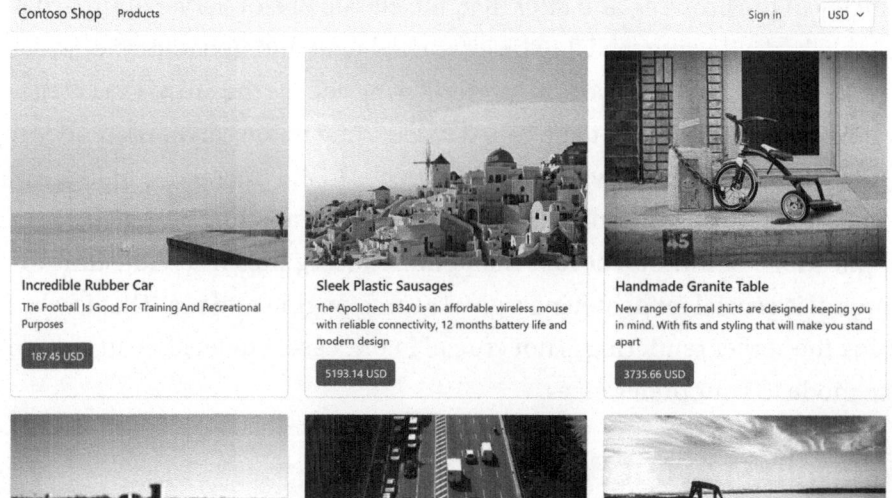

Figure 8-11. *Example application with menu and currency selection component*

The only Web Forms components in the original master page are `<asp:LoginView>`, `<asp:LoginStatus>`, and `<asp:DropDownList>`. The corresponding part of the Blazor implementation in the (Layout/ MainLayout.razor) is shown in Listing 8-9.

Listing 8-9. Converting the master page

```
@using Microsoft.AspNetCore.Components.Authorization
@using ModernizationDemo.AppNew.Services
@inject SelectedCurrencyService selectedCurrencyService
@inherits LayoutComponentBase
...
<ul class="navbar-nav mb-2 mb-lg-0">
    <AuthorizeView>
        <li class="nav-item">
```

```
            <a class="nav-link"
                href="/admin/products">Admin</a>
        </li>
    </AuthorizeView>
    <li class="nav-item">
        <AuthorizeView>
            <NotAuthorized>
                <a href="/login" class="nav-link">Sign in</a>
            </NotAuthorized>
            <Authorized>
                <!-- TODO: requires single sign-on -->
                <a href="/" class="nav-link">Sign out</a>
            </Authorized>
        </AuthorizeView>
    </li>
</ul>
<div class="d-flex">
    <select class="form-select me-2"
        @bind="SelectedCurrency"
        @bind:after="() =>↵
selectedCurrencyService.SetCurrency(SelectedCurrency)">
        <option value="USD">USD</option>
        <option value="EUR">EUR</option>
        <option value="JPY">JPY</option>
        <option value="GBP">GBP</option>
    </select>
</div>
...
@code {
    public string SelectedCurrency { get; set; }
```

```
protected override void OnInitialized()
{
    SelectedCurrency =
        selectedCurrencyService.SelectedCurrency;
    base.OnInitializedAsync();
}
}
```

The AuthorizeView usage can be understood quite easily – it displays different content to authenticated and anonymous users. The select element represents a drop-down list bound to the SelectedCurrency property, which is defined as part of the component state. When the value is changed, we call the selectedCurrencyService.SetCurrency method. This service is injected at the top of the file using the @inject directive, and it is basically a reimplementation of the PageBase methods we did not want to share between the projects.

Here is one notable difference between Blazor and the old ASP.NET technologies. Usually, ASP.NET session state was used to persist the temporary state when the user was navigating from one page to another. In the original application, the PageBase class writes and reads the selected currency to the Session collection. The data is stored in memory by default, and a cookie with a unique session ID is sent to the client the first time the session is written to. It is a widely used concept, despite the fact that using the session can introduce many problems. Many web applications relying on sessions behave quite unpredictably if you interact with them from multiple browser tabs because the session is shared between all tabs[11] (because of the underlying cookie that is shared for the

---

[11] Many years ago, I was purchasing flight tickets to attend the MVP Summit conference at Microsoft's headquarters in Redmond, Washington. Since I had a more complicated itinerary than usual, I opened multiple browser tabs to search the tickets for several segments of my journey separately. When I found the right combination, I clicked the purchase button in two tabs I had open. Unfortunately,

entire domain). Also, the session is usually configured to have a relatively short expiration period because long sessions make the application vulnerable to DOS attacks. If an attacker discovers a page that stores a considerable amount of data in the session, it is quite trivial to generate millions of new sessions and exhaust the server resources.

Blazor applications are single-page applications (SPA), and the session, as we know from the old .NET, is neither practical nor easy to use. Navigation from one page to another within the Blazor application is different from the actual browser navigation, which forgets the entire state except for the information stored in cookies or local storage. In Blazor, the page remains loaded for the entire time you interact with the application, and only the corresponding part of the UI is replaced when making the navigation URL.

Therefore, any value you hold in the C# code in scoped services or in the top-level components will remain available for the entire time the user interacts with the application. In the case of Blazor WebAssembly, the values are stored locally in the browser memory. In the case of Blazor Server, the state is kept on the server as long as the SignalR connection with the client remains active.

---

the second click has apparently overwritten the purchased ticket price in the session, and my credit card was charged twice with the amount of the second ticket purchased (naturally, the more expensive one). Luckily, customer support helped me to reclaim my money, but my action uncovered a severe security issue with the website.

When you selected the tickets and clicked the purchase button, the amount to be charged was stored in the session, and after processing the payment, the application did not verify that the actual amount matches the ticket price. This would allow anyone to purchase very expensive tickets for a fraction of their price – just click the purchase button for the expensive ticket, and before entering the credit card information, open a second tab and purchase any cheap ticket you can find. This would overwrite the price in the session, so if you proceeded with the first transaction, you were charged only with the price of the cheap ticket. You do not even need to complete the second transaction – its intent was only rewriting the price stored in the session.

Unfortunately, it is not that simple in the modernization scenario, as some pages have yet to be migrated. Users enter and leave the Blazor application quite regularly when transitioning between old and new parts, so holding the state in memory is not sufficient.

For now, we will not try to solve this issue completely, and, instead, let us focus on completing the migration of the first page. I have implemented the store for the selected currency as a scoped service holding the value in a public property. I placed the class in the Services folder and registered it in Program.cs as a scoped service, as shown in Listing 8-10.

Listing 8-10. Implementation and registration of SelectedCurrencyService

```
public class SelectedCurrencyService
{
    public string SelectedCurrency { get; private set; }
        = "USD";

    public event Action? SelectedCurrencyChanged;

    public void SetCurrency(string currency)
    {
        SelectedCurrency = currency;
        SelectedCurrencyChanged?.Invoke();
    }
}

// Program.cs
builder.Services.AddScoped<SelectedCurrencyService>();
```

Migrating First Page

The first page we will try to migrate is the product detail. In the example project, I have created a folder Components/Pages and rewritten the

ProductDetail.aspx page to ProductDetail.razor. You can find the entire page in the example repository. The interesting parts with notable changes are shown in Listing 8-11.

Listing 8-11. Migrating the product detail page

```
@page "/product/{id:guid}"
@inject ApiClient apiClient
@inject SelectedCurrencyService selectedCurrencyService

<div class="row">
    @if (Product is not null)
    {
        <div class="col col-md-4">
            <img src="@Product.ImageUrl" alt="@Product.Name"
                class="img-fluid"/>
        </div>
        <div class="col col-md-8">
            <h2>@Product.Name</h2>

                        ...
            <p class="lead">@Product.Description</p>
            <h4 class="mb-4">
                @ProductPrice
            </h4>

            ...
        </div>
    }
</div>

@code
{
    [Parameter]
    public Guid Id { get; set; }
```

```
public ProductModel? Product { get; set; }

public string? ProductPrice { get; set; }

protected override async Task OnInitializedAsync()
{
    Product = await apiClient.GetProductAsync(Id);
    ProductPrice = Utils.GetProductPriceWithCaching(
        Product.Id,
        await selectedCurrencyService.GetCurrency());

    await base.OnInitializedAsync();
}
}
```

As you can see, there is no FormView component. It was used in ASP. NET Web Forms only to allow easy data binding in the template (the binding expressions could be used only in data-oriented controls). In Blazor, we load the data in the OnInitializedAsync method, and since the loading is asynchronous, we must wrap the entire section with the if statement to ensure the content is shown only when the data is already loaded (otherwise, we would get NullReferenceException). In today's applications, displaying "skeleton loading" animations[12] is common to indicate that content is being loaded.

I call the Utils class we linked from the old application earlier to obtain the product price from the cache. It uses the HttpRuntime.Cache static member, and if you try to run the example application, you can see it works – the adapters library provides an implementation for this cache.

---

[12] For example, a popular CSS framework Bootstrap has the Placeholder widget for this purpose. See https://getbootstrap.com/docs/5.3/components/placeholders/

Sharing the Session

I mentioned earlier that the classic session in Blazor is quite difficult to use. In Blazor WebAssembly, the application runs entirely in the browser, while the session is a server-side concept. Thus, it cannot be used on the client at all. In Blazor Server, you can theoretically use it as the code runs on the server, but there are many limitations.

First, you need to set the cookie holding the session ID immediately at the first GET request when entering the application. If you try to do it later, the server has no way to send the cookie to the client, as the `HttpContext` at that moment represents the SignalR connection for the particular client. Cookies cannot be transferred over this channel – they must be sent to the client using the HTTP `Set-Cookie` response header. For security reasons, the session cookie is set as HTTP-only to prevent accessing it from JavaScript.

Even if you use other technology than Blazor (ASP.NET Core MVC or Razor Pages, for example), you will have to deal with another problem. Because both applications have different implementations of the session, the data is not synchronized, and many features may not work correctly when the user transitions between the applications.

If you run the example application, you can see that if you select a currency on the home page and then visit the product detail page, which has already been migrated, the currency will switch back to its default value. If you return to the old application, the selection was restored based on the value in the old ASP.NET session. Because we only have one page implemented in Blazor right now, if you navigate to any other page, you will exit the Blazor application, and thus the state stored in the `SelectedCurrencyService` is going to be lost.

The `SystemWebAdapters` packages can do more than just implement the old `System.Web` API to work in ASP.NET Core. The .NET Framework package `Microsoft.AspNetCore.SystemWebAdapters.FrameworkServices` we used to deal with forwarder headers earlier can provide the "remote app" experience. It establishes a secure communication channel the application can use to exchange or synchronize session (and other) information.

The channel is secured by a static API key that you need to configure in both applications. Even though the communication will most probably take place within the same server and will not enter the physical network, using HTTPS is strongly recommended. Along with sessions, possibly containing sensitive data, we will later use the same channel to share identities and claims between the applications. Therefore, it is crucial to ensure the data is not transmitted in an unencrypted form.

One of the features of the package is called Remote session. It can operate in two modes:

- Remote app session

- Wrapped session state

The second option is less important for us. It is useful if you do not want to synchronize the session between the applications and prefer to keep it independent.

In the wrapped session state mode, the old ASP.NET Session API is implemented to use the new ASP.NET Core session. This will make the legacy code that uses `HttpContext.Current.Session` work, but there are some differences worth mentioning. In the old ASP.NET, access to the session was locked in order to avoid concurrency issues. If subsequent requests wanted to access the same session, the access was made in a serial fashion. ASP.NET Core session does not provide any guarantees like that, so even though your old code will compile, it may not behave exactly the same way.

Furthermore, the old ASP.NET handled the serialization of the values automatically (e.g., if the session was stored in a database), while ASP. NET Core session works with byte arrays – you need to serialize the data yourself. The old ASP.NET used binary serialization, which is not even available in the last versions of the new .NET.

The Remote app session mode sets up an API endpoint in the old application that the new application can use for reading and modifying the session data. The session in the old application will continue working without any changes, whether it is stored in memory or configured to work in a web farm environment. The new application will configure the new ASP.NET Core Session API as well as the old System.Web API to access the values using the endpoint in the old application.

The new application can access the sessions in two ways. The first option is read-only access, which will just return the contents of the session and not issue a lock on it in the old application. The second option is to read the session with the intent of modifying it later. In that case, the remote app client will keep the GET request for the session open and wait until you make changes and call CommitAsync on the session state (which happens by default when the HTTP request ends). Only at that time, it will store the session values and release the lock. All this is handled by a middleware that the SystemWebAdapters package installs in the request pipeline. The process is illustrated in Figure 8-12.

Read-only session mode

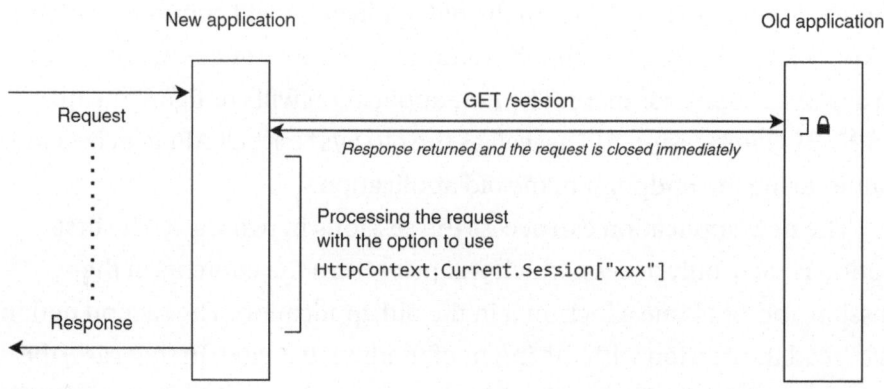

Writable session mode

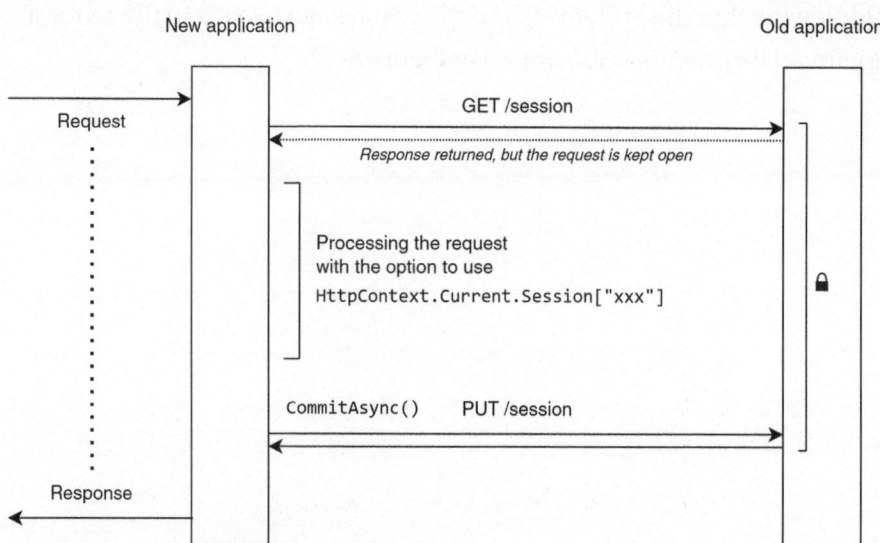

Figure 8-12. *Acquisition of the session state in read-only and writable modes by the SystemWebAdapters package*

This looks quite useful and works well in technologies with short-lived HTTP requests, such as ASP.NET Core MVC or Razor Pages (or even DotVVM). However, the SignalR-based HttpContext in Blazor Server lives for the entire time the user interacts with the application, which can be minutes or even hours. If you opened the session in the "modifiable" mode when this request starts, it would remain locked for a long time (because the request ends only as you leave the application), and you can experience deadlocks. Also, I have already mentioned the problem with creating the session cookie – it cannot be sent to the client using the SignalR connection.

Remote Session

Before I show the workaround for Blazor Server, let us see how the remote app session is configured in frameworks using short-lived HTTP requests. The AddSystemWebAdapters extension method in the new application offers additional methods that can enable session sharing, as shown in Listing 8-12.

Listing 8-12. Configuring Remote app sessions in the new ASP.NET Core application

```
builder.Services.AddSystemWebAdapters()
    .AddJsonSessionSerializer(options =>
    {
        options.RegisterKey<string>("SelectedCurrency");
    })
    .AddRemoteAppClient(options =>
    {
        options.RemoteAppUrl =
            new(builder.Configuration["ProxyTo"]);
```

```
    options.ApiKey =
        builder.Configuration["RemoteAppApiKey"];
})
.AddSessionClient();
```

As you can see, there are a couple of sections. The first section tells the `SystemWebAdapters` library to serialize session data using JSON and provides the data types for each session key. Please note that this setting does not affect how the old ASP.NET stores objects in the session – this will remain unchanged. This setting only tells the adapters library how the adapters library transfers the values between the new and old applications.

The second section configures the remote app communication channel. The new application behaves as a client and needs to know the URL of the old application (the remote app server) and an API key. The key must have a format of GUID. The correct way would be to put it in User Secrets, but we will have to specify the same key in the .NET Framework application, which does not provide an easy way to store secrets outside the `web.config` file. Therefore, I have placed the key directly in the code in the example application, but please be aware that it is not an optimal solution. If you do it the same way, make sure you use the key only for development purposes, and the value used in production is different.

The last method registers services that can work with the remote app session – most importantly, an implementation of the `ISessionManager` interface we will be using later.

In the .NET Framework application, a similar configuration is required. We need to provide the same API key to the library and advise it on how the individual session keys are serialized, as shown in Listing 8-13. The API key needs to be added to the `appSettings` section in `web.config` under the name `RemoteAppApiKey`.

Listing 8-13. Configuring Remote app session in the old ASP.NET
application

```
protected void Application_Start(object sender, EventArgs e)
{
    ...

    SystemWebAdapterConfiguration.AddSystemWebAdapters(this)
        .AddProxySupport(options =>
            options.UseForwardedHeaders = true)
        .AddJsonSessionSerializer(options =>
        {
            options.RegisterKey<string>("SelectedCurrency");
        })
        .AddRemoteAppServer(options =>
        {
            options.ApiKey = ConfigurationManager
                .AppSettings["RemoteAppApiKey"])
        })
        .AddSessionServer();
}
```

This will expose the API endpoint, providing the new application with
access to the session data. The session information will still be stored in
the old ASP.NET application as it was before, but now the new application
will be able to access it.

Now, we can start using sessions in the new ASP.NET Core application. There are two important points to be mentioned:

1. Because of performance reasons, the session is not loaded by default – you have to request it explicitly. If you use ASP.NET Core MVC or API controllers, you can use the [Session] attribute to indicate your code will need the session. Make sure you specify the IsReadOnly parameter if you do not plan to modify the session in order to prevent unnecessary locking. If you use the minimal API approach or want to request the session for all controller actions, you can call RequireSystemWebAdapterSession after calling the particular Map* method in Program.cs. Both approaches will instruct the SystemWebAdapters library to load the session at the beginning of the request pointing to the particular URL and commit the changes when such request ends.

2. The session will be accessible only through the old ASP.NET API – System.Web.HttpContext.Current. Session["key"]. If you try to access the session from the ASP.NET Core context, it will not work because the feature is not yet implemented.[13] Once you finish the migration, you can reconfigure SystemWebAdapters to use the wrapped session – it will start storing the information in the ASP.NET Core session. From that moment, you will be able to start migrating the legacy session access to the new ASP.NET Core API.

---

[13] See the GitHub issue: https://github.com/dotnet/systemweb-adapters/issues/24

Remote Session in Blazor Server

As I already mentioned, the situation is more complicated in Blazor Server. The solution I propose here worked in my scenarios, but it is by far not complete and bulletproof. Please make sure you test your application before using the code, as it may have issues. Also, please note that even though the remote app session uses locking, we will be running two independent applications, which always opens the way for both consistency issues and deadlocks.

Because we use the session in the layout page, we have to request it for all requests that use any Blazor component. We must make sure the session is created during the initial HTTP GET request, and the session cookie is included in the response sent to the client before establishing the SignalR connection. If we create the session later, there would be no way to deliver the cookie to the client.

The default API of the SystemWebAdapters library assumes that you will use the Session attribute or call RequireSystemWebAdapterSession after mapping the endpoints in the application pipeline. This approach does not work in Blazor, as the adapters library installs a middleware that loads the session state at the beginning of these HTTP requests and commits the state automatically when they finish. Therefore, you cannot use RequireSystemWebAdapterSession when mapping Blazor components.

Instead, we will create our own middleware that will obtain the session and set the cookie in Blazor's initial request. An intuitive idea would be to get the session in the read-only mode, but, unfortunately, it is not possible. If the session does not exist, the read-only mode returns an empty result without assigning a session ID. Therefore, the session cookie would not be possible to create.

Therefore, instead of using the standard methods built in the SystemWebAdapters library, we have to do the plumbing ourselves. Listing 8-14 shows how to implement a middleware that detects a Blazor request (based on the presence of the RootComponentMetadata object in the endpoint information and the correct HTTP method) and loads the session state explicitly. The session state is stored in the current request (in the Features collection), so the legacy session API can access it, and it is disposed immediately. This way, the old application will be forced to create the session and will not hold a lock on it for too long.

Listing 8-14. Requiring the session state for Blazor components

```
var app = builder.Build();
...
app.UseRouting();
app.UseAntiforgery();

app.UseSystemWebAdapters();
// TODO: After completing the migration, replace the session
// with a better mechanism for Blazor
app.LoadSessionForBlazorServer();

app.MapRazorComponents<App>()
    .AddInteractiveServerRenderMode();

...


#pragma warning disable SYSWEB1001
public static void LoadSessionForBlazorServer(
    this WebApplication app)
{
    app.Use(async (context, next) =>
    {
        // Blazor SignalR request
        if (context.GetEndpoint()?.Metadata
            .GetMetadata<RootComponentMetadata>() is not null
            && string.Equals(context.Request.Method, "CONNECT",
                StringComparison.OrdinalIgnoreCase))
```

```
        {
            // load session state explicitly
            var sessionManager = context.RequestServices
                .GetRequiredService<ISessionManager>();
            var session =
                await sessionManager.CreateAsync(context,
                    new SessionAttribute() {
                        SessionBehavior =
                            SessionStateBehavior.Required
                });

            // store it in the current request
            context.Features.Set<ISessionStateFeature>(
                new BlazorSessionStateFeature(session));

            // dispose the object so the lock is released
            session.Dispose();
        }

        await next();
    });
}
...

public class BlazorSessionStateFeature(ISessionState session)
    : ISessionStateFeature
{
    public SessionStateBehavior Behavior { get; set; }
        = SessionStateBehavior.Required;
    public bool IsPreLoad => true;
    public HttpSessionState? Session
        => new HttpSessionState(session);
    public ISessionState? State { get; set; } = session;
}
```

We have solved loading the session at the beginning of the request, but we do not deal with the case when the session needs to be modified. Because there can be a considerable time window between loading the session and the user action that requests its change, we will need to instrument the legacy code with a routine to reload the current session state before it is changed and commit the modifications afterward.

For example, if you open the example application and go to the product detail page, the session data is loaded at the beginning of the request. However, the request remains active for the entire time the user interacts with the page. If you decide to change the currency after a few minutes, the session collection may be outdated. Therefore, before changing the session state, you should explicitly request to load the session. We do not want to hold the lock longer than necessary – we should commit the changes as soon as possible.

How to implement this functionality is shown in Listing 8-15. I added the AcquireSessionLock method to the BlazorSessionExtensions class. It should be called with the using keyword, ensuring that the object is properly disposed even in the case of an exception (otherwise, the session could remain locked).

Listing 8-15. Reading and modifying the session in Blazor Server

```
public class SelectedCurrencyService(
    IHttpContextAccessor httpContextAccessor)
{
    private string? selectedCurrency;
    public event Action? SelectedCurrencyChanged;

    public async Task<string> GetCurrency()
    {
```

```
    if (selectedCurrency == null)
    {
        selectedCurrency = System.Web.HttpContext.Current
            .Session["SelectedCurrency"] as string
            ?? "USD";
    }
    return selectedCurrency;
}

public async Task SetCurrency(string currency)
{
    selectedCurrency = currency;
    SelectedCurrencyChanged?.Invoke();

    using (var sessionLock = await httpContextAccessor
        .HttpContext.AcquireSessionLock())
    {
        // modify the session state here
        System.Web.HttpContext.Current
            .Session["SelectedCurrency"] = currency;

        await sessionLock.CommitAsync();
    }
}
}

public static class BlazorSessionExtensions
{
    ...
    public static async Task<SessionLock> AcquireSessionLock(
        this HttpContext context)
    {
```

```
    var sessionState =
        context.Features.Get<ISessionStateFeature>();
    if (sessionState is null)
    {
        throw new InvalidOperationException("...");
    }

    var sessionManager = context.RequestServices
        .GetRequiredService<ISessionManager>();
    var session = await sessionManager.CreateAsync(context,
        new SessionAttribute() {
            SessionBehavior = SessionStateBehavior.Required
        });
    context.Features.Set<ISessionStateFeature>(
        new BlazorSessionStateFeature(session));

    return new SessionLock(sessionState.State);
    }
}

public class SessionLock(ISessionState session) : IDisposable
{
    public async Task CommitAsync(
        CancellationToken ct = default)
    {
        await session.CommitAsync(ct);
    }

    public void Dispose()
    {
        session.Dispose();
    }
}
```

Please note that this solution makes sense only during the migration process when the users transition between Blazor and non-Blazor parts of the application. Once you migrate all pages to Blazor, you should stop using the session at all, as the temporary session can be kept in memory or a more suitable place. You can explore other techniques available in Blazor to deal with temporary state persistence.[14]

Sharing the Authentication State

The next problem you may encounter is the need to share the authentication state. For example, if you sign in to the old application using the Forms authentication, ASP.NET creates an authentication cookie (named .ASPXAUTH by default) to store the encrypted ticket containing the username, expiration date, and other metadata. The ability to decrypt and verify the ticket depends on the machine keys, a concept that is not present in the new .NET.

There are two ways to resolve the issue. One is to set up an external identity provider and integrate both applications with it. There are many ready-made solutions you can run on your infrastructure (e.g., Duende Identity Server,[15] OpenIddict,[16] and others) as well as numerous cloud SaaS solutions, such as Microsoft Entra ID (formerly Azure Active Directory).[17] Migrating the entire authentication stack, including the user accounts, to some of these solutions may look complicated at first sight, but it may provide many additional benefits over managing and storing the user identities in your own database. Maybe there are other applications in

---

[14] You can find more methods of maintaining the state in Blazor documentation at `https://learn.microsoft.com/en-us/aspnet/core/blazor/state-management?view=aspnetcore-8.0`

[15] See `https://duendesoftware.com/products/identityserver`

[16] See `https://github.com/openiddict/openiddict-core`

[17] See `https://learn.microsoft.com/en-us/entra/identity-platform/v2-overview`

your company that would benefit from a stand-alone identity provider as well. Furthermore, if you think about introducing a mobile application that would require the sign-in functionality or have multiple APIs where you will need to set up authentication as well, all the solutions mentioned earlier provide relatively easy mechanisms to implement these experiences using OAuth, OpenID Connect, and other commonly used protocols.

The second way is to use the SystemWebAdapters library, which provides a similar mechanism for sharing the authentication state as we saw in the previous sections about sessions. This method works if your application uses Forms authentication and other authentication types that use ClaimsPrincipal and ClaimsIdentity objects. Unfortunately, the library does not yet support Windows authentication.[18]

Remote Authentication

SystemWebAdapters can set up an endpoint in the old application to provide the user identity and associated claims to the new application.

The library will set up the RemoteAuthenticationAuthHandler authentication scheme in the ASP.NET Core project. When it receives an HTTP request, it will send the Authorize and Cookie headers along with the remote app API key to the authorization endpoint set up in the old application and obtain the serialized ClaimsPrincipal object. If the authentication fails, the handler will perform the challenge action (e.g., redirects to the login page).

This mechanism will allow migrating pages as long as the old application handles user sign-in and sign-out. Since there is no mechanism that would work in the opposite direction, you will need to migrate the authentication functionality as the last step. Once you do it, you will need to reconfigure the ASP.NET Core authentication to use the native ASP.NET Core Cookie authentication and make some code changes.

---

[18] See the GitHub issue at https://github.com/dotnet/systemweb-adapters/issues/246

You can see how to enable remote authentication in both applications in Listing 8-16. If you run the example application and sign in, the correct authentication state will be visible on the product detail page we have already migrated.

Listing 8-16. Enabling remote authentication in the old and the new application

```
// new ASP.NET Core application (Program.cs)
builder.Services.AddSystemWebAdapters()

    ...
    .AddAuthenticationClient(isDefaultScheme: true);

// old ASP.NET application (Global.asax)
SystemWebAdapterConfiguration.AddSystemWebAdapters(this)

    ...
    .AddAuthenticationServer();
```

If you use multiple schemes or want to configure which headers should be provided to the authorization endpoint, the AddAuthenticationClient method allows passing another argument with custom options.

There is one caveat concerning the sign-out functionality. If you are in the migrated part of the application, the sign-in button is usually a link that points to the login page (e.g., /login). However, in the example application, the sign-out was actually a button that called the SignOut method in the master page using the ASP.NET Web Forms postback mechanism. The easiest solution is to create a Logout.aspx page in the old project and map it to the /logout URL. Once the user enters the page, you can just call FormsAuthentication.SignOut (or any other code that will reset the authentication state) and redirect back to the home page, as I did in Listing 8-17.

Listing 8-17. Logout page in the old application and updated sign-out button

```
// code-behind of the Logout.aspx page
public partial class Logout : System.Web.UI.Page
{
    protected void Page_Load(object sender, EventArgs e)
    {
        FormsAuthentication.SignOut();
        Response.Redirect("~/");
    }
}

// updated sign in / sign out button in MainLayout.razor
<AuthorizeView>
    <NotAuthorized>
        <a href="/login" class="nav-link">Sign in</a>
    </NotAuthorized>
    <Authorized>
        <a href="/logout" class="nav-link">Sign out</a>
    </Authorized>
</AuthorizeView>
```

External Identity Providers

If the remote authentication method is not possible in your scenario, or if you decide to introduce the identity provider in your solution, you will need to perform several steps.

If your application uses Windows Authentication and your company has already migrated to Microsoft Entra ID (formerly Azure Active Directory), the easiest option will be to use Microsoft Entra ID authentication. You will need to register an application in your Microsoft

Entra ID tenant and obtain the Client ID. When the user accesses any page that needs the authentication, they will be redirected to the Microsoft Entra portal where they handle the sign-in procedure (by entering credentials, using Windows Hello, a hardware token such as FIDO2 key, or any other technology). After verifying the identity, the users will be redirected back to a special endpoint in your application. This redirect will carry security tokens the application must verify. If they are valid and signed by a certificate stored in Microsoft Entra ID tenant, the endpoint will build the `ClaimsPrincipal` object using the information from the tokens, store it in an authentication cookie, and redirect the user to the desired page in the application.

In the old ASP.NET, you will need to use the `Microsoft.Identity.Web.Owin` NuGet package and follow the instructions in the documentation.[19] In ASP.NET Core, the package is called `Microsoft.Identity.Web`, and the configuration is quite similar.[20] Both libraries fit the ASP.NET infrastructure and handle most of the functionality.

If you need to use Windows Authentication with an on-premises Active Directory domain that has not been migrated to the cloud yet, there is an option to use Active Directory Federation Services (ADFS).[21] However, Microsoft recommends migrating to Microsoft Entra ID in favor of using ADFS.

If your application stores and maintains the user accounts in the database, you will probably need to import these accounts to the database of the identity provider. The process will differ based on your chosen concrete identity provider. If you want to use a Microsoft cloud offering, there is an alternative to Microsoft Entra ID called Azure Active Directory

---

[19] See https://learn.microsoft.com/en-us/entra/identity-platform/quickstart-web-app-aspnet-sign-in

[20] See https://learn.microsoft.com/en-us/entra/identity-platform/quickstart-web-app-dotnet-core-sign-in

[21] See https://learn.microsoft.com/en-us/windows-server/identity/ad-fs/ad-fs-overview

B2C.[22] Microsoft Entra ID is meant as a single place to manage accounts for all employees in the organization. Creating guest or external users in Microsoft Entra ID is possible, but this is usually restricted to partners or external contractors rather than a database of thousands or even millions of customers or other arbitrary application users.

If your application contains a database of users where most are not your organization's employees, Azure Active Directory B2C will be a better fit for this use case. You can create a separate tenant just for the application and keep all user accounts there without affecting the accounts in Microsoft Entra ID. The service supports connecting the accounts with social media providers, as well as business and government IDs. Examples of integrating ASP.NET and ASP.NET Core applications using Azure Active Directory B2C can be found in the documentation.[23]

If you prefer using on-premises options to implement an external identity provider, the most popular option in the .NET community is the Identity Server project. Version 4, which was available under Apache 2.0 license, is no longer maintained, but its creators develop and maintain its successor, Duende Identity Server, as a commercial solution. The pricing is based on the number of production deployments and client applications. They also offer a free license for smaller organizations.

Another popular choice is OpenIddict, which is open source and available for free under the Apache 2.0 license. Although it is quite low level and requires considerable knowledge of the principles of authentication protocols such as OAuth and OpenID Connect, I like it for its universality. However, be aware that it is not a turnkey solution – to use it, you will have to implement a few controllers or services and understand the authentication schemes the framework relies on.

---

[22] See https://learn.microsoft.com/en-us/azure/active-directory-b2c/overview

[23] See https://learn.microsoft.com/en-us/azure/active-directory-b2c/integrate-with-app-code-samples

Cache Invalidation

Let us look at another problem the example application has. If you open the home page and then the product detail page, the price will be stored in both application memory caches. If you sign in as the admin user and change the product price, the page invalidates the cache entry by calling the `HttpRuntime.Cache.Remove` method, but naturally the entry will be removed only in the old application. You will see an outdated price if you visit the product detail page in the new application.

A similar issue could occur if you scaled out your old application to run in a web farm when one instance of the application changed some data cached in the memory of another instance. In general, the caching in the old ASP.NET was not prepared for the distributed scenarios. Most .NET distributed caching libraries did not integrate with the built-in `HttpRuntime.Cache` API at all and offered their own API instead.

The old ASP.NET caching had features that are not present in the new .NET. For example, it offered the concept of cache dependencies (a mechanism that can invalidate cached items based on the information from an external source, e.g., the database). For example, the SQL Cache Dependency in ASP.NET relied on a special table called `AspNet_SqlCacheTablesForChangeNotification`) and used triggers to insert rows into this table whenever a change that should invalidate the cache occurred. The application then periodically polled this table (or subscribed to notifications when using higher editions of Microsoft SQL Server) and invalidated corresponding cache entries based on information in this table. Unfortunately, this method was quite cumbersome to set up and did not solve many problems in the case of web farms. This concept is not present in the new .NET at all.

ASP.NET Core, on the other hand, provides two interfaces for caching – `IMemoryCache` and `IDistributedCache`. The first one is, to some extent, similar to what the old `HttpRuntime.Cache` provides. The second one is prepared for running the application in multiple instances, and the important difference is that most methods in this interface are asynchronous, as the distributed cache will probably run in a different process or on a different machine, and there will be some communication overhead. You can find numerous NuGet packages with implementations of a distributed cache[24] – for example, Redis, Microsoft SQL Server, NCache, or Azure Cosmos DB.

Distributed Caching

If your application was already scaled out to multiple instances and you already use some distributed caching technology, your situation is much easier. If you are lucky, you are already using a library that is compatible with .NET Standard and may even already implement the IDistributedCache interface. These interfaces are declared in the Microsoft.Extensions.Caching.Abstractions package, which is available even for the old .NET Framework.

If the library provides a different API, there may still be a chance that it is supported on the new .NET. If not, you will have to replace it with some other implementation, and if there is no common library that would work in both applications, you would need to make a helper code using preprocessor directives, as we did with the Utils class.

If your application is running in one instance and you expect it may need to be scaled out in the future, you can consider migrating the caching code to the IDistributedCache. Unfortunately, this will require changing many synchronous methods to asynchronous (which can get complicated as you will need to make the entire call stack asynchronous). I do not recommend using hacks like calling GetAwaiter().GetResult() – in some edge cases, this can lead to deadlocks in old ASP.NET applications that may use some legacy synchronization context.

---

[24] See https://learn.microsoft.com/en-us/aspnet/core/performance/caching/distributed?view=aspnetcore-8.0#establish-distributed-caching-services

Please note that this refactoring may involve considerable effort, and before deciding to go this way, evaluate how many places will be affected by this change. Sometimes, adding the possibility of horizontal scaling of the application can justify such a large change.

Custom Solution Based on SignalR

Unfortunately, the SystemWebAdapters library does not include any feature to help us with caching. Therefore, in simpler scenarios with only one instance of the new application, I used a custom implementation based on SignalR Core to notify the other application that a particular cache entry was updated or removed.

Please note that this solution does not aspire to provide reliability or achieve greater data consistency. It is not distributed caching – this mechanism does not share the cached data between applications. Instead, every application is responsible for populating its own cache. This solution provides only simple broadcast notification to the other applications to inform them that a particular cache entry has been invalidated.

The solution uses SignalR Core because its client-side part can be used even in .NET Framework projects. Therefore, the new ASP.NET Core application will host a SignalR Core hub listening for notifications about invalidated cache entries and distributing them to all connected clients. Usually, there will be only one client (the old application), as this scenario is not designed for multiple instances of the new application. But if the old application has more instances, it should still work.

The old application will start a SignalR Core client that connects to the hub and tries to reconnect every five seconds in the case of any connection issue.

Because the HttpRuntime.Cache is not extensible enough and does not trigger any event when cache entries are modified or deleted, you will need to notify the other applications explicitly in any places where you update or remove cache entries.

As I already mentioned, the solution may not be reliable. If the connection between the applications is interrupted for any reason, there is a risk of losing messages. Thus, the information that a particular cache item has been invalidated may not reach the other application.

On the other hand, since both applications will probably run on the same machine, the risk of connection issues is not high. I can imagine only a few reasons for losing the connection – the most likely case is when either of the applications crashes or is restarted, which should not happen very often and would lead to clearing the entire cache anyway. The worst thing that can happen is that some outdated entries may remain in the cache because the corresponding messages got lost, but it is basically the same situation as if we did not have this solution implemented at all.

Let us start with the server-side part of SignalR Core implemented in the new ASP.NET Core application. Listing 8-18 shows how the SignalR hub looks like and how it is registered in `Program.cs`. Notice the `ShortCircuit` call that skips the authentication and authorization middlewares. This is necessary because of a bug in the Remote authentication feature of `SystemWebAdapters` that throws exceptions when the Hub tries to authenticate using the default scheme. Because of skipping the authentication middlewares, I have to check the API key in the `OnConnectedAsync` method of the Hub.

Listing 8-18. SignalR Core Hub for notifications about cache entry invalidation

```
public class CacheInvalidationHub(IConfiguration configuration)
    : Hub
{
    public override Task OnConnectedAsync()
    {
        var apiKey = Context.GetHttpContext()!
            .Request.Headers["X-API-Key"];
```

```
    if (!string.Equals(
        apiKey, configuration["RemoteAppApiKey"],
        StringComparison.OrdinalIgnoreCase))
    {
        throw new UnauthorizedAccessException();
    }
    return base.OnConnectedAsync();
}

public async Task OnCacheEntryInvalidated(string cacheKey)
{
    // client informed us that a cache entry
    // was invalidated;
    // remove it from the cache and tell the other clients
    HttpRuntime.Cache.Remove(cacheKey);

    await Clients.Others.SendAsync(
        "OnCacheEntryInvalidated", cacheKey);
}

public static void NotifyCacheEntryInvalidated(
    IHubContext<CacheInvalidationHub> hubContext,
    string cacheKey)
{
    // a helper method to be called after we
    // invalidate cache item
    Task.Run(async () => {
        await hubContext.Clients.All.SendAsync(
            "OnCacheEntryInvalidated", cacheKey);
    });
}
}
```

```
// Program.cs registration
...
app.UseSystemWebAdapters();
app.LoadSessionForBlazorServer();

app.MapHub<CacheInvalidationHub>("_migration/cache-invalidate")
    .ShortCircuit();

app.MapRazorComponents<App>()
    .AddInteractiveServerRenderMode();
...
```

The code in the old ASP.NET application is quite similar. The interesting part is the automatic reconnect logic. The WithAutomaticReconnects specifies a custom strategy that will try to reconnect indefinitely, but this logic does not take place if the initial connection made by StartAsync fails. Therefore, I use a while loop to retry the initial attempt myself. Once the connection is created, I wait for an indefinite amount of time (by passing -1 to Task.Delay) and use the cancellation token to quit gracefully when the application ends. You can see it in Listing 8-19.

Remember to add the RemoteAppUrl entry in the appSettings section in the web.config file. In the case of session and authentication, the old application behaved as the server and did not need to know the URL of the new application. However, SignalR Server is supported only in the new .NET, so the relationship must be reversed.

Listing 8-19. SignalR Core client for notifications about cache entry invalidation

```
public class CacheInvalidationClient
{
    private static HubConnection newAppClient;
    private static CancellationTokenSource cts = new();
```

```
public static void StartWorker()
{
    newAppClient = new HubConnectionBuilder()
        .WithUrl(new Uri(
            new Uri(ConfigurationManager
                .AppSettings["RemoteAppUrl"]),
                "_migration/cache-invalidate"),

            options => options.Headers["X-API-Key"]
                = ConfigurationManager
                    .AppSettings["RemoteAppApiKey"])
        .WithAutomaticReconnect(new InfiniteRetryPolicy())
        .Build();

    Task.Run(async () =>
    {
        newAppClient.On<string>("OnCacheEntryInvalidated",
        cacheKey =>
        {
            HttpRuntime.Cache.Remove(cacheKey);
        });

        while (!cts.IsCancellationRequested)
        {
            try
            {
                await newAppClient.StartAsync(cts.Token);

                // wait until the process ends
                await Task.Delay(-1, cts.Token);
            }
            catch (Exception ex)
            {
                await Task.Delay(5000, cts.Token);
```

```csharp
                }
            }
        });
    }

    public static void StopWorker()
    {
        cts.Cancel();
    }

    public static void NotifyCacheEntryInvalidated(
        string cacheKey)
    {
        Task.Run(async () =>
        {
            await newAppClient.SendAsync(
                "OnCacheEntryInvalidated", cacheKey);
        });
    }
}

public class InfiniteRetryPolicy : IRetryPolicy
{
    public TimeSpan? NextRetryDelay(RetryContext retryContext)
    {
        return TimeSpan.FromSeconds(5);
    }
}

// Global.asax
protected void Application_Start(object sender, EventArgs e)
{
    ...
```

```
    CacheInvalidationClient.StartWorker();
}

protected void Application_End(object sender, EventArgs e)
{
    CacheInvalidationClient.StopWorker();
}
```

In both applications, we need to explicitly call the static NotifyCacheEntryInvalidated method after we update or delete any cache entry. I have added a helper method in the Utils class, as shown in Listing 8-20. You can see that in the old .NET Framework, I just called a static method. In the new .NET, we need to obtain the HubContext<T> object from the service provider to be able to access the Hub API. Both implementations will run the task in the background and ignore errors if the notification cannot be delivered.

Listing 8-20. The helper method called after modifying or removing a cache entry

```
public static void NotifyCacheEntryInvalidated(string cacheKey)
{
#if !NET
    CacheInvalidationClient
        .NotifyCacheEntryInvalidated(cacheKey);
#else
    var hubContext = System.Web.HttpContext.Current!
        .AsAspNetCore()
        .RequestServices.GetRequiredService<
            IHubContext<CacheInvalidationHub>>();
    CacheInvalidationHub
        .NotifyCacheEntryInvalidated(hubContext, cacheKey);
#endif
}
```

Like in the previous cases, this solution is just a temporary workaround that should be removed after the migration is finished. Technically, you can still use the SystemWebAdapters library and its implementation of HttpRuntime.Cache, but I recommend migrating either to IMemoryCache or to IDistributedCache.

Other Considerations

The example application was implemented in a way to demonstrate the most common issues with forwarded headers, sessions, authentication, and caching. In real-world applications, you may encounter additional issues. Again, all of them will most probably originate from the fact that what used to be a single application is now two instances that act independently.

Applications designed to support running in multiple instances should be quite safe, at least to the extent that side-by-side migration does not introduce problems that were not already present.

Filesystem Access

Some web applications read or write files stored in their application folder. The old ASP.NET had a special folder called App_Data, which could be used to save files that should not be accessible to web users via HTTP. There were other folders with the App_ prefix designed for various purposes, but in general, the files from all other folders could be accessed by the web clients provided they had a file extension registered in the web server MIME map.[25] In ASP.NET Core, the general rule is that only the files in the wwwroot folder are web servable.

---

[25] See https://learn.microsoft.com/en-us/iis/configuration/system.webserver/staticcontent/mimemap

When migrating the code that works with the filesystem, you have several options. The easiest way is to move the files accessed by the application to a separate folder both applications can access. This requires changes in the code (a different mechanism of composing the path to the files), as well as moving the actual files from the applications to the new place and assigning the correct access permissions on the server.

If the files should be served to the users via HTTP, you will need to register another Static Files middleware to the pipeline to allow for this, as shown in Listing 8-21. Please be aware that if both applications try to open the same files for writing, you may experience typical filesystem concurrency issues. However, this is not a new problem – even with a single web application, you can run into a similar situation when receiving multiple HTTP requests that try to access the same files at the same moment.

Listing 8-21. Registering an external folder using the Static Files middleware

```
// register the wwwroot folder (default settings)
app.UseStaticFiles();

// map the external folder as /storage
app.UseStaticFiles(new StaticFileOptions()
{
    FileProvider = new PhysicalFileProvider(
        builder.Configuration["StoragePath"]),
    RequestPath = "/storage"
});
```

Note that web applications that write in the filesystem require additional configuration if you run them in containers. By default, the filesystem of a container is ephemeral. All changes made to it can be lost at any time when the container is deleted and recreated elsewhere, which is quite a common situation in most of today's container environments, such as Kubernetes, Azure Container Apps, and others.

In these environments, the containers are run in clusters with many nodes, and the infrastructure often needs to move containers to another node to ensure all workloads get sufficient computational resources. If you need to mark a part of a filesystem as persistent, you will need to map it as a volume[26] and ensure it is configured to be shared by multiple containers.

Another option is to use a cloud storage offering, such as Azure Blob Storage. This can be especially useful in cases where you work with huge amounts of data – hundreds of GBs or more. Transitioning to Blob Storage (or alternative services) will require code changes as these services provide a different API than System.IO, which you use to access local files.

Like transitioning to a distributed cache, the number of code changes may not be low. In the case of Azure Blob Storage, the SDK provides only the asynchronous methods, so you will probably need to make changes in the entire call stack. However, these services offer a lot of interesting benefits that may justify the effort, for example:

- They are designed to handle large amounts of data (thousands of TB) and provide very high throughput. Everything is stored in at least three replicas with support for geographic redundancy, and the service is designed to provide a strong consistency.[27]

- You can configure public read access to individual files in the storage via HTTP. Thanks to this, when the users download the files, the traffic does not go through your web server, which can be extremely useful when

---

[26] See https://docs.docker.com/storage/volumes/

[27] The strong consistency model guarantees that after the service performs a write operation, a subsequent read will return the latest updates. See https://learn.microsoft.com/en-us/azure/storage/blobs/concurrency-manage for more information.

working with large amounts of data. Several times when I diagnosed performance issues in web applications, the problem was neither CPU nor insufficient memory, but the fact that most of the bandwidth was exhausted by thousands of web users browsing the home page with many images and several videos. Moving this traffic to a CDN or a service such as Azure Blob Storage significantly speeded up the application response times.

- You can generate SAS (shared access signature) links[28] to grant time-restricted access to specific files and operations to a particular user. For example, you can generate a link that allows the user to read a single file for one hour.

- All stored data are encrypted, and you can add a second level of encryption by using customer-provided keys.[29]

There are many other interesting features, but these were the most common reasons I have used to justify migration to Azure Blob Storage. If any of these features would help your application, consider replacing the filesystem access with this or a similar cloud offering.

---

[28] See `https://learn.microsoft.com/en-us/azure/storage/common/storage-sas-overview`

[29] The data is encrypted and decrypted locally using a key stored in your infrastructure. The key never reaches the Azure Blob Storage environment – therefore, the service provider is not able to decrypt the data. See `https://learn.microsoft.com/en-us/azure/storage/blobs/encryption-customer-provided-keys`

Concurrency and Locking

It is not rare to have some logic in the application that cannot be executed concurrently. For example, if you implement a booking system, it may cause significant problems if you sell the same seat for the same time slot twice.[30]

Since most applications use a database for data persistence, the natural idea is to deal with concurrency on the database level. For example, you may have a table named Bookings with the SeatId, TimeFrom, and TimeTo columns and wrap the code accessing the table in transactions to ensure that no seat is sold twice for the same time interval. The only problem with this solution is that it does not work.

Once you start reading about various levels of transaction isolation,[31] you will find out that safety for concurrent INSERT statements can be guaranteed only when using the highest SERIALIZABLE level, but this level greatly increases the risk of deadlocks.

The correct approach would be to open a transaction with the SERIALIZABLE level. Then, you need to select all records that could conflict with the time we are going to insert (any bookings for the seat that overlap with our time slot). This would create an exclusive range lock, which means that other transactions cannot insert any records with column values falling into the range we locked – they will have to wait until our transaction ends. We must check whether the SELECT statement returned any records – if so, we can ROLLBACK the transaction and report that the seat is already occupied. If there were no conflicting entries, we can perform our INSERT statement and COMMIT the transaction.

---

[30] Unless you are an airline company that implements overbooking on purpose (see www.iata.org/contentassets/2e46aace261040b9a47fb7b9da18efc9/overbooking.pdf). But even in this case, you must not sell more seats than the overbooking limit permitted by law.

[31] See https://learn.microsoft.com/en-us/sql/t-sql/statements/set-transaction-isolation-level-transact-sql?view=sql-server-ver16

However, other transactions may access the Bookings table for different purposes, so it is quite easy to get deadlocked. Therefore, our application code would have to implement a retry logic and repeat the entire process if our transaction was killed by the database deadlock detection algorithm. What is more, it may take hundreds of milliseconds until the database discovers the deadlock, which makes the entire process quite slow.

The conditions and rules the application must verify before creating the booking are much more complex in real-world scenarios, and they often require data from other tables. You probably want to load it before even starting the transaction. Otherwise, the rare deadlocks may easily become frequent ones, hurting the application performance even more. Another disadvantage of this approach is that you will probably have to implement the same validation rules in both SQL and the application code, which leads to code redundancy and increases the risk of inconsistency whenever the validation logic changes.

Unsurprisingly, many developers resigned to deal with the issue on the database level. If you can safely assume that your application will run in a single instance, it is quite simple to wrap your code with a simple lock to ensure the bookings are created sequentially. The solution has numerous benefits – the code will be easy to understand and will not require a deep understanding of the complex model of SQL transactions and all its peculiarities, and because of avoiding the slow deadlock detection mechanism, it will probably be considerably faster.

However, once you decide to use side-by-side modernization for this application, you need to ensure the code is not called from both applications concurrently. In the beginning, the functionality is accessed from the old application. At some point, you will migrate it to the new application.

If you can do it in a way that the old application will lose the way to invoke this code, it should be quite safe – the in-process locking will just move to another place. However, this is not always possible. If both applications run on the same server, you may change the lock to Mutex[32] (both can synchronize threads across processes). Be careful of using asynchronous code inside the critical section defined by the Mutex – Mutex requires its WaitOne and ReleaseMutex operations to be called from the same thread. There is also an alternative class called AsyncCrossProcessMutex available in the Microsoft.VisualStudio. Threading NuGet package which does not have this limitation.

If your application does not run on the same machine, you will need to use a distributed locking mechanism. Various technologies exist for that. For example, Redis offers a nice mechanism of distributed locks, and there is an easy-to-use NuGet package[33] for that. Alternatively, SQL Server offers its own stored procedure[34] that can be used for this purpose.

The last approach I want to mention is a bit more universal and may require more effort to implement, but as in previous situations, it may be justified by the benefits and possibilities it provides. You can implement a separate worker service to perform these complex operations sequentially using the concept of reliable queues. When the applications need to create a booking, they will send a request in the queue. The worker will pick items from the queue and process them sequentially. This can be extended for more than one type of task, and thanks to the sequential processing, it eliminates the risk of inconsistencies or conflicts.

---

[32] See https://learn.microsoft.com/en-us/dotnet/api/system.threading. mutex?view=net-8.0

[33] See https://github.com/madelson/DistributedLock

[34] See https://learn.microsoft.com/en-us/sql/relational-databases/ system-stored-procedures/sp-getapplock-transact-sql?view=sql-server-ver16

You may already be dealing with a situation where running multiple complex actions simultaneously causes performance issues (e.g., generating reports and documents or performing some complex calculations). Moving these processes outside of the web application and ensuring sequential processing using queues may also improve the application's responsiveness.

As I mentioned, this is a more complex change and will require more effort. Sometimes, you will even need to update the user interface, as there is no guarantee that the action be processed immediately – it may take a few seconds or minutes if there are other tasks in the queue.

Migrating Remaining Pages

After you successfully deal with all the infrastructure challenges described in previous sections, you may continue migrating the other application pages. Instead of describing the differences between the ASP.NET Web Forms and Blazor markup and components, I will only highlight the most notable differences I made in the example project.

If you want to learn more, I recommend a free ebook Blazor for ASP. NET Web Forms Developers[35] written directly by authors of Blazor or a complete guide into Microsoft Blazor by Peter Himschoot.[36]

- Migration of the home page (`Components/Pages/Default.razor`) was quite easy. I had to implement a custom paging control (`Components/Controls/Pager.razor`), which obtains the page index, page size, and the total number of records. It can fire the `OnPageIndexChanged` event when the user switches

---

[35] See `https://learn.microsoft.com/en-us/dotnet/architecture/blazor-for-web-forms-developers/`

[36] Himschoot, Peter. Microsoft Blazor: Building Web Applications in .NET 6 and Beyond. Apress, 2022.

to another page. I also had to subscribe to the event emitted by SelectedCurrencyService to reload the data when the user switches the currency (and unsubscribe in the Dispose method to avoid memory leaks[37]).

- To implement the admin product list page (Components/Pages/Admin/Products.razor) with ASP.NET Web Forms GridView component, I used the GridView implementation from the BlazorWebFormsComponents[38] package I mentioned earlier. Although it does not support all the features of the Web Forms version, it saved quite a lot of work. Instead of using the SelectMethod (which does not seem to support asynchronous operations and requires paging parameters even though the control does not support them yet), it is possible to bind the collection of records directly with the Items property.

- The implementation of GridView in the package supports the most frequently used column types, but, unfortunately, you have to specify ItemType in each of them – they cannot infer it from the parent control. The ItemTemplate must specify Context="item" in order to be able to access the object bound to the current row.

---

[37] The SelectedCurrencyService is registered as a scoped dependency, but in Blazor Server, the scope lives for the entire time the user interacts with the application. If you leave the home page, the event declared in the service will still hold a reference to the OnSelectedCurrencyChanged method on the instance of the Blazor home page component, and thus this component (which may hold references to many other objects) cannot be collected by the GC.

[38] See https://fritzandfriends.github.io/BlazorWebFormsComponents/ DataControls/GridView/

- GridView does not support paging, but it is not difficult
  to implement your own paging experience that looks
  closely enough to what the users had in the Web Forms
  application. Listing 8-22 shows the excerpt from the
  GridView control migration.

Listing 8-22. Using GridView from the
BlazorWebFormsComponents package

```
@if (Items != null && ProductPrices != null)
{
    <GridView ItemType="ProductModel"
        Items="Items"
        DataKeyNames="Id"
        AutoGenerateColumns="false"
        CssClass="table table-bordered">
        <Columns>
            <TemplateField HeaderText="Image"
                ItemType="ProductModel">
                <ItemTemplate Context="item">
                    <img src="@item.ImageUrl" alt="@item.Name"
                        class="img-fluid" />
                </ItemTemplate>
            </TemplateField>
            <BoundField DataField="Name" HeaderText="Name"
                ItemType="ProductModel" />
            <BoundField DataField="Description"
                HeaderText="Description"
                ItemType="ProductModel" />
            ...
        </Columns>
    </GridView>
```

```
}
<table class="grid-pager-row">
    <NumericPager PageSize="@PageSize"
        PageIndex="@PageIndex"
        TotalRecordsCount="@TotalRecords"
        OnPageIndexChanged="@(async (pageIndex) =>
            await OnPageIndexChanged(pageIndex))"/>
</table>
```

- I had to make bigger changes on the admin product detail page in the Components/Pages/Admin/ ProductDetail.razor file. The page is quite complex as it handles both inserting and editing of products and also allows inserting, updating, and deleting of product prices for each currency (I wanted to demonstrate a more complicated form that works with dependent entities).

- The Web Forms implementation uses the FormView component, which is present in the BlazorWebFormsComponents package, but I decided not to use it as it does not add much value. To decide whether the insert or edit version of the main form should be displayed, I simply used an if block.

- To use validation, I wrapped the editable fields in the EditForm built-in Blazor component and used DataAnnotationsValidator to add support for inferring validation rules from the data annotation attributes. Because I cannot edit the model classes in the ModernizationDemo.BackendClient project as they are generated by the OpenAPI tooling, I defined the attributes in separate classes (using the same property names) and used the `TypeDescriptor` API to tell Blazor to search the validation attributes in these metadata classes, as shown in Listing 8-23.

- I again used the `GridView` control from `BlazorWebFormsComponents` to implement the price editing experience. Because the component does not support the row edit functionality, I had to define my own `EditedCurrency` property and use `TemplateField` with `if` blocks to render either the read-only or editable field.

- What is a bit unpleasant is that you cannot easily use the Blazor `EditForm` component in tables, as each table cell is in a different `<td>` element, and there is no way of inserting the `<form>` element inside the `<tr>` element. Luckily, I only had one editable field in my grid, so I could put the `EditForm` control in the table cell and use the `EditContext` object directly to call validation in the `UpdatePrice` method.

- The form to insert a new price row was made as a separate `EditFor` under the `GridView`. Because I needed to add a custom validation rule (to prevent users from inserting prices for a currency that is already defined), I had to define `ValidationMessageStore` to be able to add arbitrary validation errors there. See the `InsertPrice` method that contains the validation.

Listing 8-23. Defining validation attributes in nested classes

```
public partial class ProductCreateEditModel
{
    public class Metadata
    {
        [Required(ErrorMessage = "Product name is required!")]
        public string Name { get; set; }

        [Required(ErrorMessage =
            "Product description is required!")]
        public string Description { get; set; }

        [Required(ErrorMessage = "Product image is required!")]
        public string ImageUrl { get; set; }
    }
}

// run the following code at the application start
TypeDescriptor.AddProviderTransparent(
    new AssociatedMetadataTypeTypeDescriptionProvider(
        typeof(ProductCreateEditModel),
        typeof(ProductCreateEditModel.Metadata)),
    typeof(ProductCreateEditModel));
```

- The last page I prepared for the migration (but did not migrate entirely) is Components/Pages/Login. razor. The Web Forms implementation calls the FormsAuthentication.SetAuthCookie method that is not available in ASP.NET Core. In order to finish it, we need to configure the Cookie authentication in ASP. NET Core, which will be done in the following sections.

- Finally, the old application used the web.config file
  in the Pages/Admin folder to disallow anonymous
  users from accessing the administration part of the
  application. The same thing must be done when
  migrating the pages into Blazor. You can simply add
  the @attribute [Authorize] directive at the top of the
  pages to use the default authentication scheme. If the
  user is not signed in, they will be redirected to the login
  page at /login.

Feel free to browse the entire project in the 04-all-pages-and-handler folder in the example repository to see all details of the migration.

Migrating the Handler

In Chapter 8, we refactored the HTTP handler that generated the RSS feed with products into a DotVVM presenter, which offered a very similar API and worked in both .NET Framework and ASP.NET Core projects.

Because we now do not use DotVVM, we have to migrate the code using means of ASP.NET Core. The easiest way is to use the new Minimal API approach and call MapGet to handle GET requests pointing to the /products/rss URL, as shown in Listing 8-24. The lambda function you pass in the method can define arguments that are resolved either from the URL, request body, headers, or dependency injection, as it is in our case. The method can return a result object or manually write its output in the HttpContext.Response. Since this is how the old code produced its output, I kept using the same approach.

Listing 8-24. Mapping the ProductRssHandler in the request pipeline

```csharp
// Program.cs
...
app.MapGet("/products/rss",
    (ProductsRssHandler handler, HttpContext context) =>
        handler.BuildRssFeed(context));
...

public class ProductsRssHandler(ApiClient apiClient)
{
    public async Task BuildRssFeed(HttpContext context)
    {
        context.Response.ContentType = "application/atom+xml";
        context.Response.Headers.CacheControl =
            $"private,max-age={↵
TimeSpan.FromMinutes(30).TotalSeconds}";

        var feed = new SyndicationFeed();
        ...

        using var ms = new MemoryStream();

        // write to the MemoryStream synchronously
        await using var xw = new XmlTextWriter(
            ms, Encoding.UTF8);
        xw.Formatting = System.Xml.Formatting.Indented;
        var ff = new Atom10FeedFormatter(feed);
        ff.WriteTo(xw);
        xw.Flush();

        // write to the response stream asynchronously
        ms.Position = 0;
```

```
    await ms.CopyToAsync(context.Response.Body);
  }

  ...
}
```

The only change needed in the `ProductRssHandler` class is writing to the Response stream asynchronously. ASP.NET Core will throw an exception if you try to write the response synchronously, and, unfortunately, the `Atom10FeedFormatter` class does not provide an asynchronous version of its `WriteTo` method. Therefore, I created an intermediate `MemoryStream`. After writing to it synchronously, I call `CopyToAsync` to write the contents to the response stream asynchronously. An alternative approach would be to allow synchronous IO,[39] but please note that this setting is application-wide.

Moving Static Files

I have already mentioned what to do with the files the application writes into its own filesystem. However, most applications also contain other static files, such as scripts, stylesheets, images, fonts, or other resources.

Before we can remove the old .NET Framework project, we have to move all these assets into the `wwwroot` directory of the new project. In the example application, the `Scripts` and `Styles` folders were moved to `wwwroot/Scripts` and `wwwroot/Styles` paths in the new application.

---

[39] See https://learn.microsoft.com/en-us/dotnet/api/microsoft.aspnetcore.server.kestrel.core.kestrelserveroptions.allowsynchronousio?view=aspnetcore-8.0

If you plan to run the new version of the application on Linux, you may run into issues with case-sensitive paths if the casing of the files in the filesystem does not match the casing in the application code. This stage of the migration can be a good opportunity to clean up the inconsistencies in the filesystem paths.

I remember one project where half of the references to images used the path /assets/Images, while the other half used /assets/images. It was quite painful to unify all paths (some of them were generated by the code) when the project was moved to Linux containers.

Completing the Migration

Once you reach the point when all functionality is migrated to the new ASP.NET Core project, you can start getting rid of the old project. Please note that this process is not as simple as removing the project in Visual Studio. Some features of the SystemWebAdapters library, such as remote authentication or session, still depend on the old application being up and running.

Remove the Session

Let us start with removing the session, as it is the most problematic and fragile part of the entire solution. Anything stored in the session can be changed to a scoped service, as we saw in the original implementation of SelectedCurrencyService in Listing 8-10.

Because we changed the methods that worked with the session to be asynchronous, you can choose whether you keep them async, as shown in Listing 8-25, or refactor all their usages to be synchronous again.

Listing 8-25. Asynchronous implementation of the
SelectedCurrencyService

```
public class SelectedCurrencyService
{
    public string SelectedCurrency { get; private set; }
        = "USD";

    public event Action? SelectedCurrencyChanged;

    public Task<string> GetCurrency()
    {
        return Task.FromResult(SelectedCurrency);
    }

    public Task SetCurrency(string currency)
    {
        SelectedCurrency = currency;
        SelectedCurrencyChanged?.Invoke();
        return Task.CompletedTask;
    }
}
```

This will allow us to remove all code that concerns the remote session
implementation, including our own BlazorSessionExtensions helper
class that allows using the session in the interactive server-side mode, as
you can see in Listing 8-26.

Listing 8-26. Removing remote session registration

```
...
builder.Services.AddSystemWebAdapters()
    .AddJsonSessionSerializer(options =>
    {
```

```
        options.RegisterKey<string>("SelectedCurrency");
    })
    .AddRemoteAppClient(options =>
    {
        options.RemoteAppUrl =
            new(builder.Configuration["ProxyTo"]);
        options.ApiKey =
            builder.Configuration["RemoteAppApiKey"];
    })
    .AddSessionClient()
    .AddAuthenticationClient(isDefaultScheme: true);
...
app.UseSystemWebAdapters();
app.LoadSessionForBlazorServer();
...
```

Switch the Authentication

The only pages that could not be migrated yet are Login.aspx and Logout. aspx, as they depend on the authentication in the old application. We can now configure the ASP.NET Core Cookie authentication to get rid of the old authentication mechanism and the remote authentication stack. This is done in Program.cs, as shown in Listing 8-27.

Listing 8-27. Replacing remote authentication with cookie authentication

```
...
builder.Services.AddSystemWebAdapters()
    ...
    .AddSessionClient()
    .AddAuthenticationClient(isDefaultScheme: true);
```

```
builder.Services.AddAuthentication(
    CookieAuthenticationDefaults.AuthenticationScheme)
    .AddCookie(
        CookieAuthenticationDefaults.AuthenticationScheme,
        options =>
        {
            options.LoginPath = "/login";
        });
...
```

Next, we have to implement the sign-in functionality using ASP.NET Core cookies in Components/Pages/Login.razor. Because the call to HttpContext.SignInAsync needs to set the authentication cookie, we need to fine-tune two things:

- Currently, we set the server-side interactive mode without server prerendering for the entire application. We have to do it for all pages except for the /login page, which will need to run in the server-rendered mode. When we submit the form, it must not be done interactively using the SignalR channel. Instead, it must be the classic HTTP POST request.

- If the user navigates to the page from another Blazor page, it will be loaded using the SPA navigation. We need to check if it is the case and perform a redirect with the force reload option to ensure the page is loaded through a standard HTTP GET request.

You can see the relevant fragment of the page in Listing 8-28.

Listing 8-28. Blazor version of the login page

```
@page "/login"
@inject ApiClient apiClient
@inject NavigationManager navigation
@inject IHttpContextAccessor httpContextAccessor

<EditForm EditContext="editContext"
        OnValidSubmit="async () => await SignIn()"
        FormName="LoginForm">
    <DataAnnotationsValidator />

    <div class="mb-3">
        <InputText id="UserName"
            @bind-Value="Model.UserName" />
        <ValidationMessage For="() => Model.UserName" />
    </div>
    ...
    <div class="mb-4">
        <button type="submit" class="btn btn-primary">
            Sign In</button>
    </div>
</EditForm>

@code {
    private EditContext? editContext;

    [SupplyParameterFromForm]
    public LoginModel Model { get; set; } = new();

    protected override Task OnInitializedAsync()
    {
        // make sure we are in the server-rendered mode
        if (httpContextAccessor.HttpContext
            .WebSockets.IsWebSocketRequest)
```

```csharp
    {
        navigation.Refresh(forceReload: true);
    }

    editContext = new EditContext(Model);
    return base.OnInitializedAsync();
}

public async Task SignIn()
{
    try
    {
        await apiClient.ValidateCredentialsAsync(
            Model.UserName, Model.Password);

        var identity = new ClaimsIdentity([
            new Claim(ClaimTypes.Name, Model.UserName)
        ],
        CookieAuthenticationDefaults.AuthenticationScheme);

        await httpContextAccessor.HttpContext!.SignInAsync(
            CookieAuthenticationDefaults
                .AuthenticationScheme,
            new ClaimsPrincipal(identity));

        navigation.NavigateTo("/admin/products");
    }
    catch (ApiException ex) when (ex.StatusCode == 401)
    {
        ...
    }
}
}
```

The dynamic switching of the render mode is configured in the Components/App.razor file like in Listing 8-29.

Listing 8-29. Dynamic switching of the rendering mode

```
...
<body>
    <Routes @rendermode="PageRenderMode" />
    <script src="_framework/blazor.web.js"></script>
</body>
</html>

@code
{
    public IComponentRenderMode? PageRenderMode
    {
        get
        {
            if (httpContextAccessor.HttpContext!.Request.Path
                .StartsWithSegments("/login"))
            {
                return null;  // server-rendered mode
            }
            else
            {
                return new InteractiveServerRenderMode(
                    prerender: false);
            }
        }
    }
}
```

To handle the sign-out, we do not need to migrate the Logout.aspx page. We can just use MapGet to register a handler for the /logout URL in Program.cs, as you can see in Listing 8-30.

Listing 8-30. Mapping the logout page in Program.cs

```
app.MapGet("/logout", async (HttpContext context) =>
{
    await context.SignOutAsync(
        CookieAuthenticationDefaults.AuthenticationScheme);
    context.Response.Redirect("/");
});
```

Because we configured the login path when configuring the Cookie authentication middleware, unauthorized users trying to access administration pages should be redirected automatically to the login page.

Caching

In previous sections, we have set up the cache invalidation mechanism based on SignalR Core. Now is the time to remove it.

I also replaced the static access to HttpRuntime.Cache with IMemoryCache and updated the Utils class to use instance methods, as shown in Listing 8-31. This required several small code changes in almost all pages of the application (injecting the instance and changing the static calls to instance ones), but the code is cleaner now. As I mentioned in the previous chapter, the Utils class deserves a more meaningful name.

Listing 8-31. Updating the Utils class to use dependency injection

```
public class Utils(
    ApiClient apiClient, IMemoryCache memoryCache)
{
```

```
public async Task<string> GetProductPriceWithCaching(
    Guid productId, string selectedCurrency)
{
    var cacheKey = $"ProductPrice_{selectedCurrency}↵
_{productId}";
    var productPrice = memoryCache.Get(cacheKey) as string;
    if (productPrice == null)
    {
        double? price = null;
        try
        {
            price = await apiClient.GetProductPriceAsync(
                productId, selectedCurrency);
        }
        catch (ApiException ex) when (ex.StatusCode == 404)
        {
        }
        productPrice = price != null
            ? $"{price} {selectedCurrency}"
            : "Price unavailable";
        memoryCache.Set(cacheKey, productPrice);
    }
    return productPrice;
}

public void ResetProductPriceWithCache(
    Guid productId, string selectedCurrency)
{
    var cacheKey = $"ProductPrice_{selectedCurrency}_↵
{productId}";
    memoryCache.Remove(cacheKey);
}
}
```

```
// Program.cs

...
builder.Services.AddScoped<Utils>();
builder.Services.AddMemoryCache();

...
app.MapHub<CacheInvalidationHub>("_migration/cache-invalidate")
    .ShortCircuit();

...
```

Removing the Old Application

Now, we should be ready to remove the old application entirely. To do so,
you can remove the project from the solution and delete the corresponding
folder in the Git repository.

You may also want to remove the configuration keys from
appsettings.json and the ProxyTo environment variable from
Properties/launchSettings.json you may want to remove to keep the
repository clean.

Listing 8-32 shows how to clean up the Program.cs to remove YARP
and the remote app configuration for SystemWebAdapters. You should also
remove the Yarp.ReverseProxy NuGet package from the project.

Listing 8-32. Removing YARP and configuration of the Remote
application

```
...
builder.Services.AddSystemWebAdapters()
    .AddRemoteAppClient(options =>
    {
        options.RemoteAppUrl =
            new(builder.Configuration["ProxyTo"]);
```

```
        options.ApiKey =
            builder.Configuration["RemoteAppApiKey"];
    });
...
builder.Services.AddHttpForwarder();
...
app.MapForwarder(
    "/{**catch-all}", app.Configuration["ProxyTo"])
    .Add(static builder =>
        ((RouteEndpointBuilder)builder).Order = int.MaxValue);
...
```

I recommend keeping the AddSystemWebAdapters and
UseSystemWebAdapters in the project – they might still be necessary as the
codebase may reference the old System.Web.HttpContext objects.

Removing these artifacts is one of the next steps you should take as
soon as possible. Using two different APIs may lead to inconsistencies, and
you can experience issues that are hard to track. Also, be aware that not all
legacy APIs are implemented to use the native ASP.NET Core mechanisms.
For example, the HttpRuntime.Cache API uses a different underlying cache
than IMemoryCache. The new code will not be compatible with the old one.

You can try removing the SystemWebAdapters NuGet package and see
how many compile errors you get. In the case of the example application,
I ended up with no remaining references to the System.Web API after I
applied all the steps described in previous sections.

The only issue I encountered was the need to register the
IHttpContextAccessor I used on several pages. ASP.NET Core does
not add this service to the service collection by default, but the call to
AddSystemWebAdapters registered it. Once I removed the adapters, I had to
call builder.Services.AddHttpContextAccessor() to restore the missing
service.

Summary

Throughout this chapter, I described the process of a side-by-side modernization and the challenges you will face when it comes to sharing authentication state and session or dealing with distributed cache invalidation.

Please consider the solutions I used in the example project as examples that may not suit all scenarios. Many concrete aspects are applicable only for specific technologies, such as Blazor Server running in the server-side interactive mode. I tried to explain the underlying concepts, so you should be able to figure out how to adjust the described methods to fit your environment.

Additionally, on several occasions, I encouraged you to consider making larger changes than necessary because of gaining interesting benefits. Even if you decide not to make these improvements as part of the modernization process, keep them in your backlog and reconsider them after the migration is completed. If your application grows and gets more customers, you might sooner or later need to be prepared for horizontal scaling, running in containers without the need to deal with large persistent volumes, and so on.

CHAPTER 9

Migration of ASP.NET MVC and Web Pages

Because of the number of steps involved in side-by-side migration, I had to take a shortcut in the previous chapter. I used Blazor Server because I believe it will be the most frequent choice in modernization projects, but I did not discuss the alternatives or explain why I chose Blazor Server. In this chapter, I would like to describe other UI frameworks present in ASP. NET Core and give you a bigger picture of what options are on the table.

Available Frameworks

When it comes to building web user interfaces, ASP.NET Core currently offers three application frameworks you can use to build web user interfaces:

- Blazor is the newest addition to the family of web frameworks. It builds on a tempting idea of not having to write any JavaScript code, which turned out to be very appealing for not just a few .NET developers. Your C# code can interact with the page DOM at any time – either it runs directly in the web browser thanks to the WebAssembly technology, or it is executed on

© Tomáš Herceg 2024
T. Herceg, *Modernizing .NET Web Applications*,
https://doi.org/10.1007/979-8-8688-0617-9_9

the server and changes made to the rendered HTML
are pushed to the client through a SignalR connection.
This allows you to build very complex and highly
interactive web UI experiences.

- ASP.NET Core MVC is a successor of the old ASP.
  NET MVC. While using the same design principles, it
  integrates with the new ASP.NET Core infrastructure
  and offers new features such as Tag Helpers[1] or View
  Components.[2] ASP.NET Core MVC is great for public-
  facing applications where you need precise control over
  rendered HTML, primarily to ensure proper indexing
  by search engines. The Model-View-
  Controller pattern allows the code to be easily covered
  by tests and is generally proven to help achieve good
  code maintainability in large applications. The HTML
  is always rendered on the server – any client-side
  interactivity needs to be done by means of JavaScript.

- The Razor Pages framework is a successor to ASP.
  NET Web Pages. It provides a simpler approach to
  organizing the code than the full Model-View-
  Controller pattern and was popular for smaller-scale
  applications. Razor Pages added an MVVM-like
  experience for manipulating the page DOM, but like
  in ASP.NET Core MVC, all HTML rendering is done on
  the server.

---

[1] See https://learn.microsoft.com/en-us/aspnet/core/mvc/views/
tag-helpers/intro?view=aspnetcore-8.0
[2] See https://learn.microsoft.com/en-us/aspnet/core/mvc/views/
view-components?view=aspnetcore-8.0

For the sake of completeness, it is useful to mention two other options you can leverage when building web UIs with the new .NET:

- Using a JavaScript-based client-side framework, such as Angular, React, or Vue, in combination with an API powered by ASP.NET Core on the server. This is probably the most flexible option. You can choose from a variety of patterns to implement the web user interface – for example, React uses a functional approach to build components, while Vue and Angular are quite close to the MVVM experience. You may even avoid using any framework and implement the page interactive elements using "vanilla" JavaScript. Because the frameworks do not dictate any specific way of communication with the server, you are free to use REST, gRPC, GraphQL, or any other kind of API that suits your needs. The front-end and back-end parts are not tightly coupled, they can be owned and developed by different teams, and they can also be upgraded or modernized separately.

- In Chapter 7, I was showing DotVVM mainly as a tool for in-place migration of ASP.NET Web Forms applications. However, it is a full-featured framework running on the ASP.NET Core infrastructure and can be used to build new applications as well. It provides a similar level of comfort and simplicity for building interactive web UI experiences as Blazor (it also does not require knowledge of JavaScript) and can also be used to build highly interactive pages with complicated client-side logic. In contrast to Blazor, DotVVM needs neither WebAssembly (which imposes an initial download of a few megabytes) nor the SignalR connection (which, as we saw in the previous chapter, sometimes brings complications because of the long-term nature of scopes, problematic work with cookies, and so on). An important consideration is that DotVVM is not an official component of .NET and is developed by the community. On the other hand, it is the only framework that survived the arrival of .NET Core and maintains support for both worlds to this day – if only Microsoft provided the same level of compatibility for the built-in frameworks.

Deciding which technology will work best for your scenario is not an easy task, especially in large projects. It is important to realize that you do not have to choose just one technology. Most applications have several functional areas. Using a single framework (Razor Pages, for example) for the public-facing part and another one (Blazor) for the back-office part of the application may be a viable choice.

Additionally, the introduction of render modes in Blazor in .NET 8 and the plans for an easier combination of pure server-side rendering with interactive modes announced for .NET 9[3] tend to push out ASP.NET Core MVC and Razor Pages on the side. No matter if you need a mostly static website or a highly interactive one, it will be increasingly easy to do with Blazor, where you can combine both approaches.

On the other hand, there are also opinions that Blazor somehow does not fit the nature of typical web applications. Although both WebAssembly and WebSockets are web standards supported by all today's browsers, a considerable group of developers think that downloading megabytes of binaries or breaking the stateless HTTP request-response nature with a persistent connection does not justify the luxury of not having to write JavaScript code.

---

[3] See https://learn.microsoft.com/en-us/aspnet/core/release-notes/
aspnetcore-9.0#add-static-server-side-rendering-ssr-pages-to-a-
globally-interactive-blazor-web-app

When we decided to start building DotVVM in 2014, it was because using JavaScript was painful. TypeScript was just at the beginning of its successful journey, and TypeScript declaration files[4] were not available for many libraries. The tooling and support in IDEs could not compete with the comfort we knew from C#. Before ECMAScript 2015 was introduced, the JavaScript language did not get any updates for years, and even if there were new features, you could not use them because the old Internet Explorer 6 was still widely used. It is no surprise that many .NET developers have built up a substantial aversion to JavaScript.

Today, the situation is dramatically different. Since 2015, there have been new versions of the ECMAScript standard released every year, bringing significant feature updates to the JavaScript language. Modern JS has a nice system of modules,[5] it supports the `async`/`await` keywords,[6] and it offers plenty of other features we are used to in C#. The type safety can be successfully solved by TypeScript – its type system provides many concepts I would really like to see in .NET. And finally, the quality of developer tooling has improved to be at least on par with what we have in C#. Actually, seeing how difficult it is for Microsoft to implement the Hot Reload feature[7] to support at least the most common code edits, I often envy JavaScript developers who can just save the file and see the result immediately.

---

[4] Libraries that are written in pure JavaScript do not provide the type information for their API to the TypeScript compiler. However, it is possible to create a special `.d.ts` which augments the library with this metadata. See `www.typescriptlang.org/docs/handbook/2/type-declarations.html`

[5] See `https://developer.mozilla.org/en-US/docs/Web/JavaScript/Guide/Modules`

[6] See `https://developer.mozilla.org/en-US/docs/Learn/JavaScript/Asynchronous/Promises#async_and_await`

[7] Hot Reload allows patching the running process with changes made to the code without the need for complete recompilation and restart.

If you have an unpleasant experience with JavaScript, I recommend an amazing ebook called *You Don't Know JS*.[8] It helped me understand many (often unintuitive) JavaScript concepts and completely changed my opinion of this language. For example, the book explains why this keyword behaves in an unexpected way, how automatic type conversions work, and much more. I cannot say I started liking all JavaScript concepts, but understanding the underlying principles behind these features allowed me to make fewer mistakes when writing JS code.

Choosing the Technology

Deciding which framework to use is different when you start a project from scratch than when you already have a large codebase. In the latter case, you seek an option that will require a reasonably low number of required changes.

For new projects, look at how interactive the pages will have to be. Will the entire website be one big SPA with complicated editing UIs, heavy grids, or multistep wizards? Or is it composed of a number of static pages with just simple forms? Is the optimization for search engines crucial?

In the first case, Blazor, DotVVM, or some client-side JavaScript framework would be a good choice. Does your company have dedicated front-end teams with JavaScript experience? If so, using React, Angular, or Vue may be the most flexible option. Blazor or DotVVM will work better if your team members aspire to be "full-stack" developers or if your front-end team has only experience with CSS and never worked with complex JS frameworks.

In the second case, when the application is mostly static, using Razor Pages or ASP.NET Core MVC may be a better option. Depending on the size of the application and the number of pages, you can choose between a simpler approach of Razor Pages and the full MVC controllers.

---

[8] See https://github.com/getify/You-Dont-Know-JS/blob/1st-ed/README.md

CHAPTER 9   MIGRATION OF ASP.NET MVC AND WEB PAGES

It is worth mentioning that all frameworks built in ASP.NET Core use the same view engine (Razor). If you find out that the choice you made was not optimal, switching to another framework does not require throwing all the work away. Also, remember that you can freely combine multiple approaches in the same application. As you will see in the next chapter, focusing on good separation of business logic from the presentation concerns is what will help you greatly when you need to change the UI framework.

In modernization projects, there is always a strong motivation to select a technology that is most similar to the current codebase. The lower number of code changes reduces the risk of introducing bugs and shrinks the time required to do the migration. There is often pressure to minimize the costs of migration, which may sometimes leave you with only one option (which may not always be best from the technical perspective). Table 9-1 shows the possible migration paths. Please note that many legacy applications already combine multiple frameworks – sometimes for peculiar reasons or because of assumptions that may no longer be valid. I have seen a large .NET Framework project that used almost every technology available just because the developers wanted to try new things. Reevaluate whether it makes sense to involve all used frameworks. Using a unified approach in the entire application has its advantages, such as in easier code sharing, smoother onboarding of new team members, and more.

Table 9-1. *Common migration paths for ASP.NET web UI frameworks*

Old ASP.NET	New ASP.NET
ASP.NET Web Forms	Blazor Server (side-by-side migration) or DotVVM (in-place migration)
ASP.NET MVC	ASP.NET Core MVC
ASP.NET Web Pages	ASP.NET Razor Pages
ASP.NET Web API + client-side JavaScript framework	ASP.NET Core API + client-side JavaScript Framework or Blazor WebAssembly

The first technology – ASP.NET Web Forms – was already covered in Chapters 7 and 8. Depending on your scenario and requirements, you may choose the in-place or side-by-side modernization approach. Unfortunately, the syntax of ASP.NET Web Forms pages and components is not similar to anything available in ASP.NET Core. All views, including their code-behind files, must be rewritten to another presentation technology with a different syntax. We have seen the BlazorWebFormsComponents NuGet package or the ASPX to DotVVM Converter tool – both try to help with this process.

The last technology mentioned in the table – ASP.NET Web API – was covered in Chapter 4. If the client-side part suffers from technical debt (e.g., because of using ancient libraries such as the first version of Angular – Angular JS), you can consider rewriting the UI to Blazor WebAssembly. Since you already have an API, Blazor WebAssembly may be a better choice than Blazor Server.

When using ASP.NET MVC and ASP.NET Web Pages, migration to their ASP.NET Core successors will probably demand the least effort. The next section summarizes what has changed in the Razor view engine and the Controllers and Web Pages API.

ASPX View Engine

The Razor syntax was introduced in ASP.NET MVC 3. The previous versions of ASP.NET MVC used the ASPX view engine with the same syntax constructs as we know from ASP.NET Web Forms. I do not want to spend much time on this ancient format of the views. On the other hand, it quite nicely illustrates the path that led to the syntax we use every day and sometimes take for granted.

The old syntax in ASP.NET MVC 1 and 2 supported some server controls from ASP.NET Web Forms (e.g., `<asp:ContentPlaceHolder>` and `<asp:Content>` to implement master pages) and used the `<%` and `%>` sequences to indicate "code nuggets" – parts of the syntax inside the HTML document that use C#, VB.NET, or other configured language.

Razor uses the @ character to identify the beginning of the code block and automatically infers where the code block ends. This leads to a much cleaner syntax, as you can see in Listing 9-1.

Razor automatically HTML-encodes the printed-out content, which helps to prevent XSS vulnerabilities. The older versions of the ASPX view engine supported only the `<%= %>` sequence, where you had to do the encoding manually (e.g., by calling `Server.HtmlEncode`). The `<%: %>` sequence, which performed the HTML encoding automatically, was added only in .NET Framework 4.0.

Listing 9-1. Differences between ASPX and Razor view engine in old ASP.NET MVC

```
<!-- ASPX view engine -->

<h3>Hello <%: Name %></h3>
<ul>
    <% foreach (var item in Items) { %>
        <li><%: item.Text %> ($<%: item.Price %>)</li>
    <% } %>
</ul>

<!-- Razor view engine -->

<h3>Hello @Name</h3>
<ul>
    @foreach (var item in Items) {
        <li>@item.Text ($@item.Price)</li>
    }
</ul>
```

Instead of using the ContentPlaceHolder and Content controls, the Razor view engine comes with the concept of layouts. The template can use the @RenderBody() function call to declare the place where the content of the concrete page will be placed, and the page needs to tell the framework which layout template it will use by setting its Layout property, as shown in Listing 9-2. Thanks to this, the Razor view engine could be completely independent of the ASP.NET Web Forms infrastructure.

Listing 9-2. Defining layout in Razor syntax

```
<!-- SiteLayout.cshtml -->
<html>
    <head>...</head>
```

```
<body>
    <h1>My application</h1>
    <menu>...</menu>
    @RenderBody()
</body>
</html>

<!-- Page.cshtml -->
@{
    Layout = "SiteLayout.cshtml";
}
<h2>About</h2>
<p>This site is ...</p>
```

If your application still uses the ASPX view engine, you will need to convert the pages to Razor syntax.[9] Because of the differences between ASP.NET MVC and ASP.NET Core MVC, I recommend transforming the ASPX markup directly to the newest Razor syntax using the side-by-side migration method.

Preparing the Migration

The process of side-by-side migration is very similar for both ASP.NET MVC and ASP.NET Web Pages. You will need to set up a new ASP.NET Core application using YARP, and if the projects involve authentication or session state, you can use the SystemWebAdapters remote application functionality.

---

[9] You can find a more detailed description of the differences between ASPX and Razor syntax in the context of old ASP.NET MVC in a blog post by Scott Guthrie at https://asp-blogs.azurewebsites.net/scottgu/introducing-razor

Because both ASP.NET Core MVC and Razor Pages render the HTML on the server and do not use the long-running SignalR connection, the problems with setting session cookies are not present. Therefore, the remote session does not require any special configuration – it works out of the box.

CODE SAMPLES FOR THIS CHAPTER

The migration of data access code is demonstrated in the GitHub repository available via the book's product page at https://github.com/Apress/ Modernizing-.NET-Web-Applications. You can find the entire solution in the chapter09 folder.

The webpages folder demonstrates the migration of the ASP.NET Web Pages application.

The mvc folder demonstrates the migration of the same application written in ASP.NET MVC.

There are several subfolders showing each project in various stages:

- 01-initial-state shows the original application running on .NET Framework 4.7.2.

- 02-all-pages-and-handler shows the project after adding the new ASP.NET Core application, configuring YARP, and rewriting pages and handlers to the new syntax.

- 03-complete-migration shows the final application migrated into ASP.NET Core.

If you want to run the projects, follow the instructions in the Readme file in the chapter09 folder.

Since all solutions are configured to use the same ports, please make sure you are not running multiple versions simultaneously.

You can find the detailed steps you need to take before migrating the first page in the previous chapter. The process is the same for both ASP. NET Web Pages and ASP.NET MVC. Here is a brief summary of the actions to take:

1. Use the .NET Upgrade Assistant extension to create the new ASP.NET Core project next to the legacy application.

2. Install the `Microsoft.AspNetCore. SystemWebAdapters.FrameworkServices` NuGet package in the old project.

3. Add the remote application API key (it must have a format of `Guid`) to `web.config` in the old project and `appsettings.json` in the new project. Same as in the previous chapter, there is no good place to keep the key in the legacy project, so it would not be stored in the Git repository. Make sure you will not use the same key in production.

4. Add the registration shown in Listing 9-3 in the `Global.asax` file in the old project and the `Program. cs` file in the new project to configure the remote authentication and session.

5. Link the `Utils.cs` file in the new project and update it using preprocessor directives to compile in both target frameworks, as shown in Listing 8-5 in the previous chapter.

6. Reference the `ModernizationDemo.BackendClient` project in the new ASP.NET Core app and register `ApiClient` in the service collection, as we did in Listing 8-6.

Listing 9-3. Registration of the remote application in the old and new projects

```
// old ASP.NET project
protected void Application_Start(object sender, EventArgs e)
{
    ...
    SystemWebAdapterConfiguration.AddSystemWebAdapters(this)
        .AddProxySupport(
            options => options.UseForwardedHeaders = true)
        .AddJsonSessionSerializer(options =>
        {
            options.RegisterKey<string>("Currency");
        })
        .AddRemoteAppServer(options => options.ApiKey =
            ConfigurationManager
                .AppSettings["RemoteAppApiKey"])
        .AddSessionServer()
        .AddAuthenticationServer();
}

// new ASP.NET Core project
...
builder.Services.AddSystemWebAdapters()
    .AddJsonSessionSerializer(options =>
    {
        options.RegisterKey<string>("Currency");
    })
    .AddRemoteAppClient(options =>
    {
        options.RemoteAppUrl =
            new(builder.Configuration["ProxyTo"]);
```

```
    options.ApiKey =
        builder.Configuration["RemoteAppApiKey"];
})
.AddSessionClient()
.AddAuthenticationClient(isDefaultScheme: true);

builder.Services.AddSingleton(_ => new ApiClient(
    builder.Configuration["Api:Url"], new HttpClient()));
. . .
```

Now, we should be ready to start rewriting the individual pages to Razor Pages or ASP.NET Core MVC. Like in all previous cases, we will start with the layout page.

Please note that this time, I did not include the cache invalidation scenario in the example application. If your application uses caching, you can find the guidance in the previous chapter's "Cache Invalidation" section. Since the caching is a built-in part of ASP.NET Core infrastructure, the process is the same no matter which UI framework you use.

Like in the last chapter, the example application contains an HTTP handler that is responsible for generating the RSS feed. The migration process is also exactly the same as in the previous chapter. Refer to the "Migrating the Handler" section for more details.

Migrating ASP.NET Web Pages

Until now, the migration process has been the same for ASP.NET MVC and ASP.NET Web Pages, and as you can see, it is not much different from what we discussed in the previous chapter.

This section covers the specific case of ASP.NET Web Pages, a simplified version of ASP.NET MVC. This technology offered a simple convention-based routing, used the Razor view engine, and offered a simple "procedural" handling of HTTP requests.

ASP.NET Web Pages featured numerous extension packages (such as WebGrid or database access helpers, which allowed you to easily access the database with just one line of code), while Razor Pages chose a more spartan approach without many bells and whistles.

The experience of using Razor Pages is much more unified with using ASP.NET Core MVC. Whenever I used ASP.NET Web Pages, I always had a slightly disturbing feeling that the technology was not a native part of ASP.NET. Many concepts, such as authentication or validation, were considerably different than in ASP.NET MVC. Additionally, some defaults configured by the Web Pages collided with other technologies used in the application. Luckily, this feeling disappeared with Razor Pages, at least for me.

When creating the new project, .NET Upgrade Assistant generates the Program.cs file to work with ASP.NET Core MVC. To use Razor Pages, you need to replace registrations of ControllersWithViews with RazorPages, as shown in Listing 9-4.

Listing 9-4. Updating the new ASP.NET Core project to use Razor Pages

```
...
builder.Services.AddHttpForwarder();

builder.Services.AddControllersWithViews();
builder.Services.AddRazorPages();
...
app.MapControllersWithViews();
app.MapRazorPages()
    .RequireSystemWebAdapterSession(new SessionAttribute() {
        SessionBehavior = SessionStateBehavior.Required
    });
...
```

Notice that I proactively added the `RequireSystemWebAdapterSession` method call. We will need the session on all pages, as it is used on the layout page. This setting instructs the `SystemWebAdapters` library to fetch the session values automatically for all Razor Pages and commit the changes (if any) at the end of each request.

Routing

With ASP.NET Web Pages, all you had to do to build a page was to create a file with the `.cshtml` (or `.vbhtml` for Visual Basic .NET) extension and add it to the project. This file contained both the Razor markup and a section with code. For the sake of simplicity, Web Pages used a convention-based routing mechanism. To change this mechanism was possible only by implementing a custom route handler.[10]

For example, in ASP.NET Web Pages, an HTTP request pointing to `/admin/products` would use the following logic to locate the corresponding page:

- First, the engine would look for `/admin/products.cshtml`.

- If such file is not present, `/admin.cshtml` would be looked up, and the path segment `"products"` would be passed as a route parameter to the page accessible via the `UrlData` collection.

- If the URL does not match any of the previous paths exactly, the default documents (`default.cshtml` and `index.cshtml`) are tried:

- `/admin/products/default.cshtml`

---

[10] There were several packages that implemented this functionality, for example: `www.mikesdotnetting.com/Article/187/More-Flexible-Routing-For-ASP.NET-Web-Pages`

- /admin/products/index.cshtml

- /admin/default.cshtml (with "products" as a parameter)

- /admin/index.cshtml (with "products" as a parameter)

- /default.cshtml (with "admin" and "products" as parameters)

- /index.cshtml (with "admin" and "products" as parameters)

As you can see, ASP.NET Web Pages try to match as many route segments as possible to a relative path of the .cshtml file. If none of the segments matches, it tries to look for a default document. The parameters extracted from unused URL segments are available in the UrlData collection.

Routing in Razor Pages works in a slightly different way. By default, Razor Pages expects all files to be inside the Pages folder. You can change this root directory in Program.cs by passing a lambda to the AddRazorPages function.

In Razor Pages, the same URL – /admin/products – would only look up the /Pages/admin/products.cshtml and /Pages/admin/products/Index.cshtml pages. It would not try to look for /Pages/admin.cshtml or /Pages/admin/Index.cshml (treating the last URL segment as a parameter), unless you request it explicitly using the @page directive (e.g., @page "{id}").[11] There is no UrlData collection in Razor Pages – the parameters defined in the route work the same way as in ASP.NET Core MVC.

---

[11] See https://learn.microsoft.com/en-us/aspnet/core/razor-pages/?view=aspnetcore-8.0&tabs=visual-studio#custom-routes

Migrating the Layout Page

The Razor Page markup and code-behind are usually separated into two files, but the single-file approach is also possible[12] thanks to using code blocks (@{ ... }) and the functions block (@functions { ... }).

The Razor Pages markup file must start with the @page directive to indicate the page will be able to handle HTTP requests directly, without a controller. The page may use the @model directive to specify a model object, which can declare properties holding the state of the page and methods that respond to GET, POST, and other requests. If this resembles an MVVM approach to you, you are right – this is a new concept that was not present in ASP.NET Web Pages at all.

ASP.NET Web Pages did not provide the concept of the code-behind model object. Instead, the logic was contained in a code block, usually placed at the beginning of the file, as shown in Listing 9-5.

As you can see, the code first tried to retrieve the selected currency from the session. If the HTTP method of the request was POST and the action field was switchCurrency (this was because the page might have multiple forms, and it was necessary to be able to tell which one was submitted), the currency was set to the new value, and a redirect was issued to prevent repeating the form submission.[13]

The currency form needs to manually render the anti-forgery hidden field and generate the selected attributed to the currently selected currency.

---

[12] See www.learnrazorpages.com/razor-pages/#single-file-approach

[13] This is referred to as the POST-REDIRECT-GET pattern. It is a good practice to make a redirect after a POST request; otherwise, the form may get resubmitted when the user tries, for example, to refresh the page. See https://andrewlock. net/post-redirect-get-using-tempdata-in-asp-net-core/ for more information.

Listing 9-5. A layout page of the original ASP.NET Web Pages application

```
@{
    var currency = Session["Currency"] as string ?? "USD";

    if (IsPost
        && Request.Form["action"] == "switchCurrency")
    {
        Session["Currency"] = Request.Form["currency"];
        Response.Redirect(Request.RawUrl);
    }
}
...
<form method="post">
    <input type="hidden" name="action" value="switchCurrency"/>
    <select name="currency"
            class="form-select me-2"
            onchange="this.form.submit()">
        <option value="USD"
            selected="@(currency == "USD")">USD</option>
        <option value="EUR"
            selected="@(currency == "EUR")">EUR</option>
        <option value="JPY"
            selected="@(currency == "JPY")">JPY</option>
        <option value="GBP"
            selected="@(currency == "GBP")">GBP</option>
    </select>
    @AntiForgery.GetHtml()
</form>
...
@RenderBody()
```

Since we need this functionality on every page, it is a good idea to create a base class for the page model objects and place this shared code there. I have created the PageModelBase class, as demonstrated in Listing 9-6.

You can see that Razor Pages look for the OnGet or OnGetAsync method and invoke them automatically for HTTP GET requests. Notice that I implemented the asynchronous version, even though I do not need it in the base model. I expect the model object to be inherited in concrete pages, and they will probably need to call async methods to load data from the back-end API. Therefore, I picked the asynchronous version and declared the method as virtual. Using both versions simultaneously is impossible – the framework would not know which one to choose.

The same semantics work for POST and other HTTP methods. You can add a suffix to the method name (e.g., OnPostSwitchCurrency), which will trigger this method only when the ?handler=SwitchCurrency query string parameter is set. This is very useful to distinguish which form was submitted if there are more of them. The asp-page-handler tag helper can append this value to the URL for you.

Tag helpers[14] are registered using the @addTagHelper directive at the top of the file and allow the Razor view engine to use custom logic when rendering the HTML element. This mechanism is very powerful and is available in all Razor-based technologies in the new .NET. The other tag helper – asp-for – looks at the value of the Currency property in the model and adds the selected attribute to the corresponding <option> element. It is usual to place the @addTagHelper directive in the _ViewStart.cshtml file, which is automatically included in all Razor files.

Also, notice that all properties marked with the BindProperty attribute will be bound automatically from the corresponding form fields. This prevents the attacker from being able to set any property used in the page model – they can manipulate only with properties you explicitly allow.

---

[14] See https://learn.microsoft.com/en-us/aspnet/core/mvc/views/tag-helpers/intro?view=aspnetcore-8.0

Listing 9-6. Razor Pages version of the layout page

```
<!-- Pages/Shared/_Layout.cshtml -->

@model ModernizationDemo.AppNew.Model.BasePageModel
@addTagHelper *, Microsoft.AspNetCore.Mvc.TagHelpers
...

<form method="post"
      asp-page-handler="SwitchCurrency">
    <select name="currency"
            asp-for="Currency"
            class="form-select me-2"
            onchange="this.form.submit()">
        <option value="USD">USD</option>
        <option value="EUR">EUR</option>
        <option value="JPY">JPY</option>
        <option value="GBP">GBP</option>
    </select>
</form>

// model class
public class BasePageModel : PageModel
{
    [BindProperty]
    public string? Currency { get; set; }

    public virtual Task OnGetAsync()
    {
        Currency = System.Web.HttpContext.Current!
            .Session["Currency"] as string ?? "USD";
        return Task.CompletedTask;
    }
}
```

```
public IActionResult OnPostSwitchCurrency()
{
    System.Web.HttpContext.Current!.Session["Currency"]
        = Currency;
    return Redirect(Request.Path);
}
}
```

The First Page

To verify our base model and layout page work correctly, we can migrate the Index.cshtml page from the legacy application. As you can see in Listing 9-7, the code at the top of the file was moved to the OnGetAsync method, and the variables were changed to model object properties. Notice the FromQuery attribute, which automatically binds the query string parameter to the property.

The markup also required only a few cosmetic adjustments:

- The @page and @model directives had to be added.

- References to the products, productPrices, and pagerModel had to be changed to Model.Products, Model.ProductPrices, and so on.

- RenderPage method was changed to Html. RenderPartialAsync, and the corresponding Pager. cshtml file had to be moved to Pages/Controls/Pager. cshtml (and migrated too – luckily, there were no changes needed except for adding the @model directive at the top of the file).

Listing 9-7. Migration of the Index.cshtml page to Razor Pages

```
<!-- Pages/Index.cshtml -->

@page
@model ModernizationDemo.AppNew.Pages.IndexModel
@{
    Layout = "Shared/_Layout";
}

<div class="row row-cols-1 row-cols-md-3 g-4">
    @foreach (var product in Model.Products.Results)
    {
        ...
        <a class="btn btn-primary"
            href="@($"/product/{product.Id}")">
            @Model.ProductPrices[product.Id]
        </a>
        ...
    }
</div>

<div class="mt-4 text-center">
    @await Html.PartialAsync(
        "Controls/Pager.cshtml", Model.PagerModel)
</div>

// Pages/Index.cshtml.cs
public class IndexModel(ApiClient apiClient) : BasePageModel
{
    [FromQuery(Name = "page")]
    public int PageIndex { get; set; }

    public ProductModelPagedResponse Products { get; set; }
```

```
public Dictionary<Guid, string> ProductPrices { get; set; }

public PagerModel PagerModel { get; set; }

public override async Task OnGetAsync()
{
    await base.OnGetAsync();

    const int pageSize = 12;
    Products = await apiClient.GetProductsAsync(
        PageIndex * pageSize, pageSize);

    ProductPrices = Products.Results.ToDictionary(
        p => p.Id,
        p => Utils.GetProductPriceWithCaching(
            p.Id, Currency));

    PagerModel = new PagerModel() {
        PageIndex = PageIndex,
        PagesCount = (int)Math.Ceiling(
            (double)Products.TotalRecordCount / pageSize)
    };
}
}
```

Having the markup already using Razor syntax is a great advantage. This is very different from the ASP.NET Web Forms, where the markup had to be rewritten to use either DotVVM or Blazor, as we saw in the previous two chapters. In this case, the changes in markup are almost negligible.

Migration of Remaining Pages

The process of migrating the remaining pages follows the same principles. However, several notable differences exist, as we will see in the following sections.

Route Parameters

Because of the different way Razor Pages handle routing, the product detail pages need to declare the route attributes explicitly:

- The `Product.cshtml` page required the product ID parameter in its route. See the `@page "{id:guid}"` directive at the top of the page. To obtain the value in the model object, you can use the `FromRoute` attribute. The same page in the `Admin` folder needs to specify the parameter as optional, as it can also handle creating new products (the URL is just `/admin/product`).

- You can use the same technique to introduce the A/B testing experience easily. For example, the sign-in and sign-out need to be kept in the old application because of the remote authentication mechanism. Therefore, you cannot migrate the login page until the very last step. However, you can at least prepare it in the new project and expose it as `/login/new` by using the `@page "new"` directive. The old version will remain fully functional, and you can try whether the new implementation works (without the actual authentication – it will have to wait until the last step). Once you switch to ASP.NET Core cookie authentication, we will be able to simply remove the parameter from the `@page` directive.

Validation

ASP.NET Web Pages used a custom mechanism for validation: instead of the data annotation attributes, you had to register validation rules explicitly[15] (e.g., by calling `Validation.RequireField` or similar).

Since this API is not available in ASP.NET Core, the easiest way is moving to data annotation attributes and checking the model state in the `OnPost` method. Do not forget to mark the properties you want to bind from the POST body with the `BindProperty` attribute. You can use the attribute on the entire `Product` property, as you can see in Listing 9-8.

There is one issue when using model objects generated by OpenAPI tooling. In Blazor, we were able to declare a metadata class with properties aside from the generated classes and use the `TypeProvider` API to tell the framework to look for the validation attributes on this metadata type (see Listing 8-23). In DotVVM, the same behavior was quite easily done by implementing the `IViewModelValidationMetadataProvider` interface. Razor Pages, unfortunately, require a different approach.

One option is to create a partial class next to the generated model class and use the `ModelMetadataType` attribute to tell it where to look for the metadata properties. However, the attribute is declared in the `Microsoft.AspNetCore.Mvc.Core` NuGet package. It may not be the best idea to reference from a generic class library, which has nothing to do with ASP. NET Core. It is supposed to represent a universal REST API client that we may want to use from desktop applications as well.

Another option is to use different classes to represent the input model for Razor Pages and the model used when calling the API. Although having two classes with the same properties may seem to violate the DRY (Don't Repeat Yourself) principle, it may prove useful – in real-

---

[15] See `https://learn.microsoft.com/en-us/aspnet/web-pages/overview/ui-layouts-and-themes/validating-user-input-in-aspnet-web-pages-sites#validating-user-input`

world applications, the user interface is often not exactly a one-to-one copy of the underlying API model, and chances are that both models divert in the future. Therefore, I declared the ProductDetailModel class used as an input model in Razor Pages, which is then mapped to the ProductCreateEditModel from the shared API client project. Thanks to this, I can declare the validation attributes directly on the UI model class without rewriting built-in model metadata providers (which is quite a difficult task – the interface Razor Pages and ASP.NET Core MVC use looks much more complicated than we have in DotVVM).

Listing 9-8. Using data annotation attributes instead of Web Pages custom validation

```
public class ProductDetailModel
{
    [Required(ErrorMessage = "Product name is required!")]
    public string Name { get; set; }

    ...
}

public class ProductModel(ApiClient apiClient) : BasePageModel
{
    [FromRoute(Name = "id")]
    public Guid? Id { get; set; }

    [BindProperty]
    public ProductDetailModel Product { get; set; }

    ...

    public async Task<IActionResult> OnPostSaveAsync()
    {
        if (!ModelState.IsValid)
        {
```

```
        return Page();
    }

    var data = new ProductCreateEditModel
    {
        Name = Product.Name,
        Description = Product.Description,
        ImageUrl = Product.ImageUrl
    };
    if (Id == null)
    {
        await apiClient.AddProductAsync(data);
    }
    else
    {
        await apiClient.UpdateProductAsync(Id.Value, data);
    }
    return RedirectToPage("Products");
    }
}
```

Forms and Binding

Other changes may be needed in form controls. In ASP.NET Web Pages, the framework did not help even with basic requirements, such as persisting the user-supplied values across requests. To keep the value in the form field when validation failed, you had to set the value attribute to the corresponding Request.Form entry manually, as shown in Listing 9-9.

Razor Pages come with a useful asp-for tag helper, which you can use on the <label> element as well as on the <input>, <select>, and other form controls. It will generate the for, id, or name attribute to the elements based on the provided property path, and it will automatically populate the value attribute on form posts. The @Html.ValidationMessage helper will work in Razor Pages the same as it was before, but I like the idea of changing it to `<span asp-validation-for>` because of more readable syntax (especially if you need to set other attributes such as `class`, which requires the @ prefix because it conflicts with a C# keyword).

As you can see, tag helpers in Razor Pages can hide quite a lot of presentation logic that we had to handle manually in ASP.NET Web Pages.

Listing 9-9. Benefits of ASP.NET Core Tag Helpers in Razor Pages

```
<!-- ASP.NET Web Pages -->
@{
    Validation.RequireField(
        "Name", "Product name is required!");
    ...

    var product = new ProductCreateEditModel();
    if (IsPost)
    {
        // restore the user values on form post
        product.Name = Request.Form["Name"];
        product.Description = Request.Form["Description"];
        product.ImageUrl = Request.Form["ImageUrl"];
    }
    ...

    if (IsPost && Validation.IsValid()) {
        // save changes
        ...
    }
}
...
<div class="mb-3">
    <label for="Name" class="form-label">Product name</label>
```

```
<input id="Name" name="Name" value="@product.Name"
    class="form-control"/>
@Html.ValidationMessage(
    "Name", new { @class = "text-danger" })
</div>
...

<!-- Razor Pages -->
@model ModernizationDemo.AppNew.Model.ProductDetailModel
...
<div class="mb-3">
    <label asp-for="Product.Name"
        class="form-label">Product name</label>
    <input asp-for="Product.Name" class="form-control" />
    <span asp-validation-for="Product.Name"
        class="text-danger"></span>
</div>
```

Authorization

The last thing we can experience in our example project is authorization. In ASP.NET Web Pages, there was no built-in mechanism for it, and you had to either configure it in the web.config file or check the user authentication state directly in the page's code.

The Razor view engine in the new .NET supports the @attribute directive, which allows you to decorate the resulting class with any attribute. Listing 9-10 shows how to use it to specify the [Authorize] attribute.

Listing 9-10. Applying the Authorize attribute on a Razor Page

```
@page
@using Microsoft.AspNetCore.Authorization
@attribute [Authorize]
...
```

Unsupported Features

ASP.NET Web Pages had a modest ecosystem of accompanying NuGet packages[16] that enhanced the capabilities of this framework, often adding quite complex components or ready-made application blocks, such as authentication using social media accounts.

The framework was connected with a product called Microsoft WebMatrix, which was discontinued in 2016. This product was an attempt to provide an easy way to build websites in ASP.NET and PHP, with support for popular open source apps like DotNetNuke, Umbraco, WordPress, and more. There is a documentation page[17] listing numerous features of the product. Unfortunately, many links no longer work. Some of them reference various learning videos, and the funny thing is that the URLs of these videos contain the word Silverlight, another technology with an unhappy ending.

Some ASP.NET Web Pages applications used the WebMatrix.Data package, which provided an easy-to-use API to access the database, or the System.Web.Helpers package containing the WebGrid component.

None of these APIs are available in Razor Pages. You will need to reimplement the functionality yourself or find ready-made components with similar features. I recommend checking out the ASP.NET Core offerings of well-known component vendors – the feature set of their

---

[16] See https://learn.microsoft.com/en-us/aspnet/web-pages/overview/ ui-layouts-and-themes/installing-helpers

[17] See https://learn.microsoft.com/en-us/aspnet/web-pages/content-guide

packages is quite impressive, and it is usually much cheaper to purchase the ready-made component packages than to implement the functionality on your own.

Migrating ASP.NET MVC

Because the last step of migration – switching to ASP.NET Core cookie authentication and removing the old project – is the same for Razor Pages and ASP.NET MVC, it will be covered at the end of this chapter.

In this section, I will discuss the differences you can find when migrating from ASP.NET MVC to ASP.NET Core MVC. The process is very similar and quite seamless – do not expect many surprises.

Upgrading Controllers

The first notable difference is the option to upgrade controllers using the .NET Migration Assistant extension. When you create the new ASP.NET Core project through the wizard, as we saw at the beginning of the previous chapter, you will end up with a summary screen showing the migration status, as shown in Figure 9-1.

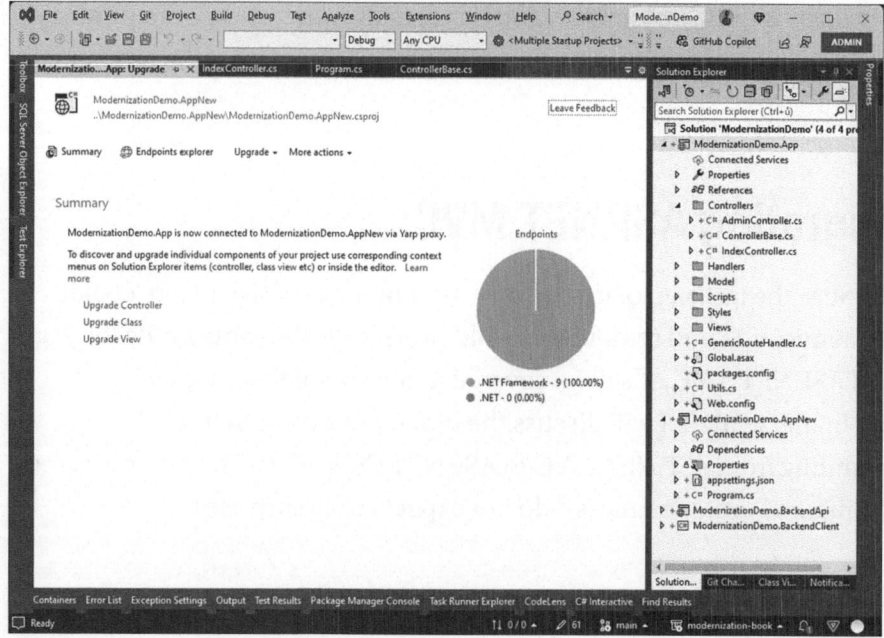

Figure 9-1. *Migration statistics in the .NET Upgrade Assistant*

There is also a second tab called *Endpoints explorer*. It shows all routes registered in both projects. There is a drop-down button featuring the *Upgrade controller* function, as you can see in Figure 9-2.

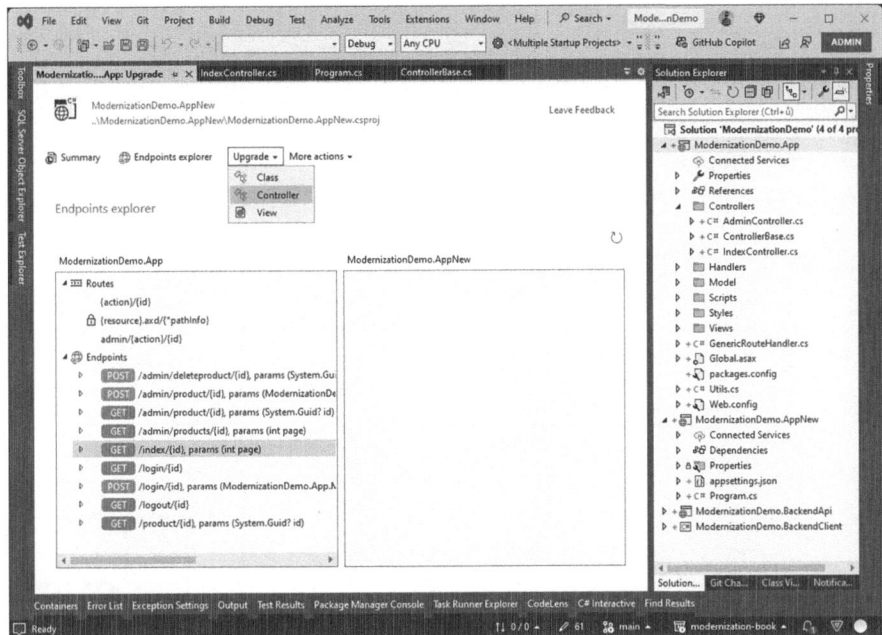

Figure 9-2. *Endpoint explorer and the Upgrade controller functionality*

In my example application, I chose to upgrade the `IndexController`. Since this controller is used by multiple views, please note that you will have to migrate all of them in a single step. If you do not want to do that, you will need to comment out the controller actions or mark them with the [`NonAction`] attribute until the associated view is ready for migration.

When you proceed with the upgrade, the wizard will inspect the controller and find all associated artifacts that shall be migrated with it – views, routes, and model classes that are used by controller actions. You can select which of them you want to migrate, as you can see in Figure 9-3.

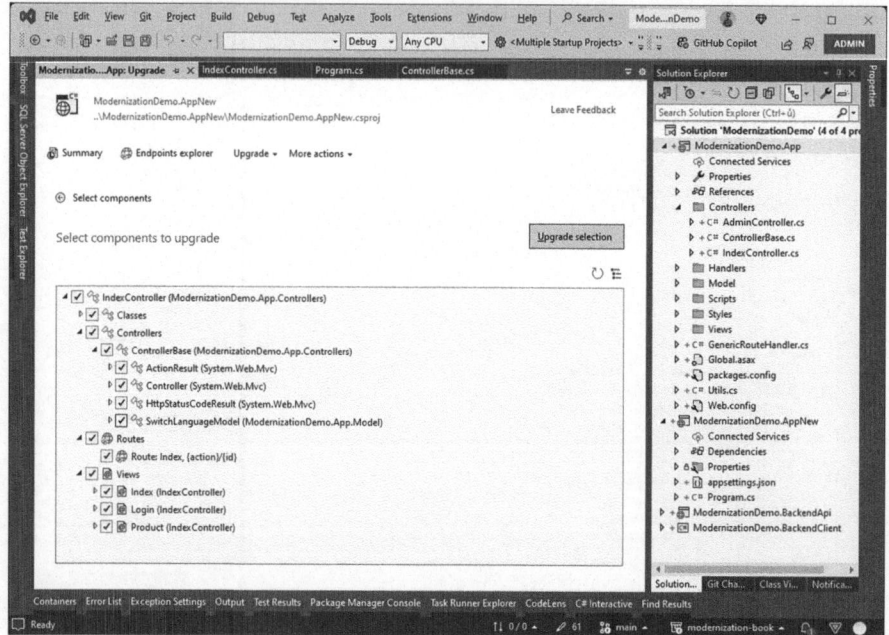

Figure 9-3. *Selecting artifacts for upgrade with the controller*

Although this functionality looks promising, it just copies the files to the new project with only minimal modifications. It is the most useful for controllers, where it can change some namespaces or add missing attributes necessary for ASP.NET Core (sometimes incorrectly, though), as shown in Listing 9-11.

The other artifacts – views, model classes, and so on – were just copied to the new project without any changes. Since the controllers used Global. GetApiClient(), the assistant automatically included even the Global. asax.cs file and the ProductRssHandler.cs referenced from there. I recommend unselecting all classes you do not want to copy – if you need them, move them to a shared class library project.

Listing 9-11. Example of code changes made by .NET Upgrade
Assistant in controllers

```
...
using System.Web.Mvc;
using Microsoft.AspNetCore.Mvc;

[ApiController]
[Route("[controller]")]
public class IndexController : ControllerBase
{
    ...
    [HttpPost("{model?}")]
    [ValidateAntiForgeryToken]
    public ActionResult Login(LoginModel model)
    {
        ...
        // TODO ASP.NET membership should be replaced
        // with ASP.NET Core identity. For more details see ...
        FormsAuthentication.SetAuthCookie(
            model.UserName, false);
        ...
    }
    ...

    [HttpGet("{id?}")]
    public ActionResult Product(Guid? id)
    {
        var product = Global.GetApiClient()
            .GetProduct(id.Value);
        return View(new ProductDetailModel()
        {
            Product = product,
```

```
            ProductPrice = Utils.GetProductPriceWithCaching(
                product.Id, currency)
        });
    }
}
```

If you look at the highlighted snippets in the code, the old ASP.NET MVC namespace was replaced by the new ASP.NET Core MVC one, and the [ApiController] and [Route] attributes were added to the controller class.

We will want to remove the [ApiController] attribute, as it is intended to be used in REST APIs and not in MVC controllers. Except for other things it does, it disables the application/x-www-form-urlencoded content type, which would break our HTML forms.

The assistant also tries to infer the route for HttpGet and HttpPost attributes, but in the Login action, it tried to use the LoginModel object as a route parameter, which will not work. The parameters of complex types are bound from the request body.

Same as in ASP.NET MVC, even in ASP.NET Core MVC, you should either ensure the model object defines only the properties that are safe to receive from the user or use the [Bind("UserName,Password")] attribute to list properties that should be bound explicitly. Otherwise, the application would be vulnerable to overposting.[18]

Fixing the Upgrade Issues

Even though .NET Upgrade Assistant helped us a bit with copying the associated views and model classes, migration of the layout page and the first views still requires some work.

---

[18] See https://learn.microsoft.com/en-us/aspnet/core/data/ef-mvc/crud?vi ew=aspnetcore-8.0#security-note-about-overposting

The example application used the controller's `Initialize` method to populate the currency field from the session. Since no such method exists in ASP.NET Core MVC controllers, I had to move this logic to a read-only property. Since the controllers in the application are not typical CRUDs, I decided to avoid the default route and specify the routes explicitly on every action, as you can see in Listing 9-12.

Listing 9-12. Explicit routes in controller and migration of the Initialize method

```
[Route("")]
public class IndexController(ApiClient apiClient)
    : ControllerBase
{
    public string Currency =>
        System.Web.HttpContext.Current.Session["Currency"]
        as string ?? "USD";

    ...

    [HttpGet]
    public async Task<ActionResult> Index(int page = 0)
    {
        ...
    }

    // temporary URL to keep the old version
    [HttpGet("login/new")]
    public ActionResult Login()
    {
        ...
    }

    // temporary URL to keep the old version
    [HttpPost("login/new")]
```

```
[ValidateAntiForgeryToken]
public async Task<ActionResult> Login(LoginModel model)
{
    ...
}

// temporary URL to keep the old version
[HttpGet("logout/new")]
public ActionResult Logout()
{
    ...
}

[HttpGet("product/{id?}")]
public async Task<ActionResult> Product(Guid? id)
{
    ...
}
}
```

This allowed me to fix the startup code generated by .NET Upgrade Assistant, as shown in Listing 9-13. The code the assistant added to Program.cs would not work anyway because the controller route was registered after the YARP catch-all middleware. As you can see, I can use just the MapControllers method without specifying the default route to use URL templates defined in controllers.

Listing 9-13. Modifying the auto-generated controller registration to use explicit routes

```
app.MapDefaultControllerRoute();
app.MapControllers()
    .RequireSystemWebAdapterSession(new SessionAttribute()
    {
```

SessionBehavior = SessionStateBehavior.Required

```
});
app.MapForwarder("/{**catch-all}", ...);

app.MapControllerRoute("Index", "{action=Index}/{id?}", new
{
    controller = "Index"
});
```

Surprisingly, the example application required only a few changes in the migrated views.

In the View/Shared/_Layout.cshtml page, the currency switching form passed the current request URL as a returnUrl parameter to the <form> element to be able to redirect the user back to the page they came from. Instead of using Request.RawUrl, we have to use Context.Request. GetEncodedPathAndQuery() and import the corresponding namespace.

The Views/_ViewStart.cshtml required an explicit use of System. Web.HttpContext.Current.Session to access the remote session. As discussed in the previous chapter, the remote session experience made by the SystemWebAdapters library does not populate the ASP.NET Core HttpContext's session but only the legacy one.

Both changes are actually symptoms of a deeper problem – we were using various HttpContext features directly in the MVC views, which is not the clean and recommended approach. Ideally, the views should gather all the information from the model object or from the ViewBag collection. Not only because these two concepts did not change at all between ASP. NET MVC and ASP.NET Core MVC – having the logic for extracting data from the HttpContext in the controller instead of in the views makes the code easily testable. Additionally, the views in ASP.NET Core do not have the Request, Response, Session, and other properties of the HttpContext – you need to access them via the Context property, which asks for other code changes.

In `Views/Index/Index.cshtml`, you can see a warning on the `@Html.Partial` line – this call should be modified to its async version: `@await Html.PartialAsync(...)`.

To be able to compile the application and try the home page, product detail, and login page, all controlled by the `IndexController`, I had to temporarily comment out the Forms authentication code. As with Razor Pages, we have to postpone migration of the sign-in and sign-out functionality since the remote authentication mechanism installed by `SystemWebAdapters` requires it to be handled in the old application. However, we can add the `/new` route suffix to the migrated views to be able to try them out.

All in all, the number of necessary code modifications in the views was very low. A huge portion of ASP.NET MVC API is available in ASP.NET Core MVC in its original form, albeit with subtle changes (asynchronous methods, and so on). The controllers are the place where you can expect more issues, and as you can see, the .NET Upgrade Assistant helped us only to a limited extent. Additionally, the controllers are sometimes shared by several views, and it may not be feasible to migrate them all at once.

I showcased the controller upgrade feature as one of the options, but feel free to migrate the views and the corresponding controller actions manually in a more granular approach. This can ensure no unwanted code is copied into the new project. The .NET Upgrade Assistant can, in some cases, bring clutter to the new project – especially if you are not cautious when selecting the classes that should be migrated.

Migration of Remaining Pages

During the migration of the remaining pages in the example application, I noticed just several differences:

- The @Html.BeginForm helper automatically includes the anti-forgery token. In ASP.NET MVC, we had to call @Html.AntiForgeryToken() manually in every form, while in ASP.NET Core MVC, this is not needed. This can help you discover places where you forgot to call @Html.AntiForgeryToken and decorate the corresponding action with the [ValidateAntiForgeryToken] attribute. ASP.NET Core MVC also added the [AutoValidateAntiForgeryToken] attribute you can apply on a controller level or globally – it will turn on the validation for all CSRF-unsafe HTTP methods. If your application contains only MVC controllers, it is a good idea to use this attribute globally, as shown in Listing 9-14.

- Like with Razor Pages, redirecting the model metadata validation using the TypeDescriptor API does not work in ASP.NET Core MVC. To avoid adding a reference to ASP.NET Core MVC NuGet packages in the shared project, I created a special AdminProductDetailModel model object with the properties required in the user interface. Please refer to the "Validation" section earlier in the chapter for more details.

Listing 9-14. Enabling automatic anti-forgery token validation in Program.cs

```
...
builder.Services.AddControllersWithViews(options =>
{
    options.Filters.Add(
        new AutoValidateAntiforgeryTokenAttribute());
});
...
```

Overall, the experience of moving from ASP.NET MVC to ASP.NET Core MVC is probably the most seamless. The HTML helper methods work mostly the same. You may eventually migrate them to the tag helpers to benefit from the new features – primarily the more readable syntax. The controllers only changed the namespace and the base class, and there may be subtle changes in routing and model binding attributes.

The code is fairly well organized, thanks to the MVC pattern, which did not change at all. I believe it adds to the smoothness of the migration.

Final Step

Once all pages are rewritten to Razor Pages or ASP.NET Core MVC and the remaining functions (such as HTTP handlers) are migrated to the new project, the last step is not different from the one we took in the previous chapter. That is why I will only provide the list of necessary steps – feel free to return to the last section of Chapter 8 to find more details.

- First, we will need to get rid of the remote session. If the legacy System.Web API is used in many places in the code, you may transition to the SystemWebAdapters wrapped session, as shown in Listing 9-15. A full migration to the new ASP.NET Core Session (we saw it in Chapter 8) is a better option as it removes the use of the legacy API, but it may be complicated because of dealing with the asynchronous API. In the example application, I used the wrapped session state to demonstrate how it works. No other code changes than in `Program.cs` were needed.

- Second, we will need to switch to ASP.NET Core authentication. Same as in Chapter 8, we will remove the call to `AddAuthenticationClient` and call the standard `AddAuthentication` and `AddCookies` methods to configure the ASP.NET Core Cookie authentication scheme, as shown in Listing 8-27.

- The commented-out `FormsAuthentication` calls need to be replaced with `HttpContext.SignInAsync` and `HttpContext.SignOutAsync`, as you can see in Listing 9-16. Also, to start using the new version of the sign-in and sign-out actions, I had to remove my custom `/new` suffix from them. In contrast to Blazor, we did not need to deal with server-side vs. interactive rendering, as both Razor Pages and ASP.NET Core MVC are always rendered on the server. Both sign-in and sign-out actions are facilitated by classic HTTP POST requests that can set cookies without any limitations.

- Since we will no longer need the remote application feature of `SystemWebAdapters`, we can remove the `AddRemoteAppClient` and the entire YARP layer the same way as we did in Listing 8-32 in the previous chapter, including the API key in `appsettings.json`.

- The last step is moving all static files (scripts, stylesheets, images) in the wwwroot folder of the new application.

- If the old project contains any code files that we linked in the new project (such as the Utils class), this is the moment to move them to the new project, with a necessary cleanup and refactoring. As we saw in Listing 8-31, I modified static methods to instance ones to allow for easy dependency injection.

Listing 9-15. Migrating to the wrapped session state in the new project

```
builder.Services.AddSystemWebAdapters()
    .AddJsonSessionSerializer(options =>
    {
        options.RegisterKey<string>("Currency");
    })
    .AddWrappedAspNetCoreSession()
    ...
    .AddSessionClient()
    ...
builder.Services.AddSession();
builder.Services.AddDistributedMemoryCache();
...
app.UseRouting();
app.UseAuthorization();
app.UseSession();
app.UseSystemWebAdapters();
...
```

Listing 9-16. The sign-in and sign-out code for ASP.NET Core
Cookie authentication

```
// sign-in code
var identity = new ClaimsIdentity([
        new Claim(ClaimTypes.Name, model.UserName)
    ], CookieAuthenticationDefaults.AuthenticationScheme);
await HttpContext.SignInAsync(
    CookieAuthenticationDefaults.AuthenticationScheme,
    new ClaimsPrincipal(identity));

// sign-out code
await HttpContext.SignOutAsync(
    CookieAuthenticationDefaults.AuthenticationScheme);
```

When all these tasks are completed, we can safely remove the old
project from the solution and from the repository. Like in the Blazor
Server version, the migrated codebase likely contains references to the old
API. That is why we may need to keep the SystemWebAdapters package in
the project. However, I recommend not giving up on further refactoring in
order to remove the legacy API.

Summary

I believe that this and the previous two chapters gave you an idea of all
the steps required to incrementally modernize ASP.NET applications.
Naturally, I was not able to cover all areas and features of the frameworks
we have discussed. The example applications were trivial, and still the
number of pages I needed to cover the modernization process was
definitely not small. What is more, all this was even easier than the real-
world applications because I moved the business logic to a separate
application providing an API. However, this simplification does not affect
the entire modernization process.

The individual steps in the modernization process will take more time in real-world projects. ASP.NET Web Forms, in particular, contained myriads of built-in components and opinionated features that can be difficult to reimplement in a functionally equivalent way. ASP.NET MVC was often used with jQuery or other JavaScript components. Although the client-side code usually does not collide with the changes on the server, you may experience various issues caused by the different behavior of JSON serialization, different formats of error responses, and so forth.

I showcased two ways of incremental modernization. The in-place method was easier to set up, as it did not require juggling with the authentication, sharing the session state, or invalidation of caches across two applications, but it required using DotVVM – an open source framework that does not possess the advantage of being officially supported by Microsoft.

The side-by-side method, on the other hand, required quite a significant effort to prepare the infrastructure. You have seen the complications brought by Blazor Server's unusual page life cycle caused by the long-term SignalR requests. The benefits of this application model are amazing and unquestionable. On the other hand, I still feel the reminiscence of the ASP.NET Web Forms view state hidden field, which also tried to break the stateless nature of the HTTP protocol.

We have experienced several dramatic revolutions in how we build web applications, and I am uncertain how Blazor Server will be looked at 10 or 15 years from now. I think that the more levels of abstraction any framework provides and the more it diverts from the principles of the underlying platform, the more difficult it is to migrate applications written in it to another technology. The modernization your application is going through may not be the last one.

CHAPTER 10

A Word on Architecture

Hundreds of books on software architecture, clean code, and other best practices were written. Developers can choose from a wide variety of architectural patterns, such as Domain-Driven Design, Onion or Hexagonal Architecture, Microservices or Modular Monolith, and others. While some of these approaches focus primarily on the organization of the business logic code and the ways of modeling the concepts from the real world, others try to define the rules and structure of the entire system.

In modernization projects, we hardly ever have a chance to introduce a new big architectural pattern. Even the time we can invest in refactoring and code cleanup is often limited by budget or other nontechnical constraints. If the codebase is not covered by automated tests, developers are (rightfully) afraid of making changes that are not inevitable, as they may have unforeseen consequences.

Throughout this book, I might have sounded a bit annoying for constantly reminding you to refactor this and that during the migration. Sometimes, I advocated for making larger changes as they could bring interesting future benefits. I always tried to avoid formulating my recommendations as "you have to..." or "in 100% of cases." Most software projects are so complex that no one can hold the entire context in their mind and make accurate predictions on what might go wrong. Every

© Tomáš Herceg 2024
T. Herceg, *Modernizing .NET Web Applications*,
https://doi.org/10.1007/979-8-8688-0617-9_10

idea needs to be carefully evaluated, and the effort should be justified by the benefits you get from the change. In general, making larger changes only makes sense if the project is expected to undergo extensive future development.

In this chapter, I am not going to explain any concrete design or architectural pattern as they are hard or even impossible to apply to existing large codebases. I just want to share an example of what you can apply to improve the maintainability and testability of the code being modernized, without adding much effort.

Actually, I somehow learned to apply these principles automatically when I write any code – no matter if it is a real-world project or a demo application for a conference. In 2022, several colleagues from RIGANTI, including me, took the Advent of Code[1] challenge, a competition that runs every December. You get a programming puzzle every day, and you are supposed to write a (relatively) simple program that can solve the presented problem. In these tasks, there is no need to apply any complicated design patterns, use dependency injection, or add other bells and whistles. I guess most developers just write a few functions and use classes or records only to represent more complex data structures. However, I found it very difficult to write code in this way. Even though I knew my code did not need to be maintainable because its life expectancy was less than 60 minutes (this was the typical time I needed to solve the tasks), I invested some effort in naming things properly, adding comments where necessary, extracting methods so the code would be easier to read and understand, and so on. Even when I look at the code now, after two years, I have no problem understanding what was happening and what the program was about to solve. I did most of the things automatically without paying special attention or thinking about them, and it was surprising how hard it was to resign to the habits built over the years.

---

[1] See https://adventofcode.com/

Clean and Readable Code

There is a great book called *Code Complete*[2] that explains and summarizes many best practices in software development. Although the book is over 20 years old, it is still very relevant today.

When I read it the first time, it was quite hard to get through the first chapter. The book started with quite high-level concepts, and at that time, I did not have enough experience to be able to relate the topics to my practical experience. But the professor in one lecture at Charles University advised us a little trick – try reading the book from the end. And it worked – I read many great recommendations on writing and structuring code and subsequently got to the high-level concepts that started making sense. I was already following many of the rules without being aware they had some names and were studied by many people. When reading a considerable amount of code written by someone else, you naturally find patterns and idioms and start applying them. I believe the process is quite similar to what large language models do. They can emit code snippets, and nobody had to explicitly teach them how to format and structure the code, use proper naming, etc. Being trained on extensive amounts of data, including large codebases where the clean code practices were followed, they were able to infer rules of how good code should look.[3]

There are dozens of practices for cleaning and readable code. I will mention only the ones I recognize as crucial. Notice that none of the points participate in the religious wars, whether to use tabs or spaces or whether the opening brackets shall be on a separate line. I never engaged in these discussions and was happy to adapt to the coding style already used on the

---

[2] McConnell, Steve. Code Complete: A Practical Handbook of Software Construction. 2nd ed. Microsoft Press, 2004.

[3] This approach has limits, especially in higher-level concepts like security. According to various research studies (e.g., `https://arxiv.org/html/2406.12513v1`), the code generated by large language exhibits significant vulnerabilities.

particular project as long as it was consistent across the entire codebase. Most development environments today support the EditorConfig files[4] that can define the unified coding style for various programming languages. This file can be stored in the Git repository, so all team member IDEs will use the same settings for indentation, brace formatting, and all other aspects:

- *Naming and hierarchy are everything*: Methods, properties, and variables should have meaningful names which express their purpose or intent. We saw an example of the `Utils` class in the example applications in previous chapters – such a name does not tell you anything. The hierarchy (in which folder, namespace, or assembly the class is located) is equally important, as it puts the name in a wider context. Always look for the added value of using a longer name. I am perfectly happy to name a variable just `i` in a typical `for` loop where it does not have any special meaning. The name of the collection being iterated is much more important. The expressions `existingProducts[index]` and `existingProducts [existingProductIndex]` do not tell you more than `existingProducts[i]`. Therefore, I prefer just `i`. However, if the collection was named `items` or `results`, it would be completely unclear what it contains no matter how well the `i` variable is named.

- *Comments are important, but they must add value*: As you can see in my example applications, there are not many comments. The functionality of most methods

---

[4] See `https://learn.microsoft.com/en-us/visualstudio/ide/ create-portable-custom-editor-options?view=vs-2022`

is trivial, and what they do should be quite obvious from their names. I use comments on methods only if something is not clearly visible from the method signature (such as special values of arguments or the wider context in which the method shall be called). In method bodies, the comments should tell you things you cannot infer easily from the code. Comments like "exit the method when customer is null" are almost useless as they just translate C# to English. Compare the value of such a comment with "customer is null when the associated order is not yet saved" – this is a description of a higher-level concept you cannot easily grasp from the code, and that is likely important.

- *Functions should be focused on a single thing*: I have seen many dogmatic rules that a function must fit on one screen, have up to 20 lines of code, or have its cyclomatic complexity[5] below 10. It is true that the readability of a function somehow correlates with these metrics, but not always. What is more important for me is whether the function is focused on a single concept. If you need to do three separate things (e.g., validate the user input, save the values in the database, and redirect the user to another page), all this logic shall not be done directly in the MVC controller function, even if it would take only ten lines of code. The controller action should only orchestrate this sequence and use other functions to perform the individual steps.

---

[5] See https://learn.microsoft.com/en-us/visualstudio/code-quality/code-metrics-cyclomatic-complexity?view=vs-2022

This works better than a strict limit on the number of lines. Sometimes, even a single thing a function needs to do is complicated by its nature.[6]

- *It is not done when the code starts working*: When you work on any complex problem, the path to the solution is often not linear. Most functions or classes I authored were not written from the first line to the last one. Instead, I started somewhere in the middle, wrapped the code with some conditions, added validation and error handling, then added even more lines in the middle, maybe extracted functions from various parts of the code, refactored variable names several times during the entire process, and so on. Eventually, the function starts to do what it is supposed to, but I do not leave it as is. I always review it once again and try to read and understand it in a "linear way" – from top to bottom, because this is how other developers will see it. I often reorder lines, perform more refactoring, and rename things once again so the code is easy to understand for an external reader who has no idea where I started and how the method evolved until it was done. This also helps me to validate the solution by looking at it from another side. I often add empty lines in method bodies to separate even smaller clusters of lines that belong together, as shown in Listing 10-1. Extracting smaller methods would not be very valuable,

---

[6] I met situations like that when writing more complex processing algorithms or parsers. Since they often need to work with complex internal state consisting of many variables, even a single step may mean many lines of code or a complicated decision logic. However, it would not make sense to break them in even smaller pieces – such pieces would not make any sense standing on their own.

as creating users and roles currently happens only
in this method and nowhere else in the application.
However, when I need the functionality elsewhere, this
method will probably split into several smaller ones.
The empty lines quite naturally show where the cuts
will happen.

Listing 10-1. Using empty lines to separate smaller code blocks

```
public static async Task SeedAdminUsersAndRoles(
    UserManager<IdentityUser> userManager,
    RoleManager<IdentityRole> roleManager)
{
    var result = await roleManager.CreateAsync(
        new IdentityRole("Admin"));
    Debug.Assert(result.Succeeded);

    var adminUser = new IdentityUser()
    {
        UserName = "admin",
        Email = "admin@test.com",
        EmailConfirmed = true
    };
    result = await userManager.CreateAsync(adminUser);
    Debug.Assert(result.Succeeded);

    result = await userManager.AddPasswordAsync(
        adminUser, "Admin1234+");
    Debug.Assert(result.Succeeded);
}
```

I have seen many legacy projects that did not follow any of these practices. The code-behind files contained functions with hundreds of lines of code, often named like `Button7_Click`. The formatting and indentation were broken, making the code hard to follow, especially when the methods or nested code blocks were long. Several times, I even heard that it was not a problem because the tooling could easily reformat the code. However, such changes confuse the Git history, making it harder to compare the versions before and after the reformatting. Also, the tooling cannot fix variable and method names that do not express their meaning.

This is a complication for anyone who tries to migrate such code. The vast majority of time will not be spent writing or moving the code but trying to understand what the code was supposed to do in the first place.

The developer who wrote the code might have saved one hour by not thinking about better naming and extracting smaller functions with a clear purpose. But now, after years and without knowing the context and circumstances under which the function was written, someone else has to spend way more time understanding and refactoring the routine. Modernization can easily become orders of magnitude more expensive than it could be, provided the code quality is better.

I do not intend to blame anyone for past mistakes – I have made many myself, and it took me years to discover ways of writing code that is not painful to maintain. Many people in the industry have never studied computer science and had to learn everything by trial and error. Even developers who attended any software development classes would probably confirm that it is extremely rare to learn these practices at school. You need to actually spend years writing code and meet multiple software projects to build the proper habits.

However, not repeating the same mistakes is crucial. No codebase will ever be perfect. There is always room for improvement, but we should do our best to leave it in better shape than it was.

Layering

The previous section can be perceived as a set of rules that apply in the scope of a single file – how to structure code inside functions and functions inside classes. Another level is how the code is organized in folders and namespaces and how it is split between projects.

In most business applications, you will probably identify three layers. They do not have to be clearly separated in the code (I already mentioned our fictional `Button7_Click` method, which most probably spans across all three layers), but they are present conceptually:

- *Data access or persistence layer*: Most applications use a database or other kinds of storage for data persistence. Many libraries, such as Entity Framework Core, try to simplify this process. A large portion of the application code in this layer will take care of loading or saving data from this persistence store and will likely provide "data entities" to the upper layers. The data access layer code may involve some validation rules to ensure the stored information's schema or referential integrity. This is especially important when using a relational database.

- *Business layer*: This is the part of the application where all business logic should take place, and it is usually the most complex layer of all. The term business logic usually refers to software representation of real-world objects and processes involving validation of business rules. There are various patterns you can use, such as CRUD[7] or Domain-Driven Design.[8] It is not unusual to have this layer split into smaller modules (e.g., domains and subdomains).

- *Presentation layer*: This top layer of the application provides a communication interface with the clients. These can be actual users interacting through a UI, but in the case of API applications, the API is the presentation layer, and the clients may be other applications. We have discussed the MVC and MVVM patterns in previous chapters. They define how the presentation layer is organized. They all use the term Model to refer to the services and data objects the business layer provides.

---

[7] CRUD stands for Create-Read-Update-Delete and is often used in simpler scenarios where the focus is primarily on storing data without the need to model complex processes for changing such data.

[8] Domain-Driven Design focuses on proper modeling of real-world entities, enforcing consistency of the model and providing a controlled way to change the state of the model. In DDD, there is usually nothing like "updating an entity" – every such update means something in the real world, and therefore it shall be represented as a separate operation and ensure the model will remain in a consistent state.

There are two impressive books on Domain-Driven Design:

Evans, Eric. Domain-Driven Design: Tackling Complexity in the Heart of Software. Addison-Wesley Professional, 2003.

Vaughn, Vernon. Implementing Domain-Driven Design. Addison-Wesley Professional, 2003.

Even when the project is not split into three assemblies representing these layers, it is necessary to keep them in mind when writing code and avoid mixing the concepts from multiple layers in a single method or class.

The problem with our example Button7_Click method is that it loads data from the database (persistence layer), handles database-specific matters such as row versioning or serialization of complex values into a single column (persistence layer), performs some validation of the user input (business layer), displays these validation results to the user if there is a problem (presentation layer), updates some entities according to the user input (business layer), and saves the changes in the database (persistence layer). Listing 10-2 shows how such a method may look like. You can see that it is not even that long – its main problem is that it handles more than a single thing and mixes concerns of multiple layers.

Listing 10-2. An example of the Button7_Click method

```
public void Button7_Click(object sender, EventArgs e)
{
    var startTime = TimeSpan.Parse(StartTimeTextBox.Text);
    var endTime = TimeSpan.Parse(EndTimeTextBox.Text);

    if (startTime >= endTime)
    {
        ErrorLiteral.Text = "The start of the reservation must↵
be earlier than its end!");
        return;
    }

    var db = new AppDbContext();

    var customerId = Guid.Parse(
        User.Identity.FindFirstValue(AppClaims.CustomerId));
    var customer = db.Customers.Find(customerId);
    if (customer.MaxReservationLength < (endTime - startTime))
```

627

```
    {
        ErrorLiteral.Text
            = "Maximum reservation length was exceeded!");
        return;
    }

    retry:
    var day = db.ReservationDays
        .Where(r =>
            r.RoomId == int.Parse(RoomComboBox.SelectedValue)
            && r.Date == DayCalendar.SelectedDay.Date)
        .Single();

    var existingReservations =
        JsonConvert.DeserializeObject<List<Reservation>>(
            day.ReservationsJson
        );
    if (!existingReservations.All(r =>
        r.EndTime <= startTime || r.StartTime >= endTime))
    {
        ErrorLiteral.Text = "The room is not available⏎
because of a conflicting reservation!");
        return;
    }

    var reservationId = Guid.NewGuid();
    try
    {
        existingReservations.Add(new Reservation()
        {
            Id = reservationId,
            StartTime = startTime,
            EndTime = endTime,
```

```
            UserId = Guid.Parse(
                User.Identity.FindFirstValue(AppClaims.UserId))
        };
        day.Reservations = JsonConvert.SerializeObject(
            existingReservations
        );

        db.SaveChanges();
    }
    catch (DbUpdateConcurrencyException ex)
    {
        // the ReservationDay entity has a RowVersion column
        // if we get the exception, someone else has modified
        // the day
        Thread.Sleep(100);
        goto retry;
    }

    Response.Redirect($"~/Reservation/Summary/{day.Id}/↵
{reservationId}");
}
```

In the ideal world, the Button7_Click method would have a better name (e.g., CreateReservation or at least CreateReservationButton_ Click to follow the naming convention of the presentation framework). Since it is declared in a web page's code-behind file, it clearly belongs to the presentation layer. Therefore, its responsibility is to gather the input from the user interface, pass it to the business layer, and present the result of the operation to the user (either by displaying validation errors or by redirecting to the reservation summary page).

The business layer will be responsible for validating user input and enforcing business rules (e.g., is the booking time valid, can the user make a reservation of the requested length, is the resource available at the requested times, and so on). For this purpose, it may need to load some data using the means of the persistence layer, and if all the checks pass, it will use the persistence layer again to save the new reservation.

We have discussed how difficult it may be to use SQL transactions to ensure consistency in this particular case. Instead of using the SERIALIZABLE transaction isolation level, I decided to serialize the reservation entries for a particular room and day as JSON and store them as a single database row. This allows me to use optimistic concurrency[9] to ensure only one user may update the record at a time. However, all this is the responsibility of the persistence layer. In the ideal world, the business layer should not be aware of this mechanism at all – the persistence layer should provide it with the tools to perform this operation safely. Naturally, there will be situations where a complete abstraction is impossible[10] – this is sometimes referred to as leaky abstraction. However, it can still be better than no abstraction, provided the limitations are documented and known to the developers.

The method in Listing 10-2 has even more problems. It uses synchronous methods, and what is worse, it uses Thread.Sleep to create a delay between individual retry attempts on conflicts. This can severely hurt the throughput of the entire website and easily exhaust the thread pool. Both ASP.NET and ASP.NET Core only provide a limited number of

---

[9] See https://learn.microsoft.com/en-us/ef/core/saving/concurrency?tabs=data-annotations#optimistic-concurrency

[10] You can find numerous examples of leaking abstractions when using ORMs, especially when using LINQ. The relational and object-oriented worlds are so fundamentally different that a perfect abstraction is probably impossible. For instance, LINQ expressions executed on in-memory collections often produce very different results when null values or string comparisons are involved.

threads (usually a few hundred[11]), and if any thread waits for synchronous operations to complete, it cannot be used to process other requests. Having the code asynchronous allows handling more requests with the same (small) number of threads.

Additionally, the method creates an instance of the Entity Framework DbContext object and never disposes it. This can lead to a similar issue – exhaustion of the database connection pool. If you are not lucky enough and the garbage collector does not dispose unused DbContext instances (which will release the underlying connections), you will get another issue. Wherever you create instances of database connections or Entity Framework contexts yourself, you are responsible for their cleanup.

Finally, the method retrieves the Customer entity for the current customer whose ID is retrieved from current identity claims. I am sure this concept will be useful in many other places of the application and should be extracted as a separate method. Otherwise, other developers will either copy and paste the code snippet into their methods or write their own implementation. Both ways lead to code duplication and worse maintainability.

Let us see how we can refactor this method on the fly when migrating it to DotVVM using the in-place method I demonstrated in Chapter 7. The same approach can be applied when migrating to Blazor or any other UI framework.

As I mentioned earlier, the responsibility of the presentation layer is to gather the input from the user, pass it to the business layer, and present the results to the user. The old implementation had to reference UI components and convert their values to the correct data types (such

---

[11] In ASP.NET, the default is 25 threads per CPU, as described at https://learn.microsoft.com/en-us/previous-versions/dotnet/netframework-4.0/7w2sway1(v=vs.100)

In ASP.NET Core, the limits are guided by the ThreadPool configuration, and there is a more sophisticated heuristic to determine the number of threads, as explained at https://learn.microsoft.com/en-us/dotnet/core/diagnostics/debug-threadpool-starvation

as converting TextBox string values to TimeSpan). In DotVVM, these conversions are handled for you by the framework's data-binding mechanism. If the user enters a value in an incorrect format, the framework will produce a standard validation error. You only need to declare the properties in the viewmodel, as shown in Listing 10-3.

Listing 10-3. Presentation layer code in DotVVM for the migrated Button7_Click method

```
public class CreateReservationViewModel(
    ReservationService reservationService)
    : DotvvmViewModelBase
{
    public CreateReservationModel Model { get; set; } = new();

    [Bind(Direction.ServerToClient)]
    public string ErrorMessage { get; set; }

    public async Task CreateReservation()
    {
        CreateReservationResult result;
        try
        {
            result = await reservationService
                .CreateReservation(Model);
        }
        catch (DomainException ex)
        {
            ErrorMessage = ex.Message;
            return;
        }
        Context.RedirectToRoute("ReservationSummary", result);
    }
}
```

```
}

// this model is declared in the business layer
public class CreateReservationModel : IValidatableObject
{
    [Required(ErrorMessage = "Please select the room.")]
    public int SelectedRoomId { get; set; }

    [Required(ErrorMessage = "Please select the day.")]
    public DateOnly SelectedDay { get; set; }

    [Required(ErrorMessage = "Please enter the start time.")]
    public TimeOnly StartTime { get; set; }

    [Required(ErrorMessage = "Please enter the end time.")]
    public TimeOnly EndTime { get; set; }

    public IEnumerable<ValidationResult> Validate(
        ValidationContext validationContext)
    {
        if (StartTime >= EndTime)
        {
            yield return new ValidationResult("The start of↵
the reservation must be earlier than its end!");
        }
    }
}
```

The first class is a pretty straightforward DotVVM viewmodel. It declares a property containing the model representing the state of the user interface and a string property used to indicate errors that may occur during the process. It uses dependency injection to obtain an instance of the ReservationService. The CreateReservation method is a nice example of what the presentation layer should do – gather the user input, send it to the lower layer, and apply the result to the user interface (by setting viewmodel properties or navigating the user to another page).

I have created a DomainException base class for all business rule violation exceptions. If the business layer throws an exception of this type, its error message will be displayed to the user. If the exception is of a different type (e.g., if the database cannot be reached), it will not be caught here and will be treated by a global error handler.

Notice also the code that makes the redirect – instead of composing the URL myself, I rely on the framework's routing engine to build the route for me. To provide the route parameters, I use directly the result object that contains properties named ReservationDayId and ReservationId. Because I always try to name things consistently, the route parameters use the same names as these properties, and thus the routing engine will be able to build the URL correctly.

The second class in the example must be defined in the business layer, as the ReservationService accepts it as a parameter. As you can see, the class tries to perform the "formal" validation of parameters using the data annotation attributes and by implementing the IValidatableObject interface.[12] This kind of validation does not involve enforcing the

---

[12] There are more strategies for object validation. Some frameworks, for example, WPF, recommend performing the validation checks in property setters. The motivation is to ensure that viewmodels will always be in a consistent state. However, this approach is not very practical in web environments where the viewmodels are often serialized and deserialized. If I checked that StartTime was before EndTime in the StartTime property setter, I would get an exception if the EndTime had not been set yet. The deserializers do not give us any guarantee in

business rules – it aims only to ensure the internal consistency of this CreateReservationModel object (ensuring the data can be parsed and the reservation does not end before it even starts).

DotVVM natively supports both data annotation attributes and IValidatableObject interface. Therefore, if the user clicks the button, the DotVVM validation framework will not even invoke the CreateReservation method. Instead, it will display the validation errors automatically and let the user correct them.

There may be numerous situations where the user interface does not exactly match the model the business layer works with. In such cases, you will need to define a "presentation model" object for the UI in the presentation layer, and the viewmodel will need to transform it into the model used by the business layer. However, this is not a problem – this kind of transformation is exactly what the presentation layer is supposed to take care of. Creating specialized "presentation model objects" that contain only the properties the user can manipulate is a recommended practice to prevent overposting.[13] When using DotVVM, please note that even the properties not displayed in the user interface are sent to the client as part of the viewmodel JSON serialization process. Therefore, always avoid having properties users shall not access in presentation models.

Let us continue with what happens in other layers. Listing 10-4 shows how the ReservationService may look like.

---

which order they will set the properties. In domain models, we commonly validate objects in the constructors to prevent inconsistent objects from even being created. This approach also does not work well for UI models that need to work throughout the process of filling the form. That is why the UI model object allows being (temporarily) in an incomplete or inconsistent state and provides means for its validation using the standard .NET Data Annotations API.

[13] See https://learn.microsoft.com/en-us/aspnet/core/mvc/models/model-binding?view=aspnetcore-8.0#bind-attribute

Listing 10-4. Implementation of ReservationService for the migrated Button7_Click method

```
public class ReservationService(
    ReservationPolicyService reservationPolicyService,
    ICurrentCustomerProvider currentCustomerProvider,
    ReservationDayRepository reservationDayRepository
)
{
    public async Task<CreateReservationResult> CreateReservation(
        CreateReservationModel model)
    {
        if (!await reservationPolicyService
            .IsValidReservationLength(
                model, currentCustomerProvider.CustomerId))
        {
            throw new MaxReservationLengthExceededException();
        }

        return await reservationDayRepository.UpdateWithRetry(
            model.SelectedRoomId, model.SelectedDay,
            day =>
            {
                var reservation = new ReservationDomainObject(
                    Guid.NewGuid(),
                    currentCustomerProvider.UserId,
                    model.StartTime,
                    model.EndTime
                );
                if (!day.TryAddReservation(reservation))
                {
```

```
        throw new
            ConflictingReservationFoundException();
    }
    return new CreateReservationResult(
        day.Id, reservation.Id);
    });
}
}
```

As you can see, the ReservationService declares three dependencies. Because the maximum reservation length can differ based on the concrete customer, and it is likely that the process may get more complicated in the future, I extracted this logic into a separate ReservationPolicyService. Thanks to this, the ReservationService does not need to care about the exact validation logic – it just asks whether the length of the reservation is allowed. If not, an exception (inheriting from our custom DomainException) is thrown. Feel free to add additional parameters to custom exceptions to allow giving more information to the users, such as the maximum permitted length.

The ICurrentCustomerProvider is an interface defined in the business layer. It needs to be implemented in the presentation layer, as it needs to find the current user's claims in the current HttpContext. Technically, I could look at Thread.CurrentPrincipal to get the current identity and its claims, but by abstracting this functionality through an interface, I will be able to cover the code by tests easily. Also, the business logic code may be called from other contexts where there is no HTTP request (e.g., some background operation triggered by a time scheduler or similar), and we will need to obtain the customer and user identifiers using a different method.

The last dependency is the ReservationDayRepository. This might raise a few eyebrows, as some people perceive hiding Entity Framework DbContext behind repositories as an antipattern. I believe the devil is

in the details – it depends on how the repository is implemented and
what exactly it provides to its consumers. I have seen many generic
implementations of IRepository<T> that did not add any extra value over
the Entity Framework's built-in DbSet<T>. Even in such cases, I would
hesitate to have a strong opinion on the usefulness of the repository. As
we saw in Chapter 5, we often need to replace the ORM in modernization
projects, and having an abstraction (no matter how leaky) can simplify the
process and minimize the number of code changes.

My repository is not a thin wrapper over the Entity Framework
Core API, as you can see in Listing 10-5. It provides a method called
UpdateWithRetry, which hides the retry logic implemented in the legacy
method using a popular library called Polly.[14] Instead of providing separate
methods to load and store objects, this UpdateWithRetry method gets
the roomId and date parameters and a lambda method that is invoked to
modify the loaded object. The method will load the specified entity and
invoke the lambda. Once the lambda returns, the repository will try to save
the changes, and in the case of a concurrency error (someone else has
modified the object at the same time), it will repeat the entire process –
load the fresh object from the database, run the lambda, and try to save the
object again.

The retry logic handles only the DbUpdateConcurrencyException
exception. Any other exceptions will be thrown out of the method. I
use this feature when there is a reservation conflict – the lambda will
throw an exception that bubbles up to the viewmodel. The lambda
method can also return a result, which is used as the result of the entire
UpdateWithRetry method.

The last thing to notice is that we add the reservation to the collection
by calling the TryAddReservation method. I did this to demonstrate
the principle of domain objects that do not allow making arbitrary
changes. Instead, there are special methods for updating the object while

---

[14] See https://github.com/App-vNext/Polly

ensuring its state remains consistent. The UpdateWithRetry method
will not give you the Entity Framework entity directly. Instead, it uses
the MapToDomainObject and MapFromDomainObject methods to convert
entities to their domain object representations and back. As you can see,
these methods deal with JSON serialization and deserialization. The
domain object is completely abstracted from these persistence concerns
and tries to model the real-world daily reservation schedule, including the
processes to update its state.

Listing 10-5. Implementation of the repository that encapsulates
concurrency logic

```
public class ReservationDayRepository(AppDbContext db)
{
    ...

    public async Task<TResult> UpdateWithRetry<TResult>(
        int roomId, DateOnly date,
        Func<ReservationDayDomainObject, TResult> updateAction)
    {
        return await Policy
            .Handle<DbUpdateConcurrencyException>()
            .RetryForeverAsync()
            .ExecuteAsync(async () =>
            {
                var entity = await db.ReservationDays
                    .Where(r => r.RoomId == roomId
                        && r.Date == date)
                    .SingleAsync();
                var day = MapToDomainObject(entity);

                var result = updateAction(day);

                MapFromDomainObject(day, entity);
```

```
                await db.SaveChangesAsync();

                return result;
        });
    }

    private ReservationDayDomainObject MapToDomainObject(
        ReservationDay entity)
    {
        var reservationObjects =
            JsonConvert.DeserializeObject<
                List<ReservationDomainObject>>(
                entity.ReservationsJson
            );
        return new ReservationDayDomainObject(
            entity.Id,
            ...
            reservationObjects);
    }

    private void MapFromDomainObject(
        ReservationDayDomainObject day, ReservationDay entity)
    {
        ...
        entity.ReservationsJson =
            JsonConvert.SerializeObject(day.Reservations);
    }
}

public class ReservationDayDomainObject
{
    private readonly
        List<ReservationDomainObject> reservations;
```

```
public Guid Id { get; }
public int RoomId { get; }
public DateOnly Date { get; }
public IReadOnlyList<ReservationDomainObject> Reservations
    => reservations;

public ReservationDayDomainObject(
    Guid id, int roomId, DateOnly date,
IEnumerable<ReservationDomainObject> reservations)
{
    Id = id;
    RoomId = roomId;
    Date = date;
    this.reservations = reservations.ToList();
}

public bool TryAddReservation(
    ReservationDomainObject reservation)
{
    if (!reservations.All(r =>
        r.EndTime <= reservation.StartTime
        || r.StartTime >= reservation.EndTime))
    {
        return false;
    }
    reservations.Add(reservation);
    return true;
}
}
```

I have intentionally omitted the code of ReservationDomainObject, as it is a plain container holding the information about the reservation. It is important to mention that its properties should be get-only – there should be no way to change them directly. If you plan to allow the users to modify reservation times, remember that this will need enforcing several business rules, and quite a complex logic may be hidden behind this entire process. The Domain-Driven Design emphasizes this – I cannot imagine any reservation system where changing the time of the booking would be just a matter of a single SQL UPDATE command.

I also skipped providing the declarations of exceptions – there is nothing special about them. You should also be able to figure out the implementation of the ICurrentCustomerProvider interface (e.g., you can use dependency injection to inject IHttpContextAccessor and use it to access the current identity) and the ReservationPolicyService.

If you think this example is too complicated, you can omit the domain objects and have the repository work just with Entity Framework entities. However, the huge benefit domain objects provide is ensuring a consistent state at all times. If you load the ReservationDay entity on some other place in the code and manipulate its properties directly, you may easily end up with conflicting reservations or violating other constraints. This is what domain objects should prevent. You do not need to apply this principle to every entity in the application – it is quite common to do it only for particular domains where complex logic is involved.

Let us stop and review the changes we made. We have split a single method into several reusable classes. I can imagine plenty of other places in a reservation system where we might need the ReservationPolicyService. The ICurrentCustomerProvider will be needed almost everywhere, and it has become a common pattern in all my business applications.

If you need to add another type of client interface, for example, expose the reservation function as an API, you have everything in place to do that. It would be impossible with the original Button7_Click method, as it accessed UI components in an ASP.NET Web Forms page. It also relied on the current user identity being stored in a particular way, which may not work for the API application.

Recently, Microsoft and other big players started integrating generative AI models into their products. Many applications introduced a chat interface that allows users to work with the application using natural language. This is just another type of client interface, and with a proper separation of business logic from presentation matters, it is easy to expose the business layer functions to automated agents.

Using libraries like Semantic Kernel, you can easily teach a language model (such as ChatGPT provided by Azure OpenAI Service) to invoke skill functions you register in the Semantic Kernel pipeline, as shown in Listing 10-6.

Listing 10-6. Registering services as language model plug-ins using Semantic Kernel

```
builder.Services.AddKernel()
    .AddAzureOpenAIChatCompletion(...)
    .Plugins
        .AddFromType<ReservationSystemPlugin>();

...

public class ReservationSystemPlugin(
    ReservationService reservationService,
    ...)
{
    [KernelFunction]
    [Description("Reserves a specified meeting room for the↲
        specified time window.")]
    public async Task<string> CreateReservation(
        string roomName,
        DateTime startDate,
        DateTime endDate
    )
    {
```

```
        // find the room id by the room name
        var roomId = ...;

        try
        {
            var result = await reservationService
                .CreateReservation(new CreateReservationModel()
                {
                    SelectedRoomId = roomId,
                    SelectedDay = startDate.ToDateOnly(),
                    StartTime = startDate.ToTimeOnly(),
                    EndTime = endDate.ToTimeOnly()
                });
            return $"Created a reservation↵
{result.ReservationId}.";
        }
        catch (DomainException ex)
        {
            return ex.Message;
        }
    }
}
```

Based on the Description attribute on the function, Semantic Kernel will generate a prompt for the language model. Hence, the model becomes aware of the plug-in's capabilities and can request to invoke the function based on the conversation. Thanks to that, the following conversation will trigger the plug-in function, correctly recognizing the input parameters and passing correct values in the roomName, startDate, and endDate parameters:

User: Hey, I need to reserve the blue meeting room next Thursday from 2PM to 4PM. Is that possible?

Assistant: Invoking plugin function
CreateReservation

Assistant: roomName: Blue meeting room

Assistant: startDate: 2024-06-27T14:00:00.000

Assistant: endDate: 2024-06-27T16:00:00.000

Assistant: Sure, it is possible. The ID of the reservation is 1bd7afd0-5fb9-4f92-9ae2-fd51574f2a1e.

Can I help you with something else?

Like in previous cases, we take advantage of the dependency injection. It is very easy to just request the ReservationService in the constructor of our Semantic Kernel plug-in and not worry about anything else. Since other parts of the application already use this service, it is ready to be used in new places and contexts. Thanks to abstractions we made, such as ICurrentCustomerProvider, we can easily provide the correct information to the business layer using a mechanism other than the one we use in the web interface.

Code Consistency and Conventions

Consistency may be the most difficult thing to achieve, especially in team projects with fluctuating team members, but it is one of the most important topics for me.

Whenever I work with a large codebase, I spend a lot of time navigating through the code, looking at how various aspects are implemented, searching for causes of reported issues, and so on. You can do many things to make navigation in the project easier.

The first aspect is **logical project structure**. In most cases, the application is not just a single project but a collection of multiple projects in a solution. Some projects are just libraries containing shared code, others represent tests, and the rest are executable applications. Most of the projects likely depend on other projects. The structure should be logical and intuitively understandable without requiring one to read the documentation (which may be outdated). You can help it by renaming projects to express their purpose, using Solution folders[15] in Visual Studio or other ways. One of my favorite ways is using .NET Aspire, a new component of .NET that helps develop distributed applications. A hidden benefit of Aspire's App host project[16] is a simple way of defining application parts and the relationships between them. Reading the AppHost `Program.cs` proved better than anything else for me to grasp the solution structure quickly.

Naming conventions are equally important. In many RIGANTI projects, we use various conventions to help understand the purpose of various classes or folders. For example, when some class name ends with `Service`, `Query`, `ListModel`, `DetailModel`, we immediately know what is inside and in what context the class shall be used. These conventions are slightly different in every project, and in many cases, they are not fully documented, even though you can infer most of them from just looking at the codebase. When working on a project, you should try to follow these conventions as much as possible. This is also one of the functions of the code review process – ensuring that the pull request complies with the rules and does not introduce clutter in the project. I noticed that AI-powered tools such as GitHub Copilot are very successful in discovering conventions even from short code snippets they have in their context

---

[15] See https://learn.microsoft.com/en-us/visualstudio/ide/solutions-and-projects-in-visual-studio?view=vs-2022#solution-folder

[16] See https://learn.microsoft.com/en-us/dotnet/aspire/fundamentals/app-host-overview?tabs=docker#app-host-project

window.[17] Generally, they produce better results when the codebase uses consistent patterns and conventions. I have not found any research to support this, but I found several other people observing similar effects.[18]

Do not reinvent the wheel. This point may be a bit difficult to explain, but I will try. I have met several developers who had great ideas and out-of-the-box thinking. It was helpful in many situations, especially when new projects were starting and we needed to experiment with new architectures, patterns, or libraries. However, once some patterns were established, they were unable to follow them and constantly tried to introduce new concepts and ways of solving problems. Even when they worked on a similar feature to the one they finished the day before, the new solution was completely different. It is natural that developers constantly learn – when I look at the code I wrote just a few months before, I immediately see things I could do better. However, I believe that a consistent approach to solving problems, especially in team environments, helps to keep the codebase in a better condition. In my experience from RIGANTI, onboarding of new team members was much more seamless on projects where the team used such a consistent approach. The new hires could be given examples of how features are usually implemented, and the "paved way" helped them go forward without having to explore the entire scope of the project. Please do not understand this point in the way that everything should be set in stone when the project starts, and there is never room for improvement. If the new solution is better and brings substantial benefits, I am all in for applying it in all places the old way was used. However, there are many cases where two solutions are equally good, and that is where I prefer choosing one of them and applying it consistently.

---

[17] Context window typically contains the file you work with, and few other files you interacted with recently. You can explicitly add additional items in the context to improve the quality of suggestions. See `https://github.blog/2023-05-17-how-github-copilot-is-getting-better-at-understanding-your-code/`

[18] See `https://medium.com/@BhabaniSwain/github-copilot-for-quality-engineers-852e3a1821c`

I am aware that this section is highly subjective, and your experience may differ. However, I always felt more comfortable working with a well-organized codebase where I could strongly rely on my intuition. Whenever I needed to find something, I looked at the project and folder structure and guessed the most probable location. Many times, the initial guess was right.

Conversely, in projects not satisfying these conditions, finding causes of bugs was always quite painful – I had to start systematically in some place in the user interface and debug through the call stack, often multiple times, because it is so simple to miss the exact moment in which the internal state of the program stops being correct.

I know that in many modernization projects, the timely and budget constraints do not allow much refactoring. There are even cases where the legacy codebase is in such a condition that there is no point trying to understand and untangle it into something more maintainable. However, you can still apply these principles to the new code and make at least small incremental improvements whenever you touch or modify any legacy functionality.

Testing

Having refactored the code in a way I presented before opens another opportunity – being able to write unit or integration tests. Let us see how such tests in our simple reservation system may look like.

Unit Tests

The unit tests ensure that individual parts of the system work correctly. They are quite easy to create, and since they work only with a small scope, they usually do not require mocking[19] any services. Most unit tests happen only in memory and do not interact with databases or external components.

For example, our ReservationDayDomainObject needs to keep its internal state consistent. You can see a test for its TryAddReservation method in Listing 10-7. It creates an instance of the domain object with several initial reservations and is executed several times with different start and end times of new reservations. After adding the reservation, the actual result is compared with the expected one.

Listing 10-7. Unit test for the domain object logic

```
[Theory]
[InlineData("9:00", "9:30", false)]
[InlineData("9:30", "10:00", true)]
[InlineData("10:15", "10:30", false)]
[InlineData("8:30", "9:30", false)]
[InlineData("8:30", "9:00", true)]
public void TestReservationConflict(
    string startTime, string endTime, bool expectedResult)
{
```

---

[19] Mocking is a process of replacing external dependencies (or components that are not subject of the particular test) with simple alternative implementations, which usually return prefabricated results or do not do anything at all. The purpose is to focus on the code being tested and omitting any mechanism that is not important for the particular test or replacing it with an alternative implementation (usually much less complex). For example, a test for a code that sends out emails may replace the mail sending routine either with an empty method or with an alternative behavior (e.g., save the email in a folder instead of actually sending it).

```
    // arrange
    var reservationDay = new ReservationDayDomainObject(
        Guid.Empty, testRoomId,
        new DateOnly(2024, 6, 23),
        [
            new ReservationDomainObject(Guid.NewGuid(),
                testUserId,
                new TimeOnly(9, 0, 0),
                new TimeOnly(9, 30, 0)),
            new ReservationDomainObject(Guid.NewGuid(),
                testUserId,
                new TimeOnly(10, 0, 0),
                new TimeOnly(11, 30, 0)),
            new ReservationDomainObject(Guid.NewGuid(),
                testUserId,
                new TimeOnly(13, 0, 0),
                new TimeOnly(16, 0, 0))
        ]
    );

    // act
    var newReservation = new ReservationDomainObject(
        Guid.NewGuid(), testUserId,
        TimeOnly.Parse(startTime), TimeOnly.Parse(endTime));
    var result = reservationDay
        .TryAddReservation(newReservation);

    // assert
    Assert.Equal(expectedResult, result);
}
```

Since domain objects rarely depend on any services and can be instantiated by providing all their state in the constructor, they are quite easy to cover by tests.

Integration Tests

Once we are sure that the domain object does not allow inserting conflicting reservations for the same room and day, we can go one step higher. We can verify whether the reservation service does what it is supposed to do.

Since the service depends on other services (the current company provider, the reservation policy service, and a repository that provides the ReservationDay domain objects), we must either provide their real implementations or try to mock them.

Because we do not want to set up the actual SQL database (which would also require seeding appropriate data for tests), we can use a mocking library such as NSubstitute.[20] This allows us to generate implementations of interfaces with the option to easily configure return values or method behavior. You could achieve the same result by manually implementing ICurrentCustomerProvider and other interfaces, but mocking libraries can do the trick with just a few lines of code. It is quite common that you need mocks with a different behavior in every test – without a mocking library, you would need to declare multiple classes per test.

Listing 10-8 shows how to use mocks to test the ReservationService.

- First, we prepare a domain object in the constructor on which the reservation service will operate. Because we do not want to use the database, we will mock the repository to return this prefabricated domain object.

- Subsequently, we create a mock for ICurrentCustomerProvider to return static values when asked for customer and user IDs.

---

[20] See https://nsubstitute.github.io/

- Then, we mock the `ReservationPolicyService` class. Since it has one argument in the constructor, we have to provide a value for that. Because the mock will not need the dependency, we can pass `null`. When configuring the behavior for the `IsValidReservationLength` method, notice the `Arg.Any<T>` arguments – this means that the behavior is set for any value of these arguments. There are other methods on the `Arg` class you can use to configure different logic based on the actual argument values. We return `Task.FromResult(true)` for any argument values – this means that any reservation length is valid in this particular test.

- The `ReservationDayRepository` is the most complicated. We need to provide an alternative body to the `UpdateWithRetry` method, which fetches data from the database, calls the lambda method, and saves the changes – all that wrapped with a retry policy. To avoid interactions with the database, I created the domain object at the beginning of the constructor. Therefore, the mock can just pick the third method argument (the `updateAction` lambda) and invoke it with the domain object as the argument.

Now, we have all the dependencies we need to build the instance of `ReservationService`. In the tests, I just call the `CreateReservation` method at different times and verify that the method either adds the reservation in the domain object's `Reservations` collection or throws the correct exception.

Listing 10-8. Mocking the dependencies to prevent the tests from using the database

```
...
private readonly ReservationDayDomainObject day;
private readonly ReservationService reservationService;

public ReservationServiceTests()
{
    // prepare domain object
    day = new ReservationDayDomainObject(
        Guid.Empty, testRoomId,
        testDay,
        [
            new ReservationDomainObject(Guid.NewGuid(),
                testUserId,
                new TimeOnly(9, 0, 0),
                new TimeOnly(9, 30, 0)),
            new ReservationDomainObject(Guid.NewGuid(),
                testUserId,
                new TimeOnly(10, 0, 0),
                new TimeOnly(11, 30, 0)),
            new ReservationDomainObject(Guid.NewGuid(),
                testUserId,
                new TimeOnly(13, 0, 0),
                new TimeOnly(16, 0, 0))
        ]
    );

    // prepare mocks
    var currentCustomerProvider =
        Substitute.For<ICurrentCustomerProvider>();
    currentCustomerProvider.CustomerId.Returns(
        Guid.Parse("897A1B7C-B7D1-44A9-A751-82AD0D0B5331"));
```

653

```
    currentCustomerProvider.UserId.Returns(
        Guid.Parse("630F65BE-A38A-4051-BFE7-385B83DA30AC"));

    var reservationPolicyService =
        Substitute.For<ReservationPolicyService>([null]);
    reservationPolicyService.IsValidReservationLength(
        Arg.Any<CreateReservationModel>(), Arg.Any<Guid>())
        .Returns(Task.FromResult(true));

    var reservationDayRepository =
        Substitute.For<ReservationDayRepository>([null]);
    reservationDayRepository.UpdateWithRetry(
        Arg.Any<int>(), Arg.Any<DateOnly>(),
        Arg.Any<Func<ReservationDayDomainObject,
        CreateReservationResult>>())
        .Returns(args =>
        {
            var updateAction =
                (Func<ReservationDayDomainObject,
                    CreateReservationResult>)args[2];
            return updateAction(day);
        });

    reservationService = new ReservationService(
        reservationPolicyService, currentCustomerProvider,
        reservationDayRepository);
}

[Fact]
public async Task MockedRepositories_SuccessfulReservation()
{
    var result = await reservationService.CreateReservation(
```

```
        new CreateReservationModel()
        {
            SelectedRoomId = testRoomId,
            SelectedDay = testDay,
            StartTime = new TimeOnly(9, 30, 0),
            EndTime = new TimeOnly(10, 0, 0)
        });

    // assert the reservation was added
    Assert.Contains(day.Reservations,
        r => r.Id == result.ReservationId
            && r.StartTime == new TimeOnly(9, 30, 0));
}

[Fact]
public async Task MockedRepositories_Conflict()
{
    // assert the reservation was added
    await Assert
    .ThrowsAsync<ConflictingReservationFoundException>(
        () => reservationService.CreateReservation(
        new CreateReservationModel()
        {
            SelectedRoomId = testRoomId,
            SelectedDay = testDay,
            StartTime = new TimeOnly(9, 25, 0),
            EndTime = new TimeOnly(10, 0, 0)
        }));
}
```

Mocks can do more than replace the original code with an alternative implementation. They also keep a history of all invocations, which you can query using the `Received` or `DidNotReceive` methods.[21] This can be useful in more complicated scenarios to make sure the code calls certain methods with correct arguments. For example, I could check that the `IsValidReservationLength` method was called.

Please note that it is better to use mocks with interfaces than with classes, where all methods you want to modify must be `virtual`. Without that, the mocking library would have no way to replace the method body. Also, whenever a non-virtual method on a mocked class is called, the actual implementation is invoked, which might have unwanted consequences. Therefore, the clean way would be to make interfaces for the `ReservationPolicyService` and `ReservationDayRepository`.

Integration Tests with Database

The last type of test I want to show is also an integration test. Instead of mocking out the dependencies, it uses a specially crafted SQL database seeded with test data. It often requires a substantial effort to prepare and maintain the seeding logic of this test database. Still, I like this approach as it can cover significant parts of the codebase in an environment that is very similar to the production.

I do not have very good experience with trying to mock the database with the in-memory provider in Entity Framework Core,[22] as it behaves very differently from the actual database. For example, the in-memory provider does not enforce referential constraints between tables, LINQ queries produce different results when comparing strings or working with null values, etc.

The crucial functionality of our little reservation system is ensuring there are no reservation conflicts. It relies on the Row version feature

---

[21] See https://nsubstitute.github.io/help/received-calls/

[22] See https://learn.microsoft.com/en-us/ef/core/testing/

of the SQL Server[23] and its implementation in Entity Framework Core. Listing 10-9 shows how to create a stress test, which tries to send random reservation requests from ten parallel threads and verifies that the domain object remains consistent after all these actions.

Listing 10-9. Stress test for concurrent reservation creation

```
public ReservationServiceConcurrencyTests()
{
    var configuration = new ConfigurationBuilder()
        .AddJsonFile("appsettings.json")
        .Build();

    var services = new ServiceCollection();
    services.AddDbContext<AppDbContext>(options =>
        {
            options.UseSqlServer(
                configuration.GetConnectionString("DB"));
        });
    services.AddScoped<ReservationPolicyService>();
    services.AddScoped<ReservationService>();
    services.AddScoped<CustomerRepository>();
    services.AddScoped<ReservationDayRepository>();

    var currentCustomerProvider =
        Substitute.For<ICurrentCustomerProvider>();
    currentCustomerProvider.CustomerId.Returns(
        Guid.Parse("897A1B7C-B7D1-44A9-A751-82AD0D0B5331"));
    currentCustomerProvider.UserId.Returns(
        Guid.Parse("630F65BE-A38A-4051-BFE7-385B83DA30AC"));
```

---

[23] See https://learn.microsoft.com/en-us/sql/t-sql/data-types/rowversion-transact-sql?view=sql-server-ver16

```
    services.AddSingleton<ICurrentCustomerProvider>(
        currentCustomerProvider);

    provider = services.BuildServiceProvider();
}

[Fact]
public async Task TestConcurrentCreateReservation()
{
    async Task InnerJob()
    {
        using var scope = provider.CreateScope();
        var reservationService = scope.ServiceProvider
            .GetRequiredService<ReservationService>();

        // generate random times
        var startTime = TimeSpan.FromMinutes(
            Random.Shared.Next(24 * 4) * 15);
        var endTime = startTime + TimeSpan.FromMinutes(
            Random.Shared.Next(8) * 15 + 15);
        if (endTime >= TimeSpan.FromHours(24))
        {
            endTime = TimeSpan.FromHours(24)
                - TimeSpan.FromSeconds(1);
        }

        try
        {
            var result = await reservationService
                .CreateReservation(new CreateReservationModel()
                {
                    SelectedRoomId = testRoomId,
                    SelectedDay = testDay,
```

```
                StartTime =
                    TimeOnly.FromTimeSpan(startTime),
                EndTime =
                    TimeOnly.FromTimeSpan(endTime)
            });
    }
    catch (ConflictingReservationFoundException e)
    {
        // no action taken, the user will see
        // an error message and leave
        // or try the operation with different times
    }
}

// create 10 concurrent tasks that
// repeatedly create reservations
var tasks = Enumerable.Range(0, 10)
    .Select(_ => Task.Run(async () =>
    {
        for (int i = 0; i < 100; i++)
        {
            await InnerJob();
        }
    }))
    .ToArray();

// wait for all tasks to finish
await Task.WhenAll(tasks);

using (var scope = provider.CreateScope())
{
```

```
var reservationDayRepository = scope.ServiceProvider
    .GetRequiredService<ReservationDayRepository>();

// load the domain object
var day = await reservationDayRepository
    .GetDay(testRoomId, testDay);

// check there are no overlapping reservations
var orderedReservations = day.Reservations
    .OrderBy(r => r.StartTime)
    .ToList();
for (var i = 0; i < orderedReservations.Count - 1; i++)
{
    Assert.True(orderedReservations[i].EndTime
        <= orderedReservations[i + 1].StartTime);
}
        }
}
```

Although the test requires the interaction of several services, the built-in dependency injection in .NET provides a very convenient way to configure the services for the tests. I copied the service registration section from the application with only minimal changes.

User Interface Tests

I did not mention another kind of test – UI tests, sometimes also called end-to-end tests. These require running the entire application and using libraries such as Selenium, Playwright, or others to launch and control an actual web browser to perform the test.

A significant advantage of these tests is that you do not need to refactor any code – the tests are completely independent of the application codebase and can be developed and maintained externally. On the other hand, UI tests suffer from several problems:

- *Difficult environment setup*: In order to use this technique, you need to install a web driver – a special application exposing an API the test can use to control the browser. Every browser uses a different driver implementation, and its version needs to match the browser's version. In RIGANTI, we spent hundreds of hours writing and fine-tuning scripts that install all browsers and corresponding versions of drivers into our continuous integration agents. There are tools, such as Selenium Manager,[24] which help with this process. Still, something in the pipeline breaks every couple of months, and we have to diagnose and fix the issue.

- *UI tests are not 100% reliable*: Because the test interacts with an actual web browser and interacts with various UI elements on a page where many operations are asynchronous, there is always the risk of various timing issues. For example, the test clicks on a button on the page and expects the UI to change in some way. However, the server response might take longer than expected, causing the test to fail. You can add Thread.Sleep behind every line in the test, but large timeouts slow down the tests significantly while still not preventing 100% of unexpected delays that might happen. Some libraries involve a retry behavior for

---

[24] See www.selenium.dev/documentation/selenium_manager/

each action (searching or interacting with elements) with exponentially increasing delays. Even though the tests may still randomly fail because the application does not respond quickly enough, the browser crashes, some script or style does not load, and so on. We have more than a thousand UI tests in the DotVVM framework's codebase, and when running them in six environments (different browsers and platforms), we usually experience at least one failed test.

- *Every change in UI can break tests*: Since most of the UI tests need to reference certain elements in the page to check their contents or interact with them, making any changes in the page structure or CSS classes that are used to identify the elements, causes the tests to fail. If you add UI tests to your project, please note that they will require constant effort and attention to keep them working.

- *UI tests are slow*: Unit and integration tests usually require milliseconds to complete, while UI tests frequently take ten seconds or more. In the DotVVM framework repository, our suite of over 1000 UI tests runs for about 20 minutes, and we had to implement various optimizations, such as reusing open browser windows across multiple tests, to get there.

I recommend starting with a few UI tests to cover the most crucial scenarios of the application. They will not require much time to create, and you can run these tests at regular intervals, even in the production environment, to ensure the application's basic functionality is not disrupted. However, keep in mind that maintaining a large suite of UI tests may require substantial effort, as this kind of test is quite fragile.

Summary

In this chapter, I tried to summarize the best practices I consider the most important and show how quite a simple refactoring can make the code easier to understand and cover with tests.

Testing is an important part of software development, and I advocate for covering any new code with tests. Good test coverage can also ensure that the migrated code remains functional. If you do not have room to cover the entire codebase with tests, try to establish a policy that every bug fix must come with a test. This will help ensure the same problems do not reappear in the future, and you will end up with a decent test suite in the long term.

Please do not get discouraged by the difficulties when writing the first test. It is always harder, as you must set up the infrastructure, prepare the test data, etc. But all this effort pays off once you add more tests of the same type – adding the second test will be much easier.

Conclusion

Throughout this book, I tried to discuss the process of application modernization from the foundational questions to the tiniest implementation details.

In the first three chapters, I explained the advantages of the new generation of .NET versions, starting with .NET Core 1.0, and gave a 10,000-foot view of the changes you will need to make. This part of the book included ideas on how to estimate the migration effort or arguments to present to nontechnical people to understand the problems legacy projects suffer with.

Chapters 4–9 took all widely used frameworks present in the old .NET Framework and showed how to migrate APIs, web services, data access code, and web pages written in ASP.NET Web Forms, MVC, or Web Pages.

In the last chapter, I discussed the topic of refactoring the code during the migration, which I believe is often overlooked. Upgrading the project to the latest version of .NET by making only the necessary changes to the codebase seems like the least risky and most efficient way. However, I tried to emphasize that you can often gain much more with just a small added effort. If your application continues to be developed and extended with new features, any code quality and maintainability investments will sooner or later return.

Naturally, there are many things missing. I ran into several interesting topics that would deserve their own chapter or even a book, but I tried hard not to miss anything important.

Before starting the modernization journey with your project, spend enough time planning and reviewing the steps you must take. There is nothing worse than finding out a task that was expected to take a

© Tomáš Herceg 2024
T. Herceg, *Modernizing .NET Web Applications*,
https://doi.org/10.1007/979-8-8688-0617-9_11

week suddenly requires a few months. You cannot avoid this in all circumstances – it is impossible to read the entire codebase and find out all Pandora's boxes that open when moving to the new .NET.

However, having a good plan is useful not only to the developer team. Other stakeholders will appreciate having at least some idea of how difficult problem the team is going to deal with and what the journey looks like. Keep the plan updated to reflect the progress and inform about the obstacles you encounter. I have seen ambitious software projects fail not because of technical reasons but because of a lack of communication. The vast majority of technical issues can be solved. Even if it is a bug in a library or a difficult performance issue, a workaround or a proper fix can be implemented with enough time and resources. The problem is when the world outside the development team does not have enough information to adjust their business plans.

Keep in mind that there are projects that do not need to be modernized. If the application is not actively developed or is already close to the end of its life, or when the budget is so limited that adding more features will be a better use of the resources, dismiss the idea of upgrading it to the latest .NET or postpone it until happier times. I have seen several businesses that suffered great losses during the COVID pandemic or because of the Russian aggression in Ukraine. Still, they recovered and were able to continue their operation. Adding a few features to their internal applications to help them survive the unpleasant situation was a much better investment than fighting technological debt at that time.

I wish you luck in your modernization journey. It is not an easy task, and it requires persistence and dedication. Do not get discouraged when your first attempts do not succeed. Try to find other ways – I am sure one of them will work.

Index

© Tomáš Herceg 2024
T. Herceg, *Modernizing .NET Web Applications*,
https://doi.org/10.1007/979-8-8688-0617-9

X, Y, Z